J. J. Keller's
Tractor-Trailer
Driver Training
Manual

2nd Edition

Based upon the FHWA Model Curriculum

Follows PTDI's required curriculum for PTDI-certified schools

J. J. Keller
& Associates, Inc.®
Since 1953

Copyright 2013

J. J. Keller & Associates, Inc.®
3003 Breezewood Lane
P.O. Box 368
Neenah, Wisconsin 54957-0368
Phone: (800) 327-6868
Fax: (800) 727-7516
jjkeller.com

Library of Congress Catalog Card Number: 2007940996

ISBN: 978-1-60287-276-9

Canadian Goods and Services Tax (GST) Number: R123-317687

Second edition, October 2013

ACKNOWLEDGEMENTS

The development of this publication would not have been possible without the contributions of many individuals and organizations. Thanks goes to Eaton Corporation and to Holland Group Incorporated for their images. Our thanks also goes to Eaton Corporation and Dana Corporation for providing the Roadranger images (Roadranger is a marketing partnership between Eaton and Dana Corporations). In addition, thanks goes to Sara M. Dougherty Noe and Badger Federal Services Inc for allowing us the use of their equipment for various pictures seen throughout the manual.

A special thanks goes to Bob Loughan, Chippewa Valley Technical College, for his professional input and guidance.

Also, special thanks and appreciation to the following persons who reviewed portions of the manuscript and provided helpful suggestions and input:

Montie Dickey, Milan Express Driving Academy

Glen Kilgour, Choctaw Express Inc.

Dave Terry, Southwest Applied Technology

My personal thanks to all.

Timothy L. Evans
Editor – Transportation Management
J. J. Keller & Associates Inc.®
Neenah, Wisconsin

Chapter 1

Chapter 2

Chapter 3

Contents

Contents

Contents

Chapter 22

Chapter 23

Chapter 24

Chapter 25

Contents

Chapter 26

Chapter 27

Chapter 28

Chapter 29

Chapter 30

Contents

Chapter 1

Orientation

OBJECTIVES

Upon completion of this chapter, you should have a basic understanding of:

- ❑ The importance of the trucking industry
- ❑ The importance of compliance with applicable regulations
- ❑ The procedure for obtaining a CDL
- ❑ The driver qualifications you are subject to in this industry
- ❑ The commercial motor vehicle

Introduction

The trucking industry is essential to our nation's economy. Trucks deliver everything from raw materials to manufacturers to completed product to warehouses, stores, and homes. Trucks deliver seed and fertilizer to suppliers and the farm and food to our nation's grocers. Virtually everything, at one time or another, is moved by a truck.

It is estimated that there are over four million tractor-trailer combinations on the roads, delivering three out of every four tons of goods. The trucking industry employs more than eight million people in jobs from the professional driver to dispatcher to warehouse worker.

This chapter will introduce you to some of the basics when it comes to the trucking industry — how it is regulated, the qualifications you must meet, and terms to become familiar with.

Trucking plays an important role in our nation's economy.

Hey driver! Welcome to the world of truck driving. Throughout this book you are going to see additional notes and thoughts in this "side-bar" section. Some of this stuff is really important, some might just be interesting, and some might put a smile on your face. Regardless of how you view it, the information in this sidebar is useful to your future success in the world of trucking. Make sure you read what's here. It just might save you from an accident, an embarrassing moment, or an unfriendly encounter with the friendly officers at that weigh station just ahead. So sit back, buckle up, and let's go truckin'!

A Regulated Industry

The trucking industry is subject to government regulation, intended in part to ensure safety for those in the industry as well as the general motoring public. Part of being a professional driver is knowing and complying with the regulations that affect you and your industry. A motor carrier may operate in Interstate Commerce, Intrastate Commerce, or both.

When discussing compliance with the regulations it is important to understand the following terms.

Interstate Commerce — You are involved in interstate commerce if you drive a commercial motor vehicle that hauls cargo from state-to-state, from overseas, or across U.S. borders. Hauling interstate cargo within a state is also considered interstate commerce.

Intrastate Commerce — You are involved in intrastate commerce if you drive a commercial motor vehicle that hauls cargo within a state and never crosses a state line. The cargo's trip must begin and end in the same state, it can not have crossed state lines by any form of transportation such as rail, air, ship, or truck.

FMCSA — The Department of Transportation's (DOT) Federal Motor Carrier Safety Administration (FMCSA) oversees motor carrier safety. Motor carriers and drivers operating in interstate commerce must comply with the agency's regulations, commonly referred to as the Federal Motor Carrier Safety Regulations (FMCSRs).

The FMCSRs establish basic safety rules and standards for motor carriers, drivers, other employees of motor carriers, and commercial motor vehicles. The following topics are covered in the FMCSRs:

- Hours of service;

- Driver qualification;

- Driver disqualification;

- Physical qualification;

- Drug and alcohol testing;

- Commercial driver's license (CDL) standards;

- Vehicle parts and accessories; and

- Vehicle inspection.

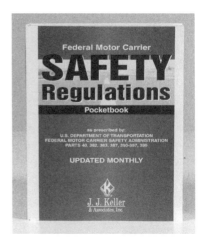

Compliance with the FMCSRs is required.

See that book on this page? As a commercial motor vehicle operator, it is your bible. You need to understand what's in that book and how it applies to you as a driver. Your instructor may have already given you one. If not, he or she probably will soon. Make sure you always have one in your truck with you and know how to use it!

Most states adopt at least some of the FMCSRs for intrastate operations. Requirements do vary from state to state. If operating in intrastate commerce, make sure you understand the state regulations before hitting the road.

The handling and transportation of hazardous materials is overseen by various organizations. These include the Pipeline and Hazardous Materials Safety Administration (PHMSA), the Occupational Safety and Health Administration (OSHA), the Environmental Protection Agency (EPA), and the National Transportation Safety Board (NTSB). The hazardous materials regulations, located in 49 CFR Parts 105 to 180 apply to all individuals who have contact with hazardous materials including individuals responsible for their preparation and transport, those transporting these materials, and emergency responders.

The regulations, as a whole, apply when hazardous materials are offered in commerce for transport to, and transported by:

- Rail, air, motor vehicle, and vessel carriers;

- Interstate, intrastate, and foreign carriers.

The hazardous materials regulations address several issues including:

- Classification;
- Emergency response;
- Incident notification and reporting;
- Labeling;
- Marking;
- Placarding;
- Shipping papers; and
- Training.

Other regulations — Drivers and their carriers are also responsible for complying with other regulations that apply to their industry, including, workplace safety, environmental, and tax laws.

Proper placarding is one of the requirements when hauling hazardous materials.

The Commercial Driver's License (CDL)

One of the first steps to becoming a professional driver is obtaining a commercial driver's license (CDL). The following is a summary of what is required to obtain a CDL. Complete details are listed in your state's CDL manual, issued by your state's licensing agency.

Application procedures — Prior to obtaining a CDL, you must meet the following requirements:

- Certify that you will be driving under one of the following categories: non-excepted interstate, excepted interstate, non-excepted intrastate, or excepted intrastate (documents provided by your state licensing agency will explain each of the classifications);

- Pass a knowledge test for the type of vehicle(s) you expect to operate, which will include a general knowledge test, a combination vehicle test, an air brake test if the vehicle you will be driving has air brakes, and written tests for any related endorsements;

- Pass a driving or skills test taken in a motor vehicle representative of the type you want to operate or pass a driving test administered by an authorized third party;

- Certify that the motor vehicle in which you take the driving skills test is representative of the type of vehicle you will be driving;

- Provide correct information required to be included on the CDL (name, address, birth date, etc.);

- Certify that you are not subject to any disqualification under Sec. 383.51 of the FMCSRs, or any license suspension, revocation, or cancellation under state law;

- Certify that you do not have a driver's license from more than one state or jurisdiction;

- Surrender your non-CDL driver's license to the state;

- Provide the names of all states where you have previously been licensed to drive any type of motor vehicle during the previous 10 years; and

- If applying for a hazardous materials endorsement, comply with Transportation Security Administration (TSA) requirements and provide proof of citizenship or lawful permanent residency status. (A lawful permanent resident of the United States must additionally provide his/her U.S. Citizenship and Immigration Services (USCIS) Alien registration number.)

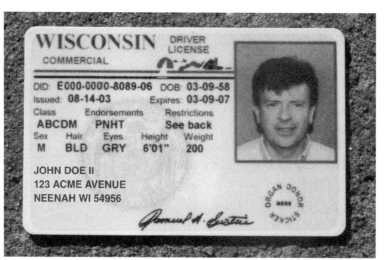

A CDL is required to operate certain groups of vehicles.

Classes of license — The federal regulations describe three vehicle groups for the purpose of the CDL. The groupings are as follows:

- **Combination Vehicle (Group A)** — Any combination of vehicles with a gross combination weight rating (GCWR) of 26,001 pounds (11,794 kilograms) or more provided the gross vehicle weight rating (GVWR) of the vehicle(s) being towed is in excess of 10,000 pounds (4,536 kilograms);

- **Heavy Straight Vehicle (Group B)** — Any single vehicle with a GVWR of 26,001 pounds (11,794 kilograms) or more, or any such vehicle towing a vehicle not in excess of 10,000 pounds (4,536 kilograms) GVWR;

- **Small Vehicle (Group C)** — Any single vehicle, or combination of vehicles that meets neither the definition of Group A nor that of Group B as contained in this section, but is designed to transport 16 or more passengers (including the driver) or is used in the transportation of a placardable amount of hazardous materials.

Endorsements — You are required to obtain endorsements for your CDL to operate certain types of commercial motor vehicles. The endorsements are as follows:

T — Double/triple trailers;

P — Passenger;

N — Tank vehicle;

H — Hazardous materials;

X — A combination of tank vehicle and hazardous materials; and

S — School bus.

States may have additional codes for endorsements and restrictions. These codes are to be explained on the license.

Driver Qualifications

As you will find throughout this course of instruction, there's more to becoming a professional driver than just obtaining a commercial driver's license (CDL) and hitting the road. This section covers regulatory qualifications you must meet in order to operate a commercial motor vehicle (CMV). These regulations are part of the FMCSR's as we mentioned earlier.

General qualifications — Section 391.11 of the FMCSRs states that you must meet certain requirements in order to operate a CMV. You are qualified if you:

- Are at least 21 years old;
- Can read, write, and speak English well enough to do your job;
- Can drive your truck safely;
- Can pass a DOT physical exam;
- Have only one current commercial driver's license;
- Have given your company a list of any violations you have been convicted of in the last 12 months;
- Are not disqualified to drive a commercial motor vehicle; and
- Passed a road test.

You must also be familiar with methods and procedures for securing cargo so that you can determine whether the cargo you transport is properly loaded, distributed, and secured. We will discuss cargo securement in a later chapter.

Hold on driver! Here's your chance to impress your instructor. You might hear a lot of fellow students and drivers talk about having an air-brake endorsement on their license. The next time you hear someone say that, smile at them and say, "Really, I was taught that there is no such thing as an air-brake endorsement. You can have an air-brake restriction on your CDL if you fail the air-brake section of the written exam (or don't take it) but you won't ever get an air-brake endorsement." They'll say, "Wow, you're really smart. I'm glad you told me that before I saw that question on a test and got it wrong." See, you're feeling smarter already!

Driver qualification file — An employer is required to maintain a driver qualification (DQ) file for each driver it employs per Sec. 391.51 of the FMCSRs. The following documents must be included in your DQ file:

- Application for employment;

- Motor vehicle record from state(s);

- Road test form and certificate, or a copy of the license or certificate accepted in lieu of a road test;

- Medical exam certificate (original or copy);

- Skill Performance Evaluation (SPE) certificate or medical exemption document;

A typical driver qualification file.

- Response of each state agency to the annual review of driving record inquiry;

- A note relating to the annual review of your driving record; and

- List of violations.

Your DQ file must be kept by your employer for the entire time you are employed and for 3 years after you leave them if you do.

Physical exam — You may not drive a commercial motor vehicle unless you are physically qualified and carry a medical examiner's certificate stating you are physically qualified. (See Sec. 391, Subpart E of the FMCSRs.)

You may not drive if you:

- Have lost a foot, leg, hand, or arm and have not been granted a skill performance evaluation (SPE) certificate;

- Have an impairment of a hand, finger, arm, foot, or leg which interferes with your ability to perform normal tasks associated with driving a commercial motor vehicle and have not been granted an SPE;

- Have diabetes requiring insulin for control;

- Have heart disease, which causes you chest pain, fainting, or shortness of breath;

- Have chest or breathing problems like chronic asthma, emphysema, or chronic bronchitis;

- Have high blood pressure likely to interfere with driving;

- Have loss of movement or feeling in part of your body;

Today, there are medical waivers for some of these conditions that may allow you to drive with additional restrictions or limitations. If you have any of these conditions it is very important that you discuss them with your doctor, inform him or her of your desire to become a commercial vehicle operator, and review possible options available to you.

- Have any sickness which is likely to cause loss of consciousness or any loss of ability to control a commercial motor vehicle;

- Have any mental problems likely to interfere with your ability to drive a commercial motor vehicle safely;

- Have poor vision that affects your ability to see objects that are far away (you may use glasses or contact lenses to correct your vision), objects to the side, or traffic signal colors (you may not drive if you see with only one eye);

- Have poor hearing (you must be able to hear a loud whispered voice in your better ear at not less than 5 feet with or without the use of a hearing aid or, pass a hearing test on a doctor's testing machine);

- Use certain drugs and dangerous substances, except that you may use such a substance or drug if the substance or drug is prescribed by a doctor who is familiar with your medical history and assigned duties and who has advised you that the prescribed substance or drug will not adversely affect your ability to safely operate a commercial motor vehicle; or

- Have a current clinical diagnosis of alcoholism.

A medical exam is required if you:

- Have not been medically examined and physically qualified to drive a commercial motor vehicle;

- Have not had a medical exam in the past 24 months; or

- Have suffered a disease or injury that affected your ability to drive a commercial motor vehicle.

As of January 30, 2012, when you apply for a CDL, you must turn in a valid copy of your medical examiner's certificate/card and file documentation certifying that you drive under one of four categories (non-excepted interstate, excepted interstate, non-excepted intrastate, or excepted intrastate) to your state driver licensing agency. Individuals who currently hold a CDL are also required to follow these procedures and have until January 30, 2014, to turn in these documents.

Until January 30, 2014, you will be required to carry a copy of your medical examiner's certificate/card while operating a commercial motor vehicle and your motor carrier will be required to maintain copy in your driver qualification file. After January 30, 2014, you will no longer be required to carry a copy of your medical examiner's certificate/card and your motor carrier will no longer be required to maintain a copy in the driver qualification file. This information will be maintained on your driving record.

Driver disqualification — A driver holding a commercial driver's license (CDL) can be disqualified from driving a commercial motor vehicle (CMV) if convicted of certain offenses while driving any type of vehicle; this includes a personal vehicle. (See Sec. 383.51 of the FMCSRs.)

Major offenses — You are disqualified from operating a CMV if convicted of any of the following major offenses while driving a CMV or non-CMV:

- Being under the influence of alcohol as prescribed by state law;

- Being under the influence of a controlled substance;

- Refusing to take an alcohol test as requested by a state or jurisdiction under its implied consent laws or regulations;

- Leaving the scene of an accident;

- Using a vehicle to commit a felony; or

- Using a vehicle in the commission of a felony involving the manufacturing, distributing, or dispensing of a controlled substance.

You are disqualified from operating a CMV if convicted of any of the following major offenses while driving a CMV:

- Having an alcohol concentration of 0.04 or greater;

- Driving a CMV when, as a result of prior violations committed operating a CMV, the driver's CDL is revoked, suspended, or cancelled, or the driver is disqualified from operating a CMV; or

- Causing a fatality through the negligent operation of a CMV.

The disqualification period for the first conviction (with the exception of using a vehicle in the commission of a felony involving the manufacturing, distributing, or dispensing of a controlled substance) is one year, provided you are not transporting hazardous materials.

If you are transporting hazardous materials, the disqualification period is three years.

The disqualification period for a second conviction is life.

If you are convicted of using a vehicle in the commission of a felony involving the manufacturing, distributing, or dispensing of a controlled substance, you are disqualified for life and not eligible for reinstatement.

Serious traffic violations — You are disqualified from operating a CMV if convicted of any combination of two or more of the following serious traffic violations while operating any vehicle (CMV or non-CMV):

- Excessive speeding, 15 mph or more above the posted speed limit;

- Reckless driving;

- Making improper or erratic traffic lane changes;

- Following the vehicle ahead too closely; or

- Violating a state or local law relating to motor vehicle traffic control (other than a parking violation) arising in connection with a fatal accident.

Slow down driver! Once you have read this section, you may want to read it again and again to make absolutely sure you know what it says. Driving a commercial motor vehicle is serious business. You can't drive one without your CDL. Don't ever let "I didn't know" be the reason you give when somebody asks you why you're sitting at home instead of out driving a big truck.

You are disqualified from operating a CMV if convicted of any combination of two or more of the following serious traffic violations while operating a CMV:

- Driving a CMV without obtaining a CDL;

- Driving a CMV without a CDL in your possession;

- Driving a CMV without the proper class of CDL and/or endorsements for the specific vehicle group being operated or for the passengers or type of cargo being transported;

- Violating a state or local law or ordinance on motor vehicle traffic control prohibiting texting while driving a CMV; or

- Violating a state or local law or ordinance on motor vehicle traffic control restricting or prohibiting the use of a hand-held mobile telephone while driving a CMV.

If you are convicted of two serious traffic violations in separate incidents during any three year period, you are disqualified for 60 days.

If convicted of three serious traffic violations in separate incidents during any three year period, you are disqualified for 120 days.

Out-of-service violation — During a trip, you may be placed out of service by an enforcement officer for a certain period of time or until a given problem has been corrected. This typically happens at a state scale (weigh station) or during a roadside inspection.

Conviction for violating such an out-of-service order subjects you to a fine and disqualification period. The disqualification period ranges from 180 days to 5 years with penalties for drivers of vehicles carrying hazardous materials being more severe. Fines for violating an out-of-service order range from $2,500 to $5,000.

Note: A driver convicted of two or more serious traffic violations while operating a non-CMV is disqualified only if the convictions result in the revocation, cancellation, or suspension of the driver's license or driving privileges.

Violation of a railroad-highway grade crossing law may result in disqualification.

Railroad-highway grade crossing violations — You are disqualified from driving if you are convicted of operating a vehicle requiring a CDL in violation of a federal, state, or local law or regulation pertaining to one of six offenses at a railroad-highway grade crossing. (See Sec. 383.51(d) of the FMCSRs for details.)

If you are convicted of a railroad-highway grade crossing violation, you are subject to a disqualification period of between 60 days and 1 year.

The fine for an employer who is convicted of knowingly allowing, permitting, or authorizing a driver to violate a railroad-highway grade crossing regulation is up to $10,000.

Drug and alcohol testing — The use of alcohol and/or drugs by a driver is a serious issue. As well as being dangerous to himself/herself and others on the road, the use of alcohol and/or drugs is illegal.

Drivers subject to the CDL standards, driving CMVs, are subject to the alcohol and drug regulations in Part 382.

Note: Drivers who are subject to the Licencia Federal de Conductor (Mexico) requirements or the commercial driver's license requirements of the Canadian National Safety Code and operate a commercial motor vehicle in the United States are also subject to the alcohol and drug regulations in Part 382.

Drug and/or alcohol use while on the job is illegal.

Alcohol misuse that could affect the performance of a safety-sensitive function is prohibited. A safety-sensitive function is defined as all time from the time you begin work or are required to be ready to work until the time you are relieved from work and all responsibilities for performing work. (See Sec. 382.107 of the FMCSRs for complete details.) Prohibited alcohol use includes:

- Use while performing safety-sensitive functions;

- Use during the 4 hours before performing safety-sensitive functions;

- Reporting for duty or remaining on duty to perform safety-sensitive functions with an alcohol concentration of 0.04 or greater;

- Use during the 8 hours following an accident, or until you undergo a post-accident test; or

- Refusal to take a required test.

If you have an alcohol concentration of 0.02 or greater but less than 0.04, you may not perform, or be permitted to perform, safety-sensitive functions for at least 24 hours.

Drug use that could affect performance of safety-sensitive functions is prohibited, including:

- Use of any drug, except by doctor's prescription, and then only if the doctor has advised you that the drug will not adversely affect your ability to safely operate a commercial motor vehicle;

- Testing positive for drugs; or

- Having an adulterated or substituted drug test result.

An employer may require you to inform your company of any therapeutic drug use.

What's the ideal amount of alcohol and/or drugs to have in your system when operating a vehicle? ZERO! Just don't do it! It's not worth losing your license over or jeopardizing your life or the lives of others. Here's one more thing to remember about alcohol...don't ever carry any in your truck; not in the cab, not in the bunk, not in your hand, NOT IN YOUR TRUCK! It's illegal to carry alcohol in a commercial motor vehicle (opened or not) and will make for a miserable day if you're caught.

Drivers of commercial motor vehicles are subject to the following tests:

1. **Pre-employment drug test** — Before you perform any safety-sensitive functions, you must submit to a drug test. The company must receive a negative result prior to allowing you to drive or perform other safety-sensitive functions.

2. **Post accident test** —

    A. As soon as practicable following an accident involving a commercial motor vehicle, you must submit to an alcohol test:

    - If any person in the accident dies; or

    - If you receive a citation within 8 hours of the accident for a moving traffic violation and any person involved in the accident is injured and is immediately taken away from the scene of the accident for medical treatment; or

    - If you receive a citation within 8 hours of the accident for a moving traffic violation and one or more of the vehicles involved is towed away from the scene.

    B. As soon as practicable following an accident involving a commercial motor vehicle, you must submit to a drug test:

    - If any person in the accident dies; or

    - If you receive a citation within 32 hours of the accident for a moving traffic violation and any person involved in the accident is injured and is immediately taken away from the scene of the accident for medical treatment; or

    - If you receive a citation within 32 hours of the accident for a moving traffic violation and one or more of the vehicles involved is towed away from the scene.

    C. If you are subject to post-accident testing you must remain available, or the company may consider you to have refused to submit to testing.

    D. If you are subject to post-accident testing, you must refrain from consuming alcohol for 8 hours following the accident, or until submitting to an alcohol test, whichever occurs first.

3. **Random testing** — Unannounced random testing is required for a certain percentage of drivers each year. Random tests must be unannounced and spread reasonably throughout the year. When you are informed of being selected for random testing you must immediately go to the testing site.

    Random testing for alcohol must be conducted while you are performing, immediately prior to performing, or immediately after performing a safety-sensitive function. Random testing for drugs may be performed at any time while you are at work for the company.

Hey driver, you are going to here a lot of talk on the CB about your rights and the fact that you do not have to take an alcohol or drug test if you don't want to. Refusing to submit to a required alcohol or drug test is treated the same as testing positive, it's just that simple! If you refuse to be tested, you cannot perform any safety sensitive functions. That means you can not drive! You're a professional. A professional truck driver that can't drive is like a heart surgeon that can't operate...not much use to anybody! Don't let this happen to you.

Selection of drivers for all random testing must be done using a scientifically valid method. The DOT only recognizes a random number table or a computer-based random number generator that is matched with drivers' Social Security numbers, payroll identification numbers, or other comparable identifying numbers as scientifically valid. Drawing names out of a hat is not considered scientifically valid.

Once you are randomly tested for drugs and/or alcohol during a calendar year, your name must be returned to the random pool for each new selection. Each driver must be subject to an equal chance of being tested during each selection process.

4. **Reasonable suspicion testing** — The regulations require you to submit to an alcohol or drug test when a company supervisor or official has reasonable suspicion to believe you are using drugs or alcohol on the job. The company supervisor or official's suspicion must be based on specific, clearly stated observations of your appearance, behavior, speech, or body odors.

   Alcohol testing is authorized only if the observations are made during, just before, or just after you perform safety-sensitive functions. The person who makes the determination that reasonable suspicion exists may not conduct the alcohol test.

   If reasonable suspicion is observed, but a reasonable suspicion test has not yet been administered, you must not perform safety-sensitive functions until an alcohol test is administered and your alcohol concentration measures less than 0.02, or 24 hours have elapsed following the determination of reasonable suspicion.

   A company may require you to submit to a drug test at any time reasonable suspicion exists while you are on duty. Supervisor observations may include indications of the chronic and withdrawal effects of drugs as well as the indications previously listed.

   The regulations do not give an employer authority to take any action, other than stated above, against you based solely on your behavior and appearance with no test result. However, the employer may take action independent of the regulations.

5. **Return-to-duty/follow-up testing** — If you fail a drug or alcohol test, you must be evaluated by a substance abuse professional (SAP) and participate in the education and/or treatment program prescribed by the SAP.

   You must successfully comply with the education and/or treatment program prescribed by the SAP and undergo a return-to-duty test with the results indicating an alcohol concentration of less than 0.02 and/or a verified negative drug test.

   You are then subject to follow-up testing. The number and frequency of the tests are determined by the SAP, but must consist of at least six tests during the first 12 months following your return to duty.

Follow-up testing may be done for up to 60 months (5 years). The SAP can terminate the requirement for follow-up testing after the first 12 month period if the SAP determines the testing is no longer necessary.

Follow-up testing for alcohol can only be performed when you are performing a safety-sensitive function, or immediately before or after performing a safety-sensitive function.

The Commercial Motor Vehicle — An Overview

There are many types of commercial motor vehicles you could be called upon to operate throughout your driving career. The following is a brief summary of some of the basic terms. This will be addressed in more detail in later chapters.

The tractor — is the power unit. It is used to pull a vehicle or vehicles (trailers, semi-trailers, tankers, flatbeds, etc.).

There are two cab styles that are most common, the conventional tractor and the cab-over-engine (COE) tractor.

Conventional tractor — The engine is located under the hood of the tractor. Like passenger vehicles, the engine is in front of the driver.

A conventional tractor

A cab-over engine (COE) tractor

Cab-over-engine — The engine is located below the cab. The driver is over the front wheels and the front of the tractor is flat.

The following are other vehicle-related terms that will be used throughout the text.

Steering axle — The front axle, responsible for controlling the vehicle direction.

Drive axle — The axle or axles that are powered and actively pull the load.

Tandem axle — An assembly of two axles (could be on the tractor or the trailer).

Duals — A pair of wheels and tires mounted together on the same side of one axle.

Trailer — The trailer is what stores and carries the cargo. There are two types of trailers, the full trailer and the semitrailer.

Full trailer — A full trailer is supported by its own axles. No part of its weight rests on the towing vehicle.

Semitrailer — The front of a semitrailer rests on the tractor, specifically the tractor's fifth wheel. When a semitrailer is disconnected from the tractor, its front end rests on legs commonly referred to as landing gear.

A semitrailer.

The fifth wheel is a coupling device located at the tractor's rear frame that is used to join the front of the trailer to the tractor. It looks like a flat rounded plate with a v-shaped notch.

The fifth wheel.

When a trailer is attached to a tractor it is called a combination vehicle. We will cover several types of combination vehicles later in this text.

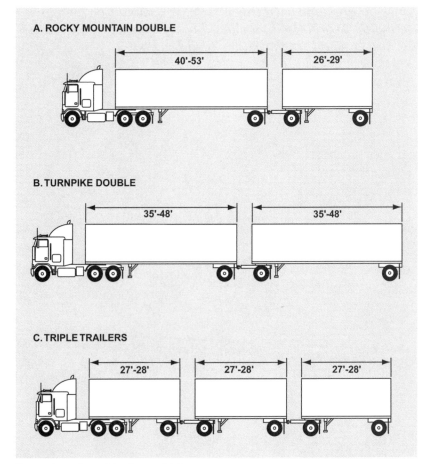

A. ROCKY MOUNTAIN DOUBLE

40'-53'   26'-29'

B. TURNPIKE DOUBLE

35'-48'   35'-48'

C. TRIPLE TRAILERS

27'-28'   27'-28'   27'-28'

Examples of combination vehicles.

Summary

In this chapter, you have learned about the first steps you must take to become a member of the trucking industry — a professional driver. As you can see, it takes more than just getting a license and driving down the road. You must meet certain qualifications and have an understanding of the industry. You must also understand what your responsibilities are to your company, the regulatory agencies, yourself, your family, and the motoring public.

O.K. driver, here's your chance to shine. You have just completed the first chapter of this book. Are you ready to see what you know? Each chapter is going to end with a quiz. This quiz will touch on some of the important things that you want to remember from the chapter.

*Also, there will be five questions in an area titled **pre-test,** just after the quiz. These could be the most important questions in the book because these are actual questions that you may see on the written exam for your CDL. You may not know any of the answers at first and you may think they aren't related at all to what you just read. Just do the best you can. You'll see these questions over and over again throughout the book so keep trying until you can answer them all correctly.*

By the time you are done with this course, you should be able to master the written test with no problem and should be well on your way toward being a successful, professional truck driver. Good Luck!

Driving a truck can be an extremely rewarding career. Are you ready to continue on this journey? Are you ready to become a professional commercial motor vehicle operator? I hope so!

Orientation Quiz

Directions: Read each statement carefully and mark the response that best answers the question.

1. **Trucking is exempt from government regulations.**

    A. True

    B. False

2. **You must pass a knowledge test and a road test to obtain a CDL.**

    A. True

    B. False

3. **Which of the following is a type of vehicle that requires an endorsement on your CDL?**

    A. Double trailer

    B. Passenger

    C. Tank

    D. All of the above

4. **According to the FMCSRs, you are qualified to operate a commercial motor vehicle if you:**

    A. Are at least 21 years old

    B. Passed a road test

    C. Have only one current CDL

    D. All of the above

5. **You may not drive a commercial motor vehicle unless you are physically qualified and carry a medical examiner's certificate.**

    A. True

    B. False

6. **The air-brake endorsement is necessary to operate a commercial motor vehicle equipped with air brakes.**

    A. True

    B. False

7. _____ is a major disqualifying offense.

   A. Jaywalking

   B. Following the vehicle ahead too closely

   C. Leaving the scene of an accident

   D. All of the above

8. **A_____ is supported by its own axles and has no part of its weight resting on the towed vehicle.**

   A. Semi trailer

   B. C.O.E.

   C. Full trailer

   D. Conventional tractor

9. **The driver of a commercial motor vehicle, subject to the CDL standards, is not subject to drug and alcohol testing.**

   A. True

   B. False

10. **The engine of a _____ is located under the hood of the tractor.**

    A. Cab-over engine

    B. Conventional tractor

    C. Full trailer

    D. All of the above

General Knowledge CDL Pre-Test

The General Knowledge Test must be taken by all applicants for a commercial driver's license

Read each question carefully and then choose the answer that is most correct.

1. **While driving you are looking ahead of your vehicle. How should you be looking?**

    A. Look to the right side of the roadway

    B. Look back and forth and near and far

    C. Stare straight ahead at all times

    D. Look straight ahead and glance in your mirrors every 45 to 60 seconds

2. **When you are driving at night, you should:**

    A. Dim your lights when you are within 300 feet of oncoming traffic

    B. Watch the white line on the left side of the roadway

    C. Adjust your vehicle speed so as to keep your stopping distance within your sight distance

    D. Keep your high beams on at all times

3. **Statistics prove that most serious skids are a result of:**

    A. Driving too fast for conditions

    B. Improper loading of the vehicle

    C. Turning too sharply

    D. Winter driving conditions

4. **If you drive through heavy rain or standing water your brakes may get wet. What can this cause when you apply the brakes?**

    A. Trailer jackknife

    B. Your brakes to heat up

    C. Hydroplaning

    D. Hydroplaning if you were traveling faster than 30 mph when you applied brakes

5. **Which of the following is true about the use of reflective emergency triangles?**

    A. The regulation requires they be placed within 5 minutes of stopping

    B. You do not need to use them if you break down as long as your 4-way flashers are working

    C. You do not need to use them as long as you have pulled your vehicle completely off the traveled portion of the roadway

    D. If you stop on a hill or curve, it is permissible to place them up to 500 feet in order to provide adequate warning

Your instructor has the answers to these questions. Ask him / her how you did, and keep trying!

Chapter 2

Control systems

OBJECTIVES

When you have completed this chapter, you should have a basic understanding of the name, location, and function of your vehicle's controls and systems. You should be able to:

❑ Describe the engine controls as well as the primary and secondary vehicle controls

❑ Identify and describe the controls for starting the engine, shifting, accelerating, braking, and parking

❑ Explain the acceptable operating range for oil, coolant, and electrical systems

❑ Identify and describe all vehicle instruments and their purpose

Introduction

As a professional driver, it is important that you understand the function of all controls and instruments of any vehicle you operate. Commercial vehicles are nothing like your family car. Commercial vehicles have numerous systems, controls, and instruments that you usually do not see in a personal vehicle.

For safety's sake, you should never operate a vehicle until you have familiarized yourself with the vehicle's instruments and controls.

A tractor's dashboard and instruments.

This chapter will introduce you to the controls and instruments found in commercial motor vehicles.

Engine Controls

The engine controls are what you use to start and shut down the vehicle's engine. Though similar in most vehicles, they do vary somewhat based on the type of engine and engine manufacturer.

Engine control switch — The engine control switch starts the engine. It must be on in order to start the engine.

Starter button — Some trucks have a starter button. If the truck you are operating has a starter button, you must turn the engine key to the on position and then push the starter button. Normal cranking time should be about 3 to 5 seconds.

Cruise control — Cruise control allows the vehicle to maintain a steady, constant speed without depressing the accelerator.

Engine control switch.

Primary Vehicle Controls

Cruise control.

Steering wheel — The steering wheel is used to steer the truck. It has a larger diameter than your car's steering wheel.

Accelerator pedal — The accelerator pedal controls the vehicle's speed. It is operated the same way on a truck as on a car. During your training you may also here this referred to as the throttle. You push the throttle down to increase speed and release it to reduce speed. Proper use of the throttle allows you to safely control the vehicle's speed, avoiding excessive use of the vehicle's service brakes.

Did you ever wonder why a truck's steering wheel is so big? Well, it's because trucks used to be operated without power steering. The larger steering wheel was necessary to create enough "leverage" to turn the vehicle safely. Today, steering wheels on big trucks are actually smaller as modern technology (power steering, set-back axles, etc) has made it much easier to maneuver big trucks. They may always be bigger than an automobile steering wheel, but at least now you know why!

Steering wheel.

Clutch, brake, and accelerator pedals (left to right).

Clutch pedal — The clutch pedal is used to engage and disengage the clutch and to shift gears. There are four basic clutch positions.

1. **Engaged** — When the clutch is engaged, the pedal is fully released (your foot isn't depressing the pedal). The engine and drive train are connected, if the vehicle is in gear.

2. **Free play** — Free play is the amount of movement possible without engaging or disengaging the clutch. Free play is necessary to prevent excessive clutch wear. Normal free play is about one to two inches.

Hey driver, make sure you don't call this a "gas pedal." It may get you some funny looks from your instructor and a little friendly harassment from your fellow students as well. Remember, you are driving a big truck...it doesn't have a gas pedal. Accelerator or throttle will work just fine!

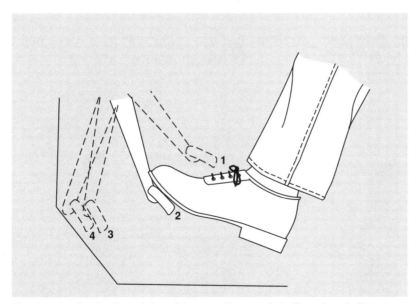

The four basic clutch pedal positions: 1. Engaged, 2. Freeplay, 3. Disengaged, and 4. Clutch brake.

3. **Disengaged** — The clutch is disengaged when the pedal is depressed about 3 to 8 inches. In this position, the engine and drive train are separated. The clutch must be disengaged in order to start the engine or shift gears.

4. **Clutch brake** — When disengaged, the transmission of a big truck "free-wheels" or spins. Because of this, the use of the clutch brake will stop the transmission from turning, allowing you to engage the next gear. This is done while at a stop, not while moving. By depressing the clutch pedal to the floor, the clutch brake will be engaged, bringing the transmission to a stop, which makes it possible to shift into the desired starting gear (forward or reverse).

Extensive damage can be caused to the transmission or drive train if the clutch pedal isn't operated properly.

Transmission controls — The transmission controls vary depending on the type of transmission in the truck.

A manual transmission uses a clutch and a gear shift lever. You have to manually change gears.

The gear shift lever may include a range selector lever, allowing you to switch between high and low ranges. The down position includes the low range of gears and the up position includes the high range of gears. A splitter valve or button allows you to split gears on 13 and 18 speed transmissions.

A semiautomatic transmission includes a clutch and gear shift lever. There could also be a control pad with push-buttons on it, instead of a gear shift lever. Some gear changes are done by an on-board computer and some are done manually.

An automatic transmission only has a gear shift lever, or touch pad. A clutch may not be needed in some models. All gear changes are done by an on-board computer and hydraulics.

Brake controls (air brakes) — The brakes are used to slow or stop the vehicle. The air brake control system is complex and involves a number of separate controls.

The brake slows and/or stops the vehicle.

- **Foot brake control valve** — The foot brake control valve (also called the service brake, foot valve, or treadle valve) operates both the tractor and trailer's service brakes. When depressed it supplies air pressure to all brake chambers.

- **Trailer brake hand-control valve** — The trailer brake control valve (also called the hand valve, trolley valve or independent trailer brake) operates the service brakes on the trailer only. It is only used in special situations. It shouldn't be used to hold equipment in place while parked or to slow the vehicle. Improper use could cause the trailer to skid or jackknife.

- **Parking brake control valve** — The parking brake control valve is a yellow four-sided knob (diamond shaped) that allows the driver to activate the parking brake. The parking brake should only be used when the vehicle is completely stopped. The parking brake should always be engaged before the driver leaves the driver's seat or turns the engine off. Failure to engage (set) the parking brake could cause the vehicle to roll, even if it is assumed that the vehicle is on level ground.

- **Trailer air supply valve** — The trailer air supply valve, the red eight-sided button, controls air supply to trailer brakes. It must be released (pushed in) for normal operation with a trailer and applied (pulled out) for operation on a tractor without a trailer. It closes automatically in the event that the airlines to the trailer are broken.

Trailer air supply valve

Antilock brakes — According to National Highway Traffic Safety Administration (NHTSA) requirements (49 CFR 571 S5.1.6.1), all truck tractors manufactured on or after March 1, 1998, must be equipped with an antilock braking system (ABS). When used properly, antilock brakes help prevent wheels from locking and losing traction, which can cause a loss of vehicle control.

The biggest difference between ABS and other brake systems is how you use the brake to stop the vehicle. With traditional brakes, you would normally pump the brake pedal. With ABS, a firm and continuous pressure on the pedal is needed to make the brakes work properly.

Auxiliary brakes and retarders — Auxiliary brakes and retarders reduce the vehicle's speed without using the service brakes. They keep service brakes from being overused and becoming overheated. They should only be used on dry road surfaces. There are four basic classes of auxiliary brakes and retarders.

1. **Exhaust brakes** — Exhaust brakes are considered the simplest form of heavy vehicle retarder. A valve is installed in the exhaust manifold that keeps exhaust gasses from escaping. This builds up back pressure in the engine, preventing it from increasing speed. Exhaust brakes are usually controlled by an on/off switch in the cab or an automatic control switch on the accelerator or clutch.

2. **Engine brakes** — Engine brakes are built into the head of the engine and alter valve timing, turning the engine into an air compressor. They're operated using a switch mounted on the dashboard and when your foot leaves the accelerator and clutch.

3. **Hydraulic retarders** — Hydraulic retarders are a type of driveline retarder. They are usually mounted between the engine and flywheel. They reduce a vehicle's speed by directing a flow of oil against the

Engine brakes.

stantor vanes. They may be activated by a hand lever or accelerator switch.

4. **Electric retarders** — Electric retarders contain electromagnets which slow the rotors attached to the drive train. They're operated by a switch in the cab.

Few trucks have all four types of auxiliary brake systems. Most trucks only have one. It is important that each driver know which type his or her truck has and how it operates.

Interaxle differential lock — An interaxle differential lock unlocks and locks the rear tandem axles. In the unlocked position, the axles turn independently of each other on a dry surface. In the locked position, power to the axles is equalized to prevent wheels lacking traction from spinning. Interaxle differential locks should never be employed any longer than is absolutely necessary.

Careful driver! You may think that Jake brake is music to you ears, and the louder it is, the better, but some communities restrict or ban the use of retarders due to noise. Be aware of the regulations/requirements of the communities you travel through. It's also not too impressive to use it in the truckstop parking lot so don't forget to turn it off when you come off the highway. Your fellow drivers will appreciate it!

Caution! Never attempt to engage your interaxle differential lock while the wheels are spinning. This could cause major damage to your differential and your transmission. Also remember, disengage the interaxle lock as soon as you don't need it any more. Prolonged travel on dry roads could also cause damage to your vehicle.

Secondary Vehicle Controls

Secondary vehicle controls assist you in safely operating your vehicle. Some are similar to the secondary controls in your car. Others are unique to trucks. The number and type of controls vary from vehicle-to-vehicle, but typically fall within the following major categories.

1. Seeing:

    *   Lights

    *   Remote mirrors

    *   Mirror heaters

    *   Windshield wipers and washers

    *   Defroster

2. Communication:

    *   Horns

    *   CB Radio (not a vehicle control but is used in communication)

    *   Lights (turn signals, four-way flashers, high beams, fog lamps, brake lights, etc.)

Lights help you see the road and help others see your vehicle.

3. Climate/Comfort controls:

    *   Heater

    *   Air conditioner

    *   Air vents

    *   Steering wheel adjustment

    *   Seat position and adjustment control

4. Driver safety:

    *   Bunk restraints

    *   Seat belts

    *   Door locks

You should be familiar with and know how to operate all secondary controls in your vehicle before hitting the road.

Vehicle Instruments

Vehicle instruments monitor and report on the operating condition of your vehicle. They warn you of potential problems. Basic instruments are listed below.

Vehicle instruments.

- **Speedometer** — A speedometer is required under Sec. 393.82 of the Federal Motor Carrier Safety Regulations (FMCSRs). The speedometer shows the speed of the vehicle in miles per hour (mph) and/or kilometers per hour.

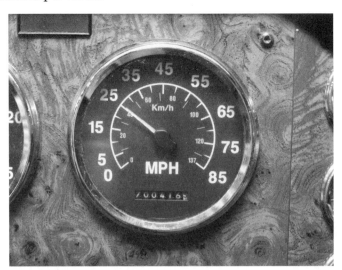

Speedometer and odometer.

- **Odometer** — The odometer indicates the total number of miles (or kilometers) traveled by a vehicle.

Hey driver, this section is just a representation of some of the more common gauges you will find in your truck. You may find out that you don't have some of these, or you may have many more. Take a few minutes when you first get in your truck and familiarize yourself with YOUR gauges.

- **Tachometer** — The tachometer shows engine speed in hundreds of revolutions per minute (RPM). It serves as a guide for shifting into the appropriate transmission gear. It also assists you in effectively using the engine and transmission when accelerating and decelerating and for fuel efficiency.

Tachometer.

Fuel gauge.

- **Fuel gauge** — The fuel gauge shows how much fuel is left in the vehicle's fuel tank(s). Since fuel gauges aren't always accurate, you should check the fuel tank(s) visually before you start a trip.

- **Ammeter** — The ammeter measures the amount of battery being charged or discharged. A normal reading is slightly to the charged side. A continuous high charge or continuous discharge are signs of problems. Ammeters are not found on all commercial vehicles. If your vehicle does not have one, refer to voltmeter for charging issues.

• **Voltmeter** — The voltmeter measures battery output in volts. The vehicle's operator's manual should be consulted to determine a normal reading for the vehicle you are operating. In most vehicles, a normal reading is between 13 and 14.5 volts. Higher or lower than normal voltage can shorten the life of a battery.

Voltmeter.

Air pressure gauge.

• **Air pressure gauge** — The air pressure gauge measures pressure of air in the reservoir, or tanks in pounds per square inch (psi). A truck may be equipped with one or two air pressure gauges. These gauges are referred to as the primary and secondary air pressure gauges. The air pressure gauge is required by law on every commercial motor vehicle equipped with air brakes.

When the engine starts, air pressure starts building. It continues to build until maximum pressure is reached (about 120 psi). If pressure drops below 60 psi, a low pressure warning device (light or buzzer) will activate, indicating that continued operation of the vehicle is unsafe. At 20 to 45 psi, the tractor protection valve closes, shutting off the air supply to the trailer. A vehicle without sufficient air pressure shouldn't be operated.

Oil pressure gauge.

- **Oil pressure gauge** — The oil pressure gauge tells you if the engine is being properly lubricated. In warm weather, oil pressure should register on the oil pressure gauge within a few seconds after the vehicle is started and gradually rise to normal operating range. Normal operating range is 30 – 50 PSI. In cold weather it could take 30 to 60 seconds to get a reading.

  Normal range varies from vehicle-to-vehicle based on engine speed and oil viscosity. If pressure is low or doesn't register, the engine isn't being lubricated properly. This can cause the engine to be ruined within a short time period. You should know the operating range of your vehicle and stop and investigate anytime there's a loss in pressure or pressure doesn't register.

- **Coolant temperature gauge** — The coolant temperature gauge measures the temperature of water and coolant in the engine block. The cooling system protects the engine from damage caused by heat. Normally, an engine operates at about 170°-195°F. This can vary. Consult the vehicle's operator's manual for specifics. If the gauge registers above the normal range, the engine may be overheating. You should immediately turn off the engine.

Coolant temperature gauge.

Engine oil temperature gauge.

- **Oil temperature gauge** — The engine oil temperature gauge indicates the temperature of the engine oil. The normal engine oil temperature is between 180°-225°F. This can vary. Consult the vehicle's operator's manual for specifics. A high oil temperature can cause thinner oil, decreasing oil pressure. This can result in engine damage.

- **Exhaust pyrometer gauge** — The exhaust pyrometer gauge shows the temperature of the exhaust gasses in the manifold. If the truck has an exhaust pyrometer, it could be used to determine when the truck has cooled enough to shut down the engine however, most trucks will have cooled down enough by the time you reach the fuel stop or dock, by a natural reduction in workload (reducing speed coming off the highway) and a continuous flow of air through the engine.

- **Axle temperature gauge** — The axle temperature gauge measures the temperature of the front and rear drive axles. Above normal readings may indicate bad bearings.

Very few trucks have a pyrometer gauge. It is not considered a critical gauge with today's engines, so don't worry if you can't find one the first time you get into your new truck.

Just like the pyrometer gauge, most trucks, other than those that are designed to pull very heavy loads, do not have axle temperature gauges. If you visually inspect your axles as part of your daily vehicle inspection, and make sure they are properly serviced by maintenance people, you should not have a problem.

Warning devices — Vehicles are also equipped with warning devices. They let you know when pressures or temperatures reach a dangerous level. Some of the more common warning devices are listed below.

- **Low pressure warning alarm/light** — The low pressure warning alarm/light indicates inadequate pressure in the air brake system.

- **Coolant level alarm** — The coolant level alarm lights up when the level starts dropping, indicating a probable leak.

- **Oil level alarm** — The oil level alarm lights up when the oil level drops below what is normal for operation.

- **Coolant temperature warning light** — The coolant temperature warning light indicates when the temperature is too high for normal operation.

- **Oil pressure warning light** — The oil pressure warning light indicates when oil pressure drops too low for safe operation.

- **Pyrometer warning light** — The pyrometer warning light indicates when exhaust temperatures are abnormal.

- **Differential warning** — The differential warning may stay illuminated when the interaxle differential is in the locked position.

- **ABS light** — This light indicates that the ABS function is not operating.

Warning lights alert you of potential problems.

Every driver needs to understand what these warning indicators mean in their truck and what may happen if they do not react to them quickly. Some trucks will shut down the engine in a very short time if a problem is detected and one of these indicators comes on. Others will reduce the speed of the engine to allow the driver time to get the vehicle off the road safely, but quickly. In any case, the driver needs to know what these mean, and what they should do if an indicator light, buzzer, or alarm comes on while driving.

Summary

This chapter has introduced you to vehicle controls and instruments. As a professional driver, you should make sure you are familiar with these components before operating a vehicle. It is also important to check the instrument panel on a regular basis while on the road. This should be part of your constant scanning motion which we will discuss later. By constantly observing these systems, the driver will be aware of any changing conditions with their truck and can react accordingly to hopefully avoid damage or breakdown.

Control Systems Quiz

Directions: Read each statement carefully and mark the response that best answers the question.

1. **Once you are on the road, it is not necessary to continually look at your gauges unless a warning buzzer sounds.**

    A. True

    B. False

2. **Primary vehicle controls include:**

    A. Steering wheel

    B. Accelerator pedal

    C. Transmission controls

    D. All of the above

3. **In order to engage the clutch you push the clutch pedal all the way to the floor.**

    A. True

    B. False

4. **A manual transmission uses:**

    A. Only a gear shift lever

    B. An on-board computer for some gear changes

    C. A clutch and gear shift lever

    D. All of the above

5. **The foot brake control valve operates both the tractor and trailer's service brakes.**

    A. True

    B. False

6. **The independent trailer brake operates the emergency brake on the trailer.**

    A. True

    B. False

7. **Auxiliary brakes reduce the vehicle's speed without using the service brakes.**

    A. True

    B. False

8. **Which of the following is *not* a secondary vehicle control?**

    A. Lights

    B. Heater

    C. Seat belts

    D. Steering wheel

9. **Vehicle instruments:**

    A. Monitor and report on the operating condition of your vehicle

    B. Slow or stop the vehicle

    C. Control the vehicle's speed

    D. All of the above

10. **Warning devices let you know when the vehicle's temperature or pressure level reaches a dangerous level.**

    A. True

    B. False

General Knowledge CDL Pre-Test

Read each question carefully and then choose the answer that is most correct.

1. **When you are driving through construction zones, you should:**

   A. Speed up and hurry through them so you aren't in them any longer than necessary

   B. Stop before entering them, get in low gear and proceed through

   C. Watch for sharp pavement drop-offs

   D. Reduce your speed only if construction workers are near the roadway

2. **If you break down on a level, straight, four-lane, divided highway, where should you place the reflective warning triangles?**

   A. One 10 feet from the rear of the vehicle, one approximately 100 feet from the rear of the vehicle and another one about 100 feet to the front of the vehicle

   B. One 10 feet from the rear of the vehicle, one approximately 100 feet from the rear of the vehicle, and one about 200 feet from the rear of the vehicle

   C. One 100 feet from the rear of the vehicle, one approximately 200 feet from the rear of the vehicle, and one about 300 feet from the rear of the vehicle

   D. One 50 feet from the rear of the vehicle, one about 100 feet from the rear of the vehicle, and one about 200 feet from the front of the vehicle

3. **According to the Commercial Driver's manual, why should you limit the use of your vehicle's horn?**

   A. If your vehicle has air brakes, the air horn may not work while you are applying your brakes

   B. It may startle other drivers

   C. You should keep both hands on the steering wheel at all times

   D. The Driver's Manual does not say that a driver should limit the use of the horn

4. **Which of the following should you NOT do?**

    A. Turn your headlights on during the day if visibility is reduced due to bad weather

    B. Flash you brake lights to warn vehicles behind you that you are slowing down

    C. Flash your brake lights when entering a construction zone if vehicles are close behind you

    D. Flash your brake lights if someone is following too closely

5. **The proper way to load a vehicle is:**

    A. Keep the load balanced in the cargo area

    B. Place the load at the front of the trailer to give your drive wheels better traction

    C. Place the load at the rear of the trailer so your rear tires have better traction

    D. It makes no difference where the cargo is placed as long as you are not over the allowable gross weight

How did you do? Check with your instructor for the correct answers. Keep trying, you'll have this mastered in no time!

Chapter 2
Control Systems

Chapter **3**

Vehicle systems

OBJECTIVES

Upon completion of this chapter, you should have a basic understanding of vehicle construction and systems including:

❑ Identification of the key parts of a tractor-trailer

❑ How the key parts of a tractor-trailer function

❑ How the key parts function together in vehicle operation

Introduction

As with any vehicle, a tractor-trailer is made up of many parts. Though these parts have individual jobs or functions, they work together to effectively and efficiently operate the tractor-trailer.

It is important that, as a professional driver, you understand the basics of vehicle construction and systems. This will help you maintain a safe vehicle and help you spot problems before they become major, causing a breakdown or accident.

As you review this chapter, keep in mind that the parts covered may not be included on all vehicles.

Frame

The frame is the structure around which the vehicle is assembled. It is the vehicle's foundation. The frame includes left and right side frame rails and cross members connecting the frame rails. This provides strength and support to the frame. The frame is connected directly or indirectly to all parts of the truck.

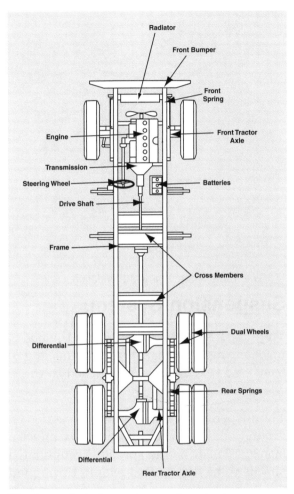

The frame, including various systems/parts.

The engine is secured to the frame by engine mounts. Axles and wheels are connected to the suspension system through the frame.

Some types of vehicles, including many cargo tanks and van trailers do not have a frame. The exterior of the vehicle carries the vehicle's weight.

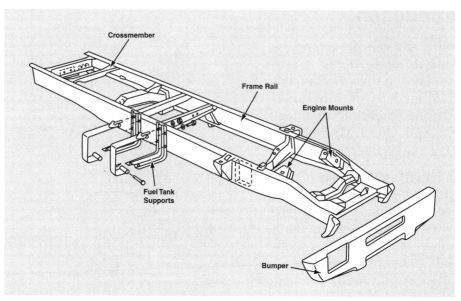

The frame is the vehicle's foundation.

Suspension System

The suspension system supports the body and frame of the truck. It is made up of springs, air bags, torque arms, and mounting brackets or hangers. The front and rear axles are attached to the suspension system, and the frame rests on it.

The suspension system allows the axles to move up and down in response to ground changes without seriously affecting the load. Securing the suspension system at points spread throughout the frame allows the stress of road shocks to be distributed evenly throughout the frame.

The strength and durability of the system is determined by the size and weight of the vehicle as well as the size and weight of the cargo being hauled.

The following are the characteristics necessary for a good suspension system:

- Capacity to support the load;

- Ability to transmit full brake effort to the chassis frame;

- A cushioned ride for the driver and cargo (laden or unladen);

- Secure axles to assure correct driveline alignment; and

- Easy maintenance and lightweight parts.

There are two main types of suspension systems, leaf spring and air bag suspension systems.

Leaf spring suspension — This type of suspension system uses metal strips of different lengths that are connected and attached to the spring mounts or hangers.

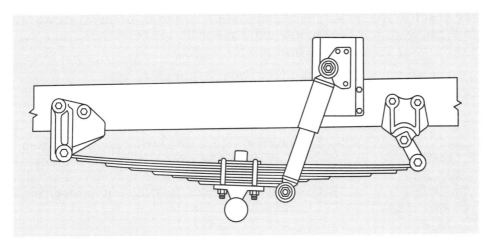

Leaf spring suspension.

Air bag suspension — Bags of air are placed between the axle and the frame in this type of suspension system. This system is most often used on trailers and truck tractors. This type of system provides a smooth ride whether the vehicle is loaded or empty.

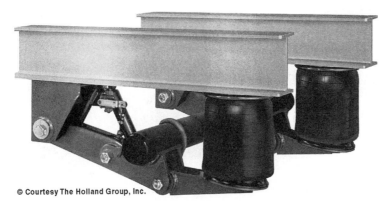

© Courtesy The Holland Group, Inc.

Airbag suspension.

In some cases these systems are combined to provide the best of both systems.

Shock absorbers — As the vehicle's wheels move over uneven surfaces, shock absorbers reduce the motion of the vehicle body. They are used in both the leaf spring and the air bag suspension systems.

Axles

In general, the axles connect the wheels to the rest of the vehicle and help support the weight of the vehicle and its cargo. Individual axles perform specific functions.

Front tractor axle — This axle is the steering axle. It connects the steering mechanism and brakes.

Rear tractor axles — These axles are the power, or drive axles. They transfer power from the engine and drive train to the wheels and serve as the connecting point for the brakes.

Axles fall into two types or categories:

1. **Dead axles** — Dead axles do not transmit power. They are used to support the load.

2. **Live axles** — Live axles transmit power from the drive shaft to the wheels through a differential gear housing. The live axle is hollow. This allows the gears and axles to transmit power through this area to the wheels.

© Courtesy of Roadranger - a marketing partnership between Eaton and Dana Corporation.

Dead axles steer and support the vehicle's load.

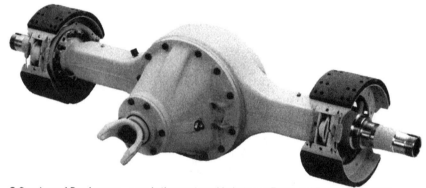

© Courtesy of Roadranger - a marketing partnership between Eaton and Dana Corporation.

Live axles transmit power.

Engine

The engine supplies the vehicle's power. It is fueled by either diesel or gasoline. In today's engines, you may also find the use of propane or natural gas as fuel. The engine on a truck-tractor is an internal combustion engine. This means the engine burns fuel within closed chambers inside the engine. The enclosed chambers are called cylinders. It is within the cylinders where the power comes from to operate the vehicle.

The engine has five basic parts:

- Engine block;
- Cylinders;
- Pistons;
- Connecting rods; and
- Crank shaft.

As previously mentioned, the engine is fueled by either diesel or gasoline. Both are internal combustion engines which use a mixture of air and fuel for ignition, but that's where the similarities end.

Today's gas engines may have a carburetor and spark plugs or they may have fuel injectors similar to a diesel engine..

The diesel engine has a series of fuel injectors. Fuel and air are mixed during compression. The compression in a diesel engine is much higher and the compression pressure actually causes ignition of the fuel/air mixture.

The engine supplies the vehicle's power.

Diesel vs. Gasoline Engines	Diesel	Gasoline
Carburetor		X
Spark plug		X
Injector	X	X
Fuel/air mix *before* compression		X
Fuel/air mix *after* compression	X	

Fuel System

The fuel system provides fuel for engine operation. It controls the amount of fuel sent to the engine and determines when the fuel is injected into the cylinders.

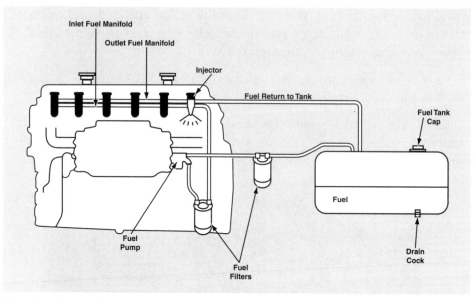

The diesel fuel system.

The fuel pump draws fuel from the fuel tanks through the fuel lines and fuel filters to the fuel injectors. The fuel injectors are operated by an injector pump and spray a fine mist of fuel into the engine cylinders.

Cleanliness is very important when it comes to the fuel system. Even the smallest amount of dirt or other particles can damage the engine. A properly operating fuel system will eliminate many impurities, but it is also important that you use great care when fueling your vehicle.

Fuel tank — The fuel tank is where the fuel is held. There may be one or two fuel tanks depending on the size and type of vehicle. Additional tanks may carry fuel for heaters and reefers.

Keep the fuel cap area clean. You don't want dirt or other particles to enter the fuel tank.

Fuel filters — A series of filters clean the fuel throughout the fuel system. These filters remove dirt, water, and rust from the fuel system.

Fuel system heaters — Fuel system heaters are especially important for vehicles operated in cold weather. In general, there are three types of heaters:

- In-tank units which heat fuel in the tank;

- In-line units which heat fuel when it is going from the tank to the injector system; and

- Filter heaters which help heat the fuel as it passes through the injection system.

Some diesel trucks do not have fuel heaters. In very large engines, some of the fuel that goes through the engine is not actually burned, but is returned to the fuel tanks by way of a fuel return line. This process heats the fuel and some companies count on this as their "fuel heating" system.

Hang on driver! Do you know how to change a fuel filter? Well you better learn how before you drive in cold winter weather for the first time. Plugged filters, due to diesel fuel gelling, is a common problem experienced by many drivers while on the road during the cold winter months. You should always carry one or two spare filters just in case, and don't forget the filter wrench! It only takes a few minutes to change one, and doing it yourself could save you a lot of money and down time.

Air Intake and Exhaust System

The air intake system delivers fresh air into the cylinders.

Fresh air is important in the operation of the diesel engine. The air intake and exhaust system are responsible for assuring that the engine processes enough fresh air to function properly.

Air intake system — The air intake system filters out dust, dirt, and water and delivers a large amount of fresh air to the cylinders.

Exhaust system — After combustion, the exhaust system collects the used gasses, passes them through the turbo charger, then expels them through a tailpipe or exhaust stack.

Turbo charger — The turbo charger converts the power it gets from the exhaust gasses into power that can be used by the engine.

Aftercooler — The aftercooler cools the intake air from the turbo charger returning it to a safe temperature level.

Pyrometer — The pyrometer is an instrument that measures the temperature of exhaust gasses. The normal temperature is between 600°-1,000° F depending on the vehicle. If the exhaust temperature is too high, the engine and the turbo can be damaged.

Lubrication System

The lubrication system has three purposes. It lubricates, cools, and cleans the engine.

1. The lubrication system delivers clean oil to parts of the engine. This allows the engine parts to move without rubbing together (friction). This increases engine efficiency and prevents damage.

Exhaust is expelled through an exhaust stack.

2.   The moving parts of the engine create a great deal of heat. Oil flowing through the engine absorbs some of this heat and removes it from the engine, keeping engine temperature at a safe level.

3.   Oil helps keep the engine clean. As it travels through the engine it picks up dirt and other particles that can damage the engine. These particles are filtered out of the engine. Oil also prevents rust and corrosion by coating surfaces that do not move within the engine.

Maintaining the lubrication system — Proper preventive maintenance can go a long way in making sure your vehicle's engine operates efficiently and effectively. It is important that the oil is changed on a regular basis according to the vehicle manufacturer's recommendations.

As part of the oil change, the condition of the oil filter should be assessed. The oil filter is where dirt and particles that the oil removes from the engine are deposited. A clean filter allows clean oil to flow through the engine.

It is also important to check the oil level in the engine on a daily basis. This can be done by using the dipstick. The dipstick is found at the side of the engine.

Check the engine's oil level daily.

To measure the engine's oil level:

1.   Turn off the engine.

2.   Put on gloves (the engine may be hot and you need to protect your hands).

3.   Remove the dipstick and wipe it off with a rag.

4.   Reinsert the clean dipstick.

5.   Again remove the dipstick.

At this point, you should be able to determine the level of the oil in the engine, which is measured in gallons. If the reading isn't clear, wipe off the dipstick, reinsert, remove, and read again.

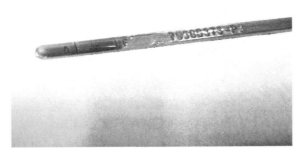

The dipstick measures the engine's oil level.

If the dipstick reads "low" or "add oil" do so before operating the vehicle again.

Oil filter system — The oil filter can help prolong the life of the engine by removing contaminants as oil passes through. There are three types of oil filter systems:

- Full flow systems;

- Bypass systems; and

- Combination bypass/full flow systems.

Cooling System

Though heat is important to engine operation, too much heat can damage an engine. The cooling system lowers the heat level of an operating engine.

Coolant (a combination of water and antifreeze) is stored in the radiator and circulated through engine water jackets by the water pump. At this point, the coolant is collecting some of the engine's heat and then returns to the radiator. In the radiator, the heated coolant travels through tubes which cool the coolant. The cooled coolant then recirculates, repeating the process.

Slow down driver, no need to be in a hurry here. You need to give your engine a few minutes for all the oil to settle before you check it. Otherwise, you may get an incorrect reading. Here's an idea...shut your engine off, pump your fuel, clean your windows, THEN check your oil. That should give the oil plenty of time to settle in the engine and give you a much more accurate reading on the dipstick.

Hey, one more thing. This is no time to get all "heated up" about your coolant system. Be careful when removing the radiator cap! Your engine's probably been working hard, is quite warm, and just might give you a very hot shower if you're not careful.

The cooling system helps prevent engine damage.

Always follow the engine manufacturer's requirements for selecting coolant. Make sure the radiator is filled with the proper amount of coolant. Too much or too little can damage the engine. Also keep in mind that different operating conditions (weather, etc.) require different levels of water to antifreeze mixture.

Electrical System

Electrical System

The electrical system serves many purposes. It is used to crank the engine and operate the vehicle's electrical equipment including lights and instruments.

The electrical system is comprised of four parts:

- Charging circuit;
- Cranking circuit;
- Ignition circuit; and
- Lighting and accessory circuits.

1. **Charging circuit** — The charging circuit produces electricity. This keeps the battery charged and runs the electrical circuits. The charging circuit is comprised of six major parts.

   - **Battery** — The battery is an electrochemical device for storing and supplying electrical energy. The battery's energy is what activates the starter.

   - **Alternator or generator** — Most vehicles on the road today are equipped with an alternator, but some still use a generator. These devices are responsible for recharging the battery. When the engine is running, the alternator creates electricity. Most of the electricity the vehicle needs is supplied by the alternator.

- **Ammeter** — An ammeter is a gauge on the vehicle's instrument panel that shows the amount of current flowing from the alternator. It shows whether the battery is being charged or is discharging.

- **Voltmeter** — The voltmeter is another gauge on the vehicle's instrument panel. It tells you how much the battery is charged.

- **Voltage regulator** — The voltage regulator is the device that controls the voltage output of the alternator or generator. The voltage regulator keeps the battery voltage from getting too high. If the battery voltage is too high, the battery could overcharge.

2. **Cranking circuit** — The cranking circuit moves electricity from the battery to a starter motor. Depressing the starter switch inside the vehicle gets this process started.

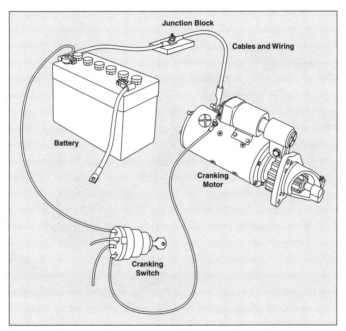

The cranking circuit moves electricity from the battery to a starter motor.

3. **Ignition circuit** — The ignition circuit is the electrical circuit that provides sparks for each cylinder, igniting the fuel and air mixture in a gasoline engine. An ignition circuit is not needed in a diesel engine.

4. **Lighting and accessory circuits** — These circuits provide electricity for the vehicle's lights, horn, instrument lights, windshield wipers, etc.

Drive Train

The drive train is a series of connected mechanical parts which take the power generated by the engine and applies it to the tractor's drive wheels.

The drive train is comprised of the following main parts:

- Clutch;
- Transmission;
- Drive shaft;
- Universal joints; and
- Differential.

© Courtesy of Roadranger - a marketing partnership between Eaton and Dana Corporation.

The drive train

These parts modify the torque/twist and engine speed produced by the engine, turning it into power to move the vehicle down the road.

1. **Clutch** — The clutch is the part of the power train that allows the driver to connect or disconnect the engine from the power train. The clutch allows the driver to shift gears. The clutch is composed of six major parts:

   - Clutch housing;

   - Flywheel;

   - Clutch disc(s);

   - Pressure plate;

   - Release assembly; and

   - Controls.

   In most trucks the clutch has three plates, one plate is squeezed tightly between two other plates. The plate in the middle is the driven member (clutch disk), which is connected to the shaft leading to the transmission. The other two plates are driving members which are connected directly to the engine. A strong spring or springs, force the two driving members together. This tightens their grip on the middle plate until they all turn as one unit.

The clutch allows the driver to connect or disconnect the engine from the power train.

   The engine flywheel is used for the first driving member. It has a smooth surface where the driven plate pushes up against it.

   The other driving member is called the pressure plate. It is a heavy cast iron ring which is smooth on one side. It is fastened to the cover, which is bolted to the flywheel, so they all turn together. It is fastened so it can slide back and forth.

   The driven plate is a flat disk of steel with friction facing on each side. The plate is fastened by splines to a shaft going to the transmission. It fits into grooves on the shaft so they can turn together, but the plate can slide backward and forward on the shaft. This disc is softer than the other plates. This allows the disc to wear out, preventing damage to other parts of the drive train.

2. **Transmission** — The transmission is a box/case of gears. It is located behind the clutch and is fastened to the clutch housing.

   The transmission adjusts the power generated by the engine. This provides the correct speed and torque needed. It transmits this power from the engine to the drive or powered axle(s) in order to propel the vehicle.

The transmission's gears control the speed of the vehicle. Though the engine moves at only one speed, the gears allow the vehicle to move at different speeds.

Another property of the transmission is torque. This is what makes something rotate. The torque of the gears in a transmission is related to the amount of power a vehicle exhibits. The gears let the driver vary the speed and force (torque) that the engine delivers to the wheels. When selecting gears, keep in mind that the more torque, the less speed there is and the more speed, the less torque there is.

By manipulating the gears in the transmission, you can change the ratio between the engine and the rear wheels to produce more speed or torque as needed.

3. **Drive shaft and universal joints** — Behind the transmission is a propeller which runs to the rear of the vehicle. This is called the drive shaft. The drive shaft is a hollow or solid steel shaft that connects the transmission to the rear of the vehicle. At the front and rear of the shaft are universal joints. They are (in most cases) made up of two U-shaped pieces at right angles to each other and fastened together by a cross having arms of equal length.

   The drive shaft transfers the twisting motion of the engine to the rear axle. The universal joints connect the shaft to the transmission and the rear axle.

   The U-shaped pieces pivot on the arms of the cross. Since there are two pivots, the two shafts can be at an angle to one another and still turn around and transmit power. They do not have to be in a straight line. This is important because they become somewhat misaligned with each bump in the road. The rear axle moves up and down with the wheels, while the transmission moves very little as it is fastened to the frame. The universal joints allow the drive shaft to keep on turning smoothly even though its two ends are not always directly in line with each other.

4. **Differential** — The differential is the part of the drive train that splits the drive axle in half, allowing one wheel to turn at a different rate of speed than another. This helps a vehicle when turning. When performing a turn, the outside wheel must rotate faster than the inside wheel so your right wheel is actually turning at a different speed than your left wheel.

Brake System

The braking system is what slows down and stops the vehicle. It is made up of three major elements:

- Service brakes;

- Emergency brakes; and

- Parking brakes.

Braking control panel.

1. **Service brakes** — Service brakes slow down and stop the vehicle. The service brakes are regulated by the driver by using the foot and trolley valves.

   There are two types of service brakes, drum and disc.

   - **Drum brakes** — This metal cylinder looks like a drum that is bolted to each end of an axle. The braking mechanism is located inside the drum. To stop, the brake shoes and linings are forced/pushed against the inside of the drum. This causes friction which slows the vehicle and creates heat. When too much heat is created the brakes can stop working, making it harder, if not (in some cases) impossible to stop.

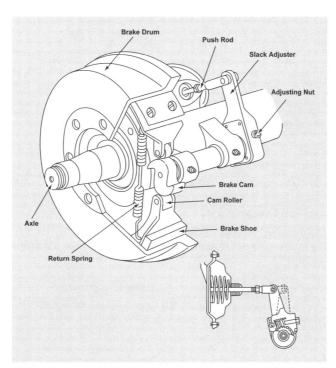

The components of a drum brake.

   - **Disc brakes** — Disc brake systems have a fixed disc attached to the inside of the wheel which rotates with the wheel. To stop, the linings are squeezed against the side of the disc which creates friction to stop the vehicle.

2. **Emergency brakes** — Emergency brakes slow down and stop the vehicle when there is a failure in the air system.

3. **Parking brakes** — Parking brakes prevent vehicle movement when parked.

Air brakes — Air brakes use compressed air to maximize braking force. The parts which make up an air brake system are listed below.

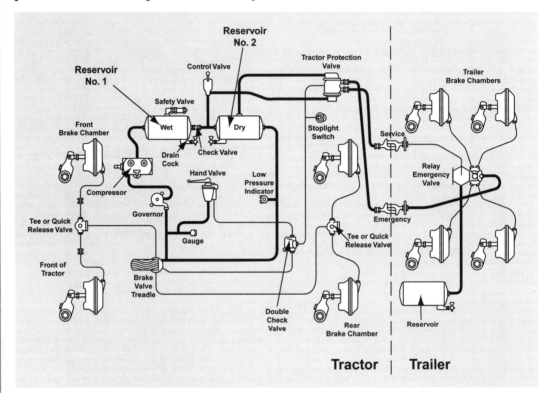

The components of an air brake system.

- **Compressor** — This device is designed to build up and maintain required air pressure in the brake system reservoir. The compressor is run by the vehicle's engine. It runs when the engine runs. The compressor may use belts and pulleys or shafts and gears, which are lubricated by the engine's lubrication system. The normal operating range is 90-125 pounds per square inch (psi). The compressor runs until the pressure in the air reservoir reaches 125 psi. It then stops until needed.

- **Governor** — The governor regulates the compressor. This allows the compressor to maintain appropriate pressure by opening and closing inlet valves.

- **Air reservoirs** — Air reservoirs hold the compressed air. There are three tanks which hold air; a wet tank, dry tank, and trailer reservoir. The wet tank removes most of the moisture and delivers the air to the dry tank. The trailer reservoir holds compressed air close to the trailer brake chambers for use in normal and emergency situations. The sizes of the tanks vary based on the number of tanks and the size of the brake chambers.

Air reservoirs.

The number of tanks on your vehicle may be different. Some tractors have only one tank, which is a wet tank and a dry combined. There also may be one or two tanks on the trailer.

- **One-way check valve** — This valve prevents air from getting back into the compressor from the air reservoirs. If air flows back, the brakes will not work.

- **Safety valves** — Safety valves, also called pressure relief valves, keep air pressure from reaching a dangerous level. A safety valve opens (usually when pressure reaches 150 psi) and releases the air into the atmosphere, lowering the pressure in the system. If the safety valve activates often or continuously, the air governor may need servicing. This should only be done by a qualified mechanic. Never make these adjustments on your own. You have probably all heard the occasional release of air while standing next to a big truck. This is the safety valve releasing and is normal.

- **Drain cocks** — Drain cocks release moisture from air brake system reservoirs. The braking system could be damaged if this moisture is not removed, especially in winter, when the moisture could freeze. To prevent damage, you should drain the moisture daily. This should be done on a level surface, with the vehicle properly chocked. Allow all of the air pressure to escape to make sure all of the moisture is released.

- **Air pressure gauge** — The air pressure gauge is located on the instrument panel. It tells you how much pressure is in the system. The normal operating range is 90-120 psi. This gauge should always be included in your visual scan of the vehicle's instruments. This will help you detect a malfunction before it becomes an emergency. Remember, this could be one gauge with two needles or two separate gauges; primary and secondary.

Just a quick note here driver. You know those "o-rings" we're talking about in your gladhands? Well, they wear out pretty easily. It's a good idea to carry some with you in your tool kit. They're pretty inexpensive, and they could save you some frustration down the road.

Do you have to know all these valves, such as the quick release valve, the relay valve, or the emergency relay valve? Not really. As a driver what you need to know is that there are a series of valves associated with your brake system that help it operate correctly. If you have a brake problem, it may be because of one of these valves but that would be determined by a mechanic. Unless you're a mechanic don't worry...be happy!

- **Low-pressure warning signal** — This signal warns you that air pressure has dropped to a potentially unsafe level (below 60 psi). Either a red warning light will light up or a buzzer will sound. If this happens, stop immediately. If you do not stop immediately, you may lose more pressure and your brakes will lock up. This must be fixed before you can continue your trip.

- **Air application pressure gauge** — This gauge shows the amount of air pressure being applied to the brakes. When pressure is not being applied to the service brakes, the gauge will read 0 psi. (Not on all trucks.)

- **Treadle valve** — The treadle valve (also called the foot brake or brake pedal) controls the air for the operation of the brakes. This valve is controlled by pushing (depressing) the brake pedal. The further down the brake pedal is pushed, the more air the system will receive, until it is at full capacity. Releasing the brake pedal releases the brakes by letting air exhaust from the brakes.

- **Independent trailer brake** — The independent trailer brake (also called the trolley valve or hand valve) is a hand-operated control that applies the trailer brakes by regulating the airflow to the trailer unit. This brake should never be used for slowing down or parking. (Not on all trucks.)

- **Tractor parking valve** — This hand controlled knob can be pushed in to release the tractor parking brake and pulled out to set the parking brake. It also operates the spring brakes.

- **Glad hands** — Glad hands are connectors mounted on the front of the trailer for connecting air lines from the tractor. When the glad hands lock, the connection is secure. An O-ring seals the coupling, preventing dirt and debris from entering and air from escaping. You should check the O-ring for damage or dirt and debris before connecting the air lines. These O-rings are color coded. The service line is usually blue and the emergency line is usually red. When the air lines are unhooked, they should be sealed with protector plates to keep out dirt and debris. Keeping the air lines clean reduces your chances of brake failure.

- **Quick release valve** — This valve (located near the brake chambers) allows the brakes to release in a short amount of time. When you remove your foot from the valve, the pressurized air in the chambers escapes quickly into the atmosphere. This allows the brake shoes to release quickly.

- **Relay valve** — This valve is used to speed up the application and release of the rear wheel brakes. In other words the relay valve is responsible for making sure that all brakes apply at the same time.

- **Emergency relay valve** — The emergency relay valve is installed either on the trailer reservoir or on the trailer frame close to the brake chambers. This valve controls brake application and also provides for automatic trailer brake application should the trailer become disconnected from the tractor. The emergency relay valve can also release the trailer brakes quickly.

- **Brake chamber** — The brake chambers are chambers of air that are installed close to each wheel. They are attached to the brakes by either a pushrod and slack adjuster (cam brake) or simply a pushrod (wedge brake). Air enters the chamber from the brake lines. From the chamber to the brake shoe and drum, the force is applied mechanically.

© Courtesy of Dana Corporation.

Air disc brake.

Air brake system operation — So how does a basic air brake system work?

1. The pressurized air is pumped by the compressor to the wet tank where moisture is removed.

2. The air then passes through the one-way check valve to the dry reservoir.

3. When you put your foot on the brake, the air flows through the service air lines to the tractor brake chambers (both front and rear). At the same time, air travels through the tractor protection valve, through the service glad hand, to the trailer brake chambers.

4. When you release the brake pedal, air escapes through the foot valve or relay valve in the tractor and the quick release valve in the trailer.

Antilock brake systems — In March 1995, the National Highway Traffic Safety Administration (NHTSA) issued rules requiring antilock brake systems (ABS) for heavy trucks, tractors, trailers, and buses. Specifically these rules require ABS for:

- All new truck-tractors manufactured on or after March 1, 1997;

- All new air-braked trailers and single-unit trucks and buses manufactured on or after March 1, 1998; and

- All new single-unit trucks and buses with hydraulic brakes manufactured on or after March 1, 1999.

The purpose of the antilock system is to control wheel lock-up, which can cause a vehicle to skid and possibly jackknife. This is accomplished by an electronic system which senses the speed of each wheel. When the wheel speed sensor detects an imminent lock-up a valve is opened and air in the chamber is released. As the wheel speed increases, the valve is closed and air is reapplied. All of this occurs automatically if the vehicle is stopping and a lock-up is sensed.

The antilock system activates when you apply pressure to the brake pedal sharply enough to lock the wheels. The computer system senses the potential for lock-up and "pumps" the brakes at a rate three to five times faster than a human could. You should never pump the brakes when operating a vehicle with an antilock brake system. Let the computer do the work for you.

Most ABS-equipped vehicles have a warning light on the dashboard. This light will turn on for a few seconds when starting your vehicle. If the light stays on or suddenly turns on while you are driving, the ABS may not be working. Though you still have properly working brakes the antilock function may not be working. Get this checked out as soon as possible.

The light also turns on for a short period of time when the brakes are applied.

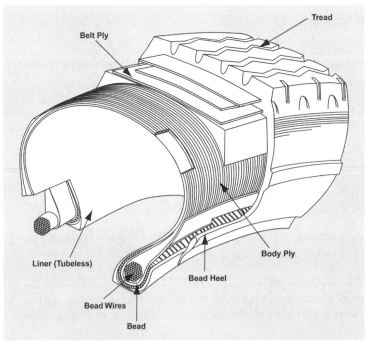

The components of a truck tire.

Wheels and Tires

Wheels — Spoke and disc wheels are the two types of wheels found on most trucks.

1. **Spoke wheels** — Spoke wheels are made up of two pieces. They are heavier and more difficult to align and balance.

2. **Disc wheels** — Disc wheels are made of aluminum or steel. They are easier to align because they are fastened together with one locking stud and nut that runs through both rims.

There are two types of wheel mounting systems used on most trucks, stud piloted and hub piloted.

1. **Stud piloted** — A stud piloted mounting system uses the studs on the wheel hub to guide and center the wheel.

2. **Hub piloted** — A hub piloted mounting system uses the wheel hub to guide and center the wheel.

The wheels are fastened by either ball-seat nuts or flange nuts.

Tires — There are three types of tires used on most trucks.

1. **Radial tires** — The body plycords run around the tire perpendicular to the tread. Radial tires also have belt plies that run circumferentially around the tire, under the tread. This type of tire construction allows for better traction and fuel mileage.

   The tread on radial tries lasts 40 to 100 percent longer because when the surface area of radials comes in contact with the road, they have greater traction while creating less friction and less heat. This gives your vehicle greater fuel mileage and better performance.

2. **Bias ply tires** — The body plycords run diagonal across the tire. The tire may also have breakers or narrow plies under the tread.

3. **Belted bias tires** — The body ply cords run diagonal across the tread and belted plies run circumferentially around the tire under the tread. The belts on this tire are of heavier construction.

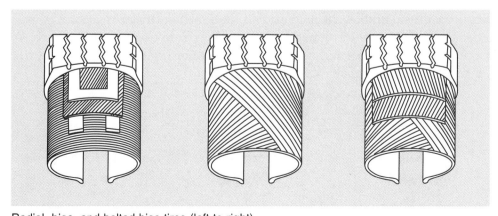

Radial, bias, and belted bias tires (left to right).

Mixing radial and bias ply tires — Generally, radial and bias ply tires should not be mixed. All tires on your vehicle should be the same size and type. The differences in traction and turning capabilities among the different types of tires can cause problems if the types of tires are improperly mixed. There are ways to properly mix the tires. Consult the tire manufacturer for guidelines/instructions.

Tire tubes — Some tires have tubes that fit between the tire and the rim. The air that keeps the tire inflated is kept in the tire tube. Flat tires are more prone to tire fires because the under inflated tube spins inside the tire, creating excessive heat.

Tubeless tires — Tubeless tires are mounted onto a single-piece wheel. The tire (instead of a tube) holds the air. Tubeless tires are lighter and easier to mount.

Tire maintenance — Proper tire inflation is important. Under inflation can increase tread wear and reduce the life of the tires. Overinflation can damage the tires and reduce stopping efficiency. Consult the vehicle's owner's manual for inflation guidance.

Tire pressure should be checked regularly. This should be done with an accurate gauge when the tire is cool.

Tread design — There are two basic truck tire tread designs.

1. **Rib tread** — The open groove design of this tread allows for a high degree of control, helping you avoid skids. This type of tread is recommended for the front wheel positions on tractors.

2. **Lug tread** — In over the road high-torque service, lug treads provide maximum protection from wear and greater traction. This type of tread is recommended for drive wheels. Generally the vehicle gets better mileage with this tread than rib tread.

Proper tire inflation — Proper tire inflation has many benefits including increased fuel efficiency, a smoother ride, and a reduced chance of blow out or tire fire. Inspect your tires often and check the pressure with a tire gauge. Refer to the manufacturer's specifications for correct pressure.

Tire pressure should be checked and adjusted when the tire is cool. If the tire is hot the pressure reading will be higher. If you do check a heated tire, and the pressure is higher than recommended, do not release any air. Wait until the tire is cool and check again.

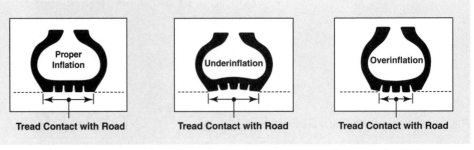

Proper tire inflation has many benefits including fuel efficiency and a smoother ride.

When inflating a tire, keep in mind the maximum pressure for the load you are carrying, making sure you do not exceed the rim or wheel rating.

During regular operation of your vehicle, the pressure of the tires should increase, as the tires get warmer. Expect increases of 10-15 psi. Greater increases, which can create an abnormal amount of heat, may indicate Under inflation, excessive speed, and/or incorrect tire size. If this happens you should stop, investigate, and correct the problem.

Under inflation of a tire — When a tire is under inflated, the following can happen:

- The tread wears down more quickly;

- The temperature within the tire increases, possibly causing the separation of the tread from the body or belt ply; and

- Deflation can occur, weakening the tire's body cords, potentially causing a blowout.

If you operate duals and one is under inflated or flat a fire can start.

Overinflation — An overinflated tire becomes rigid, making it easier for the tire to be cut or punctured by objects on the road. Overinflation also makes the ride less smooth as the tires are unable to absorb shock.

Tire care — Tires should be rotated periodically based on manufacturer recommendations. This will help in evenly distributing wear.

As well as being a good, safe practice, inspecting tires on a daily basis is required by the Federal Motor Carrier Safety Regulations (FMCSRs). Section 392.7 states that a driver must be satisfied that certain vehicle parts and accessories are in good working condition prior to driving his/her vehicle. This includes tires.

Appropriate tire condition and tread depth is also addressed in the FMCSRs. According to Sec. 393.75, you may not drive your vehicle if a tire has any of the defects listed below:

- Body ply or belt material exposed through the tread or sidewall;

- Any tread or sidewall separation;

- The tire is flat or has an audible leak; or

- The tire has a cut that exposes the ply or belt material.

Section 393.75 also states that any tire on the front wheels must have a tread groove pattern depth of at least $\frac{4}{32}$ of an inch when measured at any point on a major tread groove. All other tires must have a tread groove pattern depth of at least $\frac{2}{32}$ of an inch when measured in a major tread groove.

Matching and spacing of duals — If two tires of differing diameters are positioned together, the larger tire will begin to overheat and bulge out at the sides due to taking more of the load on its own. The smaller tire will wear irregularly because it doesn't have proper contact with the road, possibly causing the tread to separate. If the larger tire bulges too far, it will begin to touch the other tire, increasing friction and heat between the two, which can cause a blowout in one or both of the tires.

To be on the safe side, allow no more than¼ inch difference between the diameters, no matter what the tire size. Also keep the spacing between the tires at the recommended distance to prevent the tires from touching, creating a heat build-up.

Steering System

The steering system is what gives you directional control of your vehicle. The components that make up the steering system include:

- **Steering wheel** — The steering wheel controls the direction of the vehicle. It is connected to and turns the steering shaft.

- **Steering shaft** — The steering shaft connects the steering wheel to the steering gear box.

- **Gear box** — The gear box transfers the turning of the steering shaft to the Pitman arm.

- **Pitman arm** — This component is connected to the steering gear box and moves the drag link.

- **Drag link** — The drag link transfers movement from the Pitman arm to the left steering arm.

- **Steering arm** — The right side attaches the tie rod to the wheels, the left side attaches to the drag link.

- **Tie rod** — The tie rod connects the front wheels to together and adjusts their operating angle.

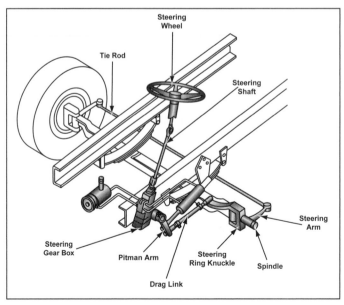

The components of the steering system.

All of the parts listed on the previous page must be correctly aligned. Incorrect alignment can cause difficulty in steering and improper tire wear.

Wheel alignment — The following alignment characteristics are built into the axle by the manufacturer. They may be changed as necessary.

- **Caster** — The caster of an axle is the amount of tilt it has. This is measured in degrees and it is recommended that the axle have positive caster (it tilts forward). When set this way, the vehicle will want to naturally move straight ahead and will recover from turns more easily. Positive caster makes it easier for you to steer.

- **Camber** — The camber of the wheels is the degree of tilt they have with respect to the road. It is best when the truck's wheels have a positive camber to support the load. In other words, the distance across the top of the wheels is greater than the distance across the bottom. When a heavy load is placed on the truck, it straightens out the tires with the road.

Other alignment characteristics are the result of wear and damage. The most notable of these are toe-in and toe-out.

- **Toe-in** — The wheels on the same axle are closer on the front than the back.

- **Toe-out** — The wheels on the same axle are closer in the back than the front.

Power steering — Power steering allows you greater control of your vehicle with less effort. There are many advantages to power steering; It takes less effort, reducing driver fatigue, road shocks are better absorbed, and it is easier to maneuver the vehicle in difficult situations.

Coupling System

The coupling system is what connects the tractor and trailer. Two main components make up the coupling system, the fifth wheel and kingpin.

Fifth wheel — The fifth wheel is a coupling device located on the tractor's rear frame. It is used to join/couple the front end of the trailer to the tractor. The fifth wheel is a flat, rounded plate with a V-shaped notch in the rear. The kingpin, which is located on the trailer, fits into the fifth wheel, allowing the tractor to pull the trailer.

There are several types of fifth wheels including fixed-mount and sliding/adjustable.

1. **Fixed-mount** — The fixed-mount fifth wheel is secured in a fixed position behind the cab and has three parts, the baseplate, bracket subassemblies, and framemounting members.

   - **Base plate** — The base plate includes the locking mechanism. It also takes on the majority of the stress of coupling.

   - **Bracket subassemblies** — The bracket subassemblies keep the base plate in place.

- **Frame mounting** — The frame mounting members are structural steel angles bolted to the fifth wheel.

© Courtesy The Holland Group, Inc.

The fixed-mount fifth wheel.

2. **Sliding/adjustable** — The sliding or adjustable fifth wheel slides backward and forward to accommodate different types of loads. The sliding fifth wheel may be locked into place with pins that fit into holes in the slider track or by a plunger that fits into a row of slotted holes.

Adjustment of the slider may be done by hand or by a control in the cab. When adjusted by hand, the driver manually moves the pins or plunger and adjusts the fifth wheel by moving it forward or backward. When adjusted from the cab, activating a switch unlocks the locking device. The driver then sets the trailer brakes and moves the tractor forward and backward until the fifth wheel is in the correct position.

The sliding/adjustable fifth wheel.

Proper maintenance of the fifth wheel is important. This includes making sure the fifth wheel has the right amount of grease so it functions properly.

The kingpin attaches to the fifth wheel.

Kingpin — The kingpin is attached to the upper fifth wheel plate, under the front of the trailer. It is a two inch steel pin that attaches to the fifth wheel to couple the tractor to the trailer.

Landing gears support the front of an uncoupled trailer.

Landing gear — Landing gears support the front end load weight of the trailer when uncoupled. They are usually cranked up or down. Landing gears have either wheels or skid feet attached to the bottom.

Summary

This chapter has covered the basics of vehicle construction and systems, helping you to maintain a safe vehicle and spot problems before they become major, causing a breakdown or accident.

Major systems covered include the frame, suspension, axles, engine, fuel, exhaust, lubrication, cooling, electrical, brake, steering, and coupling.

Vehicle Systems Quiz

Directions: Read each statement carefully and mark the response that best answers the question.

1. The _____ is a vehicle's foundation.

   A. Brake system

   B. Wheels

   C. Frame

   D. Steering system

2. Every big truck has fuel heaters so it is not necessary to treat diesel fuel when driving in the winter.

   A. True

   B. False

3. Dead axles transmit power from the drive shaft to the wheels.

   A. True

   B. False

4. Which of the following parts is *not* part of the engine:

   A. Cylinders

   B. Pistons

   C. Connecting rods

   D. Service brakes

5. Cleanliness is very important when it comes to the fuel system. Even the smallest amount of dirt or other particles can damage the engine.

   A. True

   B. False

6. Heat is important to engine operation, but too much heat can damage an engine.

   A. True

   B. False

7. **Which of the following is *not* part of the drive train:**

    A. Clutch

    B. Drive shaft

    C. Kingpin

    D. Transmission

8. **The braking system is made up of three major elements: service brakes, emergency brakes, and parking brakes.**

    A. True

    B. False

9. **The driver should check his/her oil immediately after stopping the engine to avoid settling in the oil pan causing a false reading.**

    A. True

    B. False

10. **Air brakes use compressed air to maximize braking force.**

    A. True

    B. False

General Knowledge CDL Pre-Test

Read each question carefully and then choose the answer that is most correct.

1. **When driving a vehicle with a height over 13 feet, you should:**

   A. Assume all clearances are of sufficient height

   B. Height clearance is not a concern as long as you stay on state or federal roadways

   C. If you are unsure of the clearance, stop and check before proceeding

   D. All of the above

2. **Controlled braking is:**

   A. Applying brakes hard enough for the wheels to lock up

   B. Pressing the brakes hard enough to lock-up the wheels, then releasing and then reapplying again

   C. Applying firm brake pressure but not to the point of lock-up

   D. Only used if the vehicle does not have anti-lock brakes

3. **You are driving on a straight and level roadway at 60 mph and suddenly a tire blows out on your vehicle. What should you do first?**

   A. Immediately begin light, controlled braking

   B. Immediately begin stab braking

   C. Grip steering wheel firmly with both hands and stay off the brakes until the vehicle has slowed down

   D. Immediately begin emergency braking

4. **Which of the following is true?**

   A. It is permissible to use radial and bias-ply tires together on the same axle

   B. Tires which are mismatched sizes should not be used on the same vehicle

   C. $4/32$ inch tread depth is the maximum allowed on drive tires

   D. $2/32$ inch tread depth is permissible for steering tires

5. **Why do hazardous materials regulations exist?**

   A. To provide for safe drivers and equipment

   B. To communicate a risk

   C. To contain the product

   D. All of the above

Chapter 4

Vehicle inspection

OBJECTIVES

Upon completion of this chapter, you should have a basic understanding of the vehicle inspection process. You should know how to:

❏ Inspect and check the condition of critical components of the tractor-trailer

❏ Perform accurate and efficient pretrip inspections

❏ Perform en-route inspections

❏ Perform post-trip inspections, including completion of a driver vehicle inspection report (DIR.)

Introduction

As well as being a regulatory requirement, proper vehicle inspections can go a long way in ensuring your vehicle's safe and efficient operation.

- An unsafe condition can be discovered *before* it causes an accident.

- Mechanical problems can be found before they lead to breakdowns on the road.

- By avoiding breakdowns, costly on-the-road repair service can be avoided.

- By avoiding breakdowns, your company will experience fewer delivery delays, meaning better customer service.

- Enforcement agents will not put the vehicle out of service, causing delays.

- Catching mechanical problems early will help your company's maintenance department control costs.

Types of Inspections

Three types of inspections are mandated by the Federal Motor Carrier Safety Regulations (FMCSRs).

1. **Pretrip inspection (Sec. 396.13).** This inspection is performed before taking your vehicle on the road. Doing a pretrip inspection allows you to identify problems that could cause a breakdown or accident.

2. **On-the-road (en-route) inspection (Sec. 392.9).** Watch your vehicle's gauges for signs of problems. Check all critical items each time you stop, including tires, wheels and rims, brakes, lights, electrical and air connections to the trailer, trailer coupling devices, and cargo securement devices.

3. **Post-trip inspection (Sec. 396.11).** A post-trip inspection is conducted at the end your day's work on the vehicle you are operating. This inspection includes filling out a driver vehicle inspection report (DVIR), listing any problems you may have discovered. This report helps a motor carrier make necessary repairs before the vehicle returns to the road.

What to Look at When Conducting an Inspection

As well as being a regulatory requirement, conducting vehicle inspections on a regular basis can prevent costly and time-consuming breakdowns and can prevent possible accidents due to vehicle failure. The following are critical items and issues that should be addressed regularly.

Fluid leaks — A fluid leak (oil, fuel, coolant, etc.) can lead to serious engine damage. Fluid levels should be routinely checked (pretrip, post trip, and occasionally en-route) if your vehicle's gauges indicate unusual readings). Also, watch for fluid loss (drips, puddles, etc.) underneath the vehicle.

Bad tires — A tire problem can cause a blowout, resulting in handling problems, loss of control, or even an accident. A tire blowout can also result in downtime, costing both you and your company money.

Check for proper air pressure, tread depth, and potential damage.

Watch for too much or too little air pressure as well as excessive wear. Tread depth should measure at least $4/32$ inch in the major grooves on the front tires. Tread depth should measure at least $2/32$ inch on other tires. No fabric should show through the tread or sidewall. Look for cuts, bulges, tread separation, and mismatched sizes.

Wheel and rim defects- A damaged rim could cause a tire to lose pressure or come off, causing downtime and potentially causing an accident. Watch for:

- Rust around lug nuts;

- Tightness of lug nuts;

- Missing clamps, spacers, or lugs;

- Mismatched, bent, or cracked lock rings;

- Unsafe or illegal welding repairs;

- Dented rims; and

- Loose rims.

Look for rim and wheel defects.

Braking system defects — Brake system air pressure checks are critical. You should not be able to hear any air leaks or observe a loss of air pressure on the air pressure gauge.

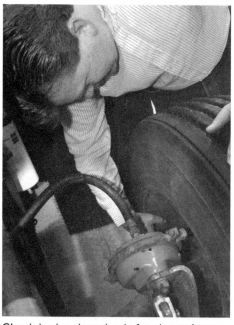
Check brake shoes/pads for signs of wear.

Air pressure should not leak more than 3 pounds per minute with the engine off and brakes released, and no more than 4 pounds per minute with the engine off and brakes fully applied (after initial application).

Check for defective gauges and low air warning devices. Section 393.51 of the FMCSRs requires that all trucks and truck tractors be equipped with a properly working warning device.

Brake drums should be checked for cracks. Shoes or pads need to be inspected for proper thickness, signs of oil or grease, and wear. Brake chambers should be securely mounted. Slack adjusters should be inspected for missing and loose parts and proper adjustment.

Brake lines (hoses) must be properly secured. They shouldn't show signs of hardening, swelling, or excessive wear or damage. They shouldn't be bent or folded over, causing possible air flow restriction. The air reservoir should be

The air reservoir should be bled daily.

properly attached to the vehicle and shouldn't contain excessive water. It should be bled daily to check for moisture.

Ever spent a cold night on the side of the road, driver? You just might find yourself doing that if you don't take care of your air system and drain those tanks every day, particularly in the winter months. If water builds up it can freeze in your air lines and then you're not going anywhere for a while. It's a long, expensive, and sometimes very cold process to thaw out a frozen brake line so get rid of that water before it's too late!

Air lines to the trailer shouldn't be tangled, restricted, or damaged. They should be correctly attached and supported. They shouldn't rub on the frame or catwalk.

Steering system defects — Steering system defects include missing parts (nuts, bolts, cotter pins, etc.) and bent, loose, or broken parts including the steering column, steering gear box, tie rods, drag link, pitman arm, and steering arm.

If your vehicle is equipped with power steering, inspect the hoses, pumps, and fluid level and keep an eye out for leaks.

Check the power steering fluid.

Check the power steering fluid.

Watch the steering wheel for looseness or "play." Steering wheel play of more than 10 degrees can make it hard to steer. Your vehicle should be put out of service if the steering wheel play is more than 30 degrees.

Section 393.209 of the FMCSRs states that steering wheel lash may not exceed the following parameters:

Steering wheel diameter	Manual steering system	Power steering system
16″ or less	2″ +	4½″+
18″	2¼″ +	4¾″+
20″	2½″+	5¼″+
22″	2¾″+	5¾″+

Frame — The frame is the vehicle's foundation. It is directly or indirectly connected to all parts of the truck. Making sure it is in good repair is mandated by Sec. 393.201 of the FMCSRs.

Make sure the frame isn't cracked, loose, sagging, or broken. The bolts securing the cab or body of the vehicle to the frame must not be loose, broken, or missing.

Suspension system defects — The suspension system supports the vehicle and its load and keeps axles in place. A broken or faulty suspension can, among other things, allow sudden shifts in cargo or steering, which can lead to an accident.

Inspect the vehicle's suspension system.

Inspect for:

- Cracked, loose, or broken spring hangers;

- Cracked, loose, or damaged torque rods;

- Cracked, loose, or damaged U-bolts;

- Missing, misaligned, or broken leaves in any leaf spring;

- Damaged air bags;

- Loose or damaged air bag mounts;

- Shock absorber leaks; and

- Loose, cracked, broken, or missing frame members.

Exhaust system defects — An exhaust system defect can allow poisonous fumes into the cab or sleeper berth.

Check for loose, leaking, cracked, broken, or missing:

- Exhaust pipes;
- Mufflers;
- Exhaust stacks;
- Mounting brackets;
- Clamps; and
- Nuts and bolts.

Exhaust system parts should not rub against fuel system parts, tires, or other vehicle parts. Also look for leaks in the exhaust system. Soot around the clamping indicates a leak.

Watch for exhaust system defects.

Inspect the entire coupling system.

Coupling system defects — A coupling system defect can cause a serious accident or damage to cargo.

Check for excessive slack or damage in the fifth wheel mechanism. Inspect the fifth wheel assembly for cracks, breaks, and security. Also make sure the fifth wheel is greased appropriately.

Inspect the area around the pivot pin for cracks or wear. Check the release arm and safety latch, making sure they are not bent or damaged.

The fifth wheel sliding mechanism pins should be securely locked in place and be free of any other damage.

Check kingpin for excessive cracking, bending, or wear.

Missing U-bolts, cracked or broken welds, or other defects in fifth wheel mounting devices should be repaired or replaced.

Cargo problems — Inspect cargo for overloading, correct balance, and securement.

Pretrip Inspection

A pretrip inspection is performed before each trip to identify problems that could cause a breakdown or accident. Section 396.13 of the FMCSRs states that before driving a motor vehicle you must:

A greased fifth wheel.

- Be satisfied that the vehicle is in safe operating condition;

- Review the last vehicle inspection report (see post-trip inspection); and

- Sign the report, only if defects or deficiencies were noted by the driver who prepared the report, to acknowledge that the report has been reviewed and that there is certification that the repairs have been performed.

The Seven-Step Pretrip Inspection

By doing a pretrip inspection the same way every time, you are less likely to forget to check an important vehicle component. The following seven-step routine is recommended.

1. **Vehicle overview** — Walk around the vehicle and note its overall condition. Look for body damage or any fluids leaking from the vehicle.

   Look for leaning, door securement, cargo security, license plates, and annual inspection stickers/documentation.

   Also check the area around the vehicle for potential hazards (pedestrians, overhead wires, other vehicles, etc.)

   Review the last vehicle inspection report. Make sure any damage or defects noted on the report have been corrected/fixed.

2. **Engine compartment** — Make sure the parking brakes are on and the wheels are chocked. Open the vehicle hood, tilt the cab, or open the engine compartment hood and check the following:

Engine compartment inspection.

- All fluid levels (oil, coolant, power steering, transmission (if applicable), windshield washer);

- All hoses for leaks, wear, or looseness;

- All belts for wear or looseness;

- The alternator, water pump, and air compressor;

- The engine compartment for leaks; and

- The electrical wiring insulation for cracks or wear.

Also check the wheels and tires, brakes, steering system, suspension, exhaust, and frame at this point. Although these items are not part of the engine compartment check, this is where these parts are most accessible.

3. **Inside the cab** — Make sure the parking brake is on and the vehicle is in neutral or (if an automatic with "park") in park. Depress the clutch and start the vehicle. Listen for unusual noises and check all gauges for normal readings including the following:

Hey, while you're sitting there waiting for your air pressure to build up, why don't you pull out your permit book and make sure your permits and other paperwork is all up to date? It doesn't do much good if your vehicle is in great operating condition, but you can't go anywhere because your permits and insurance aren't current.

Check all hoses, belts, and wiring for defects

Chapter 4
Vehicle
Inspection

- Oil pressure (read within 15 seconds; 30-45 seconds in cold weather);

- Ammeter (should register positive);

- Voltmeter (should register positive);

- Coolant temperature (will rise); and

- Air pressure (85-100 psi within 45 seconds).

Also check the following controls for looseness, sticking, damage, or improper setting:

- Steering wheel;

- Clutch;

- Accelerator;

- Brakes;

- Transmission control;

- Horn;

- Windshield wipers; and

- Lights.

Inspect and adjust all mirrors.

Inspect mirrors and windshield for cracks, dirt, and other obstructions. Clean and adjust mirrors if necessary.

Make sure all safety equipment is on the vehicle and in good condition. This includes a fully charged fire extinguisher, spare fuses (if applicable), and three emergency triangles.

87

4. **Lights** — With the parking brake set, turn off the engine and turn on the lights and emergency flashers. Get out of the vehicle, go to the front and check all lights. Also make sure the headlights' high beam and low beam settings are operational.

Turn off the headlights and emergency flashers. Turn on the vehicle's parking, clearance, side-marker, and identification lights. Turn on the right turn signal and then start the walkaround inspection on the driver's side (left front side) of the vehicle.

When inspecting headlights, make sure both high beam and low beam settings are operational.

5. **Left front side** — Make sure the window and mirror on the driver's door is clean and that all door latches and locks work properly.

Inspect the left front wheel including the condition of:

- **Wheel and rim** — Look for missing, bent, broken studs, clamps or lugs as well as signs of misalignment. Check for cracked wheels.

- **Tires** — Make sure they are properly inflated, that the valve and stem are in good condition, and that all valve caps are in place. Check for cuts or bulges. Watch for excessive tread wear.

- **Hub Oil Seal** — Not leaking.

- **Lug nuts** — Pay special attention to rusted lug nuts.

Conduct a thorough walkaround inspection.

Inspect the left front suspension checking the condition of the springs, spring hangers, shackles, U-bolts, and shock absorbers.

When inspecting the left front brake check the condition of the brake drum, hoses, brake chamber, slack adjuster, and push rod.

Front — Inspect the condition of the front axle and steering system. When checking the steering system watch for loose, worn, bent, damaged, or missing parts. Also test the steering mechanism for looseness.

Check the condition of the windshield. Look for damage and clean it if it is dirty. Also inspect the windshield wipers. Check the wiper arms for proper spring tension and the wiper blades for damage.

Inspect the windshield for damage and cleanliness.

Make sure the parking, clearance, and identification lights as well as all reflectors are clean, operating properly, and are the correct color.

Also inspect the right front turn signal light, making sure it is clean operating properly, and is the correct color.

Right side — At the right front of the vehicle, repeat the inspection of all of the items you checked on the left front (windows, door, wheels, tires, suspension, brake, etc.).

If the vehicle is a cab-over engine design make sure the primary and safety cab locks are engaged.

Inspect the right fuel tank, making sure it is securely mounted and is not damaged or leaking. The fuel crossover line should be secure and not leaking. The tanks should contain enough fuel, and the cap(s) should be secured.

Check the condition of visible parts including the:

- Rear of the engine for leaks;

- Transmission for leaks;

- Exhaust system, making sure it's secure, not leaking, and not touching wires, fuel, or air lines;

- Frame and cross members for bends or cracks;

- Drive shaft;

- Air lines and electrical wiring, making sure they're secured against snagging, rubbing, or wearing;

- Spare tire carrier or rack for damage;

- Spare tire/wheel, making sure it is the proper size, properly inflated, and securely mounted in its rack; and

- Header board.

Coupling system area — Check the fifth wheel (lower), making sure it is securely mounted to the frame and that all mounting bolts are tight. Look for missing or damaged parts. Make sure it has enough grease and that there isn't any visible space between the upper and lower fifth wheel. The locking jaws should be around the shank and not the head of the kingpin. Also make sure the release arm is properly seated and the safety latch/lock is engaged, if so equipped.

Make sure the glide plate is securely mounted to the trailer frame and the kingpin is not damaged when checking the fifth wheel (upper).

Inspect the air and electrical lines to the trailer. Inspect at both the rear of the tractor and the front of the trailer. The air and electrical lines should not drag or rub along the catwalk. The electrical cord should be firmly plugged in and secured. The air lines should be properly connected to the glad hands. There shouldn't be any air leaks and there should be enough slack for turning.

Check the sliding fifth wheel. The slide shouldn't be damaged or have any parts missing. It should be properly greased and all locking pins must be present and locked in

Inspect all air and electrical lines

place. If the sliding fifth wheel is air powered, there shouldn't be any air leaks. Also make sure the fifth wheel isn't so far forward that the tractor frame will hit the landing gear, or that the trailer will hit the cab when turning.

Right rear — Check the condition of the wheels and rims. Make sure there aren't any missing, bent, or broken spacers, studs, clamps, or lugs.

Check the condition of the tires. Make sure they are properly inflated, that the valve and stems are in good condition, and that all valve caps are in place. Check for cuts or bulges. Watch for excessive tread wear. They shouldn't rub together and nothing should be stuck between them. The tires should be of the same type and of the same size (evenly matched).

Also check the wheel bearings/seals for leaks.

Inspect the suspension, checking the condition of the springs, spring hangers, shackles, and U-bolts.

The axle should be secure and the powered axles shouldn't leak.

Check the condition of the torque rod, arms, bushings, and shock absorbers.

If the vehicle is retractable axle equipped, check the condition of the lift mechanism and if it is air powered, check for leaks.

Inspect the brakes, including:

- Brake drums, shoes, and pads;
- Hoses;
- Slack adjusters; and
- Brake chambers.

Inspect all lights and reflectors including side marker lights and reflectors. They should be clean, properly operating, and the correct color.

This includes:

Rear clearance and identification lights;

- Reflectors;
- Tail lights; and
- Rear turn signals.

Check all door hinges. Make sure the license plate is clean and secured and that splash guards are in good condition, properly fastened, and not dragging on the ground.

Inspect the landing gear.

The landing gear should be fully raised and not have any missing or damaged parts. The crank handle should be in place and secured. If it is power operated, check for air or hydraulic leaks.

Left side — In addition to the items you checked on the right side (fuel tank, engine, transmission, exhaust, frame, air lines, etc.), check the battery (if not mounted to the engine compartment) making sure it is properly secured and isn't broken or leaking.

6. **Signal Lights** — Get in the vehicle and turn off all lights, then turn on the stop lights (apply the trailer hand brake or have a helper put on the brake pedal). Also turn on the left turn signal lights.

   Get out of the vehicle and look at the left front turn signal light. It should be clean, operating, and the proper color. Then look at the left rear turn signal light and both stop lights. Make sure they are clean, operating, and the proper color.

7. **Brake System** — All brake systems should be tested, making sure they are operating properly.

   Parking brake — Release the trailer's brakes. Put the tractor parking brake on and gently pull against it in a low gear to test that the brake will hold.

   Trailer emergency brakes — Charge the trailer air brake system. Apply the trailer emergency brakes. Pull gently on the trailer with the tractor to test the brakes.

   Service brakes — Wait for normal air pressure, release the parking brake, slowly move the vehicle forward, and then firmly apply the brakes (brake pedal). Watch for the vehicle pulling to one side or delayed stopping action.

   Trailer service brakes — Check for normal air pressure, release the parking brake, slowly move the vehicle forward, and then apply the trailer brakes. You should be able to feel the brakes operate. (*Note*: Not all trucks have a way to do this.)

   Air leakage rate — Chock the vehicle, then with a fully charged air system, turn off the engine, release all of the brakes, and time the air pressure drop after the initial drop. The loss rate should be less than two pounds per square inch (psi) in one minute for a single vehicle and less than three psi in one minute for combination vehicles. Apply normal brake pressure. After the initial pressure drop, if the air pressure falls more than three psi in one minute for single vehicles and more than four psi for combination vehicles, the air loss is too great. Check for leaks before operating the vehicle.

   Low pressure warning signal — Once the vehicle has enough air pressure, shut off the engine and release the brakes. Turn on the electrical power and step on and off the brake pedal to reduce air tank pressure. The low air pressure warning signal must come on before the pressure drops to less than 60 psi in the air tank. This signal can be audible or visual. If the signal isn't working, you could lose air pressure and not know it.

Tractor protection valve — Build up normal air pressure in the air brake system and push the air supply knob in. Shut the engine off. Pump on the brake pedal several times to reduce the air pressure in the tanks. The tractor protection valve control (also called the trailer air supply control) should go from normal to the emergency position (pop out) when the air pressure falls into the pressure range specified by the manufacturer. This should be when the air pressure drops to between 30 and 45 psi. If the tractor protection valve doesn't work right, an air hose or trailer brake leak could drain all the air from the tractor. This would cause the emergency brakes to come on, possibly causing loss of control.

Rate of air pressure buildup — With the engine at operating rpm, the pressure should build up from 85-100 psi within 45 seconds in dual air systems. (This may vary, check manufacturer's specifications.) If air pressure doesn't build up fast enough, the vehicle's pressure may drop too low, requiring an emergency stop or activating the spring brakes.

Air compressor governor cut-in and cut-out pressures — Pumping by the air compressor should start at about 90-100 psi and stop at about 125 psi.(Check manufacturer's specifications for details.) Run the engine at a fast idle. The air governor should cut out the air compressor at the manufacturer's specified pressure. The reading on the air pressure gauge should stop rising. With the engine idling, step on and off the brake to reduce the air tank pressure. The governor should cut in and the compressor will start building air pressure. Once the tank pressure reaches 125 psi, the governor will cut out and the process starts again. If the air governor doesn't work as described above, it may need to be fixed. A governor that doesn't work right may not maintain enough air pressure in the system for safe driving.

En Route Inspection

There are several items you should be checking regularly while on the road including:

- Vehicle gauges;
- Air pressure gauges;
- Engine temperature gauges;
- Pressure gauges;
- Ammeter;
- Voltmeter;
- Mirrors;
- Tires; and
- Cargo including covers and restraints.

Checking these items can help you detect a problem before the problem results in a breakdown or accident.

From a regulatory standpoint, Sec. 392.9 of the FMCSRs requires the driver to follow certain inspection rules while on the road.

The vehicle's cargo and load-securing devices must be checked within the first 50 miles of a trip. Any necessary adjustments must be made at this time.

After the first 50 miles of the trip, the vehicle's cargo and load-securing devices must be reexamined:

- When the driver makes a change of duty status;

- After the vehicle has been driven for 3 hours; or

- After the vehicle has been driven 150 miles — whichever occurs first.

It may not be possible to inspect the cargo en route if the trailer is sealed and you have been instructed not to remove the seal. You should still do an en route inspection of your vehicle and inspect your cargo and its securement if at all possible.

Post-Trip Inspection

At the end of each day's work on each vehicle operated, Sec. 396.11 of the FMCSRs requires that you complete a written report (driver vehicle inspection report (DVIR)) covering at least the following parts and accessories:

- Service brakes including trailer brake connections;

- Parking brake;

- Steering mechanism;

- Lighting devices and reflectors;

- Tires;

- Horn;

- Windshield wipers;

- Rear vision mirrors;

- Coupling devices;

- Wheels and rims; and

- Emergency equipment.

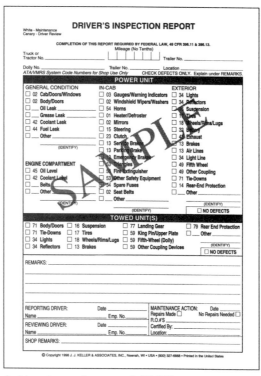

A driver inspection report (DVIR).

On the report, you must identify the vehicle and list any defect or deficiency which could affect its safe operation or cause a mechanical breakdown. If you do not find any defects or deficiencies, you need to report that as well. In all cases, after completing the inspection, you must sign the report.

On two driver operations, only one driver needs to sign the report, provided both drivers agree with what is written in the report.

Before the vehicle can be operated again, any items listed as being defective or deficient that may effect the safety of the vehicle must be repaired. The following criteria must be met:

- The motor carrier must certify (on the report) that the defect or deficiency has been corrected or that correction is not necessary to safely operate the vehicle; and

- The motor carrier must retain the original copy of each vehicle inspection report and certification of repairs for at least three months from the date it was completed.

Intermodal equipment —If you are hauling intermodal equipment and it has a defect or deficiency, you must complete a DVIR and turn it in to the intermodal equipment provider. The report must cover at least the following parts and accessories:

- Brakes;

- Lighting devices, lamps, markers, and conspicuity marking material;

- Wheels, rims, lugs, tires;

- Air line connections, hoses, and couplers;

- King pin upper coupling device;

- Rails or support frames;

- Tie down bolsters;

- Locking pins, clevises, clamps, or hooks; and

- Sliders or sliding frame lock.

The report must include the name of the motor carrier responsible at the time the defect or deficiency was discovered, the motor carrier's and intermodal equipment provider's USDOT numbers, a unique identifying number for the intermodal equipment, the date and time the report was submitted, a list of defects or deficiencies, and your signature.

Before the intermodal equipment can be transported again, any defect or deficiency that affects the safety of operation of the equipment must be repaired. The intermodal equipment provider must certify the defects or deficiencies were repaired or that repair is unnecessary.

The intermodal equipment provider must retain the original copy of each vehicle inspection report and certification of repairs for at least 3 months.

Special Rigs

Special rigs require additional, and in some cases unique inspection procedures. A summary of the additional procedures for three types of vehicles (multiple trailers, tankers, and refrigerated units) follows.

Multiple trailers — Special attention should be given to:

- Air lines, valves, and glad hands between the two trailers;
- Valve positions;
- Brake operation;
- Hook up of emergency lines and glad hands; and
- Pintle hook latches and safety chains.

Tankers — Special attention should be given to:

- Dome covers to tank compartments;
- Hoses and pumps (fastened and secured);
- Emergency shut off valves;
- Condition of the tank; and
- Proper display of hazardous materials placards (if applicable).

Refrigerator Units (Reefers) — Special attention should be given to the condition of the trailer including looking for:

- Holes in the walls, ceiling, or floor;
- Cleanliness;
- Damaged cold air circulation ducts;
- Proper locks and seals on the doors; and
- Proper securement of rails or racks on the ceiling.

The water, oil, and coolant levels should be checked in the refrigerator unit and the thermostat should be set to the appropriate temperature. The refrigeration unit should be run before loading (amount of time varies).

Summary

In this chapter, you have learned about the vehicle inspection process. This includes inspecting critical vehicle components and performing accurate and efficient pre-trip, en-route, and post-trip inspections.

Vehicle Inspection Quiz

Directions: Read each statement carefully and mark the response that best answers the question.

1. **What type of inspection is mandated by the Federal Motor Carrier Safety Regulations (FMCSRs)?**

    A. Pretrip

    B. En route

    C. Post-trip

    D. All of the above

2. **Inspecting cargo for overloading, correct balance, and securement is part of a good pretrip inspection program.**

    A. True

    B. False

3. **A_____ step pretrip inspection routine is recommended to make sure you examine all critical parts and components every time you conduct an inspection.**

    A. One

    B. Five

    C. Seven

    D. Twelve

4. **As part of your pretrip inspection routine, you should walk around the vehicle, note its overall condition, and review the last vehicle inspection report.**

    A. True

    B. False

5. **When inspecting the engine compartment, you should check:**

    A. The voltmeter

    B. The steering wheel

    C. All fluid levels

    D. All of the above

6. Section 392.9 of the FMCSRs requires you to inspect the vehicle's cargo and load-securing devices within the first _____ miles of a trip.

   A. 25

   B. 50

   C. 100

   D. 500

7. After the initial inspection of the vehicle's cargo and load-securing devices, they must be reexamined:

   A. When you make a change of duty status

   B. After the vehicle has been driven for 3 hours

   C. After the vehicle has been driven 150 miles

   D. When whichever of the above occurs first

8. At the beginning of each day's work on each vehicle operated, Sec. 396.11 of the FMCSRs requires you complete a driver vehicle inspection report (DVIR).

   A. True

   B. False

9. Lighting devices and reflectors, tires, and mirrors are all items that must be covered in the post-trip inspection.

   A. True

   B. False

10. Special rigs, such as tankers, require additional and in some cases unique inspection procedures.

    A. True

    B. False

General Knowledge CDL Pre-Test

Read each question carefully and then choose the answer that is most correct.

1. **Which of the following statements about backing a commercial vehicle to a dock is NOT true?**

   A. Since you can't see behind you, you should back slowly until you bump the dock

   B. Use a helper and communicate with hand signals

   C. You should always back toward the driver's side when possible

   D. Both A and C

2. **As alcohol begins to build up in the body, which of the following is affected first?**

   A. Muscle control

   B. Coordination

   C. Kidney control

   D. Judgment and self-control

3. **Which of the following is true concerning cold weather driving?**

   A. Exhaust system leaks are not of concern during cold weather

   B. If the temperature is below 32 degrees Fahrenheit, the engine cannot overheat

   C. Using bleach on tires will provide increased traction

   D. You should use windshield washer fluid which contains an anti-freeze

4. **Placarding, the use of hazardous material placards and labels, is an example of:**

   A. Containment

   B. Controlling the hazardous materials risk

   C. Communication

   D. All of the above

5. **Controlled braking is used when:**

   A. The goal is to keep the vehicle in a straight line while braking

   B. You must stop as quickly as possible

   C. Is only used with hydraulic brakes

   D. Is only used when the vehicle is equipped with anti-lock brakes

Chapter 5

Basic control

OBJECTIVES

Upon completion of this chapter, you should have a basic understanding of:

❑ Starting, warming up, and shutting down the engine

❑ Putting the vehicle in motion and stopping

❑ Backing in a straight line

❑ Turning the vehicle

Introduction

Operating a tractor-trailer is very different from operating your personal vehicle. Everything about a tractor-trailer, from starting the engine to backing and turning, requires a new set of knowledge and skills. This chapter will address basic control issues. It is important that you have a good understanding of these issues, as many of the skills covered in this chapter are the foundation for future lessons.

Driving a tractor-trailer differs from driving your personal vehicle.

Starting, Warming Up, and Shutting Down

There is a specific procedure that must be followed when starting and shutting down the engine of a tractor-trailer. This section will address the proper procedure for starting a four-cycle diesel engine.

Starting the engine — To start this type of engine follow these steps:

1. Apply the parking brake (if not already applied).

2. Depress the clutch pedal completely to the floor, and make sure the truck is in neutral.

3. Turn the ignition switch/key on.

4. Operate the starter (push the button). If the engine doesn't start in 15-20 seconds, turn the ignition switch/key off for at least one minute and try again.

5. Ease off the clutch.

6. Check all instruments and gauges. Make sure you know where the oil pressure gauge is. In warm weather, the oil pressure should come up to operating level in 3 to 5 seconds. If it does not, you should immediately shut the vehicle off, as severe damage could result.

Engine warm-up — Engine warm-up is generally done at a low rpm level (800-1,000 rpm). This allows the oil to warm and circulate, and oil pressure to build up.

During warm-up, the cylinder walls become coated and bearings are lubricated. Coolant temperature increases and air pressure builds up as well.

Usually a short period of idling time is required/recommended. Check the vehicle's operator's manual for specific details on the vehicle you are driving.

When driving during warm-up, keep rpm low and avoid high rpm when accelerating in first gear. Shift to the next highest gear as soon as possible. Keep all acceleration smooth and easy.

Engine warm-up is complete when the water temperature reaches 170° – 195°F. You will not typically reach this temperature by just sitting and idling so you need to proceed slowly at low rpm, until this temperature range has been reached..

Engine shutdown — To shutdown the engine follow these steps:

1.   Depress the clutch and move the gear shift to neutral.

2.   Set the parking brakes.

3.   Turn the engine (key or switch) off.

4.   If the engine has a Stop control, move it to Off.

Engine cool down can be as important as a proper warm-up. Engine damage can occur if there isn't a sufficient cool down period. Engine cool down allows heat generated during normal operation to dissipate. The appropriate cool down period will vary based on engine type as well as the nature of the trip and cargo hauled.

Excessive idling — Avoid excessive idling. Most recently manufactured engines don't need to idle for more than a few minutes. This can waste fuel and cause unnecessary wear on the engine. It also has a negative affect on the driver's fuel bonus!

Putting the Vehicle in Motion and Stopping

Putting in motion and stopping a tractor-trailer requires more specific skills and driver expertise than those required to do the same tasks in your personal vehicle. This includes:

- Testing the tractor-trailer hook-up;

- Putting the tractor-trailer in motion; and

- Stopping the tractor-trailer.

Please note that this section addresses manual transmission vehicles. If you operate an automatic transmission, consult the manufacturer's manual for details.

Testing the tractor-trailer hook-up — The coupling must be tested every time a trailer is connected to a tractor or dolly.

For vehicles with an independent trailer brake control (hand valve):

1. Release the tractor (parking) brake. This is the red 8-sided button.

2. Depress the clutch, and move the gearshift to the lowest gear.

3. Engage the independent trailer brake control to apply the trailer brakes (pull down on the Johnny bar).

4. Release the clutch to the friction point.

5. Pull gently against the locked trailer brakes. Stop as soon as you feel the engine start to drag down.

6. Disengage the clutch.

For vehicles without an independent trailer brake control (hand valve):

1. Release the tractor (parking) brake.

2. Depress the clutch and move the gearshift to the lowest forward gear.

3. Set the trailer brakes by pulling the trailer air-supply valve.

4. Partially engage the clutch and pull forward gently against the locked trailer brakes.

Putting a tractor-trailer in motion — To put a tractor-trailer in motion:

1. Release the tractor and trailer parking brakes.

2. Depress the clutch fully, engaging the clutch brake, and place the transmission in the lowest gear.

3. Increase the engine rpm slightly. (This may not be necessary in newer trucks)

4. Release the clutch to the friction point. This is the point where the clutch engages. A decrease in the rpm is a sign that the friction point has been reached. Then gradually release the clutch until it's fully engaged. As you engage the clutch, a slight increase in engine rpm may be needed to avoid stalling the engine (100-300 rpm is normal).

Specific steps must be followed when putting a tractor-trailer in motion.

5. When the vehicle starts to move, gradually increase engine rpm to increase vehicle speed, by depressing the throttle.

6. When the vehicle is in motion with the clutch fully engaged, take your foot off the clutch until you are ready to shift again or stop.

Hold on driver! Don't get too excited here or you'll damage your vehicle. Just an EASY pull against the trailer will tell you if you're connected or not. Make sure you don't pop your clutch pedal out or you may twist the drive shaft, and remember, the trailer air-supply valve is the 8-sided one. Just take it easy. You won't win this tug-of-war by seeing how hard you can pull your trailer while the brakes are locked!

7. Try to avoid excessive clutch slipping. Engage the clutch as smoothly as possible without stalling the engine. To avoid slipping the clutch, use very little additional fuel (pushing on the) until the clutch is completely engaged.

Stopping a tractor-trailer — To stop a tractor-trailer:

1. Release the accelerator pedal.

2. Depress the brake pedal.

3. As the vehicle begins to slow, downshift to the appropriate gear.

4. As the vehicle slows, release some brake pressure. When the engine is almost at idle, depress the clutch (the truck should be stopped within the next 50-75 feet).

5. After stopping, maintain enough brake pressure to keep the vehicle stationary. If you're parking the truck, put the gearshift lever in neutral, set (apply) the parking brakes, and release the clutch.

Straight Line Backing

Though backing is a basic tractor-trailer maneuver, it is one of the most difficult to master. The information below is a basic overview of and introduction to straight line backing, the simplest of all backing maneuvers. More difficult backing maneuvers will be covered in-depth in Chapter 7.

When executing a straight line backing maneuver:

1. **Position the vehicle properly** — Put the vehicle in position by moving forward until the tractor and trailer are straight in front of one another and the front (steering) wheels are straight.

2. **Clear the area—** Make sure area behind your vehicle is clear of vehicles, people, and other obstacles. Tap your vehicle's horn and turn on the four-way flashers.

3. **Watch speed** — Put the vehicle in reverse. Using an idle speed, back as slowly as possible, but don't ride the clutch or brakes.

STOP! This is serious so pay attention. NEVER move your truck backward without getting out of the seat, walking to the rear of your vehicle, and making sure everything is clear. It doesn't matter if it's cold, raining, snowing, or if you're in a hurry. None of these excuses will be acceptable when you have to call your safety manager and tell him or her that you just ran over something or even worse, someone. We'll talk more about this later but for now just remember, get off your seat and go see what's going on! Some people call this GOAL – Get Out And Look.

4. **Check behind** — Constantly check behind when backing. Make sure all doors are closed and continually check all mirrors. If you are unsure as to what may be behind your vehicle, stop .

5. **Steering** — Keep the vehicle on path and don't oversteer.

   If drifting starts, try to correct it by turning the steering wheel in the direction of the drift as soon as it occurs. Try not to oversteer. Only slight movement is required if the drift is caught right away.

   Use the push-pull method of steering to keep the trailer in line. When the trailer gets bigger in your mirror (a sign

When backing, continually check all mirrors.

that it is drifting), turn the top of the wheel toward the side that is bigger in the mirror. Once the drift has stopped, return the wheel to its original position and realign the tractor in front of the trailer.

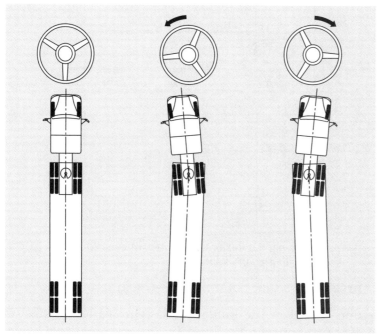
Correct vehicle drift by steering in the direction of the drift.

The biggest error in the push-pull method is not returning the wheel to the straight-ahead position immediately.

6. **Pull up and start again** — If your vehicle is too far out of position, pull up and start again. It is easier and safer to start over than to reposition the vehicle while backing.

Turning

There are four basic rules when it comes to turning:

- Know the vehicle;
- Plan in advance;
- Allow for off-tracking; and
- Watch your mirrors.

Off-tracking — Off-tracking is something that happens to all vehicles with more than one set of wheels. Put simply, the term means the rear wheels don't follow the same track as the front wheels when moving through a turn or curve. They follow a shorter path.

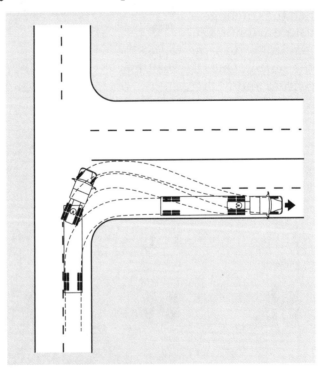

When turning, the tractor-trailer's rear wheels follow a shorter path than the front wheels.

There are three factors that determine off-tracking in a tractor-trailer unit:

- Distance between the kingpin and rear trailer wheels (the greater the distance between the kingpin and rear trailer wheels, the more off-tracking occurs);

Hey! Can you turn your head around in circles? Sometimes when you are making turns you sure feel like you need to. There are many, many things to watch and no one is going to watch them for you. Everyone seems to be in a big hurry these days but don't let that rattle you. Just keep watching your mirrors and everything going on around you as you proceed through the turn. If something doesn't look right...STOP! That impatient little car that just squeezed in between your trailer and the curb (because you left enough room for him to) doesn't realize that he's about to get squashed like a bug. Now's the time to be a professional, not prove who's bigger. Let that 4-wheeler get out of your way before you continue around the corner. Your day will be much better if you do.

- Amount of sideways drag of the rear tires (the more sideways drag, the greater the off-tracking); and

- Speed of the vehicle (at highway speed there's less off-tracking).

Right turns — Good judgement, proper speed control, and accurate steering are all important in executing safe right turns.

Judgement, speed control, and steering play a part in making safe right turns.

When approaching an intersection, adjust your vehicle's speed. The sharper the turn, the slower the vehicle should be moving. This allows you to use all available space.

Shift into the correct gear before the turn and complete the turn in the same gear. This allows you to keep both hands on the wheel during the turn.

One thing to keep in mind is that a tractor-trailer must pull further into the intersection than a smaller vehicle in order to avoid hitting the curb. One basic rule of thumb is to get about½ of the rig past the corner before beginning the turn. Once the vehicle has reached that point, turn the steering wheel to the right and complete the turn. Accelerate slightly to smooth out the turn.

Before, during, and after the turn, check both the right and left mirrors for the position of the trailer wheels.

When approaching a corner for a right turn, position your trailer so that no vehicles can come between your trailer and the curb.

Immediately after the turn is complete, turn the steering wheel back to straighten out the wheels.

The following are some of the most common errors made when executing a right turn:

- Not sizing up the corner properly;

- Approaching the intersection too fast;

- Forgetting to gear down before beginning the turn;

- Accelerating in the turn;

- Shifting gears while turning;

- Leaving to much space between the trailer and the curb;

- Forgetting to allow for off-tracking; and

- Not watching the right mirror before, during, and after the turn.

Left turns — As with a right turn, reduce vehicle speed when approaching the intersection.

When making a left turn, turn from as far right as possible.

Shift into the correct gear and keep the vehicle's wheels straight before starting the turn. As with the right turn, complete the turn in the same gear.

When executing this maneuver, turn from as far right as possible to allow plenty of room for the tractor. If you turn too soon or too tightly, off-tracking may cause the left side of the vehicle to hit another vehicle.

Watch your mirrors before, during, and after the turn. Turn the steering wheel back to the right immediately upon completion of the turn.

The most common errors made when executing a left turn are the same as those for right turns, except the errors are made from the other side.

If you are on a road with two lanes for turning left, use the outside (right most) lane.

On a right turning curve, keep the vehicle as close as possible to the center line.

Curves — Positioning is important. When approaching a right traveling curve (not a corner), keep the vehicle close to the center of the road without crossing the center line. Failure to keep toward the center could result in the rear of your vehicle running off the road, on to the shoulder, or hitting something on the right side.

Positioning is important on all curves.

When approaching a left traveling curve, keep the front of the vehicle as close to the outer edge of the road as possible. This will keep your trailer from running over the center line on a curve.

Look ahead and recognize upcoming curves. Keep in mind that there may be times that you have to stop and yield to traffic before proceeding.

Summary

As you now know, basic operation of a tractor-trailer varies from that of your own personal vehicle. There are certain, specific procedures for starting and shutting down a tractor-trailer as well as for backing and negotiating corners. Remember that maneuvers such as backing and turning require patience, planning, and skill.

Basic Control Quiz

Directions: Read each statement carefully and mark the response that best answers the question.

1. **Operating a tractor-trailer is different than operating your personal vehicle.**

    A. True

    B. False

2. **A specific procedure should be followed when starting a tractor-trailer engine.**

    A. True

    B. False

3. **The first step you should take when starting any type of tractor-trailer engine is:**

    A. Depress the clutch

    B. Pump the accelerator

    C. Apply the parking brake

    D. All of the above

4. **Engine warm-up is generally done at a low rpm level.**

    A. True

    B. False

5. **When starting to put a tractor-trailer in motion you should depress the clutch fully and place the transmission in the lowest forward gear.**

    A. True

    B. False

6. **An engine cool down period isn't necessary in newer vehicles.**

    A. True

    B. False

7. **When backing in a straight line, you should:**

    A. Position the vehicle properly

    B. Constantly check behind the vehicle

    C. Do not oversteer

    D. All of the above

8. **When turning, shift into the proper gear before the turn and stay in that gear until the turn is complete.**

    A. True

    B. False

9. **Which of the following is a common right turn error?**

    A. Not shifting gears while turning

    B. Allowing for an adequate amount of space for off-tracking

    C. Approaching the intersection too slowly

    D. Approaching the intersection too fast

10. **If you are on a road with two left turn lanes, you should use the inside lane.**

    A. True

    B. False

General Knowledge CDL Pre-Test

Read each question carefully and then choose the answer that is most correct.

1. **What is hydroplaning?**

    A. An emergency situation created when an aircraft must make an emergency landing on a highway

    B. Excessive heat built up in the radiator

    C. Something that only occurs at high vehicle speeds

    D. When your vehicle wheels lift off the roadway on a thin film of water

2. **It you are being tailgated you should:**

    A. Motion for the tailgater to pass you when it is safe

    B. Increase your following distance

    C. Turn your 4-way flashers on

    D. Slam on the brakes

3. **Which of the following conditions may produce a skid?**

    A. Driving too fast for conditions

    B. Over braking

    C. Over steering

    D. All of the above

4. **When fighting a fire, which is most correct?**

    A. Get downwind of the fire before using the fire extinguisher

    B. Get as close to the fire as possible

    C. Aim the fire extinguisher at the base of the fire

    D. Aim the fire extinguisher at the top of the fire

5. **When starting a commercial vehicle on level, dry pavement, it is not usually necessary to:**

    A. Apply the parking brake

    B. Use a slower acceleration

    C. Press on the accelerator while popping out the clutch

    D. Both A and C

Chapter 5
Basic Control

Chapter 6

Shifting

OBJECTIVES

Upon completion of this chapter, you should have a basic understanding of the procedures and skills required to shift a vehicle including:

- ❑ The key elements required to properly shift a manual transmission

- ❑ Basic shift patterns and procedures of a manual transmission

- ❑ The basics of automatic and semiautomatic transmissions

Introduction

Shifting gears is one of the more difficult skills you will learn in becoming a professional driver. Mastering this skill takes coordination, patience, and practice. This chapter will address the knowledge and skills it takes to shift safely and efficiently.

Key Elements of Shifting

Shifting controls — There are three controls used in shifting a manual transmission.

1. **Accelerator** — The accelerator controls the flow of fuel to the engine. That, in turn, determines the speed or rpm of the engine in any one gear.

2. **Shift lever** — The shift lever controls what gear the transmission is in. The gear selected determines the amount of power supplied by the engine which then transfers into road speed.

    A low gear provides a great deal of power with little road speed. Lower gears supply the power needed to build up momentum.

    A high gear provides less power, but much more road speed. High gear allows the vehicle to obtain and maintain higher road speeds once momentum is developed.

3. **Clutch** — The clutch transfers power from the engine to the transmission. Put simply, it allows you to shift gears.

    When the clutch pedal is depressed, it disengages the transmission from the engine, and gears may be safely shifted. When the clutch pedal is fully released, the transmission and engine are engaged, and gears generally can't be safely shifted.

Shifting takes skill, coordination, patience and practice.

The operation of shifting controls takes coordination and precise timing. Improper timing or a lack of coordination can cause over revving and gear grinding. As well as causing damage to the vehicle's components, improper shifting can cause problems in controlling the vehicle. Coordinating the use of the clutch and the shift lever is a simple process; first depress the clutch, and then shift gears.

When to shift — Driving conditions and vehicle needs will determine when you will upshift or downshift.

Upshifting — As mentioned earlier, low gears provide a great deal of power. This power is needed to get a stopped vehicle moving. Select the highest gear possible that will allow the vehicle to move without slipping the clutch or lugging the engine. As vehicle speed increases, upshift to a higher gear to gain additional speed. The purpose of upshifting is to allow a vehicle to increase speed.

Hey driver! This is just a general explanation of what it takes to shift a big rig. You will get a much better idea from your instructor when you actually get in the truck and start jamin' those gears. So read this section completely but really pay attention to what your instructor is telling you. Smooth shifting is a skill that good drivers master. You can too!

Downshifting — Downshifting aids in slowing a vehicle. It acts as a braking force. Downshifting can also provide more power to the vehicle when needed. Never downshift earlier than necessary. Early downshifting can cause the vehicle's engine to rev at a high level, possibly causing engine damage.

The speedometer, tachometer, and governor are all necessary tools when it comes to safe shifting.

Speedometer — The speedometer displays the speed of a vehicle in miles per hour (mph) and/or kilometers per hour. For each gear, there is a range of road speed which corresponds (matches). This varies based on the type of vehicle you are operating. When your vehicle reaches the maximum speed for a gear, you must upshift. When your vehicle reaches the minimum speed for a gear you must downshift.

Practice, practice, practice! That's how you become proficient at shifting. It won't come naturally at first to most of you, but over time it will be just like a habit. Most professional drivers pride themselves in being able to shift smoothly and efficiently without any "grinding" of the gears in any situation. It may take a little time but your instructor will help you become a pro at this if you want to.

Tachometer.

Tachometer — The tachometer displays engine speed in hundreds of revolutions per minute (rpm). It serves as a guide for shifting into the appropriate gear. When your vehicle reaches the maximum rpm for a gear, you must upshift. When your vehicle reaches the minimum rpm for a gear you must downshift.

Note: Electronic fuel pumps also limit the amount of fuel supplied to the engine, requiring you to shift to a higher gear to gain more speed.

Governor — The governor prevents the engine from excessively revving while downshifting.

Shifting gears — Most heavy vehicles with manual transmissions require double clutching to change gears. When double clutching is done properly, the gears do not grind. The following is the basic method when upshifting and downshifting.

Upshifting — To successfully upshift, follow these steps:

1. Release the accelerator, depress the clutch, and shift to neutral at the same time;

2. Release the clutch;

3. Let the engine reach the rpm required for the next gear;

4. Depress the clutch and shift to the next higher gear at the same time;

5. Release the clutch and press the accelerator at the same time.

Maintain correct engine speed when downshifting.

Downshifting — To successfully downshift, follow these steps:

1. Release the accelerator, depress the clutch, and shift to neutral at the same time;

2. Release the clutch;

3. Press the accelerator, increasing engine speed to reach the rpm required for the lower gear;

4. Depress the clutch and shift to the lower gear at the same time;

5. Release the clutch and press the accelerator at the same time.

It is important to maintain correct engine speed when either upshifting or downshifting.

Consult the vehicle's owner's manual for recommendations. One rule of thumb (in absence of manufacturer's recommendations) is when changing gears, change the rpm by about 500 rpm.

Experience also plays a part in successful shifting. Veteran drivers are often able to tell when to shift gears by using their senses and instincts. They can tell by the sound of the engine and the feel of the vehicle.

There is a third shifting skill that is required when operating a vehicle with a manual transmission. Often called hitting a gear, or hunting a gear, this skill is used when your vehicle is rolling and you must get the transmission into the proper gear. When performing this skill follow these steps:

1. Think about how the engine should feel at that speed in that gear. Experienced drivers also take into account the vehicle's speed. For each speed, there's a specific gear you should hunt for.

2. Depress the clutch and push the shift lever lightly against the gear you think is the correct gear.

3. Continue this until the shift lever goes in without excessive grinding.

If this doesn't work, move the shift lever and feel how changing the engine rpm changes the shift lever vibrations.

If the rpm is too high, you will hear a high pitched grinding noise. If the rpm is too low, you will hear a deep and hollow grinding noise. If the engine is close to the correct rpm, the shift lever vibrations are larger and farther apart. If you reach the correct rpm, the shift lever will fall into gear. When this happens, depress the clutch and push the shift lever into place. Once you have done this, you can release the clutch and press the accelerator.

There is no exact science when it comes to the skill of shifting. Again, experience may be the best aid in successfully performing this skill.

Good shifting skills are the trademark of an accomplished, professional driver. This includes:

- Good timing and coordination;
- Knowing what gear your vehicle is in at all times;
- Knowing what the top mph and rpm is for each gear on your vehicle;
- Making shifts without forcing, raking, or grinding gears;
- Never riding the clutch;
- Always using the clutch when shifting;
- Always using the proper gear for best fuel economy; and
- Anticipating changes in terrain and/or traffic.

Shifting Patterns

Not all transmissions have the same shifting patterns. This section will address five of the most common shift patterns currently being used.

Spicer Pro-Shift Seven Speed — This transmission has a no-repeat shift pattern. The shift pattern starts at the bottom left and works its way to the seventh gear on the bottom right.

Upshifting — To successfully upshift, follow these steps:

1. Depress the clutch;

2. Move the shift lever as far left as possible, finding the first gear;

3. When shifting to second, double clutch, move the shift lever up and to the right;

4. To shift through the rest of the gears, double clutch and follow the standard "H" pattern.

Downshifting — To successfully downshift, follow these steps:

1. Shift from seventh to sixth gear by double clutching and moving the shift lever forward (make sure you are matching engine speed to road speed before shifting);

2. To shift down through the rest of the gears double clutch and follow the standard "H" Pattern.

Eaton® Fuller® Nine Speed — This transmission has a low range and high range of gears. The low range has five forward gears (low through fourth) and the high range has four gears (fifth through eighth). The range control lever must be lifted or lowered to reach the high or low gears.

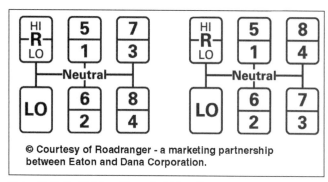

Eaton® Fuller® Nine Speed shift pattern.

Upshifting — To successfully upshift, follow these steps:

1. Depress the clutch;

2. Make sure the range lever is in the low range (down);

3. Move the shift lever to first gear;

4. When shifting to second through fourth gear, double clutch;

5. To shift from fourth to fifth gear (from low to high range), lift the range control lever up before moving the gear lever;

6. Shift from fifth through eighth gear using normal double clutching.

Downshifting — To successfully downshift, follow these steps:

1. Shift from eighth through fifth gear by double clutching (make sure you are matching engine speed to road speed before shifting);

2. To shift from fifth to fourth gear, push the range control lever down before moving the gear lever;

3. Shift from fourth through first gear by double clutching (make sure you are matching engine speed to road speed before shifting).

Eaton® Fuller® Super Ten — This transmission has five gear positions that are split. This cuts gear lever movement in half.

Eaton® Fuller® Super Ten

Upshifting — To successfully upshift, follow these steps:

1. Depress the clutch;

2. Move the gear shift lever to first gear;

3. To make a splitter shift (first to second, third to fourth, etc.), move the splitter button forward, take your foot off the accelerator, wait for the gear to engage, then accelerate;

4. To make a lever shift (second to third, fourth to fifth, etc.) move the splitter button back, double clutch, and shift normally.

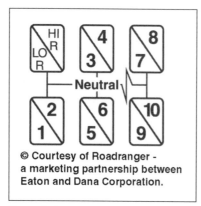

Eaton® Fuller® Super Ten shift
pattern.

Downshifting — To successfully downshift, follow these steps:

1. To make a splitter shift down (tenth to ninth, eighth to seventh, etc.) move the splitter button back, take your foot off the accelerator, wait for the gear to engage, then accelerate;

2. To make a lever shift down, move the splitter button forward, double clutch, and shift normally.

Rockwell Ten Speed — This transmission system has a low (first through fifth gear) and high (sixth through tenth gear) range of gears. A range control lever is used to reach the high range of gears.

Upshifting — To successfully upshift, follow these steps:

1. Depress the clutch;

2. Make sure the range lever is in the low range (down);

3. Move the shift lever to first gear (top left);

4. When shifting through fifth gear, double clutch;

5. To shift from fifth to sixth gear (from low to high range), lift the range control lever up before moving the gear lever;

6. Shift from sixth through tenth gear using normal double clutching.

Downshifting — To successfully downshift, follow these steps:

1. Shift from tenth through sixth gear by double clutching (make sure you are matching engine speed to road speed before shifting);

2. To shift from sixth to fifth gear, push the range control lever down before moving the gear lever;

3. Shift from fifth through first gear by double clutching (make sure you are matching engine speed to road speed before shifting).

Eaton® Fuller® Thirteen Speed — This transmission has a low range and a high range. The high range has four direct ratios and four overdrive ratios with the overdrive ratios being engaged by using a splitter switch.

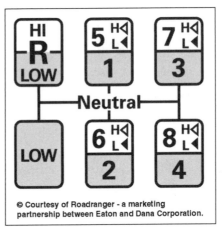

© Courtesy of Roadranger - a marketing partnership between Eaton and Dana Corporation.

Eaton® Fuller® 13 Speed shift pattern.

Upshifting — To successfully upshift, follow these steps:

1. Depress the clutch;

2. Move the shift lever to first gear;

3. When shifting through fourth gear, double clutch;

4. To shift from fourth to fifth gear (from low to high range), lift the range control lever up before moving the gear lever;

5. Shift from fifth through eighth gear using normal double clutching;

6. To go from direct to overdrive, flip the splitter switch, release the accelerator, push down and release the clutch, and accelerate;

7. To go from overdrive to direct in the next higher gear, move the gear lever to the next gear and flip the splitter switch before releasing the clutch.

Downshifting — To successfully downshift, follow these steps:

1. To go from overdrive to direct in the same gear, flip the splitter switch, release the accelerator, push down and release the clutch, and accelerate;

2. To shift from direct in one gear to overdrive in the next lower gear, flip the splitter switch to overdrive and make a normal downshift;

3. Shift from fifth to fourth gear by pushing the range lever down, double clutching, and making a normal downshift.

Semiautomatic transmission — A semiautomatic transmission uses electronic controls to help you shift. Like a manual transmission, a semiautomatic transmission has a clutch and gearshift lever. What is different is that the top gears automatically change.

Automatic transmission — An automatic transmission uses a torque converter instead of a clutch to shift gears. A lever or button is used to change gears. The following are the range selector positions found on an automatic transmission.

Neutral — Neutral is used for starting, standing, and parking the vehicle. Never coast in neutral. This can damage the transmission as well as cause you to lose control of your vehicle.

Reverse — Reverse is used for backing. The vehicle must be stopped before shifting into reverse.

Drive (2-5) — Drive is used for normal driving conditions. It begins in second and automatically upshifts to five as you accelerate. It also automatically downshifts as you slow the vehicle.

A lever or button is used to change gears on an automatic transmission.

Lower range (2-3/2-4) — This range provides engine braking and should be used when road and/or traffic conditions warrant use of a lower gear.

Low gear (2) — This gear is used when driving up a steep grade or operating in snow or mud.

Creeper gear (1) — This gear provides the greatest amount of traction and should only be used in off-road situations.

Summary

This chapter has covered the basics of shifting. Keep in mind that exact shifting patterns vary from manufacturer to manufacturer and that you should always consult the owner's manual prior to using an unfamiliar type of shifting pattern. Also remember that coordination, practice, and patience are key to mastering this professional driving skill.

Shifting Quiz

Directions: Read each statement carefully and mark the response that best answers the question.

1. **Which of the following is used when shifting a manual transmission?**

    A. Accelerator

    B. Shift lever

    C. Clutch

    D. All of the above

2. **A low gear provides little power or road speed.**

    A. True

    B. False

3. **A high gear allows a vehicle to obtain and maintain higher road speeds once momentum is developed.**

    A. True

    B. False

4. **The purpose of upshifting is to:**

    A. Allow a vehicle to maintain speed

    B. Allow a vehicle to decrease speed

    C. Allow a vehicle to increase speed

    D. All of the above

5. **The speedometer, tachometer, and governor are all tools that assist in safe shifting.**

    A. True

    B. False

6. **Double clutching causes a vehicle's gears to grind.**

    A. True

    B. False

7. **Good shifting skills include:**

    A. Riding the clutch

    B. Grinding gears

    C. Never riding the clutch

    D. All of the above

8. **A semiautomatic transmission does not have a clutch or gear shift lever.**

    A. True

    B. False

9. **A lever or button is used to change gears on an automatic transmission.**

    A. True

    B. False

10. **Good shifting skills are the trademark of an accomplished, professional driver.**

    A. True

    B. False

General Knowledge CDL Pre-Test

Read each question carefully and select the most correct answer.

1. **Shifting gears properly is important because:**

    A.   Doing so helps you maintain control of the vehicle

    B.   It helps to keep the oil flowing through the crankcase

    C.   It keeps the radiator cool

    D.   It keeps the engine at the proper operating temperature

2. **You are traveling down a long grade and you notice your brakes are not working as well as they had been. You should:**

    A.   Continue to the bottom of the grade and then stop to check your brakes

    B.   Stop as quickly as you can

    C.   Downshift one or two gears and continue

    D.   Begin pumping your brake pedal

3. **Water will extinguish which of the following fires?**

    A.   Electrical

    B.   Diesel fuel

    C.   Gasoline

    D.   Tire

4. **Convex (curved) mirrors will:**

    A.   Make objects appear to be larger than they really are

    B.   Make objects appear to be smaller than they really are

    C.   Make objects appear closer and larger than they really are

    D.   Show a wider area than flat mirrors

5. **The Driver's Manual says you should use your horn:**

    A.   To make the deer standing alongside the road to move further away

    B.   When a car gets in the way

    C.   If it may help you to avoid a collision

    D.   When you begin to change lanes

So driver, how are you doing? Are you starting to get more of these correct? Keep at it, you'll be a professional in no time!

Chapter 7

Backing

OBJECTIVES

Upon completion of this chapter, you should have a basic understanding of:

- ❏ Backing principles and rules
- ❏ Basic backing maneuvers

Introduction

Though backing is a basic tractor-trailer maneuver, it is one of the most difficult a professional driver performs. Successfully backing a tractor-trailer requires skill, practice, patience, and good judgement.

This chapter focuses on the basics of backing including safe backing and the types of backing maneuvers commonly used.

Backing is one of the most difficult maneuvers a professional driver executes.

Backing Principles and Rules

Steering principles — The techniques/procedures used for backing a tractor-trailer are very different from those used to back your personal vehicle. In most personal vehicles, the front axle serves as the steering axle. In the case of a tractor-trailer, the rear tractor axle steers the trailer.

The amount of turning or movement of the trailer is proportional to the angle between the tractor and trailer. The greater the angle, the more the trailer will pivot and the less rearward movement there will be.

Types of backing maneuvers — The following are the basic backing maneuvers you need to master in order to safely perform your job:

- Straight line backing;

- Alley dock backing;

- Parallel parking;

- Sight side backing; and

- Blind side backing.

Slow down driver! You've been going fast-forward all day to get to your customer. Now that you are there, it's time to slow down, think about what you need to do, and back in to the dock slowly and safely. This isn't a race to see who can hit the dock first. Challenge yourself to be the best backer in the lot!

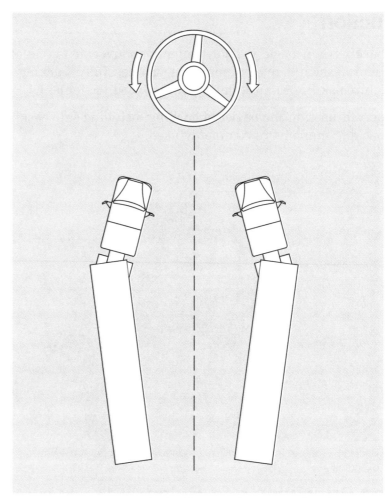

When backing, the tractor and trailer move in opposite directions.

1. **Straight line backing** — This is the simplest of the backing techniques and is fundamental in learning all other backing maneuvers.

2. **Alley dock backing** — This maneuver involves backing while turning into a space that is 90 degrees to the truck. It most often occurs at loading docks when you must back in from off the street or between two vehicles.

3. **Parallel parking** — This involves backing into a space along a curb or dock. While the principle is the same as parallel parking a car, it is one of the more difficult to learn with a tractor-trailer.

4. **Sight side backing** — This means you are backing toward the left side of the vehicle. You can see along the intended path of the trailer. Sight side backing is preferred, as you have maximum visibility.

5. **Blind side backing** — This means you are backing toward the right side of the vehicle. You can only see where you are going in your rear view mirrors. Blind side backing is more difficult and dangerous than sight side backing. You have limited visibility and have more of a chance of hitting something. Blind side backing should be avoided when possible.

Rules for safe backing — All backing maneuvers have the potential to become dangerous. In most backing situations, even a second or two is enough time for someone or something to get in the path of a vehicle.

The following safety checks should be performed prior to starting any backing maneuver:

- Get out of the vehicle and check to the rear (GOAL);

- Check above, under, and to the sides of the vehicle;

- Check for adequate swing clearance;

- Check in front of your vehicle (if pulling forward is necessary); and

- Warn others that the truck is backing.

Once the safety checks have been made, don't delay in moving the vehicle. Any delay could allow time for another potential hazard. If there is a delay, conduct the safety checks a second time.

Proper position is essential to successful backing. The easiest and safest position to start from is straight. However, most backing situations today do not give the room needed to line up in a completely straight manner. Proper backing is a learned act and you will become better and better at it, the more you practice.

Other key backing tips include:

- Being patient;

- Backing as slowly as possible, using the lowest reverse gear;

- Not accelerating (use idle speed) or riding the clutch;

- Not over steering;

- Backing to the left side (sight side) whenever possible;

- Using mirrors;

- Using the horn and flashers;

- Turning off the radio and keeping the windows open to listen for noises;

- Checking behind the rig;

Be patient, use mirrors, and don't oversteer when backing.

Not sure if you're turning too much? Try this...put your hand on the top of the steering wheel. Grasp it tight and don't let go as you back up. If you turn the wheel to a point where it's uncomfortable for your hand, or you feel like you want to let go and move your hand around the wheel...you're probably turning too far! Adjustments when backing should be slow and small. If your vehicle looks like a slithering snake while backing up, I'm sure your buddies will let you know about it when you get to the dock. They'll probably ask you how you learned to dance like that!

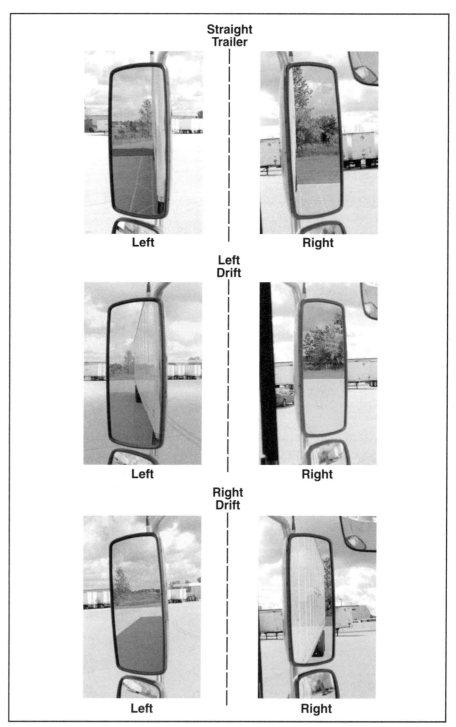

- Watching for obstacles that can tilt the trailer (curbs, ramps, etc.);

- Looking out for overhead objects (wires, tree limbs, etc.);

- Having someone watch and guide the rig from the outside (if possible); and

- Restarting the backing maneuver instead of backing poorly.

Use of a helper — Depending on company policy, you may have the option of using a helper to complete a backing maneuver.

When using a helper, you and the helper must agree on signals, with the most important signal being stop. The helper should be in front of the tractor, walking from side-to-side so you can see the helper at all times. If you can't see your helper, stop immediately.

Even though you are using a helper, you must continue to take full responsibility for your actions. You can't neglect your responsibility because a helper is available.

The Basic Backing Maneuvers

Straight line backing — This is the easiest maneuver to learn. It is the building block to learning all other backing maneuvers and should be mastered before attempting other backing maneuvers.

When executing a straight line backing maneuver the vehicle should be positioned straight and shouldn't drift to either side. Keep in mind that the earlier the drift is detected, the less steering input will be needed to correct for the drift. If drifting can't be easily corrected, start the maneuver over. It is easier to start over than to reposition the vehicle while backing.

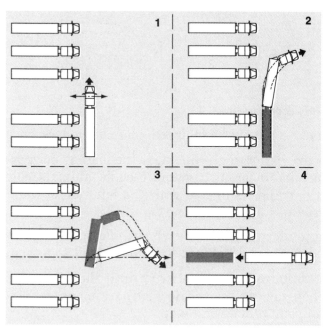

Straight line backing.

While backing, frequently check both mirrors. Select a reference point about 100-200 feet to the rear of the trailer. This will help you recognize when the vehicle is drifting.

Alley dock backing — Alley dock backing is often used at loading docks and to back into parking spaces. This maneuver combines sight side backing and straight line backing. This maneuver requires patience and extreme caution. Continually check vehicle clearance and watch for vehicles, pedestrians, or other objects that may move into the path of the vehicle after the start of the backing maneuver.

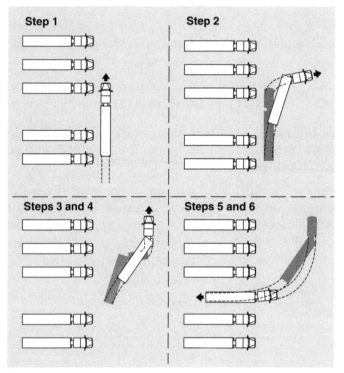

Alley dock backing.

The following steps should be followed when alley dock backing:

1. Pull forward, in a straight line near the loading dock or parking space. Check the mirrors for obstructions (people, animals, objects). When the front of the trailer is in line with the left side of the loading dock or parking space, turn hard to the right.

2. Continue to move forward (slowly, at idle speed). When the tractor is positioned at about 12 o'clock, turn to the left to a 45 degree angle.

3. Continue to move forward (slowly) until the trailer is at a 45 degree angle. When you can see the dock or parking space in your left mirror, straighten your vehicle and stop.

4. Once you have stopped, set the vehicle's brakes, exit the vehicle, and do a visual check before starting the backing maneuver. This includes the safety checks mentioned earlier in the chapter. Also check vehicle positioning. The steering tires should be straight. If you are making a delivery or picking up a load, open the trailer's doors.

5. Get back into the vehicle and start backing (slowly). Keep in mind that there may be situations in which you may have to stop the vehicle and recheck your path. Straighten out the vehicle as you proceed. Use your mirrors. Keep a close watch for drift and correct it as necessary.

6. Do not try to salvage a poor set up. It is safer to start over than to make a correction while moving backward.

Though technique is the same for all vehicles, there are some variables based on the vehicle. For example, a vehicle's overhang may cause the trailer to hit something to the side.

Parallel parking — This is one of the most difficult maneuvers to perform with a tractor-trailer. Practice, skill, and patience are required to successfully complete this maneuver.

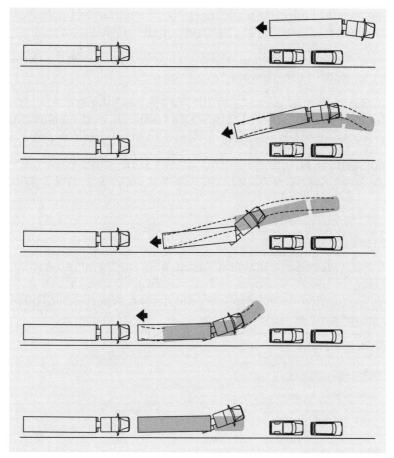

Parallel parking.

The following steps should be followed when parallel parking:

1. Your vehicle should be positioned next to the other parked vehicles. Leave about three feet of space between the vehicles.

2. Pull forward, in a straight line, near the parking space.

3. When the rear tandem axles of the trailer are about eight feet in front of the parking space, stop. Set the vehicle's brakes, exit the vehicle and do a visual check before starting the backing maneuver. This includes the safety checks mentioned earlier in the chapter. Also check vehicle positioning. Your vehicle should be positioned in a straight line with about three feet between your vehicle and other parked vehicles. The rear tandem axles should be about eight feet in front of the parking space.

4. Get back into the vehicle and start backing (slowly) with the steering wheel turned to the left. The trailer should be entering the space at about a 15 degree angle.

5. Turn the steering wheel sharply to the right and continue backing until the tractor and the trailer are in a straight line. The middle of your vehicle should be in the parking space. Continue to back until the front of the trailer is even with the front of the parking space.

6. Turn the steering wheel sharply to the right and keep backing until the trailer is parallel in the parking space.

7. When the trailer is almost parallel to the parking space, turn the wheel all the way to the left and follow the trailer into the space. Any corrections can be made by pulling forward to straighten out the units.

Should your vehicle be out of position at any time while backing, remember, it is easier to restart the maneuver than it is to try and correct what is wrong.

Summary

In this chapter, you have learned about backing principles and rules and basic backing maneuvers. Remember backing is one of the most difficult maneuvers performed by the professional driver. Practice, skill, and patience all play a part in successful backing.

One more thing about backing...it's not a crime to pull up and start over, but make sure that you correct something if you do. There's nothing more frustrating than watching a driver back up and pull forward, and back up and pull forward, never fixing what he or she is doing wrong. A five foot pull up doesn't usually correct anything. If you are going to change your direction, do something different the next time!

Backing Quiz

Directions: Read each statement carefully and mark the response that best answers the question.

1. **Backing a tractor-trailer is one of the most difficult maneuvers performed by a professional driver.**

   A. True

   B. False

2. **Which of the following is a basic backing maneuver:**

   A. Alley dock backing

   B. Straight line backing

   C. Parallel parking

   D. All of the above

3. **Prior to backing, you should get out of your vehicle and check above, under, to the sides, and to the rear of the vehicle.**

   A. True

   B. False

4. **One of the keys to successful backing is:**

   A. Riding the vehicle's clutch

   B. Backing to the right whenever possible

   C. Starting in the proper position

   D. Using extreme acceleration

5. **Another key to successful backing is:**

   A. Over steering to compensate for the backward motion

   B. Avoiding the use of mirrors because they distort objects

   C. Backing as slowly as possible using the lowest reverse gear

   D. All of the above

6. **This backing maneuver is the easiest to learn:**

   A. Alley dock backing

   B. Parallel parking

   C. Double parallel parking

   D. Straight line backing

7. **You should back to the right side whenever possible.**

   A. True

   B. False

8. **It is best to restart a backing maneuver instead of backing poorly.**

   A. True

   B. False

9. **If you are able to use a helper when backing:**

   A. You and the helper must agree on signals prior to backing

   B. The helper must be in a position so you can see the helper at all times

   C. You must still take full responsibility for your actions

   D. All of the above

10. **Straight line backing should be mastered before attempting other backing maneuvers.**

    A. True

    B. False

General Knowledge CDL Pre-Test

Read each question carefully and then choose the answer that is most correct.

1. **Which of the following is true about tire pressure?**

    A. as temperature increases so does air pressure in the tires

    B. it is not necessary to check tire pressure during a pre-trip inspection

    C. in warmer weather it is best to let out some of the air in the tires to reduce pressure

    D. all of the above

2. **Which of the following happens when a tire blows at highway speed?**

    A. you will experience an immediate and dramatic drop in speed

    B. you will feel a vibration

    C. you will hear a hissing sound

    D. the low air pressure signal device will come on

3. **What is the purpose of a pre-trip inspection?**

    A. to add an additional 15 minutes of time to your log book

    B. to avoid being cited by a law enforcement official

    C. to make sure the vehicle is safe to operate

    D. to see if any additional 1,000lbs of freight can be added to maximize revenue

4. **When you see a hazard in the road in front of you, you should:**

    A. steer and counter steer around it

    B. stop quickly and get off the roadway if possible

    C. stop quickly, stay in the roadway, set your reflective triangles, and go to the rear of your vehicle to flag down traffic

    D. turn on your 4-way flashers or flash your brakes lights to warn others

5. **At what Blood Alcohol Concentration (BOC) will you be placed out-of-service for 24 hours?**

    A. .04% or higher

    B. .03% or higher

    C. any detectable amount

    D. 1.0% or higher

Chapter 7
Backing

Chapter **8**

Coupling and uncoupling

OBJECTIVES

Upon completion of this chapter, you should have an understanding of the procedures and skills necessary for safe coupling and uncoupling of tractor-trailer units, including:

- ❑ Tractor alignment
- ❑ Backing procedures
- ❑ Trailer securement
- ❑ Tractor/trailer connections
- ❑ Landing gear retraction and securement

Introduction

Proper coupling and uncoupling skills are vital for safe tractor-trailer operations. Disaster awaits any driver not well versed in proper coupling and uncoupling procedures. Improper coupling can result in trailers being dropped, air and electrical lines being torn, cab damage, freight damage, lawsuits, fines, and other serious consequences. These consequences are always preventable.

As a professional driver, you are required to be familiar with safe coupling and uncoupling techniques so the procedure is always done in an exact sequence, every time. Know the procedures and know the hazards before ever attempting a coupling or uncoupling maneuver.

Proper coupling and uncoupling skills are vital for safe operations.

This chapter will present the step-by-step procedures and help you develop the skills necessary for safe coupling and uncoupling of tractor-trailer units.

Coupling Tractor-Trailers

The following 16-step approach to coupling will help protect you, your vehicle, your cargo, and others from damage and injury. Never attempt to couple a rig without following this sequence.

Fifth wheel with jaws locked.

Step 1: Inspect the fifth wheel and kingpin — To help ensure a safe connection, the tractor's fifth wheel and the trailer's kingpin must be inspected *before* attempting to couple the tractor to the trailer. When inspecting the fifth wheel and kingpin, you should:

Did you look at your fifth wheel plate before hooking up to that next trailer? Did you really? Think about it driver; that fifth wheel connection is the only thing that keeps the trailer connected to your tractor. Make sure it's WELL greased! If you see any rust you need to get a lot more grease on there!

Sliding fifth wheel.

1.   Check for damaged, loose, or missing parts.

2.   Make sure the mounting of the fifth wheel to the tractor is secure. Make sure there are no cracks in the frame or in any of the weld points and that all attached bolts are secure.

Fifth wheel with retention groove.

3. Grease the fifth wheel plate, if necessary. The result of an improperly greased fifth wheel will be steering problems caused by increased friction between the tractor and trailer, especially noticeable in turns.

4. Ensure that the fifth wheel is in the proper position for coupling. It should be tilted down toward the rear of the tractor, with the jaws open and the release handle in the released or unlocked position.

5. If you have a sliding fifth wheel, make sure that the fifth wheel is in the locked position and that all pins are seated correctly to prevent movement of the fifth wheel.

6. Make sure the position of the fifth wheel will not allow the tractor to strike the landing gear.

7. Check the trailer kingpin to ensure that it's not loose, bent, or broken.

Coupling must be done in an area that provides enough space to maneuver safely.

Step 2: Check area and secure trailer — The coupling procedure must be done in a location that provides enough space to maneuver safely. In addition, the trailer should be secured against movement before backing up to it, in the event your tractor makes contact with it.

1. Make sure the area around the vehicle is clear.

2. Check the cargo, if any, to make sure it will not shift when the tractor and trailer are coupled.

3. Chock the trailer wheels, or if the trailer has spring brakes, make sure they are applied.

Position the tractor.

Step 3: Position the tractor — Get into the tractor. Position the tractor squarely and directly in front of the trailer, not at an angle. Also, the kingpin should be aligned with the throat of the fifth wheel.

Backing under the trailer at an angle might push the trailer sideways and damage or break the landing gear, potentially causing the trailer to fall or hit something. If you must back at an angle, get out of the cab frequently to check the alignment of the fifth wheel to the kingpin.

When positioning the tractor, use your outside mirrors to look along both sides of the trailer and your drive axle tires. It is important that you frequently check both the left and right mirrors in order to get a true picture of the alignment between the units.

When coupling, back slowly.

If the trailer is 8 feet (96 inches) wide, the outside edge of the drive axle tires and the edge of the trailer should form a straight line. If the trailer is wider (many are now 8-½ feet (102 inches) wide), adjust your position accordingly, so the tractor tires are inside the outside edge of the trailer by a few inches.

Step 4: Back slowly into position — Begin backing the tractor up towards the front of the trailer, *slowly*. Stop just before the fifth wheel touches the trailer. Don't bump the trailer or lift it up onto the fifth wheel. At this point, you should be able to compare the fifth wheel height with the trailer height. Don't connect the air lines yet.

Step 5: Secure the tractor — Shift the transmission into neutral and engage the parking brake before exiting the cab.

Raise or lower the landing gear as needed.

Step 6: Check the trailer height — Now check the height of the trailer in relation to the fifth wheel. The trailer should be low enough that it will make contact with the middle of the fifth wheel and will be raised slightly by the tractor when the tractor is backed under it.

If the trailer is too low, the tractor may strike and damage the nose of the trailer. If the trailer is too high, it may not couple correctly or completely miss the pin, possibly striking the rear of the cab.

151

Raise or lower the trailer as needed by cranking the landing gear up or down, and/or raise or lower the fifth wheel using the tractor's adjustable air suspension, if so equipped. Secure the landing gear crank when desired height is reached.

Finally, check that the kingpin and fifth wheel are aligned, and make sure the jaws are open if the tractor has been moved any distance.

Never go under a trailer that is not supported by a tractor.

Step 7: Connect the air lines — Before connecting the tractor to the trailer, check your trailer brakes. Most trailers will already have the brakes set but if your trailer is very old (manufactured before 1973), you may need to supply air to set them. The connection must be done properly for the brakes to work correctly. It's a good idea to connect the air lines at this stage, even if the trailer is equipped with spring brakes.

There are two air lines to be connected: the "service" line and the "emergency" line. There are several ways the lines may be distinguished from one another:

Service and emergency air lines.

- They may be stamped with the words "Service" and "Emergency."

- They may be color coded, with blue or black for the service line and red for the Emergency line.

- The glad hands may be coded by shape, with square glad hands for the service line and round glad hands for the emergency line.

Check all four glad hand seals (rubber grommets) for cracks or other damage, and then connect the tractor's emergency air line to the trailer's emergency glad hand (usually on the right side when facing the trailer). Make sure the connection is firm, and then engage the safety latch or other mechanism to keep the lines together. Connect the service line in the same manner.

Make sure air lines are safely supported where they won't be crushed or caught while the tractor is backing under the trailer, and make sure there is enough slack in the lines so the glad hands won't uncouple.

Step 8: Supply air to the trailer — This step should only be done if you have determined that the brakes are not already set (pre-1973 trailer), or if you can't tell whether they are set or not. From the cab, with the engine off, push in the red air supply knob to supply air to the trailer brake system.

Hey hold on a minute! You might as well connect your electrical connection at the same time as your air lines. That way it's out of the way and won't get dragged through the grease on the fifth wheel as you continue to back up. Trust me...it happens and it's a mess!

Here's one more way to remember it. Red right...Blue left. Even if the trailer connections have the colors worn off of them, your tractor should be properly color-coded. If you always put the red gladhand from your tractor on the right connection on the trailer, you should be O.K. That's why your coiled up airlines coming off your tractor are red and blue. If they aren't, take a few minutes and mark them. It will save you a lot of grief later.

Wait until the air pressure is normal. Check the air brake system pressure gauge for signs of major air loss and listen for escaping air (a sign that a problem exists).

Apply and release the trailer brakes and listen for the sound of the trailer brakes. You should hear the brakes activate when they are applied, and hear air escape when they are released.

Step 9: Start the engine and set the trailer brakes — When you're sure the trailer brakes are working, start the engine. Make sure the air pressure is up to normal.

Apply the trailer brakes (if they are not already applied) by pulling the red air supply knob or pulling the trailer brake hand control all the way down.

Step 10: Back under the trailer — It's time to make the main connection. Put the tractor into the lowest reverse gear and release the tractor's parking brake.

Back the tractor slowly under the trailer. The trailer apron should contact the fifth wheel, lifting the trailer onto the tractor. Stop when you hear and/or feel the fifth wheel's jaws close around the kingpin. Hitting the kingpin too hard could cause extensive damage to the kingpin, fifth wheel, landing gear, and/or cargo.

Back the tractor slowly under the trailer.

Step 11: Check the connection — Put the tractor in low gear and gently pull forward, while the trailer brakes are still locked, to check that the trailer is locked onto the tractor. Stop as soon as you feel resistance from the trailer, and repeat the test once more.

Step 12: Secure the vehicle — Once the connection is solid, put the transmission in neutral and apply the tractor parking brakes. Shut off the engine and take the key with you so someone else won't move the truck while you're under it.

Step 13: Inspect the coupling — In this step, you'll make sure the coupling is safe and secure. This will require you to go under the trailer to inspect the coupling, so bring a flashlight if necessary.

Inspect the coupling, making sure it is safe and secure.

Check the following:

- Make sure there's no space between the upper (apron) and lower (platform) fifth wheel. The trailer apron and fifth wheel plate should be in full contact. If there is a space, something is wrong - fix the problem before doing anything else (the ground may be uneven, or the kingpin may be on a ridge inside the jaws or on top of the closed fifth wheel jaws, which would allow the trailer to come loose very easily).

- Go under the trailer and look into the throat of the fifth wheel using a flashlight. Make sure the fifth wheel jaws have closed and locked around the shank of the kingpin, not the head.

- Check that the release arm is in the locked position.

- Check that the safety catch is in position over the release arm, if there is one. (On some fifth wheels, the catch must be put in place by hand.)

If the coupling isn't right, don't move the vehicle.

Step 14: Connect the electrical cord and check the air lines — If you haven't already done this, plug the electrical cord into the trailer and fasten the safety catch. Don't force the connection if it doesn't fit.

Check both the air lines and electrical cord for proper securement and signs of damage. A good way to do this is to set your tractor brakes, release the trailer brakes, and listen for any air leakage.

Make sure the air lines and electrical cord won't snag any moving parts of the vehicle or rest on the catwalk.

Step 15: Raise trailer supports and remove chocks — Most landing gear cranks have two speeds, low and high. Use the low speed to begin raising the landing gear. Once the landing gear is free of weight, switch to high speed.

Raise the landing gear all the way up, making sure both legs are up. Never drive with your landing gear only partially raised, as it may catch on railroad tracks or other obstructions.

After raising the landing gear, secure the crank handle safely.

When the full weight of the trailer is resting on the tractor, do the following:

1. Check for enough clearance between the rear of the tractor frame and the landing gear. This is especially important with a tandem axle tractor and/or a sliding fifth wheel. If there isn't enough clearance, the tractor may hit the landing gear during sharp turns.

2. Check that there's enough clearance between the top of the tractor tires and the nose of the trailer.

   Step 16: Remove chocks — Finally, remove and store the wheel chocks in a safe place. Chocks are usually used only at docks. Because you may not be used to them being there, make sure you go look at and around your trailer tires.

Uncoupling Tractor-Trailers

The following 12 steps will help you to safely uncouple a tractor-trailer combination.

Step 1: Position the rig — The first step is to make sure the surface of the parking area is level and that it can support the weight of the trailer. Dirt, sand, and gravel surfaces can cause problems, as can hot blacktop. If necessary, use trailer supports, such as boards to prevent the trailer from sinking.

Align the tractor with the trailer. Pulling out at an angle can damage the landing gear.

Stop! Did you forget anything? Are you sure? If you think you've got it right, set your trailer brakes, release your tractor brakes and give a "gentle" tug against the trailer. This is a good idea particularly in the winter. Cold weather makes the grease get really thick and even though the latch looks good, it may not be latched. Now's the time to find out, not when you make your first turn and the trailer falls off the fifth wheel. Still not sure? Give it another little tug!

Properly position your vehicle prior to uncoupling.

Step 2: Secure the trailer and ease pressure on locking jaws — Pull out the trailer air supply button to lock the trailer brakes.

Ease pressure on the fifth wheel locking jaws by backing up gently. This will help you release the pressure of the locking jaws against the kingpin.

Put the tractor parking brakes on while the tractor is pushing against the kingpin. This will hold the rig with pressure off the locking jaws. Place the transmission in Neutral and turn off the engine.

Step 3: Chock the trailer wheels — Chock the trailer wheels if the trailer doesn't have spring brakes, or if you're not sure. (The air could leak out of the trailer air tank, releasing its emergency brakes. The trailer could then move if it didn't have the wheels chocked.)

Step 4: Lower the landing gear — Check the landing gear for damage, excessive rust, cracks, broken welds, or other problems. Lower the landing gear until it makes firm contact with the ground.

Make sure both supports are firmly touching the ground - if not, find more level ground before dropping the trailer.

If the trailer is loaded, after the landing gear makes firm contact with the ground, turn the crank in low gear a few extra turns to lift some weight off the tractor. This will make it easier to unlatch the fifth wheel and to couple next time. Do not lift the trailer off the fifth wheel.

Step 5: Disconnect air lines and electrical cord — Disconnect the air lines from the trailer. Connect the air line glad hands to the dummy couplers on the back of the cab, or couple them together.

Hang the electrical cord with the plug facing down to prevent moisture from entering it.

Make sure the lines are supported so they won't be damaged while driving the tractor.

Hey driver, stop and think a minute. It's pretty easy to crank down your landing gear just until it touches the ground and then dump the air out of your tractor air bags to get out from underneath the trailer. DON'T do this. It makes it extremely difficult for the next person to try and get under the trailer particularly if the trailer is loaded. You'll think it's a great idea until you are the one trying to pick up a "low" trailer. It's not fun and it's just being lazy! Take a minute and crank the landing gear down until you start to hear air releasing from your tractor air bags. Then give it another crank or two just to be nice to the next guy.

Step 6: Unlock the fifth wheel — Lift the fifth wheel release handle lock or safety latch (if so equipped). If necessary, use a hook or extension handle to reach the lock/latch.

Pull the release handle to open position.

Keep your legs and feet clear of the rear tractor wheels to avoid serious injury in case the vehicle moves.

Step 7: Lower the air suspension — If your tractor has an air suspension, release pressure from the air bags so the rear of the tractor doesn't "jump" when pulling clear of the trailer.

Step 8: Pull the tractor partially clear — Release the tractor's parking brake and pull the tractor forward until the fifth wheel just begins to clear the trailer's apron plate. Stop with the tractor frame still under the trailer, to prevent the trailer from falling to the ground if the landing gear should collapse or sink.

Step 9: Secure the tractor — Apply the parking brake, place the transmission in neutral, and exit the cab.

Step 10: Inspect the trailer supports — Make sure the ground is supporting the trailer. Make sure the landing gear isn't damaged. If necessary, use a trailer safety jack to support the trailer.

Step 11: Pull the tractor clear — Release the parking brakes, check the area, and slowly drive the tractor clear of the trailer.

Step 12: Raise the air suspension — If your tractor has an air suspension, reinflate the air bags (see Step 7 above).

Coupling Twin Trailers

The procedures for coupling twin trailers are a bit more complicated than those for single trailers. The following steps should be followed when coupling twin trailers.

The procedures for coupling a twin trailer are more complicated.

Step 1: Secure the rear trailer — If the second trailer doesn't have spring brakes (pre-1973), drive the tractor close to the trailer, connect the emergency air supply line, charge the trailer air tank, and disconnect the emergency line. This will set the trailer emergency brakes (if the slack adjusters are correctly adjusted). Chock the wheels.

Step 2: Couple the tractor and first trailer — Using the procedures for coupling tractor-trailers discussed previously, couple the tractor and the first trailer. For safe handling on the road, the more heavily loaded trailer must always be in first position behind the tractor. The lighter trailer should be in the rear.

Step 3: Position the converter dolly — Release the dolly brakes by opening the air tank petcock. Or, if the dolly has spring brakes, use the dolly parking brake control.

If the distance is not too great, roll the dolly into position by hand so it's in line with the rear trailer's kingpin. Otherwise, use the tractor and first trailer to pick up the converter dolly. Position the combination as close as possible to the dolly.

Move the dolly to the rear of the first trailer and couple it to the trailer.

Lock the pintle hook

Secure the dolly support in the raised position.

Pull the dolly into position as close as possible to the nose of the second trailer.

Lower the dolly support.

Unhook the dolly from the first trailer.

Wheel the dolly into position in front of the second trailer in line with the kingpin.

Step 4: Connect the dolly to the front trailer — Back the first trailer into position in front of the dolly tongue.

Hook the dolly to the front trailer.

Lock the pintle hook.

Secure the converter gear support in the raised position.

Step 5: Connect the dolly to the rear trailer — Make sure the trailer brakes are locked and/or the wheels chocked.

Make sure the trailer height is correct. It must be slightly lower than the center of the fifth wheel, so the trailer is raised slightly when the dolly is pushed underneath.

Back the converter dolly under the rear trailer. Raise the landing gear slightly off the ground to prevent damage if the trailer moves.

Test the coupling by pulling against the pin of the number two trailer.

Make a visual check of the coupling. There should be no space between the upper (apron) and lower (platform) fifth wheel, and the locking jaws should be closed around the kingpin.

Connect safety chains, air hoses, and electrical cord.

Close the converter dolly air tank petcock and the shut-off valves at the rear of the second trailer (service and emergency shut-offs).

Open the shut-off valves at the rear of the first trailer (and on the dolly, if so equipped).

Raise the landing gear completely on the second trailer.

Charge the trailers (push the trailer air supply knob in) and check for air at the rear of the second trailer by opening the emergency line shut-off. If air pressure isn't there, something is wrong and the brakes won't work. A valve may be closed or possibly an air line is crossed.

Uncoupling Twin Trailers

Step 1: Uncouple the rear trailer — Park your rig in a straight line on firm, level ground.

Apply the parking brakes so the rig won't move.

Chock the wheels of the second trailer if it doesn't have spring brakes.

Lower the landing gear of the second trailer enough to remove some weight from the dolly.

Close the air shut-offs at the rear of the first trailer (and on the dolly if so equipped).

Disconnect all dolly air and electric lines and secure them.

Release the dolly brakes.

Release the converter dolly fifth wheel latch. Slowly pull the tractor, first trailer, and dolly forward to pull the dolly out from under the rear trailer.

Step 2: Uncouple the converter dolly — Lower the dolly landing gear.

Disconnect the safety chains.

Apply the converter gear spring brakes or chock the wheels.

Release the pintle hook on the first trailer.

Slowly pull clear of the dolly.

Other Combinations

The methods and procedures described here apply to the most common tractor-trailer combinations. However, there are additional types of combinations, as well as other ways of coupling and uncoupling them. While they won't be covered here, it's your responsibility to learn the right way to couple and uncouple the vehicle(s) you'll drive.

Summary

The coupling/uncoupling procedure is a "nuts and bolts" skill required of everyone operating a tractor-trailer combination. This chapter has covered the step-by-step procedures used to couple and uncouple most common tractor-trailer combinations. Following the 16 coupling and 12 uncoupling steps, in order, should allow you to perform the coupling/uncoupling procedure safely in most situations. For your own safety and the safety of your equipment and the motoring public, you should practice the procedures until they become second habit and you are able to couple and uncouple your rig "by the book" every time.

Coupling and Uncoupling Quiz

Directions: Read each statement carefully and mark the response that best answers the question.

1. **After coupling, there should be no space between the upper and lower fifth wheel.**

   A. True

   B. False

2. **Failing to grease the fifth wheel plate could result in:**

   A. A dropped trailer

   B. Steering problems

   C. Excessive noise

   D. Damage to the kingpin

3. **If you must back up to a trailer at an angle, you should:**

   A. Rely on your mirrors alone to line up the fifth wheel and kingpin

   B. Lock the fifth wheel to the kingpin before connecting the air lines

   C. Get out of the cab frequently to check the alignment of the fifth wheel and kingpin

   D. Complete the maneuver as quickly as possible

4. **What is a converter dolly?**

   A. A device allowing you to connect mismatched air and electrical lines

   B. A wheeled jack used to support a trailer during coupling

   C. A steel platform, on wheels, which can connect to a trailer's landing gear and allow a driver to manually position a trailer before coupling

   D. An auxiliary axle assembly equipped with a fifth wheel, used to support a second trailer

5. **Before driving, the landing gear should be:**

   A. Lifted 3-5 inches off the pavement

   B. Raised all the way up

   C. Secured with chains or bungee cords

   D. Stowed inside the trailer

6. **Air should be supplied to the trailer brakes:**

    A. Only after connecting the tractor to the trailer

    B. Before backing under the trailer

    C. If wheel chocks are not available

    D. After the trailer supports have been removed

7. **When backing the tractor into position in front of the trailer, you should stop before the fifth wheel touches the trailer.**

    A. True

    B. False

8. **Before backing under the trailer, what should the height of the fifth wheel be in relation to the nose of the trailer?**

    A. The trailer nose should be higher than the fifth wheel, so the king-pin goes directly into the locking jaws

    B. The trailer nose should be lower than the fifth wheel

    C. The trailer nose should be aligned with the middle of the fifth wheel, so the trailer is lifted upward when the tractor is backed under it

    D. The height of the fifth wheel is not important

9. **When uncoupling, if the fifth wheel locking lever is stuck, you should:**

    A. Force the lever open using a hand tool

    B. Back the tractor up gently to ease the pressure, then put on the parking brake

    C. Pull the tractor forward gently to ease the pressure, then put on the parking brake

    D. Call your maintenance department for assistance

10. **In a set of doubles, the heaviest trailer should be positioned toward the rear.**

    A. True

    B. False

General Knowledge CDL Pre-Test

Read each question carefully and select the most correct answer.

1. **Your vehicle is 40 feet long and you are traveling at 50 mph. The safe following distance is:**

    A. 5 seconds

    B. 6 seconds

    C. 4 seconds

    D. 3 seconds

2. **After you start your engine, which of the following should occur?**

    A. oil pressure will build in 4 to 5 minutes

    B. air pressure will rise to normal in 10 to 15 minutes

    C. the water temperature will indicate a gradual rise to normal operating temperature

    D. the manifold exhaust indicator gauge will immediately rise to 190 degrees

3. **Which of the following can you NOT check at the same time?**

    A. turn signal, brake lights, and 4-way flashers

    B. headlights and clearance lights

    C. taillights and clearance lights

    D. clearance lights and 4-way flashers

4. **Which of the following is true about rear drive wheel braking skids?**

    A. the vehicle's front wheels will slide sideways

    B. it is not a cause of jackknifing

    C. the locked wheels have more traction than the wheels that are rolling

    D. if it occurs with a vehicle towing a trailer, the trailer can push the towing vehicle sideways

5. **Which of the following statements is true?**

    A. hazards are easier to see at night than during the day

    B. many commercial vehicle accidents occur between midnight and 6 A.M.

    C. most drivers are more alert at night than during the day

    D. it is recommended that you use your high beams at all times during the period from 7 P.M. to 7 A.M.

Chapter 8
Coupling and
Uncoupling

Chapter 9

Visual search

OBJECTIVES

Upon completion of this chapter, you should have a basic understanding of:

- ❑ Seeing ahead and to the sides
- ❑ The proper use of mirrors
- ❑ Seeing to the rear

Introduction

A safe driver is aware of what is going on all around his/her vehicle. The purpose of this chapter is to introduce you to the skills required to conduct an effective visual search. Developing good scanning technique allows you to gather all of the necessary information to make safe driving decisions. It also helps in reducing fatigue.

An effective visual search includes seeing ahead, to the sides, and behind your vehicle as well as proper adjustment and use of mirrors.

An effective visual search helps you make safe driving decisions.

Seeing Ahead and to the Sides

A good driver continually scans his/her entire sight area. This includes focusing on:

- The road, vehicles, and other problems (debris, etc.) ahead;

- Vehicles and other problems (debris, etc.) to the left and right; and

- Vehicles behind.

Distance scanning — Looking ahead can help you travel safely. Always look far enough ahead to:

- Give yourself time to spot a problem;

- Decide the best way to avoid it;

- Check for adverse traffic conditions; and

- Give yourself enough time to maneuver away from a potential problem situation.

As a general rule, look about 12-15 seconds ahead of your vehicle. In the city, 12-15 seconds is equal to about two to three blocks. On the highway, 12-15 seconds is equal to just over one quarter of a mile. If you can't see that far ahead, you should slow down.

When driving in the city, look 2 to 3 blocks ahead. Anticipate potential hazards.

As well as looking ahead, you should be scanning to the sides and behind your vehicle. Watch road signs and check your vehicle's instruments. Your eyes should be continually moving from far to near. When scanning ahead, pay special attention to anything that could affect your path of travel including:

- Other vehicles;

- Road signs;

- Traffic signals;

- Debris;

- Animals;

- Weather-related hazards (ice, rain, snow, etc.);

- Intersections;

- Work/construction zones;

- Stopped vehicles; and

- Emergency vehicles; and

- Accidents.

Be aware of changing conditions.

There are several benefits to distance scanning including being able to identify hazards early, and having additional time to react/respond to situations including finding ways to avoid the situation. It helps you avoid abrupt stops and radical speed changes. Also, effective scanning can help reduce fatigue. Your eyes are continually moving and are not fixed on a single object.

Scanning to the sides — When on the road, you should be periodically scanning to the sides, but there are certain situations where scanning to the sides is critical including crosswalks, intersections, and school zones.

At crosswalks you should use extra caution. As well as watching the entire area, you should pay additional attention to what is happening to your right. Pedestrians, bicycles, etc. are often hidden from your line of sight when closest to your vehicle. Also, remember to yield the right of way to pedestrians when turning on green.

At intersections, move your vehicle forward slowly. Look left, right, and left again. Start to pull into the intersection, continuing to scan as you pull through the intersection.

School zones are another place where you need to be especially careful. Watch for children, bikes, balls, etc. darting into traffic.

In cities, scanning to the sides is crucial to your safety and the safety of others. Cars parked along the shoulder create increased hazards that may not be seen if you are not constantly scanning. Often, people will walk between cars or will open their door into traffic without even looking. By scanning you can avoid a possible accident or injury caused by the inattentiveness of others.

Use of Mirrors

Mirrors provide your only view of the rear of your vehicle. You must check your mirrors before changing speed or position in traffic. You should check your mirrors about every four seconds. Also, use mirrors to assist in checking your vehicle's blind spots.

Most tractors are equipped with two types of mirrors:

- Plane or west coast; and

- Convex.

Plane or west coast — A plane or west coast mirror assists you in seeing down the sides and toward the rear of your trailer and the roadway behind. It doesn't give as wide a view as the convex mirror does, but it does allow for better visibility down the length of the trailer. The left mirror is closer and reflects a larger image which means you have a greater field of view from that mirror.

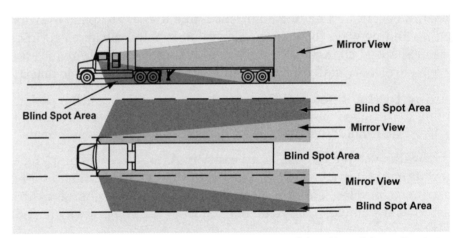

The plane or west coast mirror provides a good view of the sides of the trailer, but leaves some blind spots.

Remember that mirrors do not allow you to see everything. There are blind spots on both sides of your vehicle. This makes lane changes, passing, and other maneuvers risky. Tight turns can also pose a problem. You can't see smaller vehicles or pedestrians that are next to the vehicle. Along with using your mirrors, signal and wait a moment before changing direction or lanes.

Images in your side mirror will appear to be similar to those when you are driving your personal vehicle. When using your plane mirror in this situation, you should be able to judge the speed and distance of overtaking vehicles.

Convex — Convex mirrors are designed with an outward curvature to provide a wide-angle view. They give a broader view than plane mirrors and, if adjusted correctly, eliminate much of the blind area. Convex mirrors provide the best close-up view of the sides of your vehicle.

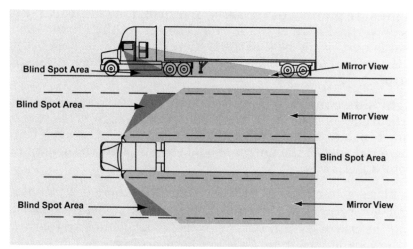

The convex mirror provides a wide-angle view.

One negative aspect of convex mirrors is that they show a distorted image. Overtaking vehicles appear smaller and farther away than they really are. When using this mirror, you need to gain a solid understanding of what you are looking at. This will take practice as this "view" is not something you are used to in a car.

When making a right turn, the convex mirror provides a larger field of vision and a wider angle of sight.

A combination of plane and convex mirrors work best. They provide maximum side and rear vision. The drawback is that the combination can be a bit confusing at first. Frequently making sure the mirrors are clean and properly adjusted can be a great aid in reducing any confusion.

Adjusting mirrors — Proper adjustment is important. It ensures that you have the best view possible to the sides and rear of your vehicle. Make sure your vehicle is straight before making any adjustments.

Left side plane/west coast — You should see the trailer body on the inside vertical edge of the mirror. The rest of the mirror should show what is next to and behind the trailer. You should be able to see a point on the ground about 30 feet away on the bottom, horizontal edge of the mirror.

Left side convex — You should see part of the trailer on the inside vertical edge of the mirror. The top, horizontal edge, of the mirror should show a point on the ground that is about 35 feet away. The bottom, horizontal edge should show a point on the ground that is about 7 feet away.

Right side plane/west coast — You should see the trailer body on the inside vertical edge of the mirror. The rest of the mirror should show what is next to and behind the trailer. You should be able to see a point on the ground about 60 feet away on the bottom, horizontal edge of the mirror.

Right side convex — You should see part of the trailer on the inside vertical edge of the mirror. The top, horizontal edge, of the mirror should show a point on the ground that is about 65 feet away. The bottom, horizontal edge of the mirror should show a point on the ground that is about 8 feet away

Some vehicles also make use of fender mirrors, which are mounted on the right and left corners of the front fenders. Companies have also started exploring the use of certain types of collision avoidance systems. Although these two types of visual aids are not on every commercial motor vehicle, they do provide an additional level of sight around the vehicle which adds to safer driving operations in many instances.

Seeing to the Rear

Continually use your mirrors to monitor the rear of your vehicle. There are several things you should be looking for when monitoring the rear of your vehicle.

Check load and cargo security. Watch for loose or falling cargo.

Keep an eye on your tires. Look for potential problems including flat or damaged tires or tire fires.

Check for vehicles beside your tractor and trailer. Be alert. Know what is going on at all times.

Use your mirrors when changing lanes or when you are forced to slow down quickly or unexpectedly. Mirror checks are required for lane changes, merging, and turns. Use of mirrors is also important when approaching alleys and intersections. Mirrors must be used more frequently when in traffic tie-ups and when approaching or driving alongside parked or stopped vehicles.

Summary

In this chapter, you have learned about the skills required to conduct an effective visual search. This includes seeing ahead, to the sides, and behind your vehicle as well as proper use and adjustment of mirrors.

Visual Search Quiz

Directions: Read each statement carefully and mark the response that best answers the question.

1. **A good driver continually scans his/her entire sight area.**

    A. True

    B. False

2. **As a general rule, you should always look about ____ seconds ahead of your vehicle.**

    A. 8-10

    B. 10-12

    C. 12-15

    D. 30-40

3. **When behind the wheel, your eyes should be continually moving, scanning ahead and to the sides.**

    A. True

    B. False

4. **There aren't any benefits to distance scanning.**

    A. True

    B. False

5. **The two types of mirrors most tractors are equipped with are:**

    A. Concave and convex

    B. Concave and straight

    C. Large and small

    D. Plane/west coast and convex

6. **Mirrors enable you to see everything to the sides and rear of your vehicle.**

    A. True

    B. False

7. **Even with the use of mirrors, there are still blind spots around your vehicle.**

    A. True

    B. False

8. **When using mirrors to monitor the rear of your vehicle, watch for:**

    A. Tire problems

    B. Cargo security

    C. Both A and B

    D. None of the above

General Knowledge CDL Pre-Test

Read each question carefully and select the most correct answer.

1. **Which of the following is a true statement?**

   A. you can always trust other drivers to turn in the direction that their turn signal is indicating

   B. mail or city delivery truck drivers are professionals and do not pose any hazard to you

   C. you do not have to worry about individuals driving cars with out-of-state license plates

   D. short-term or daily rental truck drivers are often not used to driving a large vehicle and may pose a hazard to you

2. **Bridge formulas are designed to:**

   A. determine the total gross vehicle weight of a vehicle

   B. permit the same maximum axle weight for any axle spacing

   C. permit less maximum axle weight for axles that are closer together

   D. permit less maximum axle weight for axles that are further apart

3. **When traveling down a long downgrade, you should always:**

   A. apply trailer brakes to reduce speed or maintain speed

   B. use the braking effect of the engine

   C. use stab braking

   D. apply brakes when your vehicle exceeds the "safe speed" by 5 mph

4. **What three factors add up to the total stopping distance for a commercial vehicle without air brakes?**

   A. perception distance, reaction distance, and braking distance

   B. eye lead time, reaction distance. And braking distance

   C. perception distance, reaction distance, and response distance

   D. response distance and braking distance

5. **Stab braking is not used on vehicles:**

   A. towing trailers

   B. with anti-lock brakes

   C. hauling hazardous materials

   D. it is never used on commercial vehicles equipped with air brakes

Well driver, how are you doing on these pre-tests? You should really be getting the hang of it by now. If you're still missing some of the questions, don't worry.

You'll see them again before we are done and you'll have them aced in no time!

Chapter **10**

Communication

OBJECTIVES

Upon completion of this chapter, you should have a basic understanding of:

- ❑ Communicating intent
- ❑ Communicating presence
- ❑ What is considered misuse of communications
- ❑ Communication from others

Introduction

In this chapter, you will be introduced to the basic principles of communication. This includes the appropriate processes and procedures on your part when it comes to communicating with others as well as developing the skills to understand the communications of others.

This topic has become even more important in the past few years as the number of road rage incidents have grown at a steady rate. Poor communication, which appears to be aggressive by another driver, can develop into a dangerous road rage incident. Proper communication skills can go a long way in preventing road rage incidents.

Communicating Intent

Like you, other drivers are not mind readers. They can't know what you are going to do if you don't communicate appropriately. Signaling your intentions is important. Basic methods of visibly communicating your intent include:

- Turn signals;

- Headlights;

- Four-way emergency flashers;

- Flashing brake lights; and

- Altering vehicle position.

Turn signals communicate your intent to change direction.

Turn signals — Turn signals communicate your intent to change direction. Signal anytime you plan to:

- Turn;
- Change lanes;
- Pass another vehicle;
- Merge;
- Exit;
- Parallel park; or
- Pull into traffic from the curb.

Always use your turn signal when changing lanes.

Always use your turn signal in these situations, even if you don't see any other vehicles around. Remember, your vehicle does have blind spots. The most dangerous vehicles are the ones you can't see. The following are standard turn signal guidelines you should follow.

1. **Signal early** — Signal well in advance of turning or changing lanes. In city traffic, signal one-half block before turning. On the highway, signal about 500 feet in advance. Your turn signal should blink at least three times before attempting to turn or change lanes.

2. **Signal continuously** — Keep both hands on the wheel to turn safely. Don't cancel the signal until your maneuver is complete. Remember to cancel the signal after completing the turn or lane change.

Slowing down — There will be times that you will need to let other drivers know that you are slowing down. Other drivers may not expect you to be slowing down, especially when approaching a steep grade, setting up for a turn, or stopping to load, unload, or park. A few light taps on the brake pedal (causing your brake lights to flash) should warn drivers following your vehicle. If you are driving very slowly or are stopped, use your four-way emergency flashers.

Hey, wake up!! Is your turn signal still on after you made that lane change or turned that corner? Most commercial vehicles do not have automatic cancelling turn signals and if you're not paying attention the people behind you are going to get pretty upset. So, if people around you are giving you hand signals (not friendly ones), honking their horn, or flashing their lights, as they swerve to "get out of your way," check your turn signals!

Here's another hint. If someone says on the CB, "Hey driver, are you really going to turn into that field?" they are trying to tell you something...CHECK YOUR TURN SIGNAL!

Communicate your intent to turn.

Because of the size of your vehicle and the difficulty other drivers may have seeing in front of it, it is important that you communicate early when traffic is slowing or stopping. There are many situations in which other drivers don't expect you to slow or stop, such as on the highway or in the middle of a block.

Directing traffic — One thing you should *never* do is direct traffic. Some drivers will try to help others by signaling when it is safe to pass or pull out by flashing lights, blowing the horn, or using hand signals. This could cause an accident, resulting in injury, damage, and potential liability. You could very easily be found at fault for the mistake of someone else, if you signaled them to move.

Communicating Presence

Others may not notice your vehicle, even when it is in plain sight. Communicating your presence can help prevent an accident.

Whenever you're about to pass a pedestrian, or bicyclist, assume they don't see you and could suddenly move in front of your vehicle. When it is safe and legal to do so, move your vehicle to the left of your lane, tap the horn lightly or, at night, flash your headlights off and on (if it is safe and legal). Tap the horn or flash your lights from a distance, if possible, so you don't startle the pedestrian or bicyclist.

How did they not see me! You are going to be asking yourself that almost every day. Drivers today are too busy doing everything else while they are driving, other than paying attention. Since they aren't usually watching, you need to be watching for them. So, even though you may be 70 feet long and 13 feet high, no they don't see you.

Communicating your presence can help prevent an accident.

From dusk to dawn your headlights should be turned on. They should also be turned on when it is raining, snowing, or foggy. As well as helping you see the road, this helps other drivers see you. Keep in mind that some states have laws requiring the use of headlights if weather conditions warrant the use of windshield wipers.

If you have to pull off the road and stop, immediately turn on the four-way emergency flashers.

Warning devices — Section 392.22 of the Federal Motor Carrier Safety Regulations (FMCSRs) addresses when and how warning devices must be set out on the highway.

According to Sec. 392.22 of the FMCSRs, when a vehicle is stopped on the traveled portion of the highway or the shoulder of the highway you must immediately activate your vehicle's hazard warning flashers. You then have 10 minutes to set out emergency warning devices.

When placing the devices, you should hold them in front of you to help you be clearly visible to traffic. You should remain alert for vehicles that may not see you along the roadway.

Warning devices should be placed within 10 minutes of stopping.

The placement of devices varies depending on where the vehicle is stopped. This will be covered in detail in Chapter 28.

Using your horn — The horn informs others of your presence. Only use your horn when necessary, for example to help in preventing an accident. When used unnecessarily it can be dangerous. Remember, a light tap sends a much different message than a long blast.

In general, use only your vehicle's electric horn. The air horn is extremely loud and can distract or frighten others. The horn should be used for communicating your presence and to warn of immediate danger. It isn't a toy, and should only be used for appropriate purposes.

CB radio — The citizen's band (CB) radio can be a good communication tool if used safely and legally. When used appropriately, CBs can:

- Provide information about weather and traffic conditions;

- Notify authorities about accidents or other road hazards; and

- Be used to obtain directions or other local information (although this is <u>not</u> advised).

Like your vehicle's horn, the CB isn't a toy and should be used appropriately. Avoid idle chatter and never use offensive language over the CB.

Stop driver! Don't pick up that CB mic and ask for directions to where you are going, as you enter the city limits of your destination. We will get into trip planning a little later, but this is something you should have found out BEFORE you started on this trip. Ask your dispatcher, call the customer, but DON'T ask some nut on the CB. For all you know, it could be someone that's going to lead you right down a deserted alley so they can highjack your truck! Don't take the chance, be prepared, ask ahead of time. Use the CB to tell truck driver stories and to listen for problems ahead, not to get directions!

Mobile telephone — Like the CB, a mobile telephone can be a good communication tool if used safely and legally.

Section 392.82 of the FMCSRs prohibits a driver from using a hand-held mobile telephone while driving a commercial motor vehicle. Use of a hand-held mobile telephone includes:

- Using at least one hand to hold a mobile telephone to conduct voice communication;
- Dialing or answering a mobile telephone by pressing more than a single button; or
- Reaching for a mobile phone in a manner that requires a driver to maneuver so he/she is no longer in a seated driving position, restrained by a seat belt.

Use of a hand-held mobile telephone is allowed when necessary to communicate with law enforcement officials or other emergency services.

Texting — Texting is another form of communication that is growing in use. Section 392.80 of the FMCSRs prohibits texting while driving a commercial motor vehicle. Texting is allowed when necessary to communicate with law enforcement officials or other emergency services.

Communication From Others

As the saying goes, communication is a two-way street. As a safe and professional driver, you must effectively communicate your intentions and it is just as important that you watch for and understand the communications of other drivers.

As well as the obvious means of communication (turn signals, lights, horn, etc.), there are other, more subtle communications you need to watch for when on the road.

For example, driver movement in a vehicle, such as shifting around in the seat or looking in the mirror, may indicate possible directional changes.

Observing other vehicles can give you clues as to a drivers' intentions. Sudden slowing or a slight position change in a lane may indicate a direction change. Turned front wheels or visible exhaust from a parked car may indicate the vehicle is going to pull out of a parking space.

Be alert to the obvious, and sometimes not so obvious, communication of others as ways to anticipate and avoid potential problems.

Summary

In this chapter, you have learned the importance of communication when it comes to highway safety. This includes appropriately communicating your intentions to others and understanding how others may communicate with you.

Communication Quiz

Directions: Read each statement carefully and mark the response that best answers the question.

1. **Which of the following is a way you can visibly communicate your intent when operating a tractor-trailer?**

    A. Use of turn signals

    B. Use of warning flashers

    C. By flashing the vehicle's brake lights

    D. All of the above

2. **If you don't see any other vehicles, you don't have to use a turn signal when changing lanes.**

    A. True

    B. False

3. **In city traffic, you should signal_____ before turning.**

    A. ¼ block

    B. ½ block

    C. 1 block

    D. 2 blocks

4. **On the highway, you should signal _____ before turning.**

    A. 100 feet

    B. 250 feet

    C. 500 feet

    D. 1,000 feet

5. **A few light taps on your vehicle's brakes can be used to alert other drivers that you are slowing down.**

    A. True

    B. False

6. **If you are driving very slowly or are stopped, you should use the vehicle's four-way flashers.**

    A. True

    B. False

7. **According to the FMCSRs, if your vehicle is stopped on the traveled portion of the highway or the shoulder of the highway, you have ____ to set out emergency warning devices..**

   A. 5 minutes

   B. 10 minutes

   C. 15 minutes

   D. 30 minutes

8. **When used appropriately, the CB can:**

   A. Provide information about traffic conditions

   B. Notify authorities about accidents or other road hazards

   C. Be used to obtain directions (only in an emergency)

   D. All of the above

9. **Turned front wheels or visible exhaust from a parked car may indicate the vehicle is going to pull out of a parking space.**

   A. True

   B. False

10. **A driver shifting around in his seat or looking in the mirror may indicate that he may be changing direction.**

    A. True

    B. False

CDL Combination Vehicle Pre-Test

The Combination Vehicle Test must be taken by all applicants for a class "A" commercial driver's license.

Directions: Same as General Knowledge Test; circle the most correct answer.

1. **You are hooking a tractor to a semi-trailer and have backed up but are not under it. What should you do before backing under the trailer?**

    A. Hook up the electrical service cable

    B. Hook up the emergency and service air lines

    C. Vonnect the ground cable

    D. Nothing, back up and secure the fifth wheel to the trailer

2. **After pushing in the trailer supply valve, you should not move the tractor until the whole air system is:**

    A. Charging

    B. At normal pressure

    C. Bled down to half the maximum pressure

    D. Between 50 and 60 psi

3. **There are two things that a driver can do to prevent a rollover. They are (1) Keep the cargo as close to the ground as possible, and:**

    A. Make sure that the brakes are adjusted properly

    B. Keep both hands firmly on the steering wheel

    C. Reduce speed before entering turns

    D. Keep the fifth wheel free-play loose

4. **With the engine off and the brakes released, a combination vehicle air brake system should not leak more than how many psi in one minute?**

    A. 1

    B. 2

    C. 3

    D. 4

5. **The fifth wheel locking lever is not locked after the jaws close around the kingpin. This means that:**

A. The trailer will not swing on the fifth wheel

B. You cannot set the fifth wheel for proper weight distribution

C. The hand valve is released and you may drive away

D. The coupling is not correct and should be corrected before driving the coupled unit

Chapter 11

Speed management

OBJECTIVES

Upon completion of this chapter, you should have a basic understanding of:

- ❏ The science of speed and stopping distance
- ❏ The role surface conditions play in speed management
- ❏ Adjusting speed for curves and grades
- ❏ The relationship between speed and visibility
- ❏ The influence of speed on traffic management
- ❏ The hows and whys of obeying the speed limit

Introduction

Proper speed management means operating at the appropriate speed for all road conditions. That includes taking into account the condition of the road, visibility, and traffic speed and flow.

This chapter focuses on the importance of managing your vehicle's speed in order to stop safely.

Speed management plays an important role in safe driving.

Speed and Stopping Distance

There are four factors involved in stopping a vehicle:

- Perception distance;
- Reaction distance;
- Brake lag distance; and
- Braking distance.

1. **Perception distance** — Perception distance is the distance a vehicle travels from the time you see a hazard until your brain recognizes it. The perception time for an alert driver is approximately¾ of a second. At 55 mph, a vehicle travels about 60 feet in¾ of a second.

2. **Reaction distance** — Reaction distance is the distance a vehicle travels from the time your brain tells your foot to move from the accelerator until your foot hits the brake pedal. The average driver has a reaction time of¾ of a second. At 55 mph, that accounts for another¾ of a second and another 60 feet traveled.

3. **Brake lag distance** — When operating a vehicle with air brakes, it takes about½ second for the mechanical operation to take place.

4. **Braking distance** — Braking distance is the distance it takes a vehicle to stop once the brakes are applied. Braking distance is affected by weight, length, and speed of the vehicle as well as road condition. A heavy vehicle's components (brakes, tires, springs, etc.) are designed to work best when a vehicle is fully loaded. At 55 mph on dry pavement with good brakes, a heavy vehicle travels about 170 feet and can take about 5 seconds to stop.

When you add together the perception, reaction, brake lag, and braking time and distance, at 55 mph it will take between 6 and 7 seconds to stop, and the vehicle will travel about 290 feet (almost the length of one football field) in ideal conditions. Higher speeds increase stopping distance greatly.

Speed and Surface Conditions

Traction is necessary for vehicle control. The less friction between a vehicle's tires and the road, the less traction. Certain road conditions reduce traction and lower speeds are necessary .

Rain — Rain can affect a vehicle's traction. As rain begins to fall, it mixes with oils on the road, causing the oils to rise to the road's surface. Until additional rain breaks down and washes away these oils, there is a layer of slippery oil between a vehicle's tires and the road. This condition can last anywhere from a few minutes to a few hours.

Hold on a second driver! Did you just read that right? Yes you did. It will take just about the full length of a football field to stop your vehicle in ideal conditions at 55 miles per hour! There's an awful lot of stuff that you could run over in that distance, isn't there? And when was the last time you drove at 55 miles per hour in perfect conditions? This is why you really have to pay attention to what you're doing and look WAY down the road.

Wet pavement can reduce vehicle traction.

New pavement is more slippery when wet than old pavement. New pavement has a greater concentration of oils that have yet to be washed away by years of rain. White foam on the road is an indication of oil and water mixing, a clue that the road surface is slippery.

A heavy rain that causes water to stand on the road can cause a vehicle to hydroplane. The faster a vehicle travels on standing water, the greater the chance of hydroplaning. This is due to the fact that traction is only present when a vehicle's tires have contact with the road. If the tires are riding on a wall of water, they lose traction. Even a fully load tractor-trailer can hydroplane on very little water.

When it rains, vehicle speeds should be reduced by at least⅓.

Snow — Snow causes reduced traction and limited visibility. Slowing down is required for visibility and vehicle control purposes.

A light, powdery snow often blows off the road causing few problems. If there is enough powder to cover the road, it will form a slick, smooth surface. A heavier, slushy snow can affect vehicle control. If the snow becomes hard packed, it can cause an ice hazard.

Slow down driver! If you thought it was tricky the first time you drove on ice in a car, wait until the first time you try it in a big truck. It's not fun! The best thing you can do is turn your radio off (so you can pay better attention), slow way down, and "listen and feel" how your truck is reacting to the road surface. If it's too bad, just get off the road!

Snow causes reduced visibility and traction.

Vehicle speeds should be reduced by at least ½ in snowy conditions. Remember, when determining vehicle speed in snowy conditions, you must be confident that you can safely stop and maneuver based on road conditions.

Ice — An icy road can present more dangers than a snowy road. When temperatures are near freezing, a driver has to be alert to the potential for black ice.

Black ice forms when temperatures drop rapidly and moisture on the road freezes into a smooth, nearly invisible, slippery surface. In black ice conditions, the road appears to be wet, when actually it is icy.

To check for ice formation a driver can feel the front of the vehicle's mirrors or antenna. If ice is forming there, it is also forming on the road. The driver should also watch the spray off of other vehicles. If the spray stops, ice may be forming.

A driver's actions will depend on road conditions. At the very least, a driver should slow his/her vehicle by ½ in icy conditions. As with snowy conditions, when determining vehicle speed, you must be confident that you can safely stop and maneuver based on road conditions. If the road is very slippery, the driver should get off the road as soon as safely possible

Shady portions of the road can remain slippery for a long time after ice on sunny areas of the road has melted and the pavement is dry. Slow down on shade-covered roads.

When the temperature drops, bridges can freeze before the road does. If slippery conditions are likely, avoid any change (acceleration, shifting, or braking) in driving habits while crossing the bridge. Maintain a smooth and steady speed.

Hey driver, did you ever go under an overpass and see those wet spots in the tracks of the road, right under the bridge? Usually they're not a problem, but when the temperature drops, they become a perfect place to catch a driver off guard. They may still look wet, but they're really ice and can throw your vehicle into a spin if you're not careful.

Speed and Road Shape

Curves — Remember that posted speed limits on curves are designed with cars in mind. Driving through a curve too fast (at or above the posted speed limit) can cause several problems including skidding off the road or vehicle roll over.

Slow to a safe speed before entering a curve.

Slow to a safe speed before entering a curve, at least 5 mph below the posted speed limit. Slow down as needed, but keep in mind that braking in a curve can be dangerous. It is easier to lock your vehicle's wheels and cause a skid. Never exceed the posted speed limit in a curve. Also be in a gear that will let you accelerate slightly through the curve. This will help you maintain vehicle control.

Vehicles work hard to maintain a safe speed on upgrades and downgrades.

Grades — Gravity and vehicle weight play a part in speed management when driving on upgrades and downgrades.

On an upgrade, your vehicle has to work harder to fight the pull of gravity and maintain its speed. To maintain speed you must place more pressure on the accelerator, and/or possibly shift to a lower gear.

On a downgrade, your vehicle is working with gravity, resulting in an increase in speed. Vehicle weight also has an impact on truck speeds going down a grade. Heavier trucks want to accelerate faster than lighter ones. You must use care in maintaining a safe and even speed.

Note: The procedures for dealing with uphill/downhill driving will be covered in-depth in Chapter 14.

Speed and Visibility

You should always be able to stop within your field of vision. In other words, you should be able to stop within the distance you can see ahead. When driving at night, or in poor weather conditions (rain, fog, snow, etc.) you will need to slow down so you can stop your vehicle within your field of vision.

Speed and Traffic Flow

When driving in heavy traffic, the safest speed is generally the speed of the other vehicles on the roadway provided you can maintain an adequate following distance and you are not violating the posted speed limit. If you are unable to maintain a safe following distance, slow your vehicle to 3-4 mph less than the flow of traffic.

Always maintain adequate following distance.

Often, drivers believe that exceeding the speed limit can save (or make up) time. When operating in traffic, this isn't always the case. If you are traveling faster than the speed of other traffic, you will have to pass other

Various studies have shown that split speed limits are dangerous, cause accidents, and do nothing to reduce traffic problems. In fact, they cause congestion, roadrage, and general hate and discontent toward those "slow trucks" that are always in the way! Regardless, the law is the law. As much as you don't like it, you still need to abide by the speed limit, even if you don't agree with it.

vehicles. This increases your chances of being involved in an accident. This type of driving can also add to your level of fatigue which can also increase your chances of being involved in an accident.

It is best to go with the flow of traffic when safe and legal to do so.

Obeying the Speed Limit

Speed limits are based, in part, on the principles of good speed management. They take into account several issues including sight distance limitation, road conditions, and traffic volume. There are many reasons why you should not speed. Some of these reasons are outlined in this section.

Obey the speed limit.

Stop driver! Let's think about this. Is it really that important for you to speed? It costs more in fuel, raises your stress level, and could get you in big trouble. You could even lose your license! It's pretty hard to be a truck driver if you can't drive, so think about it. Besides, if you do the math, you're only gaining minutes on the day and those few minutes could cost you months or years of driving privileges. Just don't do it!

Accidents — Accidents are more likely to occur at higher speeds. There's less reaction time and you aren't able to have as much control of your vehicle. Also, studies show that the higher the speed a vehicle is traveling when an accident occurs, the greater the chance of fatalities.

Penalties — Two or more convictions for excessive speeding (15 mph or more over the speed limit) in either a commercial or non-commercial vehicle (including your personal vehicle) can disqualify you from operating a commercial motor vehicle. Section 383.51 of the Federal Motor Carrier Safety Regulations (FMCSRs) states that you can be disqualified for a period of 60-120 days for excessive speeding violations.

All speeding convictions (whether they prompt disqualification or not) become part of your permanent driving record. Your driving record must be reviewed by your employer each time you begin work for a new motor carrier and at least once each year.

Also, speeding convictions can be costly. As well as incurring fines, speeding convictions may be tracked by your insurance carrier, prompting higher premiums.

Time to slow down a little bit! Fuel is going to be one of the highest costs involved in running your truck. Don't throw your money away, you've worked way too hard to get it! Even if you slow down just a little, you can save thousands of dollars a year, and you know what? At the end of the day, you'll be at the same truck stop as that guy that went flying by you doing 75 or 80 miles an hour. He didn't get any further down the road, he just got there 10 minutes before you did. So what! When you get your paycheck, you can buy the steak while he has to buy the hamburger because all his money went into the extra fuel he used!

Maintenance costs — Higher speeds can affect maintenance costs. Tires and brakes wear out faster at higher speeds. As speed increases, so does overall wear.

Fuel economy — Your speed has a direct and substantial affect on your fuel economy. These vehicles were never made to be race cars. You'll be doing good just to realize six miles per gallon. By adjusting your speed, even a couple miles per hour, you can positively affect your fuel mileage and save thousands of dollars over the course of a year. Think about it. If you are getting five miles per gallon at 70 miles per hour and six miles per gallon at 60 miles per hour, how much have you saved? If you drive 130,000 miles per year and fuel averages $2.85 per gallon, you've saved over $12,000 in fuel costs alone. Is it worth it to drive a little slower?

Why do drivers speed? — Shortening trip time and/or making up for lost time are two of the main reasons tractor-trailer drivers speed. Studies show that the amount of time made up by speeding is minimal.

Avoid the temptation to speed by planning ahead and making the best use of your time as possible.

Summary

In this chapter, you were introduced to the factors involved in stopping a tractor-trailer and the part speed plays in safe operation.

Speed Management Quiz

Directions: Read each statement carefully and mark the response that best answers the question.

1. **Perception distance, reaction distance, brake lag, and braking distance are the four factors involved in stopping a vehicle.**

   A. True

   B. False

2. **_____is the distance a vehicle travels from the time you see a hazard until your brain recognizes it.**

   A. Perception distance

   B. Reaction distance

   C. Braking distance

   D. All of the above

3. **_____is the distance a vehicle travels from the time your brain tells your foot to move from the accelerator until your foot hits the brake pedal.**

   A. Perception distance

   B. Reaction distance

   C. Braking distance

   D. All of the above

4. **_____is the distance it takes a vehicle to stop once the brakes are applied.**

   A. Perception distance

   B. Reaction distance

   C. Braking distance

   D. All of the above

5. **The more friction between a vehicle's tires and the road, the less traction.**

   A. True

   B. False

6. **A heavy rain that causes water to stand on a road can cause a vehicle to:**

    A. Metroplane

    B. Deplane

    C. Hydroplane

    D. All of the above

7. **You should slow to at least 5 mph below the posted speed limit when entering a curve.**

    A. True

    B. False

8. **You should always be able to stop your vehicle within your field of vision.**

    A. True

    B. False

9. **When driving in heavy traffic, it is best to travel at 5 - 10 mph faster than the surrounding vehicles.**

    A. True

    B. False

10. **It is best to go with the flow of traffic when it is safe and legal to do so.**

    A. True

    B. False

Combination Vehicle CDL Prep-Test

Select the response that most correctly answers the question

1. **A driver crosses the air lines when hooking up to an old trailer. What will happen?**

    A. The hand valve will apply the tractor brakes instead of the trailer brakes

    B. The brake pedal will work the trailer spring brakes instead of the trailer brakes

    C. If the trailer has no spring brakes, you could drive away but you wouldn't have trailer brakes

    D. The brake lights will not come on when the brake pedal is pressed

2. **After coupling a semi-trailer, you should crank up the front trailer supports (dollies) how?**

    A. Raised ½ way with the crank handle secured

    B. Raised ¾ way with the crank handle removed

    C. Fully raised with the crank handle secured

    D. Three turns off the top with the crank handle secured in its bracket

3. **Air brake equipped trailers made before 1975:**

    A. Usually do not have spring brakes

    B. Are easier to stop than newer trailers because they are heavier

    C. Usually need a glad hand converter

    D. Cannot be operated on interstate highways

4. **The hand valve should be used to park a combination vehicle when?**

    A. When you park at loading docks

    B. When you are parking for less than one hour

    C. When parking on a step grade

    D. Never

5. **Air lines on a combination vehicle are often colored to keep from getting them mixed up. The emergency line is _____.**

    A. Red

    B. Black

    C. Blue

    D. Orange

Chapter 11
Speed Management

Chapter 12

Space management

OBJECTIVES

Upon completion of this chapter, you should have a basic understanding of:

- ❑ The importance of space management
- ❑ The concept of maintaining an appropriate cushion of space
- ❑ Managing the space needed to execute a safe turn

Introduction

Proper space management means maintaining enough space around your vehicle to operate safely. This chapter focuses on the importance of managing your vehicle's speed in order to deal with the ever-changing conditions on the road.

Your Cushion of Space

When operating a tractor-trailer, you need to manage your cushion of space. This includes taking into account the space ahead, behind, to the sides, above, and below your vehicle. There must be enough space to allow you to adjust when traffic conditions change, for example, when a vehicle brakes suddenly or pulls into your lane of travel without warning.

Space ahead — The space ahead of your vehicle is the most important, and one of the easiest to monitor and adjust as needed.

The amount of space ahead of your vehicle that you should allow for depends on the speed of your vehicle and road

Monitor and adjust (when needed) space ahead.

conditions. One rule of thumb to follow (in good driving conditions) is to allow at least one second for each 10 feet of vehicle length at speeds below 40 mph. At greater speeds, add an additional second. In poor driving conditions (rain, ice, snow, fog, etc.), allow for a greater stopping distance.

Adjust space ahead based on vehicle speed and road conditions.

To determine how much space you have, wait until the vehicle ahead passes a clear landmark (pavement marking, road sign, etc.). Then count off the seconds until you reach the same spot. Compare your count with the rule of one second for every 10 feet of length and add one additional second if traveling at over 40 mph. You may hear this referred to as the "Fixed Object Count-Off Method."

For example, if you are driving a 60 foot vehicle at 55 mph (in good weather conditions), and only counted three seconds you are following too closely. You should have at least seven seconds of space ahead.

After some practice, and experience on the road, you'll be able to easily determine how far back you should follow.

Space behind — It is impossible to keep other drivers from following too closely, but there are some things that can be done to make it safer. Stay to the right, slow down, and give the tailgater plenty of chances to pass.

The following are steps you can take to help prevent an accident if you find that you are being tailgated.

1. **Avoid quick changes** — If you have to slow down or turn, signal early and gradually reduce your vehicle's speed.

2. **Increase your following distance** — Opening up room in front of you will help you to avoid making sudden speed or direction changes. This also makes it easier for the tailgater to get around you.

3. **Don't speed up** — It's safer to be tailgated at a low speed than a high speed.

4. **Avoid tricks** — Don't turn on your taillights or flash your brake lights.

Be aware of and know how to deal with vehicles that follow too closely.

Space to the sides — Commercial motor vehicles often take up most of a lane. There are several things you should try to avoid to ensure that there is plenty of space between your vehicle and other road users.

1. **Don't hug the center line** — It becomes very easy to drift across the center line into oncoming traffic.

2. **Avoid hugging the right side of the road** — A soft shoulder can cause control problems.

3. **Avoid traveling alongside other vehicles** — Another driver may change lanes suddenly, turning into your vehicle, or your vehicle may be trapped, unable to change lanes. Also, try to avoid driving alongside others in strong winds, especially cross winds. The problem is most prevalent for empty or light trucks.

Space above — Adequate space above is needed to clear bridges, overpasses, trees, and wires. Never assume the heights posted on bridges and overpasses are correct. Repaving or packed snow may reduce the clearances since the heights were posted.

Slow down driver! If the wind's blowing so much that you can feel your trailer rocking back and forth, slow down! Winds, particularly out west, can literally blow your trailer into the other lane. If you're traveling next to someone, that could become a real problem. Also, if you slow down a little it gives you more time to react to those sidewinds. The last thing you want to see is your trailer passing you, so just slow down a little!

Never assume posted heights are correct.

The weight of a vehicle's cargo can also change its height. An empty vehicle is higher than a loaded one.

Be aware of how a road is graded. Road grade can cause a high vehicle to tilt, which can be a clearance problem.

Make sure you have adequate overhead space.

If you have doubts about whether there is enough overhead space to proceed, take another route.

Space below — It's very easy to forget the space under your vehicle. That space can be very small when the vehicle is heavily loaded.

Driveways, railroad tracks, dirt roads, and unpaved lots can be a challenge. Slow and steady is the rule in these cases. This is also one of the reasons why you should always crank the landing gear up all the way.

Turning Space

Correct procedures are important when making turns. Because of wide turning and off-tracking, commercial motor vehicles run the risk of hitting other vehicles or objects during turns.

Right turns — When making a right turn, proceed slowly. This gives you as well as others time to avoid trouble. Also, scan ahead to identify potential problems.

If you are unable to make the right turn without swinging into another lane, turn wide as you complete the turn. Keep the rear of your vehicle close to the curb. Though you can position your vehicle to make it hard for drivers to pass you on the right, never assume you blocked traffic completely. Keep an eye on the right side of the vehicle, assuming that smaller vehicles may try to pass on the right.

When making a right turn, proceed with care.

Don't turn wide to the left as you start the turn. A driver who is following may think you are turning left and try to pass on the right.

If you must cross into the oncoming lane to make a turn, watch for vehicles approaching. Give them room to go by or stop, but never back up. You might hit someone behind your vehicle.

Left turns — When executing a left turn, make sure the vehicle has reached the center of the intersection before starting the turn. Starting it too soon will lead to the trailer taking a shorter path. Anything in that path will be run over (light poles, traffic signs, other vehicles).

Mirrors, mirrors, mirrors! Did I happen to say mirrors? You need to be looking EVERYWHERE when you make a turn. Don't ever assume that just because it was clear on your right when you last looked, that it's going to stay clear until you're done with the turn. And just because you're turning right don't forget everything on your left. The front bumper, the front corner of the trailer, rear trailer swing; all of these things could cause you a real headache when turning right so slow down, watch ALL around, and make your turn. Slow and steady wins the race here, driver.

Hey driver, did you see where your trailer went? Well if you didn't then you better stop! Don't think that just because your tractor has completed the turn that you can just start grabbing gears. Your trailer's not done yet! Watch your mirrors, look out your window, and make sure you're not running over the hood of that nice four-wheeler sitting at the light. He'll appreciate it!

Make sure the vehicle has reached the center of the intersection before turning left.

If there are two turning lanes, always take the lane furthest to the right. Don't start on the inside lane, as you may have to swing right to make the turn.

Space When Crossing and Entering Traffic

Because of slow acceleration and the length of your vehicle, you will need a larger gap to enter traffic than you would in your personal vehicle. Also keep in mind that acceleration varies with the load. Allow more room if your vehicle is heavily loaded.

Before starting across a road, make sure you can get all the way across before traffic reaches you. It can take 7-15 seconds to clear an intersection. If you miss a gear or cross a large intersection, it could take longer.

Summary

This chapter has covered the importance of managing all of the space around your vehicle and how to develop a safety cushion. In combination, speed and space management play an important role in safe vehicle operation.

Hey, forget about the unwritten rule that if you're in the intersection the other guy has to stop and let you finish your turn. They don't, and that's not professional! Sure, you can pull out in front of someone, take your time, and prove that you're bigger and tougher than they are by blocking all the traffic. You will not be well liked and may receive some choice hand gestures so just don't do it.

Space Management Quiz

Directions: Read each statement carefully and mark the response that best answers the question.

1. **Proper space management includes taking into account space ahead, behind, to the sides, above, and below your vehicle.**

    A. True

    B. False

2. **The space _____ your vehicle is most important.**

    A. Behind

    B. To the sides

    C. Above

    D. Ahead

3. **In good driving conditions, you should allow at least one second for each 10 feet of vehicle length at speeds below 40 mph.**

    A. True

    B. False

4. **Which of the following is a step you should take to prevent an accident if you are being tailgated?**

    A. Slam on the brakes

    B. Speed up

    C. Increase your following distance

    D. All of the above

5. **When managing your vehicle's space to the sides you should:**

    A. Hug the center line

    B. Avoid traveling alongside other vehicles

    C. Hug the right side of the road

    D. All of the above

6. **Never assume that heights posted on bridges and overpasses are correct.**

    A. True

    B. False

7. **If you have doubts about whether there is enough space overhead to proceed you should:**

    A.   Empty the vehicle's cargo and reload the vehicle after passing under the bridge/overpass

    B.   Increase your vehicle's speed

    C.   Take another route

    D.   All of the above

8. **Fast and quick is the rule when driving on an unpaved lot or dirt road.**

    A.   True

    B.   False

9. **Because of wide turning and off-tracking, tractor-trailers run the risk of hitting other vehicles or objects during turns.**

    A.   True

    B.   False

10. **Because a tractor-trailer is able to accelerate at a quicker rate, you need a smaller gap than other types of vehicles to enter traffic when at an intersection.**

    A.   True

    B.   False

Combination Vehicle CDL Pre-Test

Read each statement carefully and select the most correct answer.

1. **How do you supply air to the air tank on the trailer? You supply air to the trailer tank by:**

   A. Pushing in the trailer air supply valve

   B. Pulling out the trailer air supply valve

   C. Connecting the emergency line glad hand

   D. Applying the trolley valve

2. **In normal driving, some drivers use the trolley (hand) valve before the brake pedal in order to prevent trailer skids. Which of these statements is true?**

   A. It should never be done

   B. It results in less skidding than using the brake pedal alone

   C. It lets the driver steer with both hands

   D. It is the best way to brake in a straight line

3. **You are hooking up a tractor and semi-trailer. You have connected both air lines. Before backing under the trailer you should:**

   A. Pull forward to test glad hand connections

   B. Supply air to the trailer system, then pull out the air supply knob to lock the trailer brakes

   C. Make sure that the trailer brakes are off

   D. Blow the horn twice to alert others

4. **When backing up under a trailer, you should line up:**

   A. About 15 degrees off the line of the trailer

   B. The right mirror along the right edge of the trailer

   C. Directly in front of the trailer

5. **If the service line disconnects while you are driving, what will happen right away?**

   A. The emergency tractor brakes will come on

   B. The trailer's air tank will exhaust through the open line

   C. The emergency trailer brakes will come on

   D. Nothing is likely to happen until you try the brakes

Chapter 12
Space
Management

Chapter 13

Night driving

OBJECTIVES

Upon completion of this chapter, you should have a basic understanding of:

❑ The factors that affect night driving

❑ Procedures for driving at night

Introduction

Drivers who work the overnight hours trade the hazards of busy, congested roadways for another set of hazards including reduced visibility and impaired drivers. This chapter will address night driving factors and procedures for safely traveling at night.

Night Driving Factors

Driving at night presents several challenges for the professional driver. Potential hazards include poor lighting, reduced visibility, and impaired drivers.

Driving at night can be challenging.

There are three major factors you need to focus on when driving at night:

- Driver factors;
- Roadway factors; and
- Vehicle factors.

Driver factors — The major factors that affect you when operating at night are vision, glare, fatigue, and driver inexperience.

1. **Vision** — Put simply, we do not see as well at night as we do during the day. At night visual acuity is reduced, side vision is poorer, and the eyes have a difficult time adjusting to abrupt changes from darkness to light and back to darkness.

2. **Glare** — Glare is another problem. The bright light of oncoming headlights can temporarily blind you. The human eye requires time to recover from the effects of glare. Recovery rates vary from one-half to two seconds or more.

At 55 mph, a vehicle covers about 150 to 160 feet in two seconds. That is a substantial distance to drive with obscured vision.

Avoid looking directly into bright lights by looking toward the right side of the road when bright lights approach.

3. **Fatigue** — Fatigue is a factor when it comes to safe driving; especially at night. Fatigue can reduce your reaction time to hazards and cause blurred vision. Some of fatigue's warning signs include:

    - Drowsiness
    - Frequent or repeated yawning
    - Loss of visual focus
    - Fighting to keep your eyes open
    - Heavy/drooping head
    - Stiff or sore neck muscles
    - Lack of alertness
    - Poor memory recall
    - Dozing off for a few seconds at a time
    - Weaving from lane-to-lane
    - Making bad driving decisions
    - Erratic speed control
    - Erratic shifting
    - Intermittent shifting
    - Following vehicles ahead too closely

4. **Driver inexperience** — Inexperience with operating a tractor-trailer under nighttime conditions is also a factor. As with all other aspects of driving this type of vehicle, the more practice and experience you have, the better you will be able to deal with the challenges of driving at night.

Roadway factors — Roadway hazards faced at night include poor visibility, lack of familiarity with your route and its hazards (road construction, curves, etc.), impaired drivers, and other road users.

1. **Poor visibility** — At night, hazards aren't as easy to see and may not be recognized as quickly as during daylight hours.

    In rural areas, you need to depend on your vehicle's headlights for lighting.

    In urban areas, lighting levels can vary. Since levels vary, your eyes are required to adjust to different levels of lighting.

Hey driver think about this. Humans are not normally nocturnal animals. What that means is we typically sleep at night! So if you don't have to drive at night then just don't do it. Sometimes it can't be avoided but as you'll read about in this chapter, when driving at night the hazards are increased, reaction time is decreased, and the potential for accident or mishap is much greater. Here's just one thing to think about. What time do bars close? Do you really want to be on the road when all the locals are on their way home from tipping a few...maybe a few too many??

How's your windshield? Is it dirty, streaked, or pitted? At night these things can greatly reduce your visibility so make sure your windshield is clean and in good shape at all times.

2. **Familiarity with route** — Though caution should be used on all roads (familiar or unfamiliar) when driving at night, slow down and use extra caution on unfamiliar roads. Make sure you have enough stopping distance.

3. **Impaired drivers** — Impaired drivers are a hazard to everyone on the road. Extra caution should be used around closing times for bars and taverns. Keep an eye out for vehicles that weave from lane-to-lane, stop without reason, have trouble maintaining a constant speed, or show other signs of impaired or erratic driving.

4. **Other road users** — In many cases, the cover of darkness impairs your view of other road users including those who jog, walk, or bike along the side of the road. Pay special attention to roadways that are lined by woods and/or tall grass. Deer, raccoons, and other animals are often on the move at night and can dart into the roadway.

Vehicle factors — Vehicle condition plays a part in safe night driving. A vehicle's lights, turn signals, windshield, and mirrors should be kept clean and in good working condition.

1. **Headlights** — At night, headlights are the main way to see and be seen on the highway. In good weather, low beams allow you to see about 250 feet ahead and high beams about 350-500 feet ahead. Speed may need to be adjusted so the vehicle can be stopped within the range of the headlights.

Headlights are the main way to see and be seen.

Always drive within the range of the headlights. Driving outside the range of the headlights (over driving the headlights) can adversely affect your ability to recognize hazards.

Headlights should be clean and in proper adjustment. Dirty or poorly adjusted headlights can cut illumination by as much as one-half.

2. **Other lights** — Marker lights, reflectors, clearance lights, taillights, and identification lights must also be clean and working properly.

All lights and reflectors should be clean and properly adjusted.

Look in your mirror. How close is that vehicle? At night, vehicles behind you look much different in your mirrors. Headlights shining in your convex mirrors make a vehicle look further away than it actually is so make sure you know what you're looking at. If you're not sure, look again!

3. **Turn signals** — The importance of communicating your intention to turn or change lanes is multiplied at night. Other drivers may have a hard time seeing your vehicle and understanding your intent. The turn signals may be the only way to communicate this information.

4. **Windshield and mirrors** — A clean windshield and mirrors are very important at night. Bright lights hitting dirt on a windshield or mirror can create a glare. Dirt on the windshield can also cause problems if driving into a sunrise or sunset.

Night Driving Procedures

Preparing to drive at night — Being prepared to drive at night can go a long way when it comes to safety. A prepared driver is focused on the task ahead and doesn't have to be concerned with issues such as route planning or whether the vehicle's headlights are working appropriately.

1. **Get yourself ready** — Make sure you are rested and alert. The cover of darkness can magnify the effects of fatigue, making night driving more dangerous.

   If you wear eyeglasses, make sure they are clean and free of scratches. Scratches can magnify glare, reducing your ability to see clearly. Never wear sunglasses at night.

2. **Plan your route** — Know where you are going. Know where you may have to exit or enter a roadway and where construction zones are located. Know where rest stops are located. If you are familiar with your route, keep in mind where hazards are located.

3. **Get your vehicle ready** — Do a complete pre-trip inspection of your vehicle. When conducting this inspection, pay special attention to the lights, reflectors, and windshield. Clean and replace as needed.

When driving at night — There are additional issues you need to consider when driving at night compared to driving during daylight hours.

Plan your route.

Maximize your visibility when driving at night.

1. **Avoid blinding others** — Glare from your vehicle's headlights can cause problems for drivers coming toward you. They can also bother drivers going in the same direction as you are, when your vehicle's lights shine into their rearview mirrors. If you are using high beams, dim them before they pose a glare problem for others. This includes dimming your lights within at least 500 feet of an oncoming or leading vehicle.

2. **Don't blind yourself** — Don't look directly at the lights of an oncoming vehicle. Look slightly to the right.

3. **Maximize visibility** — Use high beams when it is safe and legal to do so. Remember, high beam headlights should be dimmed within 500 feet of an oncoming vehicle. Turn off the vehicle's dome light and adjust the brightness of the instrument lights. This makes it easier to see outside the vehicle. Also, don't forget to scan your mirrors. As well as maximizing visibility, this helps fight fatigue by helping you avoid staring at one point for a period of time.

4. **Adjust basic driving techniques** — This means making adjustments to how you communicate and how you manage speed and space.

Communication — At night, communication is limited to your vehicle's lights and horns. Signaling your intentions is more critical at night. Signal all stops, slowdowns, and direction changes a bit earlier than you would in daylight. Avoid blinding others with lights as a way of signaling. Use the horn sparingly.

Speed and space — Increase following distance at night by at least one second. This will give you extra time and space to spot and react to hazards.

As previously mentioned in this chapter, drive within the range of the headlights. Over driving the headlights can adversely affect visibility as well as your ability to stop for hazards.

When rounding a curve, headlights shine straight ahead (off the road) reducing vision. Reducing vehicle speed is the best way to deal with curves.

Summary

In this chapter, you have learned about the special issues associated with driving at night. This includes the factors that contribute to the increased danger of night driving and the procedures that need to be followed in order to complete a safe nighttime trip.

Stop driver! The worst thing you can do is signal your fellow driver to come back over after passing you, by flashing your high beams at them. Think about it. They are looking in their passenger side mirror to see if they've cleared you and at the same time, you BLIND them with your high beams. Does this sound like a smart thing to do? Either flash your headlights off and on or don't use your lights to signal at all. Either way is better than blinding the other driver right when they are about to pull in front of you. Just don't do it!

Night Driving Quiz

Directions: Read each statement carefully and mark the response that best answers the question.

1. **At night, visual acuity is reduced, side vision is poorer, and the eyes have a difficult time adjusting to abrupt changes from darkness to light and back to darkness.**

   A. True

   B. False

2. **Drowsiness, repeated yawning, and lack of alertness are all signs of_____.**

   A. Driver inexperience

   B. Poor visibility

   C. Fatigue

   D. All of the above

3. **At night, hazards may not be recognized as quickly as during daylight hours.**

   A. True

   B. False

4. **A vehicle that weaves from lane-to-lane or has trouble maintaining a constant speed may indicate:**

   A. There is fog ahead

   B. Nothing in particular

   C. An impaired driver is behind the wheel

   D. All of the above

5. **In good weather, low beam headlights allow you to see about _____.**

   A. 150 feet

   B. 250 feet

   C. 500 feet

   D. 1,000 feet

6. **In good weather, high beam headlights allow you to see about** _____.

   A. 150 to 200 feet

   B. 200 to 250 feet

   C. 250 to 300 feet

   D. 350 to 500 feet

7. **To avoid blinding others, highbeam headlights should be dimmed within at least** _____ **of an oncoming vehicle.**

   A. 250 feet

   B. 300 feet

   C. 500 feet

   D. All of the above

8. **To avoid being blinded by the headlights of another vehicle, you should:**

   A. Look directly at the oncoming vehicle's lights

   B. Look slightly to the right

   C. Look slightly to the left

   D. All of the above

9. **At night, you should signal all stops, slowdowns, and direction changes a bit later than you would in daylight.**

   A. True

   B. False

10. **Over driving your vehicle's headlights can adversely affect visibility.**

    A. True

    B. False

Combination Vehicle CDL Pre-Test

Read the question and select the answer that is most correct.

1. **After hooking up, you should check the fifth wheel connection by:**

   A. Driving away at 20 mph and pulling down the trailer hand valve

   B. Backing up with the trailer brakes released

   C. Pulling the tractor ahead sharply to release the trailer brakes

   D. Pulling the tractor ahead gently with the trailer brakes locked

2. **When hooking up a tractor to a trailer, you'll know the trailer is at the right height when the:**

   A. Trailer dolly wheels are fully extended

   B. Kingpin is about 2-¼ inches above the fifth wheel

   C. Beginning of the kingpin is even with the top of the lower fifth wheel

   D. The coupling surface of the trailer is just below the middle of the tractor fifth wheel

3. **You are driving a combination vehicle when the trailer brakes away and pulls apart the air lines. You should expect:**

   A. The tractor to lose all air pressure

   B. The tractor brakes to keep working properly

   C. The trailer supply valve to stay open

   D. The tractor brakes to lock up

4. **How much space should be between the upper and the lower fifth wheel plates?**

   A. About 1 inch

   B. About ½ inch

   C. About ¼ inch

   D. None

5. **When not pulling a trailer, why is it a good idea to lock the glad hands together or to a dummy coupler?**

   A. It keeps air from escaping

   B. The brake circuit becomes a secondary air tank

   C. It keeps dirt and water out of the lines

   D. All of the above

Chapter 13
Night Driving

Chapter **14**

Extreme driving conditions

OBJECTIVES

Upon completion of this chapter, you should have a basic understanding of:

- ❏ Operating in adverse driving conditions including snow, ice, and cold temperatures
- ❏ Operating in hot weather conditions
- ❏ The challenges of mountain driving

Introduction

Extreme driving conditions demand increased preparation and awareness. Both you and your vehicle must be in top form. This chapter will introduce you to the challenges of operating a tractor-trailer in extreme driving conditions.

Extreme driving conditions present a special set of challenges.

Adverse Weather

Adverse weather conditions, including winter driving, rain, and fog, demand increased preparation for you and your vehicle. Reduced traction increases stopping distances and decreases vehicle maneuverability and control. Reduced visibility decreases your ability to clearly see hazards.

Conditions can change quickly in the winter and being prepared is key to successfully operating in snow, ice, and extreme cold. In addition to your regular vehicle inspections, pay close attention to the items listed below.

1. **Coolant level and antifreeze concentration** — Make sure the cooling system is full and that there's enough antifreeze in the vehicle's system. A low coolant level can affect the engine's performance as well as the operation of the vehicle's defroster and heater. Antifreeze concentration can be checked with a tester designed for this purpose.

2. **Defrosting and heating equipment** — Make sure the vehicle's defrosters and heater are working and that you know how to operate this equipment. Also check the heaters for the mirrors and fuel tank(s).

3. **Windshield wipers and washers** — Make sure the wiper blades are in good condition. The wiper blades need to press against the window hard enough to wipe the windshield clean. This is important in keeping snow off of the windshield. Also make sure the windshield washer works and that there's an appropriate type and amount of washer fluid (fluid that will not freeze in cold weather) in the reservoir. Also check the reservoir for cracks or other damage.

Let's face it driver. If you drive a truck for a living, sooner or later you are going to have to drive in bad weather. It's not the end of the world. Read this chapter thoroughly, pay attention to what you are doing, and you should be fine. The most important thing to remember about bad weather is SLOW DOWN! You're a professional. You can handle just about anything that gets thrown at you, but you just need to slow down a little so you can react without ending up in the ditch!

I used to have an unwritten rule that I went by; "If it's bad enough for chains, it's bad enough to stop." You may not have this option if you drive for a company that requires you to continue driving in these types of conditions but keep in mind, it's your life out there and no one has more control over it than you.

4. **Tires** — Check tire tread depth. The drive tires must provide enough traction to operate on wet pavement and snow. The steering tires must have enough traction to steer the vehicle. The front wheels must have a tread depth of at least $\frac{4}{32}$ inch on every major groove to be legal. Other wheels have to have a tread depth of at least $\frac{2}{32}$ inch to be legal. Also check tire mounting and inflation.

5. **Tire chains** — You may be faced with conditions which require the use of chains (per state or local law). Prepare

Appropriate tread depth is important.

for this possibility by carrying the proper size and number of chains as well as extra cross-links. Check the chains for broken hooks, worn or broken cross-links, and bent or broken side chains. Make sure chain slack adjusters are also available if you need them.

6. **Brakes** — Brake balance should be checked. The brakes should apply pressure equally at the same time. Check adjustment, and take up any slack. Be careful when setting your brakes in very cold weather. If there is a lot of moisture on them, they could freeze together and you may not be able to release them. One way to avoid this is to lightly ride your brake when exiting the highway or while going through the parking lot. This will help warm the brakes and get rid of moisture.

Also, keep air tanks as moisture-free as possible. Drain both tractor and trailer tanks daily. Moisture in the air lines can cause the vehicle's brakes to freeze. If your vehicle has other moisture-control equipment (alcohol evaporators, spitter valves, etc.), make sure they are working properly.

7. **Lights and reflectors** — Visibility of lights and reflectors is very important in poor weather conditions. Make sure the vehicle's lights and reflectors are clean (free of dirt, snow, ice, road salt, etc.) and check them often. In poor weather, the condition of your lights and reflectors play a big part in determining your range of sight and how well others can see your vehicle.

8. **Windows and mirrors** — Remove all ice, snow, and debris from the windshield by using a snow brush and/or scraper and the windshield defroster.

9. **Hand holds, steps, and deck plates** — Reduce your chances of slipping and falling by removing all ice and snow from the handholds, steps, and deck plates.

10. **Winterfront** — Make sure the winterfront isn't closed too tightly. This can cause the engine to overheat. *Note:* Winterfronts are not recommended for all types of engines. Check the vehicle's owner's manual for specifics.

11. **Exposed wiring and air lines** — Remove ice and snow from wiring and air lines. At or below zero degrees, plastic air lines can become brittle and can brake very easily. Snow and ice build-up can cause them to sag and possibly get snagged on the tractor, trailer, or the tires.

12. **Fuel tank** — Make sure the fuel tank is full before starting out and kept topped off regularly if bad weather is expected. This will help keep water out of the fuel, which can freeze in fuel lines and filters. This is also a good precautionary measure to make sure you don't run out of fuel and are stranded in a dangerous situation. It's also a good idea to always know where your next fuel stop is, even if it's not the one you planned on stopping at.

13. **Exhaust system** — Loose exhaust system connections can cause carbon monoxide to leak into your vehicle. Carbon monoxide is poisonous. It can kill you if you are exposed to it, especially if you are in an area with poor ventilation, like a truck cab with the windows rolled up.

14. **Coupling devices** — Before coupling, remove all snow and ice. (In below freezing temperatures, the jaws of the coupling device may not lock if the grease is frozen.) Double check the locking mechanism and make sure the fifth wheel is lubricated with a winter-grade lubricant. This will help prevent binding and help steering on slippery roads.

15. **Interaxle differential lock (if vehicle has this)** — Check the owner's manual for proper operation.

When is a good time to check all these things? Before you get in the middle of a snowstorm or down-pour! Get in the habit of doing a "bad weather pre-check" BEFORE you get in the bad weather. It's just a lot easier.

16. **Emergency equipment** — When it comes to your vehicle you should have the following items:

- Windshield scraper;
- Snow brush;
- Extra windshield washer fluid;
- Small shovel;
- Flashlight;
- Spare batteries;
- Jumper cables; and
- Warning devices.

Make sure you have the necessary emergency equipment and that it is in good condition.

As for your protection and safety, you should have the following items:

- Drinking water;

- Extra food;

- Medicine (as needed);

- Hats;

- Boots;

- Gloves;

- Extra clothes and blankets; and

- Proper outerwear (heavy jacket, heavy coveralls).

17. **Weather reports** — Stay up to date on the latest weather and road conditions. The National Weather Radio Service (162.4-162.55 MHz) broadcasts updated information on weather conditions for many areas around the country. Many states also provide road reports via the Internet and/or toll-free phone numbers. Also stay in contact with your dispatcher, as he/she may be able to provide up-to-date information from various sources.

Tire chain installation — Tire chains are constructed to grip the tire around the sides and provide traction across the tread. Chains can increase traction by as much as 500 percent. Installed on the drive wheels, they improve uphill traction. On trailer wheels, they improve traction for downhill braking. Chains help keep your vehicle on the road, and they decrease your chances of getting stuck.

Hey driver! It's a nice warm day, you're waiting for a load, do you know what you should do? Put your tire chains on. I know, it sounds crazy but trust me, it's a lot easier to put them on the first time when it's warm and dry than when you're approaching a mountain in the middle of a snowstorm! If you figure out how to do it now, it will be quick and easy when you really have to do it later. Besides...you were bored anyway, so just go out and do it!

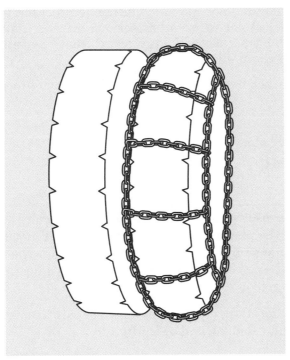

Tire chains increase traction in heavy snow.

Chains are most effective in heavy snow. In light, dry snow they provide little traction advantage, but do provide some stability. Most chains are not effective on glare ice.

When installing chains, they should be snug, but not too tight. They are designed to creep or move on the tires to prevent gouging or breakage. Chains should be regularly checked and re-tightened as necessary to prevent slap against the trailer or catching on to the suspension or fuel tank.

Use extreme caution when installing chains:

- Pull well off the road (most areas that require chains have "chain-up" areas)
- Park on a level surface
- Work facing traffic
- Know where you are going if confronted by an out of control vehicle
- Watch your footing
- Watch your own vehicle, making sure it doesn't slide

Many states have laws and/or regulations addressing the type and number of chains that must be used on certain highways and the dates in which they must be carried in the vehicle and used if necessary. Depending on the state you're in, you could get a fine just for not carrying the required number of chains, even if you don't want to use them, so know the rules!

Cold weather starting — The colder it is, the harder it is to start any type of engine. There are a number of devices that can help in starting your vehicle's engine.

1. **Ether and ether-based fluids** — There are both good and bad points to using ether to help start your vehicle in cold temperatures. On the good side, ether has a very low flash point and can ignite easily at cold temperatures. On the bad side, if ether is not used properly or is used too often, it can damage the engine. Also, it can be dangerous to use as it is highly flammable. Too much either could crack your engine block, cause vapor lock, or cause other serious internal damage. Should you spill some on your clothes, stay away from cigarettes, lighters, and heaters and change immediately.

   Ether and ether-based fluids come in a variety of forms including:

   - Capsules;
   - Aerosol sprays;
   - Pressurized cylinders; and
   - Driver-controlled, automatic injection systems.

   Capsules, aerosol sprays, and pressurized cylinders are used manually and require the placement of ether near (but not in) the air cleaner. The automatic injection system is activated by either the driver turning on a switch in the cab or the vehicle automatically injecting ether when the vehicle is started.

   No matter what form of ether you may use, always use extreme caution to prevent an accident and/or injury.

2. **Glow plugs** — Glow plugs are electric heating elements that warm air coming into the engine from the air intake. Consult your vehicle's owner's manual for specific operating instructions.

3. **Preheaters** — Preheaters keep the engine warm while your vehicle is parked for an extended period of time. Most truck tractors use an in-block type of preheater. In-block heaters fit into the freeze plug holes in the lower water jacket. They are then plugged into an electrical outlet. Coolant is heated to 160ûF and the heated coolant is circulated throughout the engine. This eliminates warm-up, allowing you to use normal starting procedures.

   In extremely cold areas, coolant heaters are frequently supplemented with battery box heaters, oil sump heaters, and fuel heaters. Consult your vehicle's owner's manual and maintenance personnel for proper operation.

   If your engine doesn't start — If your vehicle's engine won't start with the use of starting aids, check the fuel and electrical systems. To make sure your vehicle is getting enough fuel, watch the exhaust stack while cranking your engine. If you don't see vapor or smoke, the engine may not be getting fuel. Don't continue to crank the engine, as this will run down the battery. Check the fuel tank and fuel lines for ice blockage. Also check the fuel tank vent.

   Never crank the engine for more than 15 seconds. If the engine is getting fuel, but isn't starting, there could be a problem in the electrical system. Check the battery for terminal corrosion, loose connections, cracks in cables, and moisture on cables.

   If your vehicle has an air starter, it needs an air supply to start. If there is no air, you'll need to resupply air from either an air compressor or another tractor. Check the vehicle's owner's manual for specific procedures.

Operating hazards — There are two main hazards when driving in adverse winter weather conditions, reduced visibility and reduced traction.

1. **Reduced visibility** — When snow and ice build up on your vehicle's lights, windows and mirrors your visibility is reduced in all directions (front, side, and rear). If operating properly, your vehicle's defroster and windshield wipers will keep the windshield clean and clear. However, you will need to stop to clean off the side windows and mirrors. Never drive if you cannot see in all directions.

   As mentioned earlier in this chapter, snow, ice, and dirt can build up on your vehicle's lights and reflectors. This reduces your visibility and the ability of other drivers to see your vehicle. Frequently clean all lights and reflectors.

   Snow and ice can greatly reduce your visibility. Adjust your speed in bad weather to compensate for limited visibility. If you are unable to see, do not continue driving. Pull off the road at the nearest safe place and stop until conditions improve.

2. **Reduced traction** — Different surfaces have a different amount of traction. For example, a snow-packed or ice-covered surface will have only one-fifth (20 percent) of the traction that the same surface does when it's wet.

Slippery surfaces reduce traction, causing a vehicle's drive wheels to spin easily. This impairs your ability to maneuver the vehicle. Proper tire inflation and tread as well as proper weight on the drive wheels increases traction and improves maneuverability.

If traction is poor, reduce vehicle speed.

Traction is needed for accelerating, turning, and braking. As vehicle speed increases, more traction is needed. If traction is poor, you must reduce your speed.

On a wet surface, you may need to reduce your speed by one-fourth or more. For example, if you normally travel at 65 mph on a stretch of road, you will need to reduce your speed to about 45-48 mph.

As a general rule, you can drive about one-half your normal speed on packed snow. If you usually travel at 65 mph, you should cut your speed to about 30-32 mph.

On ice, cut your speed to about one-third of your normal speed. Again if traveling at 65 mph, slow to about 18-20 mph.

Black ice is one of the most dangerous road conditions, as most drivers aren't aware of black ice until it is too late. Black ice forms when temperatures drop rapidly and hover around the freezing mark (32°F). Any moisture on the road freezes into a smooth, nearly invisible, slippery surface.

Hey driver! These speeds are only guidelines. You're the professional out there. Only you can decide what's the right speed to go based on the conditions, so don't let someone tell you that you are going too slow! You drive your truck and let them just go on by. No need to get in a "discussion" about who's right and who's wrong. You have other things to worry about!

On cold days, when the road is wet, pay extra attention to the spray thrown from other vehicles. If the spray suddenly stops, black ice may be forming.

The most common places for black ice to form include:

- Bridges;

- Beneath underpasses;

- Dips in the road where water can collect and freeze;

- Shaded areas from buildings, trees, hills, and embankments; and

- The lower side of banked curves.

Also, watch for rain turning into freezing rain as temperatures drop. Listen for a change in the sound of your tires on the road. Watch for spray from other vehicles suddenly disappearing. Feel for ice on the front of your outside mirror. Watch the vehicle's antenna for signs of ice formation.

Skidding and jackknifing — There are three basic causes of skidding and jackknifing: over acceleration, over braking, and over steering.

1. **Over acceleration** — Too much acceleration sends too much power to the drive wheels, causing them to spin.

2. **Over braking** — Braking too hard for conditions causes wheels to lock-up.

3. **Over steering** Turning the steering wheel too quickly can cause the front wheels to slide, the drive tires to slide, or the trailer to skid or swing out.

Slippery surfaces — Drive slowly and deliberately on slippery roads. If the road is so slippery that it is unsafe to proceed, stop at a safe place and wait for conditions to improve. Take the following steps when operating on what could be a slippery road:

- Don't hurry. Give yourself plenty of time to get a feel for the road.

- Make turns as gently as possible.

- Don't brake any harder than necessary.

- Don't use the engine brake or speed retarder.

- Never pump antilock brakes (if your vehicle is so equipped).

- Don't pass slower vehicles unless necessary.

- Go slow and steady. Avoid having to slow down and speed up.

- Take curves at slower speeds and don't brake while in curves.

- Know that roads become more slippery as temperatures rise to the point where ice begins to melt. Road temperatures and air temperatures can vary widely.

Stop driver! This is really important stuff on this page so maybe you should read it again. Jackknifing in a big rig is serious business so learn what to do if it happens but more importantly, learn what to do to avoid it!

Hey, pay attention! So how do you get out of a jackknife? Get rid of the power (take your foot off the accelerator and push in the clutch), don't touch the brake, look in your mirror, and steer away from your trailer. How can you avoid all this? SLOW DOWN OR GET OFF THE ROAD!

- Don't drive next to other vehicles.

- Keep a larger following distance.

- If you see a traffic jam ahead, slow down or stop until it has cleared.

- Try to anticipate stops so you can slow down gradually.

Wet brakes — When driving in heavy rain or deep standing water, your vehicle's brakes will get wet. Water in the brakes can reduce their effectiveness, apply unevenly, or grab. This can cause a lack of braking power, wheel lock-ups, pulling to one side or the other, and vehicle jackknife (if pulling a trailer).

If possible, avoid driving through deep puddles or flowing water. If you can't avoid this, take the following steps:

1. Slow down.

2. Place the vehicle transmission in a low gear.

3. Increase engine speed (rpm).

4. Cross the water while keeping light pressure on the brakes.

When out of the water, keep light pressure on the brakes for a short distance. This heats up and dries out the brakes. Make a test stop if it is safe to do so. Check behind you to make sure no one is following, then apply the brakes to make sure they work correctly. If they aren't working correctly, again apply light pressure on the brakes and travel a short distance. Do not apply too much brake pressure and accelerate at the same time. This can cause the brake drums and linings to overheat.

Freeing a stuck vehicle — The best way to deal with freeing a stuck vehicle is by not getting stuck in the first place. The best way to prevent getting stuck is by avoiding soft shoulders, deep snow, muddy roads, and icy/slippery surfaces.

If you do get stuck, don't panic, and take the following steps:

1. Avoid spinning the drive wheels and rocking. This digs the vehicle in deeper. On ice or snow, spinning wheels warm the ice or snow under the tires, reducing traction even more.

2. Use traction aids. Dig out from in front of the wheels. Scatter sand or gravel in the wheel path. Lay loose chains in front of the vehicle's tires.

3. When ready to try pulling out, start with the steering wheel facing straight ahead. Don't turn the wheels until the vehicle is moving.

4. Start in second or third gear, using very little power. This keeps the wheels from spinning and gives a smoother application of force.

5. Accelerate smoothly and gently. Ease off at the first sign of spinning or slipping. Allowing the wheels to continue spinning can cause you to dig in deeper and/or cause a spin out.

Towing — If all of the procedures to free your vehicle fail, you may need to call a tow truck. Remember, even if towing is necessary, you are still responsible for your vehicle and cargo. You need to stay in charge of the situation, not the tow truck operator. Supervise the operation. If the tow truck operator does something wrong or unsafe, stop the operation, and correct the problem.

The tow chain or cable should be hooked to the vehicle following these steps:

1. Make sure there's enough chain or cable, so once freed, your vehicle doesn't lurch into the tow truck.

2. In hooking up, pass the chain or cable through the hole in the bumper, but do not hook it to the bumper.

3. Attach the chain or cable to a solid portion of the frame or a frame cross member. (Some vehicles are equipped with tow hooks protruding from the frame.) Be careful not to get the chain around the steering tie-rod or spring shackles along with the axle.

Before towing, agree on a procedure to be followed. Know the direction the tow truck will pull and the direction your vehicle is to be steered. Agree on a signal that you can both clearly hear or see for stopping (if you run into problems) or for when your rig is clear. Also, make sure all bystanders are out of the way just in case a chain or cable snaps.

As the towing procedure starts, accelerate the tractor gently, just enough to turn the wheels slowly. When you have been pulled clear, signal the tow truck driver to stop accelerating immediately. Apply the tractor-trailer brakes. This prevents your vehicle from rear ending the tow truck.

Breakdowns — A vehicle breakdown can be dangerous at any time, but it is especially dangerous in adverse weather conditions. Exposure to wind and cold can cause frostbite. Blowing and drifting snow can be disorientating. If your vehicle breaks down in adverse conditions, stay in the cab.

Put on extra clothing to stay warm. Use your food and beverage supply cautiously. Depending on weather conditions and the amount of traffic on the road, you could be stranded for a while. If the vehicle's engine is able to run, idle the engine to keep the truck warm.

Don't try to walk for help unless it is absolutely necessary. If you must leave your vehicle, leave a note on the steering wheel stating when you left, where you were headed, and when you think you may return.

Rain and Fog

The dangers of driving in rain or fog are similar to those of winter driving. However, there are some situations unique to operating in rain or fog.

Reduced visibility is one concern when driving in rain and/or fog.

Rain — When rain first starts to fall, roads become slippery. As rain begins to fall, it mixes with the dirt, oil, and grease that cover the road's surface. Until additional rain breaks down and washes away this slippery mixture, the pavement is very slick. This condition can last anywhere from a few minutes to a few hours.

When traveling in rain, reduce your vehicle's speed, allow for more space behind other vehicles, and allow for more time to stop.

A heavy rain that causes water to stand on the roadway can cause a vehicle to hydroplane. The faster a vehicle travels on standing water, the greater the chance of hydroplaning. This is due to the fact that traction is only present when a vehicle's tires have contact with the road. If the tires are riding on a wall of water, they lose traction. This loss of traction causes you to lose steering control of your vehicle.

The best way to prevent hydroplaning is by slowing down.

Visibility is also a concern when driving in the rain. Take advantage of "path of light" driving. Make use of the reflections that occur when roads are wet.

Also, make sure your vehicle's windshield wipers are functioning properly, the windshield washers are full and functioning properly, and the defroster is operating properly.

Here's a suggestion. If a downpour happens, or fog starts getting thick, turn your head-lights on, slow down, and move into the left lane for a little while. The reason you move over is two-fold. 1. Most four-wheelers DRAMATICALLY slow down in the right lane and sometimes just stop! 2. The yellow line on the inside of the road is easier to see than the white line on the outside shoulder. It gives you something better to use as a guide until the weather gets better, or until you can get off the road.

Fog — The greatest challenge in foggy conditions is reduced visibility. Slowing down is key. A safe speed in fog may be 20 - 30 mph if you can see six car lengths ahead. If you can see only two car lengths ahead, slow down to 10-15 mph. How fast a vehicle should travel in foggy conditions is often best left to your judgement.

Low beam headlights should be used in the fog. They serve two purposes. As well as helping you see the roadway, low beam headlights allow others to see your vehicle.

High beam headlights should never be used in the fog. The water particles that make up fog tend to reflect more light back at you than on the roadway when high beam headlights are used.

Windshield wipers should be used to clear the fog's fine mist off of the windshield.

If visibility is extremely poor, find a safe place to stop until visibility improves.

Hot Weather

When you think of extreme driving conditions, snow, ice, and fog are often the first things that come to mind. Excessive heat is also an extreme driving condition that can cause additional stress on you and your vehicle.

When conducting pre-trip and on-the-road inspections in hot weather, you should pay extra attention to the following vehicle components.

1. **Tires** — Tires should be inspected every two hours or 100 miles when driving in hot weather. Check tire mounting and inflation.

    Air pressure increases with temperature. Don't let air out of the tire to reduce pressure. The air pressure will drop as the tire cools off. If you let air out of the tire, the pressure will be too low when the tire cools off.

    If you have to change a hot tire, never place it in your vehicle's spare rack unless it has cooled off. Placing a hot tire in a spare rack can also cause a tire fire.

2. **Engine oil** — The engine's oil helps keep the engine lubricated and cool. Make sure your vehicle's engine has the right amount of oil. Also check the vehicle's oil temperature gauge, making sure it is within the proper range while driving.

3. **Engine coolant** — Make sure the engine's cooling system has enough water and antifreeze before starting out.

    Once on the road, check the water temperature or coolant temperature gauge from time-to-time, making sure it remains in the normal range. If the gauge goes above the highest safe temperature, stop as soon as safely possible and try to find out what's wrong. Ignoring a high reading could lead to engine failure or an engine fire.

Caution driver! DO NOT DRIVE WITH YOUR EMERGENCY FLASHERS ON! Many accidents have been caused by this type of miscommunication. If your flashers are on you should be on the side of the road, not driving. If you see flashers ahead of you, don't assume they are moving. Slow down, pay attention, and avoid a bad situation.

Use great care if you need to add coolant to the engine. The engine generates a great deal of heat and you could be severely burned if you do not follow proper, safe procedures.

- Shut off the engine.

- Wait until it has cooled.

- Use thick gloves or a thick cloth to protect your hands.

- Release pressure by turning the radiator cap slowly to the first stop. This releases the pressure seal.

- When all pressure has been released, press on the cap and turn it the rest of the way to remove it.

- Visually check the coolant level, and add more if necessary.

- Replace the cap and turn it all the way to the closed position.

In hot weather, pay extra attention to the water temperature gauge.

Hey! Turn your engine fan on! If you have a manual fan switch just turning your fan on before you start up a long incline in hot weather can help avoid a lot of problems. If you don't have a manual switch and things start getting hot under the hood, shift down and race the engine. You will go up the hill slower but your engine will run faster and will hopefully cool itself down a little bit. If all else fails, don't sweat it, pull over and let things cool down before you continue.

4. **Engine belts** — Check belts for cracking and other signs of wear. Also check for looseness. Loose belts will not turn the water pump and/or fan properly, resulting in overheating.

5. **Hoses** — Check coolant hoses for cracks, breaks, or wear. A broken hose can lead to engine failure or an engine fire.

General hot weather driving tips — In desert areas, even a simple thunderstorm or brief downpour can cause serious driving problems. In heavy rain, a road can flood quickly. Be on the alert for changing road conditions if you encounter rain in a desert area.

When driving in extremely hot conditions, watch for bleeding tar on the road surface. Tars or oils often rise to the road's surface in these conditions, causing slippery spots on the road.

Also pay special attention to your vehicle's tires. The higher the vehicle's speed, the more heat is generated, increasing the risk for tire failure.

Breakdowns — As well as being dangerous to your vehicle, exposure to excessive heat and sunlight is dangerous for you. Prolonged exposure to heat and sun can cause dehydration and/or sunstroke. Should your vehicle breakdown, stay out of the sun. Stay in your cab or wait in the shade of your vehicle for help to come.

Mountain Driving

In mountain driving, gravity plays a major role on both upgrades and down-grades. Because of this, it is important that your vehicle's brakes are in top condition. If your vehicle is equipped with an air brake system, you should check for the following:

It is difficult to maintain a steady, constant speed.

- Compressor maintaining full reservoir pressure;

- Pressure drop on full application within limitations;

- Slack adjusters for full push rod travel, within specifications;

- Audible air leaks, applied and released;

- Drums for overheating; and

- Trailer protection valve operation.

Upgrades — The force of gravity causes all vehicles to slow down on upgrades, making it difficult to maintain a constant speed.

The steepness and length of the grade, as well as the weight of the load on the vehicle, all play a part in which gear you select to safely travel on an upgrade. The steeper and/or longer the grade and the heavier the load, the lower the gear you should select. If you select a gear that is too high for conditions your vehicle could overheat and possibly stall.

The vehicle's gauges should also be monitored as the vehicle heads uphill. The task of traveling uphill causes all of the vehicle's components to work harder than when traveling on a flat roadway.

This additional work causes the engine to create more heat. If the vehicle's gauges indicate high temperatures, a decrease in engine oil pressure, or if water and exhaust gas temperature readings are abnormal, pull over in a safe area and allow the engine to cool down.

When traveling uphill on a multi-laned road, travel in the right lane. This will allow smaller, faster vehicles to pass safely. Continue to pay attention to the traffic surrounding your vehicle. Especially to the left and rear.

Downgrades — Gravity's pull forces all vehicles to speed up on downgrades. To help combat the forces of gravity when traveling downhill, select:

- An appropriate speed;

- A low gear; and

- Proper braking technique.

An appropriate speed is one that is slow enough to allow a vehicle's brakes to hold the vehicle without the brakes overheating and fading. If you have to continually increase the pressure applied to the brakes to get the same stopping power, the brakes will eventually fade until there's little to no stopping control.

When selecting an appropriate speed, consider the total weight of the vehicle and its cargo, the grade's steepness and length, and weather and road conditions.

Gravity's pull forces vehicle speed to increase on downgrades.

As with upgrades, stay to the right, allowing other vehicles to pass. Also be aware of any warning signs along the roadway. The signs may indicate maximum vehicle size or safe rate speed for handling the grade.

The braking effect of the engine should be used as the primary way to control the vehicle's speed. The engine's braking effect is greatest when it is near the governed RPMs and the transmission is in the lower gears.

Before starting down a grade, shift the transmission into a low gear. Once a vehicle's speed has been built up, it will be difficult, if not impossible to downshift.

If you attempt to downshift with a manual transmission, the vehicle may get stuck in neutral. This can cause a vehicle to coast downhill and lose all braking effect, creating what can be a very dangerous situation.

Forcing an automatic transmission to shift into a lower gear can damage the transmission and can cause the vehicle to lose all braking effect.

How brakes can fail — Anytime a brake is used, heat is created. The rubbing of the brake pad against the brake drum or disc is what creates this heat. Excessive heat, caused by excessive braking can cause brakes to fail.

All brakes must be adjusted and operating properly to safely and efficiently control a vehicle.

If some brakes are out of adjustment, others may become overworked, causing them to overheat and fade, leaving a driver with little or no braking control.

As with all vehicle components, brake adjustment should be checked often, but it should be given even more attention when you are ready to head downhill.

Braking technique — The following is proper braking technique for a vehicle traveling in the proper, low gear.

1. Identify a safe speed for the load and grade.

2. When that speed is reached, apply the brakes hard enough to feel a definite slowdown.

3. Once the vehicle's speed has been reduced by 5 mph below the vehicle's safe speed, release the brakes. The application of the brakes should last about 3 seconds.

4. When the vehicle's speed increases back to or above the safe speed, repeat the first two steps.

For example, if the vehicle's safe speed is 30 mph, don't apply the brakes until the vehicle's speed has reached 30 mph. Then, the brakes should be applied just hard enough to gradually reduce the vehicle's speed to 25 mph. Once at 25 mph, the brakes may be released.

Driver, it is very important that you get the big picture here. Read all the signs at the top of the hill and know what grade you are about to go down. The higher the number, the steeper the hill. Take note of the posted speed, how far it is to the next escape ramp, and total miles to descend the hill. Knowing these numbers and understanding what to do, will save your life!

An escape ramp can help stop a runaway vehicle.

Escape ramps — Escape ramps are found on steep mountain downgrades. They are designed to help in safely stopping a runaway vehicle. These ramps can help save lives when a vehicle's brakes fail. There are four basic types of escape ramps.

1. **Gravity ramps** — Gravity ramps are found on steep ascending grades. They are constructed of a pea gravel surface with mounds of sand or gravel at the end of the ramp.

2. **Sand piles** — Sand piles contain mounds or ridges tall enough to drag the undercarriage of a vehicle.

3. **Arrester beds** — Arrester beds have large masses of loose material (at least 18 inches deep), causing a vehicle to sink.

4. **Ramp and arrester bed combinations** — This combination relies on both loose surface material and long grades to slow a vehicle.

Summary

In this chapter, you have learned about the special issues associated with operating in extreme conditions. This includes dealing with extreme weather (snow, ice, heat) and mountain driving.

Escape ramps are for emergencies ONLY! If you are a professional driver, you shouldn't ever have to use an escape ramp unless you have equipment failure that was beyond your control. At the top of the hill, if there's a sign that says, "check your brakes before proceeding," DO IT! Forget about those other guys that are flying by the brake-check area. They'll be at the bottom of the hill with smoke billowing off their brakes...if they make it that far.

Extreme Driving Conditions Quiz

Directions: Read each statement carefully and mark the response that best answers the question.

1. **When operating in winter driving conditions, you should pay close attention to _____ when conducting vehicle inspections.**

    A. Coolant level

    B. Windshield wipers and washers

    C. Coupling devices

    D. All of the above

2. **Tire chains are most effective on:**

    A. Glare ice

    B. Light, dry snow

    C. Heavy snow

    D. All of the above

3. **A windshield scraper, snow brush, and small shovel are just some of the emergency items you should carry in your vehicle.**

    A. True

    B. False

4. **_____ occurs when moisture on the road freezes into a smooth, nearly invisible, slippery surface.**

    A. Brown ice

    B. Black ice

    C. Blue ice

    D. Plaid ice

5. **The three basic causes of skidding and jackknifing are:**

    A. Dry powdery snow, rain, and wind

    B. Under acceleration, under braking, and under steering

    C. Over acceleration, overbraking, and oversteering

    D. All of the above

6. **When driving on a slippery surface:**

   A.   Get the feel of the road

   B.   Go slow

   C.   Watch far enough ahead to keep a steady speed

   D.   All of the above

7. **If you believe a road is too slippery to safely proceed, you should:**

   A.   Stop at the first safe place and wait for conditions to improve

   B.   Reduce your vehicle's speed to 5 mph

   C.   Pass other vehicles with extreme caution

   D.   Keep on driving so you aren't late in making your delivery

8. **Water in the brakes can cause a lack of braking power.**

   A.   True

   B.   False

9. **When operating in hot weather conditions, you should pay close attention to _____ when conducting vehicle inspections.**

   A.   Coolant level

   B.   Windshield wipers and washers

   C.   Coupling devices

   D.   All of the above

10. **_____ plays a major role in mountain driving.**

   A.   Amount of sunshine

   B.   Temperature

   C.   Gravity

   D.   All of the above

General Knowledge CDL Pre-Test

Read each question carefully and then select the answer that is most correct.

1. **While driving you are looking ahead of your vehicle. How should you be looking?**

   A. Look to the right side of the roadway

   B. Look back and forth and near and far

   C. Stare straight ahead at all times

   D. Look straight ahead and glance in your mirrors every 45 to 60 seconds

2. **When you are driving at night, you should:**

   A. Dim your lights when you are within 300 feet of oncoming traffic

   B. Watch the white line on the left side of the roadway

   C. Adjust your vehicle speed so as to keep your stopping distance within your sight distance

   D. Keep your high beams on at all times

3. **Statistics prove that most serious skids are a result of:**

   A. Driving too fast for conditions

   B. Improper loading of the vehicle

   C. Turning too sharply

   D. Winter driving conditions

4. **If you drive through heavy rain or standing water your brakes may get wet. What can this cause when you apply the brakes?**

   A. Trailer jackknife

   B. Your brakes to heat up

   C. Hydroplaning

   D. Hydroplaning, if you were traveling faster than 30 mph when you applied the brakes

5. **Which of the following is true about the use of reflective emergency triangles?**

    A.   The regulation requires they be placed within 5 minutes of stopping

    B.   You do not need to use them if you break down as long as your 4-way flashers are working

    C.   You do not need to use them as long as you have pulled your vehicle completely off the traveled portion of the roadway

    D.   If you stop on a hill or curve, it is permissible to place them up to 500 feet in order to provide adequate warning

This is the second time you are seeing these questions. Did you get them all correct this time? If not, go back and find the answers so that you can "ace" the written exam!

Chapter **15**

Hazard perception

OBJECTIVES

Upon completion of this chapter, you should have a basic understanding of:

- ❑ Hazard recognition
- ❑ Road hazards
- ❑ User hazards
- ❑ The importance of planning ahead

Introduction

Any road user or road condition can be a potential hazard. Learning to recognize hazards is a skill that you should continually work on and will continually develop as you proceed in your professional driving career. This chapter will introduce you to the nature of hazards, and the clues to recognizing them.

Any road user or road condition can be a potential hazard.

Hazard Recognition

A hazard is any road condition or road user that can pose a potential danger to the motoring public. Being aware of and anticipating potential hazards is key to effective hazard perception which in turn helps in preventing accidents.

In some ways, hazard perception is like doing detective work. You should be continually looking for clues, signs that you could be dealing with a potential hazard. This includes scanning the road ahead and the area around your vehicle. The clues or signs you are looking for fall into two major categories:

- Road hazards; and
- User hazards.

Road Hazards

Road hazards appear in many different forms. They may be naturally occurring, man-made, or a combination.

Road hazards are outstanding characteristics of the road surface that could adversely affect your ability to control your vehicle or see clearly.

Hey driver! Do you know how long it takes to stop your vehicle? Do you really? Well get this...at 55 mph in ideal conditions, it will take you 290 feet to stop your truck. That's almost the full length of a football field! Next time you are behind the wheel, visualize a football field in front of you. What's in that distance? Can you stop without running over it? If not, you better change something quick.

Road hazards include:

- Pavement drop-offs;

- Road construction/work zones;

- Road debris;

- Off-ramps; and

- On-ramps.

Pavement drop-offs — Sometimes, the pavement drops off sharply near the edge of the road. Driving too close to the edge can cause a vehicle to suddenly tilt. This can cause a vehicle to hit roadside objects (tree limbs, signs, etc.). Also, it can be hard to steer when crossing a drop-off.

Driving through a work zone can be dangerous.

Be careful driver! This is where you really need to pay attention. Construction zones are bad! Everyone seems to be in a hurry, and no one wants to move over into the lane they are supposed to be in. It's not your job to be the "construction police" so just pay attention, drive your own vehicle, and let the four-wheelers mess up on their own!

Road construction/work zones — A construction crew working on a road is hazardous. There may be narrow lanes, sharp turns, poor visibility, unclear lane markings, or uneven surfaces. Other drivers are often distracted and may drive unsafely. Workers and construction vehicles may get in the way.

Road debris — Foreign objects (debris) can be a road hazard. Debris can be a danger to tires and wheel rims, damage electrical and brake lines, and get caught between dual tires causing severe damage.

Some obstacles which appear harmless can be very dangerous. A box or bag that appears to be empty may contain a heavy material, causing damage.

It is very important to keep an eye out for objects in the road, and see them early enough in order to avoid them without making unsafe, sudden moves.

Off-ramps — Freeway and turnpike exits can be particularly dangerous. Off-ramps often have speed limit signs posted, but, the posted speed is the recommended speed for an automobile, and may not be safe for a larger vehicle. Exits that go downhill and turn at the same time can be especially dangerous. The downhill grade makes it difficult to reduce speed.

On-ramps — A driver entering a freeway or turnpike may not be paying attention. He/she may not notice a vehicle approaching from behind or the side. In some cases, on-ramps have a short upgrade. This makes it difficult for a heavy vehicle to get up to speed and merge.

Use extra caution at on-ramps.

User Hazards

Anticipating a situation is key to avoiding a user hazard. The following are considered user hazards:

- Intersections;
- Blocked vision;
- Parked vehicles;
- Children and animals;
- Disabled vehicles;
- Inattentive/distracted drivers;
- Confused drivers; and
- Accidents.

Intersections — Vehicles may be hidden by a blind intersection or alley. A driver may not have a clear view of traffic and may pull into the intersection or roadway. Always be prepared to stop.

Always be prepared to stop at an intersection.

This is a good time to start talking to yourself. No, I don't think you're crazy, what I mean is you need to identify hazards and ask yourself, "What if?" What if that car pulls out right in front of me? What if that child runs between those two cars? What if that guy tries to cut me off just before his lane ends in that construction zone? Asking yourself, "What if?" and always having a plan can save you a lot of grief and can get you through most situations without a problem. So go ahead and talk to yourself and ask, "What if?" Don't worry...no one else is listening.

Blocked vision — People who can't see others can be a danger. It is important to be alert for drivers whose vision is blocked. Vans, loaded station wagons, and cars with rear windows blocked are some examples. Rental trucks should also be watched carefully. In many cases, rental truck drivers aren't used to the limited vision they have to the sides and rear of the truck. In winter, vehicles with ice or snow covered windows are a hazard.

Parked vehicles — A parked vehicle can be hazardous when it is starting to pull out into traffic or is suddenly starting up and driving into traffic. Watch for movement inside the vehicle or movement of the vehicle itself that shows people are inside. Keep an eye out for brake lights, backup lights, exhaust, or other clues that a driver is about to move.

Children — Children tend to act quickly without checking traffic. They may dart into the road or between parked vehicles to retrieve a ball or chase another child.

Disabled vehicles — Drivers changing a tire or working on an engine may not pay attention to traffic. Jacked-up wheels or raised hoods are hazard clues.

Inattentive drivers — People who are distracted can be a hazard. Watch where they are looking. If they are looking elsewhere, they can't see you.

Confused drivers — Confused drivers often change direction or stop without warning. Confusion is common near freeway or turnpike interchanges and major intersections.

Tourists unfamiliar with an area can be hazardous. Clues to watch for when looking for tourists include car top luggage, trailers, and out-of-state license plates.

Hesitation is another sign of confusion. Keep an eye out for vehicles driving very slowly, frequent use of brakes, or drivers looking at signs or maps.

Accidents — People involved in an accident may not look for traffic. Passing drivers tend to look at the accident. People often run across the road without looking and vehicles may slow down or stop suddenly.

Plan Ahead

Strong observation skills as well as the ability to think fast and quickly develop a plan are important. A hazard can easily turn into an emergency situation. Good preparation can improve safety for everyone on the road. You should:

- Stay alert;

- Aim high (scan at least 12-15 seconds ahead of your vehicle);

- Scan, see the whole picture, use your mirrors;

- Identify your options; and

- Execute (carry out your plan).

Good observation skills and planning are important.

Summary

In this chapter, you have learned about the types of hazards that can pose a potential danger to the professional driver as well as ways to identify these hazards well in advance. These skills are important when it comes to accident prevention and keeping you and your vehicle safe.

Hazard Perception Quiz

Directions: Read each statement carefully and mark the response that best answers the question.

1. **A hazard is any road condition or road user that can pose a potential danger to the motoring public.**

    A. True

    B. False

2. **_____ hazards are outstanding characteristics of the road surface that could adversely affect your ability to control your vehicle or see clearly.**

    A. User

    B. Pedestrian

    C. Road

    D. All of the above

3. **_____ is a road hazard.**

    A. Children

    B. Pavement drop-offs

    C. Disabled vehicles

    D. All of the above

4. **An object which appears to be harmless (paper bag or box) can actually pose a danger to you and your vehicle.**

    A. True

    B. False

5. **The speed limit posted on an off-ramp is the safe, recommended speed for all vehicles.**

    A. True

    B. False

6. **Blocked vision, parked vehicles, and disabled vehicles are _____.**

    A. User hazards

    B. Pedestrian hazards

    C. Road hazards

    D. All of the above

7. _____ is a user hazard.

    A.   An inattentive driver

    B.   A confused driver

    C.   An accident

    D.   All of the above

8. **Driver hesitation, changing direction, or stopping without warning are signs of a confused driver.**

    A.   True

    B.   False

9. **When it comes to hazard perception, strong observations skills are not important.**

    A.   True

    B.   False

10. **Good preparation on your part can improve safety for all road users.**

    A.   True

    B.   False

General Knowledge CDL Pre-Test

Read each question carefully and select the most correct answer.

1. **When you are driving through construction zones, you should:**

   A. Speed up and hurry through them so you aren't in them any longer than necessary

   B. Stop before entering them, get in low gear and proceed through

   C. Watch for sharp pavement drop-offs

   D. Reduce your speed only if construction workers are near the roadway

2. **If you break down on a level, straight, four-lane, divided highway, where should you place the reflective warning triangles?**

   A. One 10 feet from the rear of the vehicle, one approximately 100 feet from the rear of the vehicle and another one about 100 feet to the front of the vehicle

   B. One 10 feet from the rear of the vehicle, one approximately 100 feet from the rear of the vehicle, and one about 200 feet from the rear of the vehicle

   C. One 100 feet from the rear of the vehicle, one approximately 200 feet from the rear of the vehicle, and one about 300 feet from the rear of the vehicle

   D. One 50 feet from the rear of the vehicle, one about 100 feet from the rear of the vehicle, and one about 200 feet from the front of the vehicle

3. **According to the Commercial Driver's manual, why should you limit the use of your vehicle's horn?**

   A. If your vehicle has air brakes, the air horn may not work while you are applying your brakes

   B. It may startle other drivers

   C. You should keep both hands on the steering wheel at all times

   D. The Driver's Manual does not say that a driver should limit the use of the horn

4. **Which of the following should you NOT do?**

   A. Turn your headlights on during the day if visibility is reduced due to bad weather

   B. Flash you brake lights to warn vehicles behind you that you are slowing down

   C. Flash your brake lights when entering a construction zone if vehicles are close behind you

   D. Flash your brake lights if someone is following to closely

5. **The proper way to load a vehicle is:**

   A. Keep the load balanced in the cargo area

   B. Place the load at the front of the trailer to give your drive wheels better traction

   C. Place the load at the rear of the trailer so your rear tires have better traction

   D. It makes no difference where the cargo is placed as long as you are not over the allowable gross weight

Chapter 15
Hazard
Perception

Chapter 16

Railroad crossings

OBJECTIVES

Highway-rail grade crossings can be deadly. This chapter is designed to help you learn how to cross railroad tracks safely in a commercial motor vehicle. Upon completion of this chapter, you should understand the importance of and methods for:

❑ Determining when stopping is required

❑ Stopping at and crossing tracks safely

❑ Recognizing crossing signs, gates, and other engineering devices

❑ Emergency procedures

Introduction

In 2005, there were more than 3,000 collisions and 350 deaths at highway-rail grade crossings in the United States, according to the Federal Railroad Administration. Approximately one-fourth of those accidents involved a train colliding with a large truck or tractor-trailer. In almost every case, human error is the cause.

An example of a highway-rail grade crossing.

A highway-rail grade crossing is the area where a roadway (highway, road, street, etc.) crosses a railway at grade, that is, where both the roadway and the railway are at the same level at the crossing point, as opposed to grade-separated overpasses or underpasses.

With 200,000 miles of railroad tracks, 147,000 public highway-rail grade crossings, and 94,000 private highway-rail grade crossings in the United States, every driver must know how to cross railroad tracks safely. That is especially true for drivers of long, heavy vehicles like tractor-trailer combinations and other commercial vehicles that move slowly, may offer poor visibility, and can easily obstruct or get stuck at a crossing.

This chapter will address safely crossing railroad tracks including regulatory requirements, emergency procedures, and recognition of safety devices and signs.

Active Vs. Passive Crossings

There are two basic types of crossing warning devices for at-grade crossings:

1. **Active warning devices** — Active warning devices are devices that are activated automatically at the approach of a train. These devices include flashing lights, bells, horns, traffic signals, message boards, gates, and other physical barriers. Active devices offer greater protection than passive devices.

This crossing has active warning devices.

2. **Passive warning devices** — Passive warning devices do not give notice of the approach of a train. Passive devices are designed to direct the attention of the driver to the crossing so they may exercise caution. These devices include crossbuck signs, stop signs, yield signs, pavement markings, and constantly flashing lights.

About three-fourths of all highway-rail crossings in the United States have passive warning devices or traffic control devices. That means it's up to you, the driver, to make sure no trains are approaching before you cross.

Engineering Considerations

Various technologies are in use at both active and passive highway-rail grade crossings to help avoid collisions. To use these technologies appropriately, you must know what they look like and what they are trying to tell you. These technologies include signs, flashing lights, bells, gates, and barriers.

The following is an overview of the most commonly used engineering devices.

Crossbuck signs — A crossbuck sign is one of the oldest warning devices. It is a white regulatory, X-shaped sign with the words "Railroad Crossing" in black lettering, located alongside the highway prior to the railroad tracks.

In most cases, the crossbuck sign is installed on the right-hand side of a public roadway on each approach to the highway-rail grade crossing. A crossbuck sign is a passive yield sign and is considered the same as a "Yield" sign. The crossbuck sign is required at all public highway-rail grade crossings.

Advance warning sign — An advance warning sign is a round yellow warning sign with a black "X" and "RR." These signs are located alongside the highway in advance of the crossing, and serve to alert motorists to the crossing.

The advance warning sign is usually the first sign you see when approaching a highway-rail grade crossing.

Flashing light signal — This is a device installed on a standard mast which, when activated, displays red lights flashing alternately. Flashing light signals activate upon the approach or presence of a train at a highway-rail grade crossing, and require a complete stop by the highway user.

Flashing light signals are mandatory with gates. When both are activated, the gate arm light nearest the tip will be illuminated continuously and the other two lights shall flash alternately in unison with the flashing light signals. The typical flashing light signal assembly on a side-of-the-roadway location includes a standard crossbuck sign and, where there is more than one track, an auxiliary "number of tracks" sign, all of which indicate a highway-rail grade crossing ahead. A bell may be included in the assembly and operated in conjunction with the flashing lights.

Advance warning sign.

The flashing light signal has been activated at this crossing.

Flashing light signals are found at all types of public highway-rail grade crossings. They normally are placed to the right of the approaching highway traffic on all roadway approaches to a crossing.

Standard bell — A standard bell is a device which, when activated, provides an audible warning. It may be used with flashing light signals and gates, and is most effective as a warning to pedestrians and bicyclists.

A standard bell is designed to ring loudly when a train is approaching, to warn people in the surrounding area. When used, the bell is usually mounted on top of one of the signal support masts. The bell is usually activated whenever the flashing light signals are operating.

A new innovation being used by most railroads is the electronic bell, the volume of which can be adjusted.

Standard gates — A standard gate assembly is an active traffic control device used with flashing lights and normally accompanied by a crossbuck sign, flashing light signals, and other passive warning signs. It consists of a drive mechanism and a fully reflectorized red and white striped gate arm with lights, and which in the down position extends across the approaching lanes of highway traffic about 4 feet above the top of the pavement. The flashing light signal may be supported on the same post with the gate mechanism, or separately mounted.

When no train is approaching or occupying the crossing, the gate arm is in an upright, vertical position. In a normal sequence of operation the flashing light signals and the lights on the gate arm in its normal upright position are activated immediately upon detection of a train. The gate arm is designed to start its downward motion not less than 3 seconds after the signal lights start to operate, reach its horizontal position before the arrival of any train, and remain in that position as long as the train occupies the crossing. When the train clears the crossing, and no other train is approaching, the gate arm ascends to its upright position.

Flashing light signal with gate.

Long arm gate — A long arm gate is structured the same way as a standard gate assembly, but with a longer arm. The intent of the longer arm is to reduce the driver's ability to run around the gates. A long arm gate will cover at least 75 percent of the roadway.

Four quadrant gates — These gate assemblies have an additional pair of dual gate arms to completely seal off the intersection. Gate arms are lowered on each side of a bi-directional crossing, preventing potential gate violators from driving around the gates.

The mechanical operation of the four quadrant gates are very similar to the standard gate assembly and the long arm gate. All three of the gate assemblies have gate mechanisms and gate arms that are designed to warn traffic of an oncoming train. They restrict motorists from entering a highway-rail grade crossing by lowering the gate arm when the presence of a train is detected.

Barrier gates — These are a new variety of warning gates that lock into a post when in the down position, which prevents vehicles from driving around them at a crossing.

Median barriers — These barriers consist of a pre-fabricated mountable island placed in the center of the roadway leading up to a highway-rail grade crossing. The barrier provides an obstacle so that a vehicle cannot attempt to drive around a crossing gate arm. Yellow and black reflectorized paddle delineators are mounted to the curb barrier. The delineators are mounted on either a rubber boot or concrete. If a roadway is not wide enough to accommodate a median barrier, yellow and black tubular markers, mounted directly to the roadway's centerline, can be used.

Wayside horns — A wayside horn is a stationary horn system that is designed to sound like a train horn and is activated by the railroad-highway grade crossing warning system. It is mounted at the crossing, rather than on the locomotive, to deliver a longer, louder, more consistent audible warning to motorists and pedestrians while eliminating noise pollution in neighborhoods for more than one-half mile along the rail corridor.

Stop driver! Don't become another train/truck crash statistic. There's just no reason for it! If the arm is down or the lights are flashing, just stop. No excuses! It's not worth your life just to gain a few minutes in your trip, so relax, set your brakes, and wait for the train to pass. Getting in a fight with a train is a fight you will never win.

Exempt sign.

Exempt sign — This sign is placed in advance of and at crossings authorized by state law or regulation to inform placarded hazardous materials vehicles, buses, and other highway users that a stop is not required, except when a signal, train crew member, or uniformed police officer indicates that a train, locomotive, or other railroad equipment is approaching the crossing.

Yield sign — The yield sign assigns right-of-way. Vehicles controlled by a yield sign need to avoid interference with other vehicles, including trains, which are given the right-of-way.

Yield sign.

Do not stop on tracks sign.

Stop sign.

Do not stop on tracks sign — This sign is a black and white regulatory sign placed at a crossing when an engineering study or experience determines there is a high potential for vehicles stopping on the tracks.

Stop sign — A standard, red regulatory stop sign with lettering intended for use where motor vehicle traffic is required to stop. This sign can be added to the crossing, requiring all vehicles to come to a complete stop before crossing the railroad tracks.

Tracks out of service sign — This sign is for use at a crossing in lieu of the crossbuck when a railroad track has been abandoned or its use discontinued.

Parallel track sign — This sign is a diamond-shaped yellow advance warning sign located on a roadway parallel to the railroad tracks, indicating the road ahead will cross the tracks. This sign is intended to warn motorists making a turn that there is a highway-rail grade crossing immediately after the turn.

Low ground clearance sign — Of particular importance to truck drivers, the "low ground clearance" sign is a new symbol sign for railroad grade crossings where conditions are sufficiently abrupt to create hang-up of long wheelbase vehicles or trailers with low ground clearance. This sign is currently used by the New York State Department of Transportation.

Tracks out of service sign.

Parallel track sign.

Low ground clearance sign.

Number sign — At multiple-track crossings, a sign indicating the number of tracks will be on the post below the crossbuck.

Pavement markings — The white letters "R&R" can be set into the surface of, applied to, or attached to, the pavement in advance of a crossing, to advise, warn, or guide traffic.

Number sign.

Pavement markings.

Regulatory Considerations

According to Sec. 392.10 of the Federal Motor Carrier Safety Regulations, drivers of the commercial motor vehicles listed below must always stop before crossing railroad tracks:

1. A bus transporting passengers.

2. A commercial motor vehicle transporting any quantity of a Division 2.3 chlorine.

3. A commercial motor vehicle required to be marked or placarded with one of the following markings:

   - Division 1.1;

   - Division 1.2, or Division 1.3;

   - Division 2.3 Poison gas;

   - Division 4.3;

   - Class 7;

   - Class 3 Flammable;

   - Division 5.1;

   - Division 2.2;

   - Division 2.3 Chlorine;

   - Division 6.1 Poison;

   - Division 2.2 Oxygen;

   - Division 2.1;

   - Class 3 Combustible liquid;

   - Division 4.1;

   - Division 5.1;

   - Division 5.2;

   - Class 8; or

   - Division 1.4.

4. A cargo tank motor vehicle, whether loaded or empty, used for the transportation of any hazardous material as defined in the Hazardous Materials Regulations (Parts 107 through 180).

5. A cargo tank motor vehicle transporting a commodity which at the time of loading has a temperature above its flash point as determined by Sec. 173.120.

6. A cargo tank motor vehicle, loaded or empty, transporting any commodity under exemption in accordance with the provisions of Part 107 Subpart B.

Before crossing at grade railroad tracks, these vehicles must first:

- Stop the commercial motor vehicle within 50 feet of, and not closer than 15 feet to, the tracks;

- Listen and look in each direction along the tracks for an approaching train;

- Determine that no train is approaching; and

- When it is safe to do so, drive the commercial motor vehicle across the tracks in a gear that allows the vehicle to complete the crossing without a change of gears (Do not shift gears while crossing the tracks).

Whether required or not, it is best to stop at all railroad tracks.

You are not required to stop at the following:

- A streetcar crossing, or railroad tracks used exclusively for industrial switching purposes, within a business district, as defined in Sec. 390.5.

- A railroad grade crossing when a police officer or crossing flagman directs traffic to proceed.

- A railroad grade crossing controlled by a functioning highway traffic signal transmitting a green indication which, under local law, permits the commercial motor vehicle to proceed across the railroad tracks without slowing or stopping.

- An abandoned railroad grade crossing which is marked with a sign indicating that the rail line is abandoned.

- An industrial or spur line railroad grade crossing marked with a sign reading "Exempt."

Slowing required — Drivers of commercial motor vehicles not subject to Sec. 392.10 are required to at least slow down at railroad crossings. Section 392.11 says that, upon approaching a railroad grade crossing, these vehicles must be driven at a rate of speed which will allow the vehicle to be stopped before reaching the nearest rail of the crossing and must not be driven upon or over the crossing until "due caution" has been taken to make sure that the course is clear.

Penalties — The penalties for violating the railroad crossing regulations can be severe. The commercial driver's license (CDL) regulations in Part 383 state that a driver who holds a CDL can be disqualified if convicted of highway-rail grade crossing violations. Disqualification means the loss of your license for a specified period of time, as follows:

- A first-time offender is disqualified for at least 60 days;

- A second conviction within a three-year period results in disqualification for at least 120 days; and

- A third or subsequent conviction within a three-year period results in disqualification for at least one year.

The following are the violations which could result in disqualification:

- The driver is not required to always stop, but fails to slow down and check that tracks are clear of an approaching train;

- The driver is not required to always stop, but fails to stop before reaching the crossing, if the tracks are not clear;

- The driver is always required to stop, but fails to stop before driving onto the crossing;

- The driver fails to have sufficient space to drive completely through the crossing without stopping;

- The driver fails to obey a traffic control device or the directions of an enforcement official at the crossing; and

- The driver fails to negotiate a crossing because of insufficient undercarriage clearance.

What's the biggest penalty for crossing a railroad track when there is an approaching train? DEATH! Don't you want to see your family and friends again? Of course you do, so like I said before, just don't do it!

Safety Considerations

The regulations requiring you to slow down or stop at railroad crossings are the bare minimum requirements. As a professional driver, you need to do more. The following are some of the "best practices" you should follow when traversing highway-rail grade crossings, in addition to the regulatory requirements.

- Never fail to be alert when you approach a crossing, even if you cross it every day and have never seen a train at that crossing.

- Check for traffic behind you and make sure they know your intentions.

- Use a pull-out lane, if available. Turn on your flashers in traffic, if necessary.

- Choose an escape route in the event of brake failure, unexpected problems, or traffic tie-ups in front of or behind you.

- If required to stop, stop between 15 and 50 feet from the nearest rail.

- Roll down your window and turn off the fan, radio, CB, and other noisy equipment to better hear a train.

- While slowing or stopped, look carefully in each direction for approaching trains, moving your head and eyes to see around obstructions such as mirrors, pillars, and windshields.

- Be alert for optical illusions. It's easy to underestimate the speed of an approaching locomotive when you look down the tracks, because the train will look smaller and slower than it actually is. It is almost impossible to accurately judge the speed of a train when looking down the tracks. If you can see a train, assume that it cannot stop in time to avoid you. Be even more careful at night and at passive crossings.

- When waiting for a train to pass, set your emergency brakes so you won't move onto the track.

- Obey all rail-crossing signals and never drive around a lowered gate, even if you can't see a train approaching. If you think the railroad signals are malfunctioning, contact your dispatcher, local law enforcement, or the 800 number posted at the crossing, if available, and then find another route.

Never drive around a lowered gate.

- Watch for additional trains. As you approach a crossing, be aware of any signs indicating how many tracks are part of the crossing. If the crossing involves multiple tracks, don't assume it's all clear when the first train passes. Wait until you can see down all the tracks before starting across, to be sure another train is not approaching on a different track.

- If you drive a low-bed trailer, such as a moving van, car carrier, or lowboy, you may not be able to get across some grade crossings where there is not enough clearance. These "hump" crossings are not always marked. When in doubt, turn around and find another crossing.

- If it won't fit, don't commit. Every driver needs to know the size of their vehicle and the size of the "containment area" at railroad crossings, that is, the amount of space available on the other side of the tracks. If a crossing has a stop sign or traffic light on the far side, be sure there is enough room to completely clear the tracks. If there is any doubt about the amount of space available, don't start across. If you drive a regular route, learn the highway-rail grade crossings on it and how your truck fits those crossings.

- Check the crossing signals one final time before proceeding.

- If you stopped in a pull-out lane, signal and pull back onto the road when there is a safe gap in traffic. Expect traffic in other lanes to pass you.

- Use the highest gear that will allow you to cross the tracks without shifting. Do not change gears when crossing the tracks.

- If the red lights at the crossing begin to flash after you have started over the track, keep going. Lights should begin flashing at least 20 seconds before the train arrives.

- Always be aware of overhang, both yours and the train's, especially if you are hauling bulky cargo like steel or logs. Don't get caught with your "tail" hanging over a track. Trains also extend over the rails, by at least three feet on both sides, so you must be well beyond the track to ensure your safety.

When stopped, at 80,000 pounds pulling a 53-foot trailer on a level road with good surface conditions, it will take you at least 14 seconds to clear a single track, and more than 15 seconds to clear a double track.

If you get stuck on the tracks, you should follow the steps listed below.

1. Get out of the vehicle immediately. Take your cell phone (if available).

2. Move far away from the vehicle in the direction of any approaching train, to avoid being near the point of impact.

3. Look for an emergency telephone number posted at the crossing and call it. If you don't have a phone, flag someone down.

4. Give your exact location, using landmarks and the DOT number from the crossing.

5. If there is no posted emergency number, call the police or 911 immediately.

Summary

In this chapter, you learned about the serious dangers associated with crossing highway-rail grade crossings, the various engineering controls that may be in place at those crossings and their purpose, the regulations requiring you to slow down and/or stop at such crossings, and the "best practices" you should use to safely approach, analyze, and cross railroad tracks.

Railroad Crossings Quiz

Directions: Read each statement carefully and mark the response that best answers the question.

1. **It's up to you, the truck driver, to avoid an accident because:**

   A. Trains can't stop quickly

   B. Trains always have the right of way

   C. Trains cannot swerve to avoid collisions

   D. All of the above

2. **When approaching a railroad crossing, if you are not required to stop, you should:**

   A. Slow down and proceed with caution

   B. Sound your horn

   C. Stop anyway

   D. Ignore any flashing red lights

3. **If there are multiple tracks, it's okay to shift gears while crossing, in order to get across more quickly.**

   A. True

   B. False

4. **If you are required to stop at railroad crossings, you should stop:**

   A. Within 15 feet of the nearest rail

   B. Between 15 and 50 feet from the nearest rail

   C. At least 50 feet from the nearest rail

   D. None of the above

5. **A round, yellow sign with a large "X" and the letters "RR" tells you:**

   A. There is a railroad yard nearby

   B. There is a train approaching

   C. There is only one railroad track ahead

   D. To slow down, because you are approaching a railroad crossing

6. **A sign with the words "Railroad Crossing" on two crossed white boards is called a:**

   A. Advance warning sign

   B. Cantilever

   C. Crossbuck

   D. Track sign

7. **As you start driving over some tracks, the red lights begin to flash and the gates start to come down. You should:**

   A. Call the railroad to report a faulty signaling device

   B. Keep going and clear the tracks

   C. Back up and clear the tracks

   D. Stop and abandon the vehicle

8. **If your vehicle gets stuck on the tracks, you should:**

   A. Remain with the vehicle and call 911

   B. Stand next to the vehicle and wave at any approaching trains

   C. Abandon the vehicle immediately

   D. Honk your horn continuously until help arrives

9. **Why shouldn't you cross the tracks when an approaching train appears to be far away?**

   A. The train may be closer and faster than it appears

   B. The train may unexpectedly speed up

   C. You may not be able to clear the tracks in time

   D. Both A and C

10. **Most truck/train collisions can be attributed to:**

    A. Poorly designed roadway/rail intersections

    B. Faulty gates

    C. Train speed

    D. Driver error

General Knowledge CDL Pre-Test

Read each question carefully and select the most correct answer.

1. **When driving a vehicle with a height over 13 feet, you should:**

   A. Assume all clearances are of sufficient height

   B. Height clearance is not a concern as long as you stay on state or federal roadways

   C. If you are unsure of the clearance, stop and check before proceeding

   D. All of the above

2. **Controlled braking is:**

   A. Applying brakes hard enough for the wheels to lock up

   B. Pressing the brakes hard enough to lock-up the wheels, then releasing and then reapplying again

   C. Applying firm brake pressure but not to the point of lock-up

   D. Only used if the vehicle does not have anti-lock brakes

3. **You are driving on a straight and level roadway at 60 mph and suddenly a tire blows out on your vehicle. What should you do first?**

   A. Immediately begin light, controlled braking

   B. Immediately begin stab braking

   C. Grip steering wheel firmly with both hands and stay off the brakes until the vehicle has slowed down

   D. Immediately begin emergency braking

4. **Which of the following is true?**

   A. It is permissible to use radial and bias-ply tires together on the same axle

   B. Tires which are mismatched sizes should not be used on the same vehicle

   C. $4/32$ inch tread depth is the maximum allowed on drive tires

   D. $2/32$ inch tread depth is permissible for steering tires

5. **Why do hazardous materials regulations exist?**

   A. To provide for safe drivers and equipment

   B. To communicate a risk

   C. To contain the product

   D. All of the above

Chapter 16
Railroad
Crossings

Chapter **17**

Emergency maneuvers

OBJECTIVES

Upon completion of this chapter, you should have a basic understanding of:

- ❑ The role of emergency maneuvers
- ❑ Evasive steering
- ❑ Emergency stopping
- ❑ Off-road recovery
- ❑ How to handle brake failure
- ❑ How to deal with a tire blowout

Introduction

Emergencies occur when one or more drivers fail to observe safe operating practices. As a professional driver, you can reduce the likelihood of being involved in an emergency situation by practicing safe driving skills. Unfortunately, even the safest and most conscientious professional drivers face emergency situations during their careers. This chapter will address the importance of recognizing an emergency situation and the methods and techniques for safely dealing with the situation.

The Role of Emergency Maneuvers

The safest and best way to avoid an emergency is to prevent it from happening in the first place. Proper driving skills, hazard perception technique, and preventive maintenance can go a long way in preventing many emergencies.

In many cases, driver error plays a major role in an emergency. Failure to observe safe operating practices is a prime cause.

Evasive Steering

Generally, steering to avoid an emergency is safer than trying to stop. If an escape path is available, evasive steering provides a better chance of avoiding a collision than attempting to stop. Constant scanning for hazards, adequate following distance, and good driver and vehicle preparation are key.

Even the safest professional drivers face emergency situations from time-to-time.

The two most common escape routes are another lane of traffic and the shoulder of the road. If a lane is available, a quick lane change is the best escape route. If a lane change is impossible or dangerous, the shoulder of the road provides an alternate escape route.

Evasive steering, when done correctly, is generally safe. A number of factors can affect the outcome of an evasive steering maneuver. Be aware of these factors. React accordingly. The best results are achieved when you are hauling stable cargo with a low center of gravity and are able to steer onto a firm road or shoulder.

General procedures — When evasive steering, minimize the amount of turning necessary. Start the maneuver as soon as possible; as soon as you see the emergency/hazard. The earlier an evasive maneuver starts, the less steering input is needed to avoid the emergency/hazard.

Remember, the other lane is always the first choice over the shoulder. This is because the shoulder could be soft and give way, or could have debris that could damage your vehicle. What ever you do, do not freeze! You need to react and do it quickly.

Turn only as much as needed. Avoid over steering. Keep in mind that the larger the steering input, the greater the chance of a jackknife or rollover.

Turn as quickly as possible. Use hand-over-hand steering. Each turn of the wheel should be about 180 degrees. Placing your hands in the 9:00 and 3:00 positions while driving allows you to turn 180 degrees without letting go of the steering wheel.

Avoid braking while turning. Braking could cause the tractor and trailer wheels to lock-up, which can result in a loss of control.

Brake before turning. A firm braking application reduces your speed before turning. This allows your vehicle to turn more sharply and reduces the chance of a jackknife or rollover.

After making the evasive turn, be prepared to countersteer immediately. Smooth, quick countersteering is required to keep your vehicle from going outside its escape path; off the shoulder or into another lane of traffic. Begin to countersteer as soon as your vehicle clears the obstacle.

Though important at all times (and required by law in almost all states), the use of a seat belt is extremely important when involved in an evasive maneuver. A quick turn could cause you to slide out of the driver's seat, causing you to lose control of your vehicle if you are not wearing a seat belt.

Details of how an evasive maneuver is performed depend on the specific situation. These special maneuvers may be needed for emergencies involving:

- Oncoming vehicles;

- Stopped vehicles; and

- Merging vehicles.

Oncoming vehicle — Evade an oncoming vehicle by steering to the right. Sound your horn to get the driver's attention. This may startle the driver, causing him/her to correct his/her action. Don't steer to the left. Entering the left lane may cause a head-on collision.

Stopped vehicle — If the left lane is clear, turn into that lane. Swerving to the right could cause you to sideswipe a vehicle next to you. The height of your cab should allow you to see ahead to determine if the left lane is clear. Also be aware of what is next to your vehicle. Check your mirrors when determining if is safe to make a lane change.

If you're next to a clear shoulder, you may be able to go to the right if the left lane is blocked.

Stop and pay attention to this! If a driver is coming at you in your lane, and the other lane is now empty, your first thought might be to go into the other lane, but don't do that! If the other person, who may be sleeping, ill, or whatever, suddenly becomes aware of where they are, their natural reaction is going to be to go back into their own lane. If you are now there...head-on collision! If this happens to you go to the right, even if it means going off the road.

If you're in the middle lane of a multi-lane road, choose to steer into the lane which presents the least danger. Otherwise, evade to the right. It is better to force a vehicle onto the shoulder than to force another vehicle into oncoming traffic.

Merging vehicle — When another vehicle converges (merges) causing an emergency situation, sound your horn. This generally gets the other driver's attention, causing him/her to stop or correct his/her action. This can minimize the amount of evasive steering you will have to do. Remember, though a horn sounding may frighten or annoy another driver, it will communicate your presence, warning the other driver of a problem.

If the vehicle continues to converge (merge), swerve away from the vehicle. Don't try to steer behind it. If the other vehicle should stop, this would cause a collision.

Sounding your vehicle's horn may prevent a collision.

Never steer away from a converging (merging) vehicle if it puts you into the path of oncoming traffic. It's better to collide at an angle with the merging vehicle than to swerve into the path of an oncoming vehicle.

Emergency Stopping

Over application of the brakes will lock-up your vehicle's wheels, causing your vehicle to skid and possibly jackknife. You could also lose control of your vehicle. Proper emergency braking allows you to bring your vehicle to a stop within a minimum distance while allowing you to maintain control of the vehicle.

Proper braking allows you to stop your vehicle and maintain vehicle control.

Hey driver, you should always be looking for an "out." This is an escape route from the path you are currently traveling. You need to be planning ahead in case something happens directly in front of you. Only you can decide whether moving left, right, or just stopping is the best choice, but don't wait until something's right in front of you to make this decision.

There are two emergency braking techniques that can be used to safely stop your vehicle:

- Controlled braking; and

- Stab braking.

Controlled braking — In controlled braking, you maintain a steady pressure on the brakes, applying them just short of lock-up. Keep in mind that it is difficult to precisely anticipate the point of lock-up. Developing this skill requires practice in the vehicle you're operating.

Stab braking — When stab braking, fully apply the brakes. Then release the brake pedal partially when the wheels lock. Applying the brakes achieves maximum braking. Releasing or backing off the brakes, avoids a skid. When the wheels roll again, reapply the brakes. Make sure you allow time for the wheels to roll again between each stab. Reapplying the brakes too quickly will cause a skid. Repeat the stab braking sequence until your vehicle has slowed enough for a safe stop or turn maneuver.

Off-Road Recovery

Don't be afraid to use the shoulder if you have to. Just remember, it may be soft so hold on to the steering wheel tightly, make gradual movements, and return to the highway as soon as it is safe to do so. Remember, going off the road should be your LAST choice. It may be safer to hit that deer or tire than to swerve and lose control.

In many emergencies, the roadside provides the best escape path. As previously stated, the use of the roadside is better than colliding with another vehicle.

Drivers are often fearful of leaving the roadway. Many fear that an accident/crash will be the result of their using the roadside for an evasive maneuver. The fact is that many of the reported roadside crashes are the result of fatigued or impaired driving. Keep in mind that many evasive maneuvers are successful and are never reported.

Successful off-road recovery often requires leaving the roadway *immediately*. Too often drivers react too late. Most crashes/accidents that involve off-road recovery are due to incorrect technique.

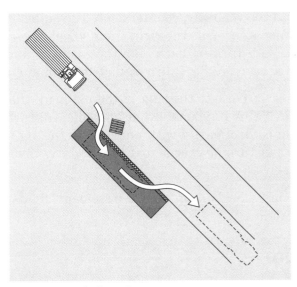

An example of off-road recovery.

Off-road recovery is generally safe when the roadside is wide enough to accommodate the vehicle and firm enough to support the vehicle.

General procedures — If you need to leave the road to avoid a collision, brake before turning, reduce speed as much as possible, and use controlled or stab braking to prevent loss of control. If you are operating a vehicle with an antilock braking system (ABS), keep braking until a safe speed is achieved.

Steering control is important. Avoid braking while turning as the vehicle is more likely to skid during braking, unless you have full ABS. With full ABS you can brake and steer at the same time without losing control of your vehicle.

Minimize turning. Keep one set of wheels on the pavement if possible. This will aid in traction and help you maintain control. Maintain as straight a course as possible. Remember, each turn creates the danger of a skid.

If the roadside is clear, fight the tendency to return to the roadway. Grasp the steering wheel firmly and concentrate on steering.

Stay on the roadside until your vehicle comes to a complete stop. Allow engine compression to slow and help stop the vehicle. Apply your brakes only after speed has been reduced. When the situation has passed, signal and check your mirror before returning to the travel lane.

If the roadside is blocked by a parked vehicle, sign, or other obstacle, you'll need to return to the road more quickly. If this happens, allow your vehicle to slow as much as possible before returning to the road. Then turn the steering wheel sharply toward the roadway. Attempting a gradual return to the roadway can cause you to lose control of your vehicle. Turning sharply allows you to determine the point of return to the road and allows you to countersteer.

Upon returning to the roadway, countersteer. Turn quickly in the direction of the roadway. Turn as soon as the right front wheel (steering axle) rides up onto the surface. Both turning back onto the roadway and countersteering should be executed as a single, integrated steering maneuver.

Often, if a truck is too close to the edge of the roadway, the wheels will drop off the pavement. If this happens, avoid immediate return to the roadway. You can maintain control easily with one side of the rig on the pavement. The vehicle may overturn or veer across the roadway if you try to return to the road too quickly.

When your vehicle's wheels drop off the pavement, follow the same procedure as off-road recovery.

Brake Failure

A well-maintained brake system rarely fails completely. Despite this, brake failures do occur. The result, a vehicle that is not under your control. Like all other emergency situations, keeping your cool is key to bringing your vehicle under control in this situation.

Causes — There are four common causes of brake failure:

- Loss of air pressure;

- Air blockage;

- Brake fade; and

- Mechanical failure.

Loss of air pressure — A warning buzzer will sound and/or a light will illuminate on the instrument panel when air pressure is too low. Stop immediately. Continued loss of air pressure could cause your brakes to completely fail. This will lock up your brakes and not allow your vehicle to move.

Your brakes should apply automatically when air loss reaches a critical level (between 20-40 psi). This happens when there is still enough air in the system to stop your vehicle. Do keep in mind that even when everything works as designed, air loss could happen too quickly, and the air could be exhausted before the vehicle is stopped. Also, the independent trailer brake valve won't activate the trailer brakes, as they also depend on the air system.

The brakes will activate automatically on a vehicle equipped with spring-loaded parking brakes when air pressure fails. This will generally bring the vehicle to a stop, unless it is on a steep grade.

1. **Air blockage** — A blockage can prevent air from reaching the brakes. This is commonly caused by water freezing in the air system or dirt through the glad hands.

2. **Brake fade** — On long downgrades, brakes may overheat and fade. The brakes will lose their ability to stop wheel rotation. The brakes won't cool quickly.

3. **Mechanical failure** — Brake failure can result from a failure in the mechanical linkage. Rarely are all brakes affected at once. Usually, in this situation, the vehicle can be stopped.

General procedures — The following steps should be followed if your vehicle's brake system fails:

1. **Downshift** — If on a relatively flat road, putting a vehicle into a lower gear will help to slow it down. Continue to downshift until your vehicle has slowed to a point that you can apply the parking brake. Do not try to downshift if you are on a downgrade.

2. **Escape route** — While slowing your vehicle, look for an escape route. A safe escape route may include an open field, side street, or escape ramp. Turning uphill is another way to slow and stop your vehicle. If you do use a hill to slow your vehicle, make sure it doesn't start rolling backward after stopping by applying the parking brake.

Downgrade procedures — If your vehicle's brakes fail on a downgrade, you will have to look outside your vehicle for something to help slow and stop. One option is the use of an escape ramp. Escape ramps are intended to safely stop a runaway vehicle. Escape ramps use a soft material such as gravel or sand to slow and stop a vehicle.

If an escape ramp isn't available, an open field or side road that is flat or turns uphill are options.

Make a move to slow your vehicle as soon as you are aware that your brakes aren't working. The longer you wait, the greater the vehicle's speed and the harder it is to stop.

Blowouts

The term "blowout" refers to a sudden loss of tire inflation. Blowouts can result from worn tires, cracks in the tire casing, or damage from debris, potholes, or nails. Remember, a careful pre-trip inspection can prevent blowouts caused by wear.

Don't kid yourself driver. Blowouts with a big rig, unlike what you see in the movies, rarely cause the vehicle to go out of control. Don't expect to go flipping over and over if your tire blows, just because you saw that happen in your favorite movie the night before! Keep a firm grip on the steering wheel and pull off the road as soon as you can safely do so. Flat tires (blowouts) are more of a nuisance than a major accident, if you just pay attention to what you're doing.

A careful pre-trip inspection can help prevent blowouts.

A blowout of a front tire disrupts steering and can cause the vehicle to veer in the direction of the blowout. With a rear tractor tire blowout, you may feel the rear of the tractor slide from side-to-side. A trailer tire blowout is harder to detect. You may hear the tire blowing out, see it in your mirrors, or you may experience some difficulties in handling the vehicle.

The sooner you are aware of a tire blowout, the more time you have to react. The major signs of tire failure are:

- Sound;

- Vibration; and

- Feel.

Sound — The loud bang of a blowout is an easily recognizable sign. Any time you hear a tire blow, assume it is one of your vehicle's tires.

Vibration — If your vehicle thumps or vibrates heavily, it may be a sign that one of the tires has gone flat.

Feel — If steering feels heavy, it's probably a sign that one of the front tires has failed. At times, rear tire failure will cause a vehicle to fishtail or slide back and forth.

Procedure — There are five steps to follow to safely handle tire failure.

1. Be aware the tire has failed.

2. Accelerate to overcome drag.

3. Hold the steering wheel firmly. If a front tire fails, it can twist the steering wheel out of your hands.

4. Stay off the brake. Braking when a tire has failed can cause loss of control. Unless you're about to collide with something, stay off the brake until the vehicle has slowed down. Then brake gently, pull off the road, and stop.

5. After stopping, get out of the vehicle and check all tires. If one of your dual tires goes, a visual check may be the only way to discover this problem.

Summary

In this chapter, you have learned about the importance of properly executing emergency maneuvers including evasive steering, emergency braking, and off-road recovery. You have also learned the common techniques to apply when dealing with brake failure and tire blowouts.

Emergency Maneuvers Quiz

Directions: Read each statement carefully and mark the response that best answers the question.

1. **The best way to avoid an emergency is to prevent it from happening in the first place.**

    A. True

    B. False

2. **Attempting to stop provides a better chance of avoiding a collision than evasive steering.**

    A. True

    B. False

3. **The best way to evade an oncoming vehicle is by:**

    A. Braking hard

    B. Steering to the left

    C. Steering to the right

    D. All of the above

4. **_____ braking are two emergency braking techniques that can be used in an emergency situation.**

    A. Jacking and chasing

    B. Controlled and stab

    C. Steer and countersteer

    D. All of the above

5. **Successful off-road recovery often requires leaving the roadway immediately.**

    A. True

    B. False

6. **A common cause of brake failure is:**

    A. Loss of air pressure

    B. Brake fade

    C. Mechanical failure

    D. All of the above

7. **When air is low in a vehicle's brake system, a warning buzzer or alarm should sound.**

    A.   True

    B.   False

8. **If your vehicle's brakes fail you should:**

    A.   Find an escape route

    B.   Increase the vehicle's speed

    C.   Jump from the vehicle

    D.   All of the above

9. **A front tire blowout can disrupt steering.**

    A.   True

    B.   False

10. **If a tire fails, you should:**

    A.   Hold the steering wheel firmly

    B.   Stay off the brake

    C.   After stopping, check all of the tires

    D.   All of the above

General Knowledge CDL Pre-Test

Read each question carefully and select the most correct answer.

1. **Which of the following statements about backing a commercial vehicle to a dock is NOT true?**

    A. Since you can't see behind you, you should back slowly until you bump the dock

    B. Use a helper and communicate with hand signals

    C. You should always back toward the driver's side when possible

    D. Both A and C

2. **As alcohol begins to build up in the body, which of the following is affected first?**

    A. Muscle control

    B. Coordination

    C. Kidney control

    D. Judgment and self-control

3. **Which of the following is true concerning cold weather driving?**

    A. Exhaust system leaks are not of concern during cold weather

    B. If the temperature is below 32 degrees Fahrenheit, the engine cannot overheat

    C. Using bleach on tires will provide increased traction

    D. You should use windshield washer fluid which contains an anti-freeze

4. **Placarding, the use of hazardous material placards and labels, is an example of:**

    A. Containment

    B. Controlling the hazardous materials risk

    C. Communication

    D. All of the above

5. **Controlled braking is used when:**

    A. The goal is to keep the vehicle in a straight line while braking

    B. You must stop as quickly as possible

    C. Is only used with hydraulic brakes

    D. Is only used when the vehicle is equipped with anti-lock brakes

Chapter 18

Skid control & recovery

OBJECTIVES

Upon completion of this chapter, you should have a basic understanding of:

❑ The factors that affect vehicle control

❑ The major causes of skids

❑ Common types of tractor-trailer skids, how they are caused, and prevention

❑ Skid recovery technique

Introduction

Put simply, a skidding vehicle is an out of control vehicle. It is much easier to prevent a skid than to correct a skid. This chapter will address what causes a vehicle to skid, types of vehicle skids, and techniques for safely dealing with the situation.

A skidding vehicle is an out of control vehicle.

Skid Dynamics

Factors that affect vehicle control include traction, wheel load, and force of motion. If there is an imbalance among these vehicle control factors, a skid will occur.

1. **Traction** — Traction is the grip your tires have on a road surface. Traction plays a part in determining how much control you have over your vehicle. If traction is poor, control of your vehicle is poor which can lead to a skid.

2. **Wheel load** — Wheel load is the downward force of weight on a wheel. Weight of the vehicle and load distribution determine wheel load. Keep in mind the fact that although wheel load can increase downward force and the amount of tire tread on the road, this may not improve traction.

3. **Force of motion** — Force of motion is determined by the weight and speed of the vehicle. The heavier the vehicle and its cargo, and the faster it travels, the greater the force. Speeding up, braking too quickly, or changing direction too quickly can affect the force of motion.

Causes of Skids

The major causes of skids include overbraking, oversteering, and overacceleration.

Overbraking — Overbraking is braking too hard and locking up the vehicle's wheels.

> Stop driver! Did you get that? A skidding vehicle is an out of control vehicle. Don't kid yourself in thinking that if you "survive" a skid, that means you kept your vehicle under control. If your vehicle was under control, you wouldn't have gotten into a skid in the first place!

Oversteering — Oversteering is turning the wheels more sharply than the vehicle can turn.

Overacceleration — Overacceleration is supplying too much power to the drive wheels, causing them to lose traction.

The most common skid is one in which the rear wheels of the tractor lose traction due to excessive braking or acceleration. Skids caused by overacceleration most often occur on slippery surfaces, rain, ice, or snow.

Tractor-Trailer Skids

Tractor-trailer skids are classified based on what occurs during the skid. There are four major kinds of skids:

- Trailer jackknife;

- Tractor jackknife;

- Front wheel skid; and

- All-wheel skid.

1. **Trailer jackknife** — Overbraking or oversteering can cause a trailer jackknife. When a trailer jackknife occurs, the trailer's tires are locked, causing it to skid.

   When overbraking, the trailer will continue to move forward at a higher speed than the tractor. Not being able to move forward, it will slide around.

   When taking a curve too fast for surface conditions, the rear of the trailer may continue in the same direction as it was originally heading while the tractor and the front of the trailer turn.

Pay attention driver! This is serious stuff. You might of thought it was fun to slide around in your car or pickup when you were a kid, but there's nothing fun about losing control of 80,000 pounds of vehicle going down the highway. When conditions start getting right for a skid to happen you need to be aware of even the slightest change in handling. If not, you may be dancing in circles with an 80,000 pound partner...not a pretty picture.

Face it driver. You're in this mess because you made a mistake! Skids don't just happen, they happen because of driver error. The best thing you can do once you get into a skid is stay calm, remember what you learned, and try to get out of it. Then, learn from your mistake!

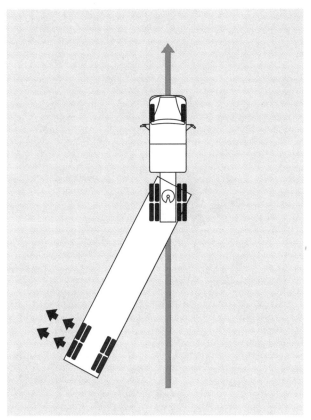

A trailer jackknife.

To prevent a trailer jackknife:

- Inspect your air system, and check brake adjustments;

- Adjust your speed to suit conditions;

- Read the road ahead;

- Avoid braking in curves (brake before entering the curve); and

- Avoid hard braking.

2. **Tractor jackknife** — A tractor jackknife occurs when the drive wheels lose traction. This can be caused by wheel lock-up or over-acceleration. In this situation, the drive wheels attempt to take over the front wheels, causing the rear of the tractor to swing out. The tractor follows the path of least resistance while the trailer continues in its original direction. Then, as the trailer pivots, it pushes the rear of the tractor outward, resulting in a jackknife.

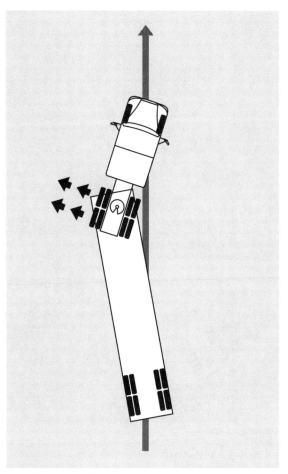

A tractor jackknife.

To prevent a tractor jackknife:

- Avoid overbraking, overacceleration, and sudden downshifts;

- Load your cargo properly, making sure it is secure; and

- Pay special attention to the brake system and tire tread when performing your pre-trip inspection.

3. **Front wheel skids** — Front wheel skids are caused by reduced front wheel traction. Reduced front wheel traction can be caused by an excessive load on the fifth wheel, lack of tread on the front tires, hydroplaning, oversteering, or brake system malfunction.

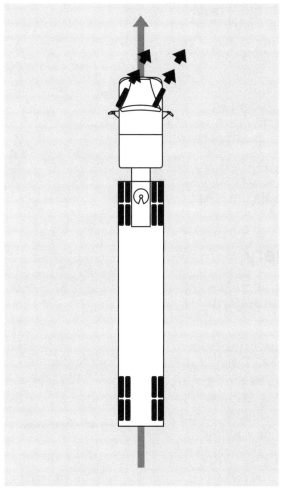

A front wheel skid.

A good inspection of the following vehicle components can aid in preventing front wheel skids:

• Tires;

• Front wheel alignment;

• Suspension system; and

• Fifth wheel lubrication.

A reduction of vehicle speed on wet or slippery pavement can also help in preventing skids.

4. **All-wheel skids** — In an all-wheel skid, all wheels are locked. Friction/ traction changes from rolling to sliding as the wheels are not turning. Usually, during an all-wheel skid, your vehicle continues in a straight line in spite of your efforts to steer. The main cause of this is overbraking on slippery surfaces.

The best way to prevent an all-wheel skid is by avoiding excessive speed and braking, especially on slippery surfaces.

Skid Recovery

The following technique can be used to recover from the majority of tractor skids.

1. **Stop braking or accelerating** — Disengage the clutch and steer. If you have an automatic, shift it into neutral. This allows the drive wheels to roll again, keeping them from sliding any further.

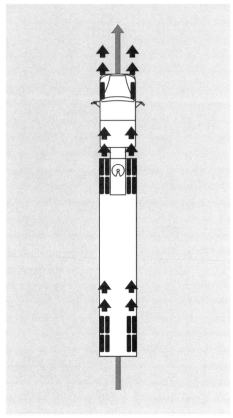

An all-wheel skid.

2. **Turn quickly** — When your vehicle begins to slide sideways, quickly steer in the direction you want the vehicle to travel.

3. **Countersteer** — As your tractor turns back on course, it has the tendency to keep turning. Countersteering prevents your vehicle from skidding in the other direction.

Once your vehicle is again traveling in a correct path, you can use your brakes to stop. A light, steady application is the preferred technique.

Front wheel skids — Most front wheel skids are caused by driving too fast for conditions. Other causes include lack of tread on the front tires and improper loading of cargo (not enough weight on the front axle).

In a front wheel skid, the front end tends to go in a straight line regardless of how much you turn the steering wheel. On a very slippery surface, you may not be able to steer around a curve or a turn.

When a front wheel skid occurs, the only way to stop the skid is to let the vehicle slow down. Stop turning and do not brake hard. Slow down as quickly as safely possible.

Just a note here...Even though an all-wheel skid may result in your vehicle staying in a straight line, it seldom remains in the same direction. What I mean is that it may not jack-knife, but it usually won't continue straight forward either. Slope of the road, varying weight on each tire, tire pressure, and brake adjustment all play into the direction your vehicle may be headed. Let's face it. It doesn't matter how many wheels you lock up, a skid just isn't fun!

Summary

In this chapter, you have learned about the causes of skids and skid prevention. You have also learned about the common techniques used to recover from a skid.

Skid Control and Recovery Quiz

Directions: Read each statement carefully and mark the response that best answers the question.

1. **The factors that affect vehicle control include friction, wheel load, and forces of motion.**

    A. True

    B. False

2. **The major causes of skids include:**

    A. Overbraking

    B. Overacceleration

    C. Oversteering

    D. All of the above

3. **One way to avoid a trailer jackknife is by adjusting your speed to suit conditions.**

    A. True

    B. False

4. **Another way to avoid a trailer jackknife is by using a hard braking technique at all times.**

    A. True

    B. False

5. **A tractor jackknife occurs when the drive wheels lose traction.**

    A. True

    B. False

6. **To prevent a tractor jackknife, you should over brake and over accelerate when road conditions are icy or snowy.**

    A. True

    B. False

7. **Front wheel skids are caused by reduced front wheel traction.**

    A. True

    B. False

8. _____ can help in preventing front wheel skids.

   A. Use of hard braking technique

   B. Increasing speed on wet or slippery pavement

   C. Reducing speed on wet or slippery pavement

   D. None of the above

9. **In an all-wheel skid_____ of the vehicle's wheels are locked.**

   A. None

   B. About 3 to 5

   C. All

   D. None of the above

10. **The best way to recover from a skid is to:**

   A. Do nothing

   B. Stop braking, turn the steering wheel, disengage the clutch, and countersteer

   C. Brake hard, hold the steering wheel tightly, and engage the clutch

   D. None of the above

CDL General Exam Pre-Test

Read the question carefully and select the answer that is most correct.

1. **What is hydroplaning?**

    A. An emergency situation created when an aircraft must make an emergency landing on a highway

    B. Excessive heat built up in the radiator

    C. Something that only occurs at high vehicle speeds

    D. When your vehicle wheels lift off the roadway on a thin film of water

2. **It you are being tailgated you should:**

    A. Motion for the tailgater to pass you when it is safe

    B. Increase your following distance

    C. Turn your 4-way flashers on

    D. Slam on the brakes

3. **Which of the following conditions may produce a skid?**

    A. Driving too fast for conditions

    B. Over braking

    C. Over steering

    D. All of the above

4. **When fighting a fire, which is most correct?**

    A. Get downwind of the fire before using the fire extinguisher

    B. Get as close to the fire as possible

    C. Aim the fire extinguisher at the base of the fire

    D. Aim the fire extinguisher at the top of the fire

5. **When starting a commercial vehicle on level, dry pavement, it is not usually necessary to:**

    A. Apply the parking brake

    B. Use a slower acceleration

    C. Press on the accelerator while popping out the clutch

    D. Both A and C

Chapter **19**

Special rigs

OBJECTIVES

Upon completion of this chapter, you should be able to identify various types of special rigs and their unique operating characteristics and hazards, including:

❏ Multiple articulation vehicles (doubles, triples, and B-trains)

❏ Oversize, low-clearance, and high center-of-gravity vehicles

❏ Unstable loads (tankers and livestock haulers)

❏ Reefers (refrigerated trailers)

❏ Other special rigs

Introduction

A "special rig" is any combination vehicle that differs from the standard tractor and dry freight trailer with five axles and up to 18 wheels. This definition includes vehicles:

- That have more than one point of articulation (joints);

- That are over length, over height, over width, or over weight;

- That have very low ground clearance;

- That have a high center of gravity when loaded;

- That have load stability problems;

- That require special handling and permits, or

- That are used for certain special cargos.

Special rigs require special knowledge and skills to operate safely.

Most of the material covered in this manual is applicable to the operation of all tractor-trailer combinations, but special rigs can require special procedures. This chapter will describe the most common special rigs, their handling characteristics, and the special skills required to operate them.

(*Note:* Federal and state regulations often restrict operation of special rigs in some way. These restrictions should be well known to companies that use special rigs.)

Multiple Articulation Vehicles

Multiple articulation vehicles (also known as long combination vehicles) are those with several joints, or points at which two parts of the vehicle are joined. A typical tractor-trailer unit has only one joint, at the connection between the kingpin and fifth wheel. Multiple articulation vehicles, as the name implies, have two or more joints and include various types of doubles and triples.

Doubles — Doubles consist of a tractor and two semi-trailers, with the second trailer converted to a full trailer using a converter gear (a set of wheels with a fifth wheel, called a converter dolly). The converter dolly is connected to the first trailer by one or two drawbar(s) with an eye(s) connected to a pintle hook(s) on the back of the first trailer.

A dolly with a single drawbar (the most common type) is known as an A-dolly, and a rig equipped with an A-dolly is known as an **A-train** . A dolly with two parallel drawbars is called a B-dolly, and a rig equipped with a B-dolly is called a **C-train** (B-trains will be discussed later). Being equipped with two drawbars, a C-train eliminates the rear trailer's ability to rotate at the hitch point.

Is your head spinning yet? Nobody told you we were going to learn about trains did they? Well don't worry, this stuff is pretty straight forward. Just read through it, listen to what your instructor has to say, and get on-board!

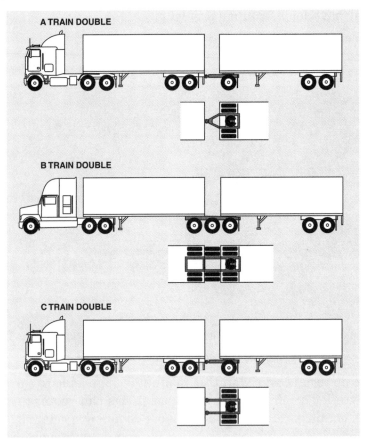

The A-train, B-train, and C-train.

While a standard tractor-trailer unit has one point of articulation or joint, doubles have three:

1. Front trailer kingpin and fifth wheel.

2. Pintle hook and eye.

3. Converter gear fifth wheel and kingpin of the second trailer.

Following are some defining characteristics and handling requirements of several types of doubles.

Western doubles — A western double is a standard A-train with two equal-length trailers, typically 24-31 feet long, and an overall length of 60-75 feet.

The trailers may be dry vans, tankers, flatbeds, or dumps.

There are several special handling concerns when pulling western doubles:

- Avoid backing. This typically difficult maneuver is made even more difficult with a double trailer unit not designed to be backed.

- Smooth steering is required. Jerking or aggressively moving the steering wheel is greatly magnified in the second trailer. (To create a picture in your own mind, think of a group of ice skaters playing "crack the whip.")

- The heaviest trailer must always be ahead of the lighter one. This adds stability for turning and braking.

- Don't apply brakes in a curve, because this will cause the second trailer to dip.

- The greater length of the rig requires the driver to plan further ahead. Additional time is needed for passing, changing lanes, and crossing intersections.

- It's very difficult to make tight turns with close coupled rigs.

- Bumps and potholes may cause the tops of the trailers to strike each other.

- On curves, be aware of the vehicle's tracking so you stay within your lane while going around the curve.

Doubles add steps to the normal coupling and inspection procedures. The drawbar and pintle hook must be properly in place and hooked. Safety chains need to be in place, electrical cords need to be attached, all air lines must be hooked up properly, and valves must be opened or shut as required. These items must be checked closely during pre-trip and en-route inspections as well.

Finally, before operating a western double, you'll need a Double/Triple Trailers endorsement on your commercial driver's license (CDL) and you'll have to learn the rules of the road.

Many states limit or prohibit the operation of doubles, depending on the weight and length involved. You may need to obtain state permits before driving in certain states.

Turnpike doubles — A turnpike double has longer trailers than a western double, generally 35-48 feet, with an overall vehicle length of around 100 feet or more. They typically are equipped with nine axles. Such rigs are often found on the turnpikes of the Eastern United States.

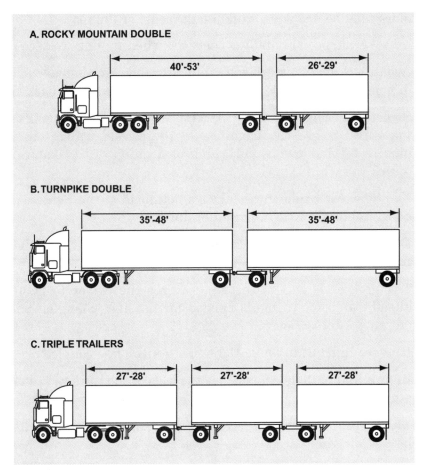

Rocky mountain and turnpike doubles and a triple trailer.

Typically, a high-output engine and multiple gear range transmission are required for turnpike doubles.

Other major characteristics, handling, and special requirements are essentially the same as for western doubles, if magnified somewhat by the additional length. However, a driver who pulls turnpike doubles does need to be aware of areas where their use is restricted, as well as special permits that are required. A company that regularly uses turnpike doubles should be aware of current federal and state regulations concerning their operation. A Double/Triple Trailers endorsement is required for operating a turnpike double.

Rocky mountain doubles — A rocky mountain double, as the name suggests, is generally used in the Western United States and is composed of a longer trailer in the front and a shorter trailer in the rear. Generally, the front (semi) trailer is 40-53 feet long, and the rear (full) trailer is 26-29 feet long. Overall length is generally 80-100 feet.

Other major characteristics, handling, and special requirements are essentially the same as for western doubles, though the long front trailer does require extra room for maneuvering. As with other doubles, a Double/Triple Trailers endorsement is required.

B-trains — A B-train is composed of two semi-trailers. On the first trailer, tandem rear axles are to the rear of the trailer body so the second axle is under the nose of the second semitrailer. A fifth wheel mounted above the second axle eliminates the need for a converter dolly. This also eliminates one articulation point normally found on a double rig. B-trains have two articulation points rather than three.

Trailer and overall length will vary depending on the geographical locations of B-train operations. Generally, there will be two 40-foot trailers or one 40-foot and one 27-foot trailer. B-trains are more common in Canada than in the United States. You also may see a lot of them in Michigan.

Again, other major characteristics, handling, and special requirements are essentially the same as for western doubles, with adjustments for trailer length. Backing is easier with B-trains, though it should still be avoided. A Double/Triple Trailers endorsement is required.

Requirements for Double/Triple Trailers Endorsement

Applicants for a Double/Triple Trailers endorsement will be expected to know:

- Procedures for assembly and hookup of the units.

- Proper placement of the heaviest trailer.

- Handling and stability characteristics, including off tracking, response to steering, sensory feedback, braking, oscillatory sway, rollover in steady turns, and yaw stability in steady turns.

- Potential problems in traffic operations, including problems the motor vehicle creates for other motorists due to slower speeds on steep grades, longer passing times, possibility for blocking entry of other motor vehicles on freeways, splash and spray impacts, aerodynamic buffeting, view blockages, and lateral placement.

Triples — Triple trailers, also known as triples, are becoming a much more common sight on America's highways, especially in the West. Triples are made up of three semi-trailers, with the second and third converted to full trailers using converter gear and connected, as with doubles, by drawbar and pintle hook.

There are three kingpin/fifth wheel connections and two eye/pintle hook connections. Trailers are typically 27-28 feet long, with overall lengths of up to 100 feet.

Triple trailers require drivers to have more advanced operating skills. Their length requires additional time and space for making turns, stopping, and performing other maneuvers. Some maneuvers, such as backing, should never be attempted. Areas and highways where triples are allowed are limited, and a Double/Triple Trailers endorsement is required. This and other regulatory information should be kept current by any company using triples in its operations.

Oversize Vehicles

Oversize-vehicle trailer types may include lowboys, drop frames, flatbeds, open-top vans, and extendable trailers. There can be a number of wheel and axle combinations depending on weight, size of cargo, and state regulations. Many oversize vehicles are equipped with outriggers to support oversized loads. Converter dollies may be attached to the trailer or tractor by fifth wheel and kingpin, or to the cargo itself to distribute weight over more axles and support longer loads.

Hang on driver! You may think those oversize loads look really cool going down the road and you want to jump right in and pull them. This is not a good place to start as it requires a lot of additional training. This could be a good goal to work toward but don't try and pull these big jobs right out of school. You may be very frustrated and could easily get involved in an accident or injury. Learn the basics first, then let your load grow as your knowledge grows!

Oversize vehicle.

Typically, the cargo that creates or makes necessary an oversize vehicle is over dimensional or overweight. This could include such cargo as power-plant equipment, industrial dryers, or heavy construction equipment. Oversize vehicles are usually operated with special permits and on designated highways. Requirements will vary depending on type of cargo, size, weight, and state regulations.

Driving an oversize vehicle generally requires special knowledge and skills, and may require a Double/Triple Trailers endorsement on your CDL.

Some examples of these types of trailers include:

- **Double-drop low bed with two axles** — The deck on this semi-trailer is at a standard flatbed height over the fifth wheel and dual rear axles, but drops close to the ground in between. These trailers are used to carry large, heavy loads. Outriggers may be used to extend the sides of the trailer to support wider loads.

- **Removable gooseneck low bed** — Typically equipped with 2, 3, or 4 axles, these low-bed trailers have a removable gooseneck, allowing the trailer to rest on the ground for easier loading and unloading of heavy equipment. Often used for front loaders, bulldozers, backhoes, etc. Outriggers may be used to extend the sides of the trailer.

- **Folding gooseneck low bed** — Similar to the removable gooseneck trailer above, but the gooseneck folds to the ground to allow loading and unloading

- **Hydraulic sliding axle trailer** — A sliding axle trailer, as the name implies, has rear axles that can slide forward and a bed that slopes to the ground, allowing for easier loading and unloading of heavy equipment.

- **Hydraulic tail low bed** — This type of trailer, with a fixed gooseneck, has a hydraulically operated ramp in the rear, allowing for the loading/unloading of heavy equipment.

- **Low bed with jeep dolly** — A low-bed semi-trailer can be attached to a multi-axle jeep dolly to increase the trailer's capacity. Part of the cargo rests on the dolly and part on the trailer.

Low-Clearance Vehicles

There are two basic kinds of low-ground-clearance vehicles:

1. **Double-drop frame** — Drops right behind the kingpin and right in front of the trailer axles, close to the ground.

2. **Single-drop frame** — Has a single drop located right behind the kingpin; only drops about half as much as a double-drop frame.

Low-clearance vehicles are designed to haul heavy, oversized cargo or to accommodate greater cubic capacity loads. Operation of low-clearance vehicles sometimes requires special licenses and permits, as well as restricted road use, depending on trailer type, size, weight of cargo, and individual state requirements. Special training and skills are required before operating these trailers.

Both types of trailers are designed with enough clearance behind the kingpin to prevent the back of the tractor from hitting the dropped portion of the trailer, as long as the unit is properly adjusted. The driver must ensure that the fifth wheel is back far enough to allow for adequate clearance.

Double-drop frames are especially susceptible to bottom clearance problems at curbs, railroad crossings, and other places where the pavement is uneven. Special skills and knowledge are required to operate these vehicles. A double-drop low bed is also known as a lowboy, while double-drop vans are often called furniture, warehouse, or electronics vans. Furniture vans are commonly used in the household goods moving industry, due to their larger load capacity. In addition, the dropped well allows for easier hand loading.

Furniture van.

Single-drop frames can handle taller loads than conventional trailers, and bottom clearance problems are not as significant as with double-drop trailers. A single-drop low bed is also called a drop-deck or step-deck trailer. As with a double-drop van, a single-drop van may also be known as a warehouse, furniture, or electronics van.

High Center-of-Gravity Vehicles

In a high center–of–gravity vehicle, the majority of the weight is high off the ground, so the greatest danger is in their tendency to tip, especially in curves. There are relatively few regulatory restrictions, other than those in place for regular commercial motor vehicles, but much greater care is required in vehicle handling. High center–of–gravity vehicles require the driver to plan ahead to avoid abrupt steering and braking. Examples of high center–of–gravity vehicles include dry bulk tankers, liquid tankers, livestock trailers, some reefers (refrigerated units), and some oversized vehicles.

Whenever feasible, this type of vehicle should be loaded with the heaviest material low in the trailer and forward (weight permitting) for improved handling.

Dry bulk tankers are generally cylindrical in shape and are used to haul dry bulk goods such as cement, limestone, flour, sugar, fly ash, etc. They are generally loaded through the top and unloaded through the bottom.

Dry bulk tanker.

Liquid tankers require many special skills to operate safely. Liquid surge is what makes handling difficult. To avoid rollover, drivers must accelerate and turn slowly, and avoid braking in corners. A Tank Vehicle endorsement is required on the driver's CDL. A Hazardous Materials endorsement may also be required, depending on the load. See Unstable Loads for more information.

Livestock trailers, also called cattle liners, have a flat or double-drop design and are used to carry live animals, including cattle, sheep, pigs, etc. See Unstable Loads for more information.

Unstable loads — The two most common unstable-load vehicles are liquid tankers and trailers designed for hauling livestock or carcasses. Liquids and animals both can contribute to the instability of a vehicle because of their propensity to shift about.

Liquid tanker.

Liquid tankers — Liquid tankers are generally semi-trailers, either oval, round, or occasionally even square in shape. There are cold tankers, hot tankers, and pressurized tankers. Often tankers are used to transport hazardous materials.

Liquid tankers vary in length. They may contain one compartment or several. They may or may not contain baffles. Handling can be difficult to master because of surging loads that make for an unstable vehicle.

Examples of liquid tankers include:

- Petroleum or chemical tankers;

- Acid tanks;

- Liquefied gas tanks (high pressure);

- Insulated tanks; and

- Food grade (milk, cooking oils, etc.).

Some specific training is necessary for tanker drivers depending on the type of trailer and cargo. Road use may be restricted and permits required, based on the type of trailer and cargo.

Driver inspections must include checking for leaks, checking all hoses, valves, fittings, the emergency valve release, and any special emergency equipment. Thereafter, the standard inspection procedures apply. See Chapter 4 for vehicle inspection details.

Livestock transport — Livestock transport includes hauling live cattle, hogs, horses, sheep, and a variety of other less common living freight. A semi-trailer with a flat floor or double-drop frame is used. Slots or holes in the sides allow livestock to breathe. Livestock trailers often have side doors in addition to, or instead of, rear doors.

Trailer length will vary and will have a fixed tandem or spread axle. Smaller animals such as pigs or sheep are often carried in trailers converted to accommodate two or three decks.

Livestock trailer.

Live cargo can create problems. Put simply, animals shift. You need to maintain a speed at which you can safely keep the vehicle under control. When stopping, tap brakes lightly to set the animals, then gradually apply brakes. Never attempt to haul livestock without proper training. Livestock hauling is unique in that the driver is responsible for the animals' health and safety en route.

Refrigerated trailers — Refrigerated trailers, or reefers, come in basically two types, nose mounts and belly mounts. Nose mounts have the refrigeration unit mounted on the upper front of the trailer. Belly mounts, as the name implies, have the refrigeration unit mounted under the trailer.

Reefer or refrigerated trailer.

Reefers are most often van- or box-type trailers. Some have racks or rails suspended from the roof, on which animal carcasses are hung, and which can make them unstable. Handling requires the same care as liquid tankers and livestock transport.

Others have separate compartments to keep some cargo frozen while other cargo is kept cool. Slotted floors allow for air or gas circulation. Floors, walls, and roofs are insulated.

Vegetables, fruit, meat, and other foodstuffs are common reefer cargo, as are some chemicals. Hanging meat is a particularly difficult cargo because it can swing and cause stability problems.

Refrigerated trailers have their own engines powered by diesel fuel or liquefied petroleum gas. Obviously, they also have their own fuel tank.

Special reefer inspection procedures include checking for holes in walls, checking ceiling and floor ducts, and inspecting the doors and door gaskets. Fuel, coolant, oil, and refrigerant levels must also be checked regularly. Trailer temperature must also be maintained to avoid cargo damage.

Note: Some states require reefers to stop at agricultural inspection stations.

Special Cargo Vehicles

Special Cargo Vehicles

A special cargo vehicle is any vehicle designed to haul primarily one particular type of cargo. Two of the most common types of special cargo vehicles are pole trailers and auto transporters.

Cargo securement requirements for these and other special cargo vehicles are addressed in Part 393, Subpart I of the Federal Motor Carrier Safety Regulations (FMCSRs).

Pole trailers — Pole trailers are designed to carry poles, steel girders, logs, and other types of long, narrow cargo. These trailers can be lengthened or shortened as needed to fit the load. Generally, a pole trailer is equipped with two U-shaped cradles (known as bunks) to hold the cargo in place. In some cases, the load itself becomes the body of the trailer; in others, a steel beam forms the body.

Pole trailer.

Auto transporters — Auto transporters generally hold 6-10 automobiles. Sometimes, a rack holds a car atop the tractor itself. These trailers are equipped with ramps in the rear to be used for loading and unloading. Auto transporters have a very low ground clearance. Overhead clearance may vary with each load of vehicles being transported.

Auto transporter.

Summary

Merely being able to identify a special rig is not enough to be able to operate one. Adequate driver training is essential for the operation of the special rigs discussed in this chapter. Each has its own unique operating characteristics and hazards, and each may require its own training, endorsements, and permits before being operated.

Special Rigs Quiz

Directions: Read each statement carefully and mark the response that best answers the question.

1. **Which of the following qualify as a special rig?**

    A. Western doubles

    B. Low-clearance vehicles

    C. Refrigerated trailers

    D. All of the above

2. **Which of the following is not a characteristic of a refrigerated trailer?**

    A. Reefers are most often van-type trailers

    B. Reefers have their own engines and fuel supplies

    C. Live cattle are often carried in reefer units

    D. The refrigeration unit may be at the upper front of the trailer or under the trailer

3. **A special rig is any combination vehicle that differs from the standard tractor and 48-53 foot dry freight van trailer with five axles.**

    A. True

    B. False

4. **What do liquid tankers and livestock trailers have in common?**

    A. Refrigeration units are used to cool the cargo

    B. Cargo movement can create serious handling problems

    C. Trailer length is always 45 feet

    D. A removable gooseneck allows for easy loading

5. **What's the difference between western doubles and turnpike doubles?**

    A. A western double does not require a special CDL endorsement

    B. The lead trailer in a turnpike double has a rear-mounted fifth wheel

    C. A turnpike double is longer than a western double

    D. A western double is longer than a turnpike double

6. **The greatest danger with high-center-of-gravity vehicles is their tendency to tip.**

   A. True

   B. False

7. **One danger associated with double-drop trailers is:**

   A. Their inability to carry heavy loads

   B. Low ground clearance

   C. Their tendency to tip

   D. Their length

8. **A double trailer rig in which the front trailer is 45 feet long and the rear trailer is 27 feet long would be known as:**

   A. Rocky mountain double

   B. Western double

   C. B-train

   D. C-train

9. **An A-train uses two drawbars to connect the rear trailer to the front trailer.**

   A. True

   B. False

10. **When hauling western doubles, you should always:**

    A. Place the lightest trailer ahead of the heaviest one

    B. Avoid backing

    C. Apply your brakes as you are going through curves

    D. Tap your brakes lightly to "set" the cargo before fully applying the brakes

General Knowledge CDL Pre-Test

Read each question carefully and select the most correct answer.

1. **Which of the following statements about causes of vehicle fires is true?**

   A. An overheated radiator is the most common type of vehicle fire

   B. Carrying a properly charged and rated fire extinguisher will help to prevent fires

   C. Under-inflated or flat tires will NOT cause a vehicle fire

   D. Poor trailer ventilation can cause cargo to catch fire

2. **"Over-the-counter" medication used to treat the common cold:**

   A. Is permissible as long as the dispatcher has given the O.K. to use it

   B. Can only be taken when driving during daylight hours

   C. Often can make you sleepy and should not be used while driving

   D. Is O.K. as long as you take just half a dose

3. **Can federal inspectors inspect your truck or bus?**

   A. Yes, and they have the authority to place you out-of-service

   B. Yes, but they have no authority to place you out-of-service

   C. Yes, but only at a port-of-entry

   D. No

4. **How many missing or broken leaves in a leaf spring will cause your vehicle to be placed out-of-service?**

   A. One-fourth of the total

   B. One-half of the total

   C. One-third of the total

   D. Any

5. **First offense for driving a CMV under the influence of alcohol or drugs will cause you to lose your CDL for at least:**

   A. Three years

   B. One year

   C. Two years

   D. Six months

Chapter 20

Preventive maintenance

OBJECTIVES

In order for a safe, efficient, and economical fleet to exist, vehicles need to be inspected and maintained on a regular basis. A driver's keen eye and attune ears are the first line of defense against a mechanical defect that can result in an accident, late delivery, or disabled vehicle.

Upon completion of this chapter, you should have a basic understanding of:

❑ A driver's role in vehicle inspection and maintenance

❑ Types of maintenance

❑ Maintenance requirements under the Federal Motor Carrier Safety Regulations (FMCSRs)

❑ Preventive maintenance as a cost deterrent

Introduction

Each motor carrier will determine how much maintenance a driver is expected to take part in. At some carriers, even the smallest of details are assigned to a mechanic, while at others, there will be an expectation that a driver is responsible for simpler, more routine tasks such as adding coolant or oil. Owner-operators may be expected to, and often do, possess substantial mechanical skills and do much of their own maintenance. It is important to note that a driver should never attempt to repair something he or she is not trained or skilled in.

A driver should report malfunctions as revealed through instruments, sight, sound, feel, smell, and vehicle operation characteristics. Drivers and mechanics must work together as a team to achieve safe, economic operation of vehicles.

Fleet-performed maintenance can be achieved through a variety of avenues, such as an in-house maintenance staff, a dealership, an independent garage, or a leasing company.

Preventive maintenance plays an important role in the operation of a safe and efficient vehicle.

Types of Maintenance

The three kinds of maintenance covered in this chapter are:

- Routine servicing;
- Scheduled preventative maintenance (PM); and
- Unscheduled maintenance and repair.

Routine servicing — There will be times when a driver will need to add oil or coolant, or drain moisture from fuel and air systems. Though these tasks are considered routine, if they are overlooked, it could lead to problems down the road.

Scheduled preventive maintenance — Most motor carriers follow some sort of preventive maintenance schedule for their vehicles. Preventive maintenance (PM) schedules can be arranged according to mileage, engine hours, or time.

You really need to get to know you truck, driver. If you take care of it, it will take care of you. Think about it...you will probably spend more hours in your truck going down the road then you do in your house, your personal vehicle, or with your family. Doesn't it make sense to take care of something you are so intimately connected to?

Routine servicing and scheduled preventive maintenance can go a long way in keeping your vehicle on the road.

Unscheduled maintenance — Unscheduled maintenance is an unexpected expense. Examples would include repairs that are noted on a driver's vehicle inspection report, and repairs due to accidents and breakdowns.

As a professional driver, you know your truck better than anyone. When you keep a watchful eye on its condition, you are ensuring safety for yourself on the road, as well as for other drivers traveling the highways with you. Fully participating in your company's PM effort can save the company money in the long run and can save you wasted time that results when you experience unexpected periods of downtime.

Worn, failed, or incorrectly adjusted components can cause or contribute to accidents. Preventive maintenance and periodic inspection procedures help to prevent failures from occurring while you are on the road.

A company's preventive maintenance and inspection program should recognize the following safety-related components as their failure directly affects vehicle control.

- Braking system;

- Steering system;

- Coupling devices;

- Tires and wheels; and

- Suspension system.

You are ultimately responsible to make sure that the vehicle you are driving is in safe operating condition. Thorough inspection reports assist in assuring this. You are also in the best position to detect vehicle deficiencies and refer them to maintenance for repairs. But you need to understand that some vehicle deficiencies cannot be detected by periodic preventive maintenance and inspection procedures.

As a professional driver, you can do the following to help keep your vehicle's components in good working order:

- Be proficient in detecting maintenance and repair needs as you travel, and refer them to the correct place for handling;

- Be expert at doing good pre-trip and post-trip inspections - check all pertinent components each time you do an inspection;

- Be certain that an annual vehicle inspection has been conducted on the vehicle; and

- Stop to check out any potential problems you think may be developing with your vehicle.

Don't continue with your trip until you are satisfied that everything is OK, and it's safe to do so. Federal and state regulations require that you not drive a vehicle unless you are satisfied that it is in safe operating condition.

Your driving behavior can help in getting the most out of your vehicle at the least cost. Now let's look at four major vehicle areas (brakes, tires, clutch, and engine). The way you drive can be a significant help in your company's preventive maintenance efforts.

Brakes — Your braking system is one of the "key" safety systems. Sudden failure can lead to loss of control and inability to recover. Progressive brake deterioration, such as brake shoe wear without corresponding adjustment, can be even more troublesome because it may appear harmless during normal driving, but may cause an accident during emergency braking situations. To help assure that your brakes are performing well:

Test your brakes for stopping performance before heading out on the highway;

- Assure yourself that your brakes are properly adjusted;

- Learn how to determine if the air system is operating correctly;

- Check to be sure that low air warning devices are functioning properly; and

- During a trip, before entering severe downgrades, stop and check your brake adjustment.

Having your brakes adjusted properly is one of your most important maintenance tasks. One thing you can do to keep your brakes functioning well is to check the slack adjusters. Some vehicles are equipped with automatic slack adjusters while others are adjusted manually. Checking slack adjustment is especially important if you do a lot of mountain driving. When you adjust, remember that each brake should be adjusted to the same degree so they are performing the same amount of work when they stop the vehicle.

Hey driver! While you're laying under your vehicle adjusting those brakes just before you go down that big mountain, take a look at all the brake parts. Is anything loose, broken, or missing? Better to find out now than when you push on the pedal and nothing happens.

Tires — The best way to extend the life of your tires is to watch your load weight. Know the load rating of the tires you have on your truck and the weight of the load you are carrying. As well as being illegal, driving overloaded is extremely hard on your tires. Exceeding the load rate on the tires can contribute to a blowout. And blowouts can cause accidents and injuries, as well as delay your schedule.

Reduce the wear and tear on your tires by making sure they are inflated correctly. Ideally, tire pressure should be checked when a tire is cold, but it can be checked during a trip. The heat generated by an under inflated tire and highway speeds can

Proper inflation reduces wear and tear on tires.

reduce a tire's tread life, or worse yet cause the tread to physically separate from the tire body, causing breaks in the body cords.

You should also make sure you are not overinflating your tires. Such a tire doesn't absorb road shocks well, and has more of a chance of being punctured or suffering other damage. Another problem with overinflated tires is traction. Tread doesn't make proper contact with the road surface, and traction is reduced.

Clutch — Good driving practices can also help extend the life of your vehicle's clutch. The clutch initially compensates for the difference in rotation between the running engine and a stopped vehicle. When you engage the clutch, you are putting 35 tons or more of equipment and cargo into motion. Proper specifications and good maintenance are important in keeping the clutch operating well. A clutch cannot last forever, but its lifespan can be extended if it is properly spec'ed for the vehicle, properly maintained, and properly treated during operation.

Your experience behind the wheel combined with good observation skills can help you avoid downtime when it comes to dealing with clutch problems. Keep your eyes open for problems with the clutch and report them as soon as possible to your maintenance department. Be as detailed as you can be in describing the clutch problem. In many cases, with early detection the problem can be easily handled, and at low cost. Here are some common problems you may encounter with your truck's clutch:

- Unusual noise in the clutch may mean you have been riding or slipping the clutch, but it also could mean poor lubrication.

- Clutch slippage can be a sign of worn facings or a lack of clutch pedal freeplay.

- Clutch drag can be caused by something as simple as poor adjustment or something as serious as a warped disc.

- There should be 1-2 inches of freeplay at the top of the clutch pedal. If not, it may need to be adjusted.

- Overloading can be a problem as well. If the clutch you are dealing with is not spec'ed for the weight you are carrying, burnout is likely, and extensive damage can happen.

To increase the lifespan of your clutch, follow some simple guidelines. Start out in the correct gear, engage the clutch properly, and don't ride the clutch or cause it to slip. Clutch problems can also be caused by improper shifting technique. Don't skip gears or shift up before the vehicle has reached adequate speed. These bad habits force the clutch to work extra hard and also generate excessive heat.

Engine — There are a couple of easy ways to improve the lifespan of your truck's engine. They are progressive shifting and good observation skills.

- **Progressive shifting** — This practice reduces equipment wear and also saves on fuel. Generally, it doesn't take any longer to bring a vehicle up to full speed with progressive shifting than it does with other shifting techniques.

  So what is progressive shifting? Normally you shift when you have accelerated up to the governor. In progressive shifting, however, you only accelerate enough to bring engine RPM up to peak torque where you can shift gears. Peak torque is where the engine develops maximum pulling power. This usually occurs in the mid-range of engine RPMs.

  In the lower gear ranges, you don't need to accelerate up to the governor before shifting. The major advantage of progressive shifting is that the engine doesn't work as hard as in standard shifting, thus extending life of both the engine and the drive train, and increasing fuel mileage.

- **Good observation skills** — Even the best of drivers occasionally have to deal with engine problems. One of the most obvious signs of engine trouble is oil consumption. If your oil consumption increases to a point where you are getting less than 200 miles per quart, you could very well be dealing with engine problems. Increased oil consumption is often accompanied by loss of power, increased fuel consumption, and reduced compression. In large diesel engines, oil is usually measured and replaced by the gallon, not the quart. Typically, if your engine is running correctly, you may use as little as one gallon every 12,000 to 15,000 miles.

Another indicator of trouble is injectors that become erratic. When you give the engine the throttle, the vehicle will act like it's choking or "missing". Many times plugging, poor spray patterns, or over fueling is the culprit. These can all be caused by malfunctioning fuel injectors.

Regulatory Requirements

Part 396 of the Federal Motor Carrier Safety Regulations (FMCSRs) addresses vehicle inspection and maintenance. The regulations address systematic maintenance, daily inspections, and annual or periodic inspections.

Systematic maintenance — Section 396.3 of the FMCSRs states that every motor carrier must systematically inspect, repair, and maintain all vehicles in its control or make provisions for systematic inspection, repair, and maintenance.

The term systematic means a regular or scheduled program to keep vehicles in safe operating condition.

It is up to the motor carrier to determine the time-frame for conducting systematic vehicle inspections as long as they are reasonable and systematic. They may be based on mileage, time, etc.

Pre-trip inspection — Section 396.13 of the FMCSRs states that before driving a motor vehicle the driver must:

- Be satisfied that the vehicle is in safe operating condition;

- Review the last vehicle inspection report (see post-trip inspection); and

- Sign the report, only if defects or deficiencies were noted by the driver who prepared the report, to acknowledge that the report has been reviewed and that there is certification that the repairs have been performed.

On-the-road inspection — Section 392.9 of the FMCSRs requires the driver to follow certain inspection rules while on the road.

The vehicle's cargo and load-securing devices must be checked within the first 50 miles of a trip. Any necessary adjustments must be made at this time.

After the first 50 miles of the trip the vehicle's cargo and load-securing devices must be reexamined:

- When the driver makes a change of duty status;

- After the vehicle has been driven for 3 hours; or

- After the vehicle has been driven 150 miles — whichever occurs first.

These on the road inspection rules do not apply to the driver of a sealed vehicle who has been ordered not to open the vehicle to inspect its cargo. Also, the rules do not apply to the driver of a vehicle that has been loaded in a way that makes inspection of the cargo difficult or impossible.

DRIVER'S VEHICLE INSPECTION REPORT
AS REQUIRED BY THE D.O.T. FEDERAL MOTOR CARRIER SAFETY REGULATIONS

CARRIER: _____

ADDRESS: _____

DATE: _____ TIME: _____ A.M. _____ P.M.
CHECK ANY DEFECTIVE ITEM AND GIVE DETAILS UNDER "REMARKS"

**TRACTOR/
TRUCK NO.** _____ ODOMETER READING _____

☐ Air Compressor	☐ Front Axle	☐ Safety Equipment
☐ Air Lines	☐ Fuel Tanks	Fire Extinguisher
☐ Battery	☐ Horn	Flags - Flares - Fusees
☐ Belts and Hoses	☐ Lights	Reflective Triangles
☐ Body	Head - Stop	Spare Bulbs and Fuses
☐ Brake Accessories	Tail - Dash	Spare Seal Beam
☐ Brakes, Parking	Turn Indicators	☐ Starter
☐ Brakes, Service	☐ Mirrors	☐ Steering
☐ Clutch	☐ Muffler	☐ Suspension System
☐ Coupling Devices	☐ Oil Pressure	☐ Tire Chains
☐ Defroster/Heater	☐ Radiator	☐ Tires
☐ Drive Line	☐ Rear End	☐ Transmission
☐ Engine	☐ Reflectors	☐ Trip Recorder
☐ Exhaust		☐ Wheels and Rims
☐ Fifth Wheel		☐ Windows
☐ Fluid Levels		☐ Windshield Wipers
☐ Frame and Assembly		☐ Other

TRAILER(S) NO.(S) _____

☐ Brake Connections	☐ Hitch	☐ Suspension System
☐ Brakes	☐ Landing Gear	☐ Tarpaulin
☐ Coupling Devices	☐ Lights - All	☐ Tires
☐ Coupling (King) Pin	☐ Reflectors/Reflective Tape	☐ Wheels and Rims
☐ Doors	☐ Roof	☐ Other

Remarks: _____
_____
_____
_____
_____
_____
_____
_____
_____

☐ CONDITION OF THE ABOVE VEHICLE IS SATISFACTORY

DRIVER'S SIGNATURE: _____

☐ ABOVE DEFECTS CORRECTED

☐ ABOVE DEFECTS NEED NOT BE CORRECTED FOR SAFE OPERATION OF VEHICLE

MECHANIC'S SIGNATURE: _____ DATE: _____

DRIVER'S SIGNATURE: _____ DATE: _____
ORIGINAL
© Copyright 2007 J. J. KELLER & ASSOCIATES, INC., Neenah, WI
USA • (800) 327-6868 • Printed in the United States

Driver's Vehicle Inspection Report

Post-trip inspection — At the end of each day's work on each vehicle operated, Sec. 396.11 of the FMCSRs requires the driver complete a written report (driver vehicle inspection report (DVIR)) covering the following parts and accessories:

- Service brakes including trailer brake connections;
- Parking brake;
- Steering mechanism;
- Lighting devices and reflectors;
- Tires;
- Horn;
- Windshield wipers;
- Rear vision mirrors;
- Coupling devices;
- Wheels and rims; and
- Emergency equipment.

On the report, the driver must identify the vehicle and list any defect or deficiency which could affect its safe operation or cause a mechanical breakdown. If the driver does not find any defects or deficiencies he/she needs to report that as well. In all cases, after completing the inspection, the driver must sign the report.

On two driver operations, only one driver needs to sign the report, provided both drivers agree with what is written in the report.

Before the vehicle can be operated again, any items listed as being defective or deficient that may effect the safety of the vehicle must be repaired. The following criteria must be met:

- The motor carrier must certify (on the report) that the defect or deficiency has been corrected or that correction is not necessary to safely operate the vehicle; and
- The motor carrier must retain the original copy of each vehicle inspection report and certification of repairs for at least three months from the date it was completed.

Also, there are post-trip inspection reporting requirements that you must follow if you are hauling intermodal equipment and discover a defect or deficiency. See Chapter 4 for complete details.

Roadside inspections — Section 396.9 of the FMCSRs is the regulation that provides agents of the Federal Motor Carrier Safety Administration (FMCSA) with the authority to perform inspections on your vehicle while in operation — being driven on a highway.

Drivers and their vehicles are subject to roadside inspections.

This regulation also authorizes these same agents to declare a vehicle "out of service" if they believe continued operation of the vehicle is likely to cause an accident or breakdown due to a safety-related defect or deficiency. If placed out of service, the vehicle cannot be operated again until any and all defects and deficiencies have been repaired. In addition, your company must not allow, permit, or require you to violate an out-of-service order. Fines for violating an out-of-service order range from $2,100-$3,750 for drivers, and $3,750-$16,000 for employers.

During the actual inspection of your vehicles during a roadside inspection, most states and provinces use the North American Uniform Out-of-Service Criteria, which was developed by the Commercial Vehicle Safety Alliance (CVSA). CVSA is the leading commercial vehicle enforcement organization in North America, including membership from enforcement agencies and industry representatives from Canada, U.S., and Mexico.

The Out-of-Service Criteria identifies critical vehicle inspection items and provides criteria for placing a vehicle out-of-service. No motor carrier shall require or permit any person to operate nor shall any person operate any motor vehicle declared and marked "out-of-service" until all repairs required by the "out-of-service notice" have been satisfactorily completed.

Pitfalls of Poor Vehicle Maintenance

If drivers do not communicate potential or visible defects to their motor carriers, they are adding to a very dangerous formula for catastrophe. Or, at very minimum, adding to their carrier's operational costs.

Breakdown costs include more than the parts and labor to get the vehicle up and running once again. An incapacitated vehicle may incur additional expense, such as:

- Cost of towing;
- Driver wages, meals, and lodgings when unable to drive;
- Cost of renting another vehicle;
- Late delivery charges;
- Lost customers; and/or
- Cargo transfer fee.

The cost of a breakdown includes more than just the part(s) needed to repair the vehicle.

Every minute a truck is in the shop or placed out of service, it is not being used to bring in revenue to a carrier. Sometimes the cost of a downed truck cannot always be quantified, as it includes phone calls, administrative time, and the like, all of which take from the profitability of a motor carrier.

If a defective part causes an accident, the costs incurred can include insur-ance deductibles, higher insurance rates, and a tarnished safety record for the carrier.

Summary

In this chapter, you have learned about the importance of preventive maintenance. Preventive maintenance, though an initial expense, can very easily be justified. Even if a breakdown, accident, or out-of-service order does not happen, a vehicle which is not well-maintained will not operate efficiently. Its cost per mile will eat into profits. In addition, a truck which does not stick to a strict preventive maintenance program will wear out sooner and may have to be replaced before its time.

Preventative Maintenance Quiz

Directions: Read each statement carefully and mark the response that best answers the question.

1. **The four major vehicle areas that a driver should keep an eye on include brakes, clutch, tires, and engine.**

    A. True

    B. False

2. **Under the pre-trip inspection requirements in Sec. 396.13 of the FMCSRs, a driver must:**

    A. Be satisfied that the vehicle is in safe operating condition

    B. Take the word of the previous driver of the vehicle that everything is working fine

    C. Complete an inspection sometime during the course of the day at the driver's convenience

    D. None of the above.

3. **Which is *not* true of a driver's vehicle inspection report (DVIR)?**

    A. It is completed as part of the post-trip inspection

    B. It is required under Sec. 396.11

    C. All defects must be listed and repaired before the vehicle is operated again

    D. Reports are kept for 30 days after the report is completed

4. **A pre-trip inspection only needs to be completed twice a week.**

    A. True

    B. False

5. **Out-of-service orders are suggestions, and a driver can drive the truck back to the terminal.**

    A. True

    B. False

6. **If preventive maintenance is not practiced:**

    A. It could result in greater mechanical damage to the truck

    B. It could result in an accident

    C. It will cost carriers more in the long run

    D. All of the above

7. **A driver should make all attempts to fix a mechanical problem, no matter his/her training.**

    A. True

    B. False

8. **Breakdown costs include:**

    A. Cost of parts and labor

    B. Missed utilization of the truck while in the garage

    C. Lost or dissatisfied customers

    D. All of the above

General Knowledge CDL Pre-Test

Read each question carefully and select the most correct answer.

1. **Shifting gears properly is important because:**

   A. Doing so helps you maintain control of the vehicle

   B. It helps to keep the oil flowing through the crankcase

   C. It keeps the radiator cool

   D. It keeps the engine at the proper operating temperature

2. **You are traveling down a long grade and you notice your brakes are not working as well as they had been. You should:**

   A. Continue to the bottom of the grade and then stop to check your brakes

   B. Stop as quickly as you can

   C. Downshift one or two gears and continue

   D. Begin pumping your brake pedal

3. **Water will extinguish which of the following fires?**

   A. Electrical

   B. Diesel fuel

   C. Gasoline

   D. Tire

4. **Convex (curved) mirrors will:**

   A. Make objects appear to be larger than they really are

   B. Make objects appear to be smaller than they really are

   C. Make objects appear closer and larger than they really are

   D. Show a wider area than flat mirrors

5. **The Driver's Manual says you should use your horn:**

   A. To make the deer standing alongside the road to move further away

   B. When a car gets in the way

   C. If it may help you to avoid a collision

   D. When you begin to change lanes

Chapter 21

Diagnosing and reporting malfunctions

OBJECTIVES

Upon completion of this chapter, you should have a basic understanding of:

❑ The diagnosis and reporting of vehicle malfunctions

❑ Troubleshooting

❑ Procedures for reporting vehicle malfunctions

Introduction

In this chapter, you will learn about the importance of diagnosing and reporting malfunctions as well as your role in troubleshooting. You should understand that you know your vehicle best. Diagnosing and reporting problems while they are small/minor can keep you and your vehicle on the road and in service.

Diagnosing and Reporting Malfunctions

Driver awareness — You should be aware of your vehicle's condition at all times. Your ability to spot a potential problem can help in diagnosing a vehicle malfunction. As well as being alert for warning lights and alarms/ buzzers, pay attention to your senses. Sights, sounds, smells, and/or the feel of the vehicle can indicate a potential problem. Report to your company anything that doesn't seem quite right and have it checked out.

> **Sight** — Look at your vehicle's gauges. Know what the proper readings are and what readings indicate a potential problem. Watch for defects in all vehicle components when performing vehicle inspections.
>
> **Sound** — Listen for unusual or abnormal equipment sounds. Squeaks, squeals, thumps, and rattles can be the first sign of vehicle malfunction.
>
> **Smell** — Be aware of unusual smells including burning rubber, hot oil, or fuel.
>
> **Feel** — Be aware of vibration, swaying, or other movement that isn't normal for your vehicle.

Early detection — Catching a problem in the early stages, reporting it to your company, and having the problem checked out will save you and your company time and money. It's cheaper to do this than suffer a breakdown or accident.

Driver responsibility — As a professional driver, you are responsible for safely operating your vehicle. This responsibility includes reporting any problems with your vehicle to your company and making sure these issues are looked into.

Your responsibilities when it comes to actual maintenance will depend on the policy of the company you work for. Most companies expect you to fix simple problems, but do not expect or want you to make other repairs. Never attempt to fix a problem if you do not have the appropriate training, knowledge, or tools.

Hey driver, what color is your smoke? You might think this is an odd question, but just paying attention to the color of the smoke coming out of your stacks can tell you a lot about how your engine is running. So what color is your smoke? Is it blue...black...white? Know what these colors mean!

Mechanic responsibility — The mechanic is responsible for making sure your vehicle is in safe operating condition. When you report a problem with your vehicle, it should be checked out and appropriate repairs should be made (if applicable).

Driver and mechanic responsibility — Communication between a driver and mechanic is important. Your on-the-road observations can go a long way in diagnosing vehicle problems. Working together can aid in making sure a vehicle is repaired properly and in an efficient manner.

Note: Many companies have specific policies and procedures dealing with driver and mechanic communication. This helps in assuring that all parties have the same understanding of the vehicle problem.

Driver and mechanic communication is important.

You don't need to be a mechanic, but you do need to know what you can fix and what you need help with. Do you know what tools you should carry? What about pieces of hose, clamps, fuel filters, JB Weld, duct tape, electrical tape...the list goes on, and it's important that you know what to carry in your truck. There's a troubleshooting guide in the back of this book. Check it out. Make a list of what you can carry based on some of the problems and quick-fixes listed there, and help keep yourself rolling!

Troubleshooting

Vehicle knowledge — Knowing your vehicle can go a long way when it comes to troubleshooting. This includes knowing the vehicle's systems, where they are located, and how they work (both independently and together).

Warning signs — In many cases, a vehicle will give you clues that there could be a problem. Some things to watch for that may signal a possible problem include inconsistent/erratic gauge readings, unusual sounds (rattling, whining, grinding, etc.), or a sharp drop in fuel mileage.

Detection of problems — If you notice a problem, stop your vehicle as soon as practical. If you can, try to identify the source of the problem. If the problem is one you can fix based on your knowledge/experience and company policy, do so. If you cannot fix it, report it to your company. Make sure you include a description of what you observed and how the vehicle acted/responded. Get mechanical help as soon as possible.

Reporting Requirements

Post-trip inspection — Section 396.11 of the Federal Motor Carrier Safety Regulations (FMCSRs) requires a driver to prepare and sign a written driver vehicle inspection report (DVIR) at the completion of his/her day's work on each vehicle he/she operates. The driver is to indicate any problems with the vehicle on this report.

The company is then required to have the problem checked out and determine whether repairs are warranted. The mechanic who checked out the problem must then certify on this report that either the problem was corrected or that no corrective action was necessary.

When the driver next operates this vehicle, he/she must review the action(s) taken and sign the report indicating the needed repairs were done.

Though this report is required by the regulations, it should not replace direct communication with your company and the mechanic who will be doing any necessary repairs. Knowing what you observed, in addition to what you indicate on the DVIR will help in determining your vehicle's problem.

Any vehicle problems must be noted on the DVIR.

Summary

In this chapter, you have learned about the importance of diagnosing and reporting malfunctions, your role in troubleshooting, and reporting requirements. Remember, you know your vehicle best. Diagnosing and reporting problems while they are small/minor can keep you and your vehicle on the road and in service. Waiting until the problems are large/major can take you off the road for long periods of time, costing both you and your company time and money.

Diagnosing and Reporting Malfunctions Quiz

Directions: Read each statement carefully and mark the response that best answers the question.

1. **Your ability to diagnose a vehicle malfunction can prevent a potential problem, reduce downtime, and enhance safety.**

   A. True

   B. False

2. **Abnormal _____ can indicate a problem with the vehicle.**

   A. Smells

   B. Sounds

   C. Feel

   D. All of the above

3. **As a professional driver, it is not your responsibility to report vehicle problems.**

   A. True

   B. False

4. **Communication between a driver and mechanic is important.**

   A. True

   B. False

5. **_____ may signal a problem with your vehicle.**

   A. A slippery highway

   B. An increase in fuel mileage

   C. Unusual sounds

   D. All of the above

6. **If a vehicle problem is one you can fix based on your knowledge/ experience and company policy, you should do so.**

   A. True

   B. False

7. **A driver vehicle inspection report (DVIR) is only required when your vehicle has a problem.**

   A. True

   B. False

8. **Completing a DVIR can replace direct communication with your company and the mechanic who will be doing any necessary repairs on your vehicle.**

    A. True

    B. False

CDL General Knowledge Pre-Test

Read each question carefully and select the most correct answer.

1. **Which of the following is true about tire pressure?**

    A. As temperature increases so does air pressure in the tires

    B. It is not necessary to check tire pressure during a pre-trip inspection

    C. In warmer weather it is best to let out some of the air in the tires to reduce pressure

    D. All of the above

2. **Which of the following happens when a tire blows at highway speed?**

    A. You will experience an immediate and dramatic drop in speed

    B. You will feel a vibration

    C. You will hear a hissing sound

    D. The low air pressure signal device will come on

3. **What is the purpose of a pre-trip inspection?**

    A. To add an additional 15 minutes of time to your log book

    B. To avoid being cited by a law enforcement official

    C. To make sure the vehicle is safe to operate

    D. To see if any additional 1,000lbs of freight can be added to maximize revenue

4. **When you see a hazard in the roadway in front of you, you should:**

    A. Steer and countersteer around it

    B. Stop quickly and get off the roadway if possible

    C. Stop quickly, stay in the roadway, set your reflective triangles, and go to the rear of your vehicle to flag down traffic

    D. Turn on your 4-way flashers or flash your brakes lights to warn others

5. **At what Blood Alcohol Concentration (BAC) will you be placed out-of-service for 24 hours?**

    A. .04% or higher

    B. .03% or higher

    C. Any detectable amount

    D. 1.0% or higher

Chapter 22

Handling cargo

OBJECTIVES

Upon completion of this chapter, you should have a basic understanding of:

- ❏ The importance of properly handling cargo
- ❏ The principles and methods of cargo securement
- ❏ The principles of weight distribution
- ❏ Safe loading responsibilities
- ❏ Common tools used to load/unload a vehicle

Introduction

The proper handling of cargo is just one of many tasks the professional driver faces on a daily basis. This chapter will address the importance of proper handling of cargo, cargo securement, and weight distribution principles.

The Importance of Proper Cargo Handling

As a professional driver, it is your job to safely and efficiently transport cargo to the customer, making sure it arrives on time and damage-free.

Each year, cargo claims from damaged and lost freight cost the motor carrier industry over $200 million. Proper loading and securement of cargo can go a long way in making sure you don't contribute to this statistic.

Section 392.9 of the Federal Motor Carrier Safety Regulations (FMCSRs) addresses the basic requirements when it comes to inspection of cargo and cargo securement devices and systems.

The regulation states that a commercial motor vehicle may not be driven unless the load is properly distributed and adequately secured, and does not obscure your view.

You must examine the load and any load-securing devices within 50 miles of the start of the trip. The cargo and load-securing devices must be reexamined periodically during the trip and necessary adjustments to load-securing devices must be made.

Periodic examinations must be made:

- When you make a change of duty status;

- After the vehicle has been driven for 3 hours; or

- After the vehicle has been driven for 150 miles — whichever occurs first.

Note: You are not required to check the cargo on a sealed load that is not to be opened, or if checking the cargo is impractical.

Your responsibility for the cargo starts as it is being loaded onto your vehicle and continues until delivery. Follow applicable regulations, including state and local requirements in the areas where you are traveling.

Principles and Methods of Cargo Securement

As cargo is being loaded, you need to take steps to secure it. Shifting cargo can be easily damaged and can also pose a safety hazard. Securement is required under Part 393, Subpart I of the FMCSRs.

A commercial motor vehicle must be secured to prevent cargo from shifting upon or within the vehicle. It must be loaded, equipped, and secured to prevent the cargo from leaking, spilling, blowing, or falling from the vehicle.

Hey driver! The most important thing to remember about this whole chapter is that the freight (cargo) is YOUR responsibility as long as it is in or on your trailer. It's up to you to make sure it is loaded and secured correctly. If you don't like the way the freight is being loaded, stop the process and call your dispatcher! Waiting until everything is all loaded and the forklift operator has moved on to his or her next truck is not the time to complain about the load. Do it now!

Cargo securement devices and systems must be designed, installed, and maintained to ensure that the maximum forces acting on the devices or systems do not exceed the working load limit for the devices.

Aggregate working load limit — The aggregate working load limit of any securement system used to secure an article or group of articles against movement must be at least one-half times the weight of the article or group of articles.

The aggregate working load limit is the sum of:

- One-half of the working load limit of each associated connector or attachment mechanism used to secure a part of the article of cargo to the vehicle; and

- One-half of the working load limit for each end section of a tiedown that is attached to an anchor point.

Immobilization of cargo — Cargo must be firmly immobilized or secured. There are several methods and devices that can be used for cargo securement, such as blocking, bracing, dunnage, load locking bars, tiedown assemblies, and tarps.

Blocking and bracing — Blocking is a cargo securement procedure where you fit blocks snugly against the cargo's front, back, or sides to prevent the cargo from sliding. Normally, blocking is secured to the cargo deck or sides. Bracing (putting pressure on a piece of cargo to keep it in place) is generally used between cargo and the trailer ends or sides to keep an object stationary.

Dunnage — Dunnage is filler material used in the empty spaces between cargo. Dunnage keeps the cargo from shifting. Wood, cardboard, airbags, extra pallets, bubblewrap, and plastic are types of material used as dunnage.

Load locking bars — Load locking bars can be used vertically or horizontally. The bars have rubber feet that are placed against the vehicle walls or ceiling and floor. The bars are placed snugly against the cargo and then tightened with a jacking device until they are tightly wedged in place against the cargo.

Tiedown assemblies — When an article is not blocked or positioned to prevent forward movement by other means (other cargo, blocking devices, etc.) you may use tiedowns, such as belts, straps, chains, or ropes, to secure your cargo. It must be secured by at least:

- One tiedown for articles 5 feet or less in length, and 1,100 pounds or less in weight.

You need to know your equipment driver. Only you can determine what is safe and correct when securing a load so know your freight and what it takes to keep it safely on or in your trailer.

Locking bars help secure this load.

- Two tiedowns if the article is:

  - Five feet or less in length and more than 1,100 pounds in weight; or

  - Longer than 5 feet, but less than or equal to 10 feet in length, irrespective of weight.

- Two tiedowns if the article is longer than 10 feet and one additional tiedown for every 10 feet of article length, or fraction thereof, beyond the first 10 feet in length.

When using tiedowns:

- Always check the rated load limit of the tiedown to make sure it's the proper strength for your load.

- Before using, check the tiedowns for signs of wear or weakness. Don't use tiedowns that have been knotted or repaired.

- Place the tiedowns flat on the load and secure them to the vehicle using hooks, bolts, rails, rings, or other approved devices. The tiedowns should be tight against the load, but not so excessively tight that they damage the load.

- If the trailer you are using has rub rails, all tiedowns and other cargo securement components should be inboard of the rub rails whenever practical.

- Edge protection must be used whenever a tiedown may be subject to damage (abrasion or cutting).

- After use, store tiedowns in a clean, dry space.

The working load limit of a tiedown may be determined by using either the tiedown manufacturer's markings or by using working load limit tables. Working load limit tables are located in Sec. 393.108 of the FMCSRs.

Part 393, Subpart I also includes commodity-specific cargo securement requirements for items such as logs, dressed lumber, metal coils, paper rolls, concrete pipe, intermodal containers, automobiles, heavy equipment, crushed vehicles, roll-on/roll-off containers, and boulders. Consult the regulations for specific requirements before hauling any of these commodities.

Tarps — If you carry freight in an open cargo area, you may need to use a tarp. Tarps prevent loose material like sand, gravel, or salt from blowing or falling out of a vehicle. They can also be used to protect cargo from the weather. If you use a tarp, make sure it fully covers your load and is secured at all securing points. While traveling, check your mirrors frequently to make sure the tarp has not become loose, causing a hazard for you and/or others on the road.

Principles of Weight Distribution

Definitions — As a professional driver, it is your responsibility to make sure your vehicle is not overloaded. The following are some definitions of weight measurements you should know.

If you are not sure of your weight...scale the load! It only takes a few minutes and can save you time and money down the road.

Gross vehicle weight (GVW) — The total weight of a single vehicle, plus its load.

Gross combination weight (GCW) — The total weight of a powered unit, plus trailer(s), plus load.

Gross vehicle weight rating (GVWR) — The value specified by the manufacturer as the loaded weight of a single vehicle.

Gross combination weight rating (GCWR) — The value specified by the manufacturer as the loaded weight of a combination (articulated) motor vehicle.

Axle weight — The amount of gross weight that rests on any one axle.

Tire load — The maximum safe weight a tire can carry at a specified pressure. The rating is usually stated on the side of the tire.

Coupling device capacity — Coupling devices are rated for the maximum weight they can pull or carry.

Legal weight limits — Your vehicle must stay within legal limits. Federal requirements outlined in 49 CFR 658.17 are as follows.

The maximum gross vehicle weight (GVW) is 80,000 lbs. except where a lower GVW is dictated by the bridge formula.

The maximum gross weight on any one axle, including any one axle of a group of axles, or a vehicle, is 20,000 lbs.

The maximum gross weight on tandem axles is 34,000 lbs.

Vehicles are not allowed on Interstate highways if the gross weight on two or more consecutive axles exceeds the limitations prescribed in the Bridge Gross Weight Formula, described below.

$$W = 500\left[\frac{LN}{N-1} + 12N + 36\right]$$

W = the maximum weight in pounds that can be carried on a group of two or more axles to the nearest 500 pounds.

L = the distance in feet between the outer axles of any two or more consecutive axles.

N = the number of axles being considered.

This formula limits the weight on groups of axles in order to reduce the risk of damage to highway bridges. Allowable weight depends on the number of axles a vehicle has and the distance between those axles. However, the single- or tandem-axle weight limits supersede the Bridge Formula limits for all axles not more than 96 inches apart.

Note: Each state has its own weight limitations. Be aware of the regulations for the states you travel through.

It is your responsibility to make sure your vehicle is not over loaded.

Overloading — Overloading can adversely effect a vehicle's steering, braking, and speed control. An overloaded truck moves slowly on upgrades and can gain too much speed on downgrades. Stopping distance increases and brakes can fail if worked too hard.

Keep in mind that in bad weather or when traveling through a mountainous area, it may not be safe to operate at the legal maximum weight.

Top-heavy loads — The height of a vehicle's center of gravity is important for safe handling. A high center of gravity (heavy cargo on top or cargo piled too high) makes it easier for your vehicle to tip over. A high center of gravity is also dangerous when in a curve or when you have to swerve to avoid a hazard. Load your vehicle so the heaviest cargo is on the bottom and the lightest on top. Also, distribute cargo so it's as low as possible.

Weight balance — Poor weight distribution can make vehicle handling unsafe.

Too much weight on a steering axle can cause hard steering and cause damage to the steering axle and tires.

Under loaded front axles (cargo weight is too far to the rear) can make the weight on the steering axle too light to steer safely. Too little weight on the driving axles can cause poor traction. The drive wheels may spin easily.

Safe Loading Responsibilities

You are responsible for making sure your vehicle is loaded safely and legally. It must meet all cargo securement and weight distribution requirements.

Know what you are hauling and the amount you are hauling. Make sure the commodity and amount on your vehicle matches your bill of lading or shipping papers. Report any discrepancies to the shipper and document this on your bill of lading or shipping papers. If you have any questions about accepting the shipment, call your supervisor.

Also check and document the condition of the cargo. Report any damages to the shipper and document this on your bill of lading or shipping papers. Again, if you have any questions about accepting the shipment, call your supervisor.

Note: For more information on cargo documentation see Chapter 23.

Loading/Unloading Tools

When loading or unloading your vehicle, set the parking brake, turn off the vehicle, put the keys in your pocket, and chock the vehicle's wheels. (*Note:* You may not need to chock the vehicle's wheels if loading/unloading from a dock equipped with a dock lock.) The following are just some of the tools you may use when loading or unloading your vehicle.

Forklift — A forklift is a mechanical device used for moving materials. It is powered by an electric motor or internal combustion engine. A forklift may only be operated by an individual who has successfully completed a training program as mandated by the Occupational Safety and Health Administration (OSHA) under 29 CFR 1910.178.

Forklifts are often used to load/unload vehicles.

Pallet jacks — When you must move cargo on pallets, you may use a pallet jack.

Hand pallet jacks are best for short distances and on low grades.

A pallet jack can aid in moving cargo.

Powered pallet jacks are useful for heavier loads or when you have to move cargo greater distances. A powered pallet jack may only be operated by an individual who has successfully completed a training program as mandated by OSHA under 29 CFR 1910.178.

Although relatively easy to use, pallet jacks must be used carefully. When using a pallet jack:

- Always check the pallet jack for any defects that might affect its operation or safe use.

- Make sure the items on the pallet are properly balanced and secured. Heavier items should be on the bottom with lighter ones on the top.

- Position the forks well into the pallet before raising the load. If the load is too heavy, take some of the items off.

Two-wheel dolly — A dolly is a simple piece of equipment that will let you haul several items at one time or move heavier items with greater ease. Although it's a simple device, if not used carefully, it can crush toes, injure ankles, strain backs, and damage cargo.

To use a dolly properly:

- Make sure the load is securely stacked and balanced. If so, tip the load forward slightly and push the "tongue" of the dolly completely under the load.

- The load should not limit your view. If you cannot see above and around the items, split the load, if possible, and make multiple trips.

- Test the load by moving it a short distance. You want to be sure it can be moved without shifting or falling.

- Once you're certain you can move the load safely, check your path to make sure no people or obstacles are in your way.

- Use your leg muscles to move the dolly. Keep your back straight and use one hand to steer and the other to balance the load.

- Do not try to push the dolly too fast.

- Make sure the floor is clean and flat before lowering the load.

- When lowering the load, use your leg muscles, not your back, to set the load on the floor.

Summary

In this chapter, you have learned about the proper handling of cargo, cargo securement, and basic weight distribution principles. All play an important part in safely and efficiently getting a shipment to its destination.

Handling Cargo Quiz

Directions: Read each statement carefully and mark the response that best answers the question.

1. **The Federal Motor Carrier Safety Regulations (FMCSRs) require you to examine your vehicle's load and load securing devices within _____ of the start of your trip.**

   A. 20 miles

   B. 25 miles

   C. 50 miles

   D. 75 miles

2. **The FMCSRs require periodic examination of your vehicle's cargo _____.**

   A. When you make a change of duty status

   B. After the vehicle has been driven for 3 hours

   C. After the vehicle has been driven for 150 miles

   D. When whichever of the above occurs first

3. **According to the FMCSRs, you are not required to check the cargo on a sealed load that is not to be opened, or if checking the cargo is impractical.**

   A. True

   B. False

4. **_____ is a filler material used in empty spaces between cargo to keep cargo from shifting.**

   A. Tiedown

   B. Dunnage

   C. Tarps

   D. All of the above

5. **_____ is a cargo securement procedure where you fit blocks snugly against the cargo (front, back, and/or sides) to prevent it from sliding.**

   A. Tarps

   B. Dunnage

   C. Tiedown

   D. Blocking

6. Never use tiedowns that have knots or have been repaired.

   A. True

   B. False

7. _____ prevents loose material like sand or gravel from blowing or falling out of a vehicle.

   A. A tarp

   B. Dunnage

   C. A tiedown

   D. Blocking

8. Overloading a vehicle can adversely effect a vehicle's steering, braking, and speed control.

   A. True

   B. False

9. A high center of gravity makes it harder for a vehicle to tip over.

   A. True

   B. False

10. Too little weight on a vehicle's driving axles can cause poor traction.

   A. True

   B. False

CDL General Knowledge Pre-Test

Read each statement carefully and select the most correct answer.

1. **Your vehicle is 40 feet long and you are traveling at 50 mph. The safe following distance is:**

   A. 5 seconds

   B. 6 seconds

   C. 4 seconds

   D. 3 seconds

2. **After you start your engine, which of the following should occur?**

   A. Oil pressure will build in 4 to 5 minutes

   B. Air pressure will rise to normal in 10 to 15 minutes

   C. The water temperature will indicate a gradual rise to normal operating temperature

   D. The manifold exhaust indicator gauge will immediately rise to 190 degrees

3. **Which of the following can you NOT check at the same time?**

   A. Turn signal, brake lights, and 4-way flashers

   B. Headlights and clearance lights

   C. Taillights and clearance lights

   D. Clearance lights and 4-way flashers

4. **Which of the following is true about rear drive wheel braking skids?**

   A. The vehicle's front wheels will slide sideways

   B. It is not a cause of jackknifing

   C. The locked wheels have more traction than the wheels that are rolling

   D. If it occurs with a vehicle towing a trailer, the trailer can push the towing vehicle sideways

5. **Which of the following statements is true?**

   A. Hazards are easier to see at night than during the day

   B. Many commercial vehicle accidents occur between midnight and 6 A.M.

   C. Most drivers are more alert at night than during the day

   D. It is recommended that you use your high beams at all times during the period from 7 P.M. to 7 A.M.

Chapter 22
Handling Cargo

Chapter **23**

Cargo documentation

OBJECTIVES

Upon completion of this chapter, you should have a basic understanding of:

❏ The terms/definitions most commonly used in conjunction with cargo documentation

❏ The basic forms used to document cargo movement

❏ Pickup and delivery procedures

Introduction

As a professional driver, you will be dealing with some form of freight documentation. You need to know what documents are required and what your responsibility is in handling them. This chapter will cover the basics of cargo documentation including a general overview of the bill of lading and freight bill and procedures you should follow when making pickups and deliveries. First, we will look at the many definitions associated with freight documentation.

Basic Definitions

Carrier — An individual or company in the business of shipping goods.

Shipper (consignor) — The individual or company originating the order for transport of goods.

Receiver (consignee) — The individual or company to whom the goods are shipped or consigned.

Freight broker — An individual or company who arranges, for compensation, the truck transportation of cargo belonging to others, utilizing authorized for-hire carriers to provide the actual truck transportation. A broker does not assume responsibility for the cargo and usually does not take possession of the cargo.

Freight forwarder — An individual or company that accepts small shipments from various shippers and combines them into one larger shipment.

Understanding freight documentation is an important part of a professional driver's job.

Originating (pickup) carrier — The carrier who picks up a shipment from a shipper.

Connecting carrier — The carrier who delivers a shipment to an interchange point where goods are then transferred to another company to continue shipment.

Terminal carrier (agent) — The carrier who delivers the shipment to the consignee.

Bill of lading — A written transport contract between the shipper and carrier. It identifies the freight, who it is consigned to, place of delivery, and terms of agreement.

Straight bill of lading — Provides that goods be delivered to the consignee indicated. The consignee doesn't have to surrender his copy to receive the goods.

Through bill of lading — Covers a shipment by more than one carrier at a fixed rate for the entire service.

Manifest — A document describing the contents of an entire shipment on a vehicle.

Packing slip — A detailed list of packed goods prepared by the shipper.

Delivery receipt — A receipt signed by the customer receiving the goods indicating acceptance of the goods from the driver.

Warehousing receipt — A receipt for goods placed in a warehouse.

Charges and services — Both goods and transportation services have to be paid for. Payment for goods is usually arranged between the shipper and consignee. In rare cases, the carrier is required to collect. When this occurs, the driver can't deliver or relinquish possession of freight unless these charges are paid. Because of this, it is important for you to understand the following terms.

Prepaid — The transportation charges are paid for or will be paid at the shipping point.

COD — The payment for goods is made at the delivery point. The driver must collect payment before the cargo is unloaded. Policies regarding this vary from company-to-company.

Order notify shipment — The payment of goods on an Order Notify Bill of Lading. The driver must collect a copy of the bill of lading from the person receiving the goods as payment for the goods.

Basis of rates — Rates are charges based on the value of the transportation and additional services performed by the carrier. Mileage rates are determined by a fee per mile. Class rates are set by grouping goods into classifications according to characteristics such as density, stability, ease of handling, and liability.

Value of cargo — Cargo is valued as either actual valuation or released valuation.

- **Actual valuation** — The actual value of goods shown on the bill of lading when the rate applied is dependent on that fact.

- **Released valuation** — The value of goods set by the shipper as limits of carrier liability and as the basis of rates charged.

Weight and distance — The primary determiner of shipping charges. Rates are expressed in terms of per pound of cargo and per mile traveled.

Services performed by carrier — A list of services that a carrier performs and the rates for those services.

Tariffs — Rates on transportation charges based on the type of service.

Minimum rate — The lowest lawful rate that may be charged.

Maximum rate — The highest rate that can be charged for a specific type of shipment.

Duties — Government tax on imports and exports which must be collected.

Services and surcharges — Basic rates, services, and duties are determined in advance by rules and agreements between the shipper and carrier. Services and surcharges are based on such things as type of cargo (valuation), weight, destination, and type of service. Additional services and rates may be specified on the bill of lading. It is important to know and understand what each of the following terms mean so you can perform the services indicated as required.

Inside delivery — The freight is unloaded and delivered inside instead of at curbside.

Tailgate delivery — The freight is unloaded and delivered at the truck's tailgate (back of truck).

Helper service (lumper) — The arrangement and compensation for loading/unloading should appear on the bill of lading, but seldom does. Usually what is listed is that the load is either shipper/receiver "load and count" or it is driver "load and count." A driver may hire a helper service (lumper) to load/unload if there is one available. This is usually paid for by the driver's company and is included in the freight rate.

Residential delivery — The freight is to be delivered to a residential address. The bill of lading will specify the conditions of delivery and method of collection of payment.

Dunnage and return of dunnage — Dunnage is cardboard, lumber, or other material used to stabilize and secure a shipment. It is not packaging. The bill of lading should list the weight of dunnage. Usually there is no charge for dunnage weight. If return of dunnage is specified, the driver must keep the dunnage and return it to the carrier or shipper as indicated.

Storage and delay charges — Additional charges are made for storage or if the carrier is delayed from making a delivery.

Demurrage (detention) — The detention of a vehicle beyond a specified time. Payment is made to the carrier for this delay (detention time).

> Don't worry driver. You don't have to memorize all of these definitions. You just need to be aware that there is a "language" associated with freight that includes many terms that may be new to you. You should become familiar with them over time.

Basic Documents

As a professional driver, there are two basic documents you will deal with on a regular basis when picking up and delivering cargo. These documents are the bill of lading and freight (expense) bill.

Bill of lading — The bill of lading is the document used in transactions between a shipper and common carrier. The front or face of the bill of lading is where the required information for transportation of the freight must be entered. The reverse side or back of the bill of lading usually contains the terms and conditions of carriage.

There are three distinct and important functions served by the bill of lading:

1. It is a receipt issued by the carrier to a shipper for goods received for transportation. The bill of lading:

    *   States the place and date of shipment;
    *   Describes the goods, their quality, weight, dimensions, identification marks, condition, etc.; and
    *   Sometimes the goods quality and value.

2. It is a contract naming the:

    *   Parties involved;
    *   Specific rate or charge for transportation; and
    *   Agreement and stipulations regarding the limitations of the carrier's common law liability in the case of loss or injury to the goods.

3. It also lists other obligations assumed by the parties or to matters agreed upon by them.

Certain bills of lading provide documentary evidence of title to the goods being transported. The "Order" or "Negotiable" bill of lading designates the consignee as the owner of the freight and the carrier may only deliver the cargo to the person in possession of the bill of lading. When a bill of lading is "negotiated", the person to whom it is negotiated receives title to the cargo. Use of this bill of lading is very limited.

Bills of lading must be legibly written in ink, indelible pencil, or preferably, typed. It is important that all information be written or typed in the exact space provided for it.

The following information must be included on the bill of lading.

Name of consignor — The individual or company originating the order for transport of goods.

Name of consignee — The individual or company to who the goods are shipped or consigned to.

Address — The street address of the consignee should always be listed in the space provided. A post office box is not acceptable for delivery.

Destination — The destination must be accurate. An error of illegibly written or misspelled destination can cause a great deal of trouble and expense. If there are two destinations of the same name within a state, insert the name of the county to indicate the correct destination clearly.

Date — This should be the exact date of delivery of the merchandise to the carrier. This can help prevent misunderstandings regarding what rate of tariff applies to the shipment.

Description of goods — The description of goods covered by the bill of lading should be complete and exact regarding quality and quantity. Other information may be necessary to allow the carrier to classify and properly rate the shipment.

Special marking and instructions — Special marks shown on the shipping units should be reproduced on the bill of lading. Special instructions (freezable, transit privileges, pick-up allowances, etc.) should be included.

Payment of freight charges — Carriers may require prepayment of freight charges on certain commodities or on freight consigned to certain points, and they have the right under law to require prepayment on all freight as long as they avoid discrimination. Generally, it is the option of the shipper to determine who will pay the charges and at what point.

Bill of lading forms must indicate who is responsible for transportation charges. The charges may be "prepaid" or "collect."

Section 7 — The box on the face of the bill of lading referring to "Section 7 of conditions," sometimes known as the "no recourse clause," deals with the payment of freight charges. It is explained in Section 7 of the terms and conditions on the back of the bill of lading, and basically provides that the shipper/consignor is primarily responsible for payment of the freight and other lawful charges, unless the shipper stipulates in writing in the space provided, that the carrier makes delivery without requiring pre-payment.

Shippers who leave the Section 7 area blank, or unsigned, in effect are telling the carrier that if they do not, or are unable to collect the charges from the consignee, the carrier may return to the shipper (consignor) for payment of the freight charges, even though the terms for payment of freight charges on the bill of lading are collected on delivery.

Whether or not Section 7 is executed has a direct impact on the carrier's ability to collect freight charges from the consignor when the charges are due and uncollectible from the consignee.

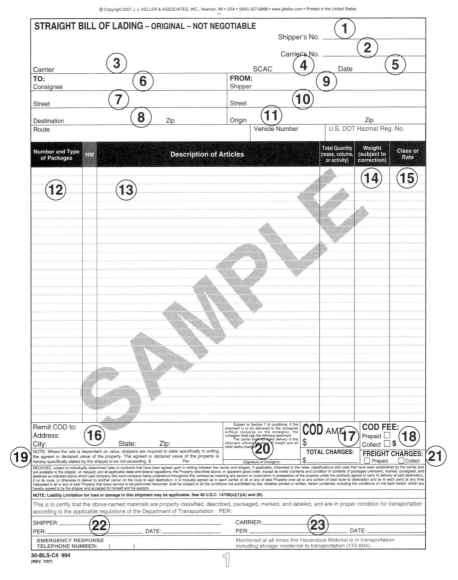

A straight bill of lading.

Key:

1. Shipper assigned BOL number.

2. Carrier assigned pro number

3. Name of carrier

4. Standard Carrier Alpha Code assigned by NMFTA required by some carriers

5. Date the shipment is accepted by the carrier

6. Name of consignee.

7. Street name and number

8. Destination state and zip code

9. Name of shipper/consignor

10. Street name and number of pickup.

11. Origin state and zip code.

12. Number of units to be handled.

13. Description of goods, special marks, exceptions

14. Weight.

15. Class or rate if known for information only

16. Exact name and address of the COD amount received by the carrier.

17. Collect on Delivery amount

18. Carrier COD charge paid by shipper or consignee

19. Shipper's valuation declaration.

20. Non-recourse clause executed only by shipper at time of shipment

21. Indicates prepaid freight charges unless collect box is checked

22. Signature of shipper and date.

23. Driver signature and date

Unilateral Amendments — Amendments, or changes, to the bill of lading contract made by only one party to the contract are not binding upon the parties. Any changes or amendments must be accomplished by both parties, with amended copies of the contract provided.

Bill of lading retention period — To satisfy Federal Motor Carrier Safety Administration (FMCSA) requirements, a bill of lading must be retained by a motor carrier, broker, household goods freight forwarder, or water carrier for a period of one year from the date of the document, or until any claim or dispute involving the transportation of freight based upon the document is resolved.

Basis of rates — Rates are charged based on the value of the transportation and additional services performed by the carrier. Mileage rates are determined by a fee per mile. Class rates are set by grouping goods into classifications according to characteristics such as density, stability, ease of handling and liability.

Freight (expense) bill — Every motor common carrier must issue a freight or expense bill for each shipment transported.

PLEASE PRESS HARD WHEN WRITING

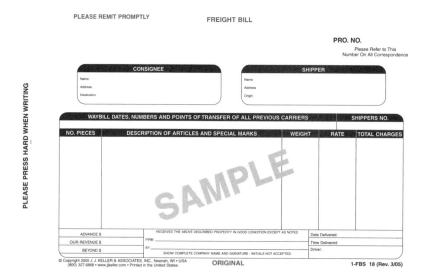

A freight bill.

The freight or expense bill must include:

- Names of consignor and consignee;

- Date of shipment;

- Origin and destination points;

- Number of packages;

- Description of freight;

- Weight, volume, or measurement of freight (if applicable to the rating of the freight);

- Exact rate(s) assessed;

- Total charges due, including the nature and amount of any charges for special service and the points at which such service was rendered;

- Route of movement and name of each carrier participating in the transportation;

- Transfer point(s) through which shipment moved; and

- Address where remittance must be made or address of bill issuer's principal place of business.

No person shall cause a motor carrier to present false or misleading information on a document for payment about the actual rate, charge, or allowance to any party to the transaction.

The shipper or receiver owing the charges shall be given the original freight or expense bill and the carrier shall keep a copy as prescribed in 49 CFR 379.

Pickup and Delivery Procedures

Freight pickup — By signing the bill of lading, you are stating that your company accepts the contract terms. Since you are acting as your company's agent, your signature legally binds the company. It also means that you accept responsibility for the freight and that the actual freight matches the type and amount listed on the bill of lading.

Before signing the bill of lading, make sure the freight is properly described.

Always count, inspect, and determine, in general, that the freight is properly described before signing the bill of lading. You should refuse or note in writing, on the bill of lading, if the freight is short, damaged, or poorly packed.

Freight delivery — There are several things you need to keep in mind when delivering freight.

- Make sure the delivery is made to the right person (consignee);

- Handle payment for merchandise correctly;

- Handle freight changes correctly;

- Get the proper signatures on the bill of lading (and freight bill if applicable); and

- Always follow your company's policy dealing with short shipments, damages, or any other freight problems.

If another party is unloading the freight, observe/supervise the unloading process (if possible). Remember, the freight is yours until the consignee signs for it.

Split shipments — A split shipment is one in which cargo is picked up at more than one address. A receipted bill of lading must be furnished at each address. The bill of lading must also contain the address for each delivery.

When dealing with a split shipment, be especially careful. Check each piece against the bill of lading and/or freight bill very carefully, making sure the correct freight is delivered to the correct address.

Interline freight — Interline freight is freight picked up from or delivered to another carrier. Use the same care when dealing with interline freight as you would when dealing with any other consignor or consignee.

- Check for cargo shortage or damage before signing the connecting carrier's bill of lading or freight bill;

- Don't sign the bill of lading or freight bill if the connecting carrier refuses to acknowledge things such as shortages or damages;

- If equipment interchange is involved (leaving your trailer and/or hooking up a trailer belonging to another company), inspect the trailer and its contents before signing for possession; and

- Always check with your company for instructions.

Summary

In this chapter, you have learned about bills of lading, freight bills, and the terms associated with these documents. You have also learned the basics of freight pickup and delivery.

Cargo Documentation Quiz

Directions: Read each statement carefully and mark the response that best answers the question.

1. **The shipper is also called the _____.**

    A. Consignor

    B. Consignee

    C. Receiver

    D. Bill of lading

2. **The receiver is also called the _____.**

    A. Consignor

    B. Consignee

    C. Shipper

    D. Bill of lading

3. **A written transport contract between a shipper and carrier which identifies the freight, who it is consigned to, place of delivery, and terms of agreement is called the _____.**

    A. Consignor

    B. Consignee

    C. Freight broker

    D. Bill of lading

4. **Payment for goods is usually arranged between the shipper and consignee.**

    A. True

    B. False

5. **A bill of lading must be legibly written in ink, indelible pencil, or must be typed.**

    A. True

    B. False

6. **A freight bill is a document a motor carrier may issue for selected shipments.**

    A. True

    B. False

7. **When signing a bill of lading, you are acting as your company's agent, accepting the contract terms.**

   A. True

   B. False

8. **When picking up freight, you should always count, inspect, and determine that the freight is properly described before signing the bill of lading.**

   A. True

   B. False

9. **A split shipment is one in which more than one container is picked up at a shipper.**

   A. True

   B. False

10. **_____ is freight picked up from or delivered to another carrier.**

    A. Consignor

    B. Consignee

    C. Interline freight

    D. Split freight

CDL Air Brake Pre-Test

Read each statement carefully and select the most correct answer.

1. **The air loss rate for a straight truck or bus with the engine off and the brakes applied should not be more than:**

   A. 1 psi in 60 seconds

   B. 1 psi in one minute

   C. 2 psi in 45 seconds

   D. 3 psi in one minute

2. **Which of the following statements about brakes is true?**

   A. The heavier a vehicle or the faster it is moving, the more heat the brakes have to absorb to stop it

   B. Brakes have more stopping power when they get very hot

   C. Brake drums cool very quickly

   D. All of the above are true

3. **The purpose of engine retarders is to:**

   A. Provide emergency brakes

   B. Help slow the vehicle while driving and reduce brake wear

   C. Apply extra braking power to the non-drive axles

   D. Help prevent skids and slides

4. **If your vehicle has an alcohol evaporator, it is there to:**

   A. Get rid of alcohol that condenses in the air tanks

   B. Let the driver skip the daily tank draining

   C. Increase tank pressure the way superchargers boost engines

   D. Reduce the risk of ice in the air brake valves in cold weather

5. **The air supply pressure gauge shows the driver how much pressure:**

   A. Has been used in this trip

   B. Is available in the air tanks

   C. Is being sent to the brake chambers

   D. None of the above

Chapter 23
Cargo
Documentation

Chapter 24

Hazardous materials

OBJECTIVES

Upon completion of this chapter, you should have a basic understanding of:

- ❏ What a hazardous material is
- ❏ The CDL hazmat endorsement
- ❏ Hazard classes and divisions
- ❏ Why hazmat shipping papers must be filled out properly and easily accessed
- ❏ Loading and unloading hazmat
- ❏ What needs to be done when transporting hazmat

Introduction

Transporting hazardous materials safely and securely today is more important than ever. Hazmat drivers need to receive special training associated with what they do on the job, as well as training in all aspects of general transportation. If you are hired by a carrier to transport hazmat, additional training will be provided to you. This chapter will provide you with some background on requirements pertaining to the hazardous materials transportation process.

What Is a Hazardous Material?

The Hazardous Materials Regulations (HMR) defines a hazardous material as a substance or material capable of posing an unreasonable risk to health, safety, and property when transported in commerce. The term includes hazardous substances, hazardous wastes, marine pollutants, elevated temperature materials, materials designated as hazardous in the Hazardous Materials Table, and materials that meet the defining criteria for hazard classes and divisions.

Transporting hazmat safely and securely is more important than ever.

CDL Endorsements

Generally, a hazmat endorsement is required on a driver's commercial driver's license (CDL) in order to haul placarded amounts of hazardous materials. An endorsement is also required for any quantity of a material listed as a select agent or toxin in 42 CFR Part 73.

In order to receive a hazmat endorsement, you will need to be fingerprinted and will need to pass a criminal background check as part of the Homeland Security Regulations pertaining to the transport of hazardous materials.

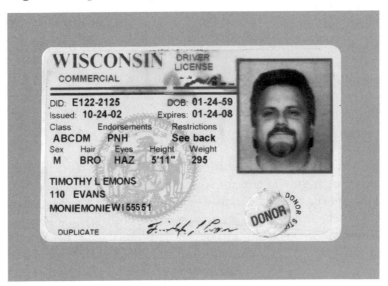

The commercial driver's license (CDL).

Hazard Classes and Divisions

Hazardous materials are classified by a hazard class or division number.

A hazard class is the category of hazard assigned to a hazardous material in the HMR. A material may meet the defining criteria for more than one hazard class, but is assigned to only one hazard class.

A division is a subdivision of a hazard class.

There are nine hazard classes, with some of the classes broken down into divisions.

- Class 1 — Explosives
- Class 2
  - Division 2.1 — Flammable gas
  - Division 2.2 — Non-flammable gas
  - Division 2.3 — Poison gas
- Class 3 — Flammable and combustible liquid
- Class 4
  - Division 4.1 — Flammable solid
  - Division 4.2 — Spontaneously combustible
  - Division 4.3 — Dangerous when wet

Hey driver! This is important stuff. You will receive much more training in the transportation of hazardous materials from your employer if you are going to haul them, but the basics are important and that's what we are covering here. Even if you "think" you will never haul hazmat, this is good stuff to know!

- Class 5
  - Division 5.1 — Oxidizer
  - Division 5.2 — Organic peroxide
- Class 6
  - Division 6.1 — Poisonous material
  - Division 6.2 — Infectious substance
- Class 7 — Radioactive
- Class 8 — Corrosive material
- Class 9 — Miscellaneous hazardous material

Shipping Papers

No one wants to be involved in an accident, let alone one involving hazardous materials. However, accidents do happen. Accidents involving hazardous materials can potentially threaten lives, property, and the environment. That's why shipping papers have such an important role in the hazmat transportation process.

A hazardous materials straight bill of lading.

A hazmat shipping paper provides key information about the hazardous material being transported. Emergency responders use that information at the scene of an accident to determine what steps must be taken to keep damages to the lowest level possible. It is up to you, the driver, to make certain that information is correct and the shipping papers are easily accessible.

- The UN or NA identification number

  The HMR requires that a shipping paper have the basic description for each hazardous material being transported. For domestic transportation, the basic description must include in this order:

- The proper shipping name

- The hazard class or division number

- The subsidiary hazard class or division number entered in parentheses

- The packing group (PG), if any.

The total quantity of the hazmat must be entered before and/or after the basic description. It must also include the appropriate unit of measure, which may be abbreviated. The number and type of packages must also be indicated.

You, the driver, should never accept a hazmat shipment unless you are certain the shipping papers have been properly prepared.

Shipping Paper Accessibility

Shipping papers must be readily accessible to authorities in the event of an accident or inspection. The driver must:

- Clearly distinguish the hazmat shipping paper from other papers by tabbing it or having it appear first.

- Keep the shipping paper within immediate reach while at the vehicle controls and restrained by the lap belt, and visible to anyone entering the driver's compartment or in a holder mounted to the inside of the driver's door.

- Keep the shipping paper in a driver's side door pouch or on the driver's seat when you are not at the vehicle controls.

Loading and Unloading

Set parking brake — During the loading and unloading of any hazmat the vehicle parking brake must be set and all precautions taken to prevent movement of the vehicle.

Tools — Any tools used in loading or unloading hazmat must be used with care not to damage closures on packages or containers, or to harm packages of Class 1 material and other hazmat in any way.

I know, I know...it seems like all we talk about is paperwork. But when it comes to hazmat, the paperwork is extremely important. If you are in an accident and can't communicate with emergency personnel, the paperwork might be the only thing that saves you and those around you. Emergency responders need to know exactly what you are hauling in order to know how to respond safely and correctly. Give yourself and those around you a chance...make sure the paperwork is correct and complete before you pull away from the dock!

No smoking — Smoking on or near any vehicle while loading or unloading any Class 1, Class 3, Class 4 (flammable solid), Class 5 (oxidizer), or Division 2.1 is forbidden. Care should be taken to keep all fire sources (matches and smoking materials in particular) away from any vehicle hauling the previously mentioned materials.

Securing packages — Packages containing any hazmat not permanently attached to a vehicle must be secured against any movement, including shifting or movement between packages during normal transportation. Packages having valves or other fittings must be loaded to minimize the likelihood of damage during transportation.

Placards — The HMR requires most vehicles hauling hazmat to be placarded. The shipper is responsible for providing the appropriate placards. You, the driver, are responsible for putting them correctly on your vehicle and maintaining them during transportation.

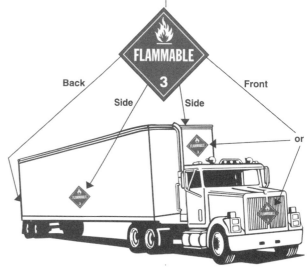

Placards should be placed/displayed correctly.

On the Road

Fueling — The engine of a placarded vehicle must be shut-off and someone must be in control of the fueling process at the point where the fuel tank is filled.

Smoking — No smoking or carrying lighted smoking materials is allowed on or within 25 feet of a placarded vehicle containing any Class 1, Class 5 (oxidizer) or flammable materials classified as Divisions 2.1, 4.1, 4.2, Class 3, or any empty tank vehicle that has been used to transport Class 3 or Division 2.1 materials.

Routing — Hazardous materials drivers must abide by designated hazardous materials routes that are posted around many cities and residential areas. Even if the route is not specified or pre-determined, placarded vehicles should avoid heavily populated areas, tunnels, narrow streets or alleys except when:

- There are no practicable alternatives;

- It is necessary to reach your destination, or facilities for food, rest, fuel, or repairs; or

- Emergency conditions require a deviation.

Tire checks — The tires of placarded vehicles must be checked at the beginning of each trip and each time the vehicle is parked. If any defect is found, the tire should be repaired or replaced immediately.

Be careful driver. You can not fuel your truck the way you might do when hauling regular freight. Don't stick one hose in one tank and turn it on, stick the other hose in the other tank and turn it on, and walk around cleaning your windshield, kicking tires, etc. This is not allowed! You need to be in control of the fueling process AT ALL TIMES! this means one hose at a time, with your hand on the nozzle. This is no time to set your pumps and go get a cup of coffee!

Check tires at the start of each trip and each time the vehicle is parked.

Sorry driver. If you are hauling hazmat, that over-night trip through the house may not happen. Parking a hazmat load in a residential area is usually a big no-no so make other plans...maybe just a phone call this time and a little longer stay next time around.

Parking — Placarded vehicles should not be parked on or within five feet of the traveled portion of any roadway. However, except for certain explosives, the vehicle may be stopped for brief periods when operational necessity requires parking and it would be impractical to stop elsewhere. Standard warning devices are to be set out, as required, when stopped along a roadway.

Summary

In this chapter, you have learned about CDL endorsements, hazard classes and divisions, shipping papers and accessibility, and procedures for loading and unloading hazardous materials. These are some of the basic requirements when it comes to transporting hazardous materials. Keep in mind that if you do transport hazardous materials for an employer, you will receive additional training.

Hazardous Materials Quiz

Directions: Read each statement carefully and mark the response that best answers the question.

1. **Every driver transporting hazardous materials needs a hazmat endorsement.**

    A. True

    B. False

2. **There are ___ hazard classes of hazardous materials.**

    A. 9   B. 7   C. 11   D. 5

3. **What items make up the basic description for a hazardous material on a shipping paper?**

    A. The UN or NA identification number; the proper shipping name; the hazard class or division number; the subsidiary hazard class or division number; and the packing group (PG), if any

    B. The proper shipping name; the vehicle DOT number; the UN or NA identification letter; and the proper group (PG) number, if any

    C. The proper shipping name; the vehicle DOT number; the date; and the packing group (PG), if any

    D. The proper chemical name; the hazard class or division number; the UN or NA identification number; and the product group, if any

4. **The total quantity of the hazmat must be entered:**

    A. Before the basic description

    B. After the basic description

    C. Before and/or after the basic description

    D. Any of the above

5. **The driver should take the shipping papers with him/her when not at the vehicle controls.**

    A. True

    B. False

6. **It is the shipper's fault if the wrong placards are on the vehicle.**

    A. True

    B. False

7. **Tires must be checked every 2 hours or every 200 miles.**

    A. True

    B. False

CDL Air Brake Pre-Test

Read each statement carefully and select the most correct answer

1. **Which brake system applies and releases the brakes when the driver uses the brake pedal?**

    A. The emergency brake system

    B. The service brake system

    C. The parking brake system

    D. None of the above

2. **When using the parking brakes or emergency brakes, what type of pressure is being used?**

    A. Fluid pressure

    B. Spring pressure

    C. Air pressure

    D. Any of the above

3. **Three different systems are found on modern air brake systems; service brakes, parking brakes, and the:**

    A. Emergency brakes

    B. Foot brakes

    C. S-cam brakes

    D. Drum brakes

4. **Air loss in a single vehicle (not a combination unit) should not be more than _____ with the engine off and the brakes on.**

    A. 1 psi in 30 seconds

    B. 1 psi in one minute

    C. 2 psi in 45 seconds

    D. 3 psi in one minute

5. **The vehicle must have a warning device which comes on when the air pressure in the service air tanks falls below:**

    A. 40 psi

    B. 50 psi

    C. 60 psi

    D. 80 psi

Chapter 25

Hours of service

OBJECTIVES

Upon completion of this chapter, you should have a general understanding of the:

- ❏ 11-hour driving rule

- ❏ 14-hour duty limit

- ❏ Mandatory break provision

- ❏ 60-hour/7-day and 70-hour/8-day limit

- ❏ Sleeper berth option

- ❏ Driver's record of duty status and how to complete this document

- ❏ 100 air-mile radius exemption

- ❏ Short-haul provision (Non-CDL)

Introduction

Originally created over 70 years ago, the hours-of-service regulations were designed to keep tired drivers off the road and to protect them from the unscrupulous actions of dispatchers and shippers.

The hours-of-service regulations limit your driving and on-duty time.

These regulations, which all drivers of property-carrying vehicles are required to comply with, limit the number of hours you can drive, as well as the number of hours you can be on duty. The hours-of-service regulations also require that you maintain a record of your duty status (driver's log). The specific requirements are covered in this chapter.

Who Must Comply?

All motor carriers and drivers operating property-carrying commercial motor vehicles in interstate commerce must follow the hours-of-service regulations, located in Part 395 of the Federal Motor Carrier Safety Regulations (FMCSRs).

If you operate any of the vehicles described below, you must comply with the hours-of-service requirements covered in this chapter:

- A vehicle with a gross vehicle weight rating, gross combination weight rating, gross vehicle weight, or gross combination weight (whichever is greater) of 10,001 pounds (4,537 kilograms) or more; or

- Any size vehicle transporting a placardable amount of hazardous materials.

There are also hours-of-service requirements for drivers of certain types of passenger-carrying vehicles. Refer to Part 395 for details.

Note: Many states also have hours-of-service requirements that apply to intrastate operations within that specific state. State requirements may match federal requirements in whole or in part.

11 Hours Driving Time

All time spent behind the wheel is considered driving time. After 11 hours of driving time, you must have at least 10 consecutive hours off duty before you can drive again.

Adverse driving conditions — Adverse driving conditions include snow, sleet, fog, or unusual road and traffic conditions that are unexpected. This would be conditions that were not known prior to starting a trip.

Driver, you have GOT to learn this stuff. Your ability to properly operate your vehicle and record your actions (log book) is paramount to your success as a professional driver. If you can't (or don't) do this correctly, you will face continuous stress, fines, and lost revenue. It could even get you fired and hinder your ability to get hired by someone else. It's that important!

If you encounter adverse conditions, you may be allowed an additional two hours of driving time.

If you experience an adverse driving condition and cannot safely complete a run that normally would have been able to be completed within the legal driving hours, you may drive for an additional 2 hours within your 14 consecutive hours of duty time.

14 Consecutive Hours on Duty

Your 11 hours of driving time must fall within a period of 14 consecutive hours of duty time.

The 14 hours are consecutive from the time you start your tour of duty. Lunch breaks or other off-duty time do not extend this 14-consecutive-hour period.

Once you have reached the end of this 14-hour period, you cannot drive again until you have been off duty for at least 10 consecutive hours. You may continue to work after the 14th hour, but you must not drive.

For example, if you begin your work day at 6 a.m. you may not drive after 8 p.m. You must have at least 10 consecutive hours off duty before you may then drive again.

Short haul exception — There is an exception to the 14-hour duty limit that you can use on a periodic basis if you regularly return to your normal work reporting location.

Under this exception, you are allowed to accumulate 11 hours of driving time within 16 consecutive hours of duty once every 7 days, provided you:

- Return to your work reporting location on that day, and are released from duty at that work reporting location for the previous 5 on-duty days;

- Are released from duty within 16 hours after coming on duty (no additional on-duty time after 16 hours); and

- Have not used this exception within the previous 6 consecutive days (unless you have complied with the 34-hour restart provision (see 60-hour/7-day and 70-hour/8-day rules)).

Mandatory Break Provision

Under the mandatory break provision, you may not drive if more than 8 hours have passed since the end of your last off-duty or sleeper-berth period of at least 30 minutes. This 30-minute break can be taken at any time during your first 8 hours on duty. The break counts towards your 14-hour limit and does not extend your work day.

If you are required to be in attendance on a vehicle containing Division 1.1, 1.2, or 1.3 explosives, you may use 30 minutes or more of attendance time to meet the break requirement. In order to be considered a break, you may not be performing any other on-duty tasks while in attendance on the vehicle, must record the attendance time as on-duty time on your log, and include a remark or note indicating that this is your mandatory break.

Sleeper Berth

By using the sleeper berth option, you can accumulate the required 10 hours off duty in two sleeper berth periods provided:

Use of the sleeper berth can help you maximize your driving and on-duty time.

- At least 8 consecutive hours (but less than 10 consecutive hours) are spent in the sleeper berth; and

- A separate period of at least 2 consecutive hours (but less than 10 consecutive hours) is spent either in the sleeper berth, off duty, or any combination of the two

Calculation of driving time includes all driving time. Compliance must be re-calculated from the end of the first of the two periods.

Calculation of the 14-hour duty limit includes all time except any sleeper-berth period of at least 8 but less than 10 consecutive hours. Compliance must be re-calculated from the end of the first of the two periods.

When using this option, you may not return to driving under the normal limits until you take:

- At least 10 consecutive hours off duty;

- At least 10 consecutive hours in the sleeper berth; or

- A combination of at least 10 consecutive hours of off duty and sleeper berth time.

The 60-Hour/7 Day and the 70-Hour/8 Day Rules

To better understand this rule, you must understand the definition of on-duty time. On-duty time is defined as all time from the time you begin work or are required to be ready for work until you are relieved from work and all responsibility for doing work. This includes time spent:

- Waiting to be dispatched;

- Inspecting, servicing, or conditioning a commercial motor vehicle;

- Driving (at the controls of your vehicle);

- All time (other than driving time) in or on your commercial motor vehicle (CMV) except:

    ○ Time spent resting on a parked vehicle (except when attending to a CMV containing Division 1.1, 1.2, or 1.3 (explosive) material);

    ○ Time spent resting in a sleeper berth; or

    ○ Up to 2 hours riding in the passenger seat of a property-carrying CMV moving on a highway immediately before or after a sleeper-berth period of at least 8 consecutive hours;

- Loading or unloading your vehicle;

- Repairing, obtaining assistance, or attending a disabled vehicle;

- Performing any other work for a motor carrier;

- Complying with drug or alcohol testing requirements; and

- Performing work for pay for any other employer (motor carrier or non-motor carrier).

Under the 60-hour/7 day rule, you may not drive after having been on duty for 60 or more hours in 7 consecutive days.

Under the 70-hour/8 day rule, you may not drive after having been on duty for 70 hours in any 8 consecutive days.

Any non-driving work done after reaching either limit must be added to your total on-duty hours.

A company that does not operate commercial motor vehicles every day of the week must use the 60-hour/7 day schedule.

A company that operates vehicles every day of the week may use either the 60-hour/7 day schedule or the 70-hour/8 day schedule.

A monthly summary sheet is one way to keep track of the 60 or 70 hour limit.

Remember, the 7 or 8 consecutive days does not mean a "work week." It means any 7- or 8-consecutive day period.

You don't "start over" counting hours. The oldest day's hours drop out of consideration as each new day's hours are added.

34-hour restart — The regulations include an optional "restart" provision. This allows you to "restart" the 60- or 70-hour clock.

In order to use the restart, you must have at least 34 consecutive hours off duty that includes two periods of time between 1:00 a.m. and 5:00 a.m.

You may only use the restart once within a period of 168 hours (7 days).

For example, if you go off duty at 3:00 p.m. on Friday, in order to use the 34-hour restart, you may not report for duty again until 5:00 a.m. on Sunday. You may not use the restart provision again until 3:00 p.m. or later the following Friday.

These provisions do not prohibit you from taking more than one period of 34 or more hours off duty in a week, but only one of the periods can be used to restart your 60-hour/7-day or 70-hour/8-day schedule. If you do take more than one period of more than 34-consecutive hours off duty, you must indicate on your record of duty status which is being used as your restart.

The Driver's Record of Duty Status

The regulations require you to record your duty status (in duplicate) for each 24-hour period.

You must use a form that includes a vertical or horizontal graph grid and the following information:

- Date;
- Total miles driven today;
- Truck or tractor and trailer number;
- Carrier's name;
- 24-hour period starting time (selected by the driver's home terminal);
- Driver's signature/certification;
- Main office address;
- Remarks;
- Co-driver's name (if applicable);
- Total hours in each duty status (at end of grid); and
- Shipping document number(s), or shipper name and commodity.

Even though a monthly recap is not required, it is strongly recommended. It is a good tool to help keep you out of "logging" trouble, particularly if you find yourself running close to being out of hours quite often. Even a mistake by as little as 15 minutes could get you shut down...this charts helps avoid that mistake.

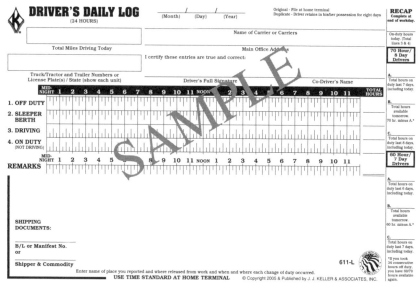

A driver's record of duty status form.

Completing Your Record of Duty Status

You must complete the record of duty status in your own handwriting. Certain items, such as carrier name and main office address may be preprinted.

There are four categories to use when recording your time:

- Off duty;
- Sleeper berth;
- Driving; and
- On duty (not driving).

The total in all four categories must add up to 24 hours.

The record must be legible and kept current to the time shown for the last change of duty status.

The location (city, town, village and state) of all changes of duty status must be recorded in the remarks section. If the change of duty status occurs at a location other than a city, town, or village the location can be recorded as the:

- Highway number and nearest milepost followed by the name of the nearest city, town, village and state;
- Highway number and name of the service plaza followed by the name of the nearest city, town, village and state; or
- Highway numbers of the two nearest intersecting roadways followed by the name of the nearest city, town, village and state.

You are going to hear all kinds of stories about "creative log book writing" and the many ways to "get around" the rules. Here's my suggestion...Run it legal and log it as you ran it. Don't get creative or try and beat the system. Eventually, the system will catch up with you and it will cost you lost time and revenue.

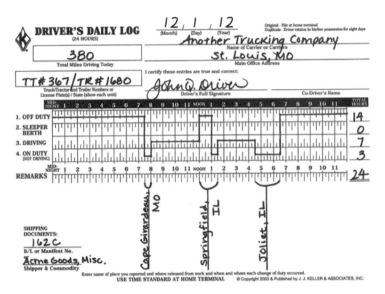

A completed driver's record of duty status.

You must submit the original record of duty status to your motor carrier within 13 days of completion.

You must have in your possession a copy of each record for the last 7 consecutive days as well as the original record for the current day. They must be available for inspection while you are on duty.

A motor carrier must keep records of duty status, along with all supporting documents for a period of 6 months from the date of receipt.

100 Air-Mile Radius Exemption

You are not required to complete a record of duty status (driver's log) if the following criteria are met:

- You operate within a 100 air-mile radius of your normal work reporting location;

- You return to your normal work reporting location and are released from work within 12 consecutive hours;

- At least 10 consecutive hours off duty separate each 12 hours on duty;

- You do not drive more than 11 hours following 10 hours off duty; and

- Your motor carrier maintains your time records for 6 months showing the:

  ○ Time you report for duty each day;

  ○ Time you are released from duty each day;

  ○ Total number of hours you are on duty each day; and

○ Total time on duty for the preceding 7 days (if you are used for the first time or intermittently).

Keep in mind that when using the 100 air-mile radius exemption you are not exempt from the 60-hour/7-day or 70-hour/8-day limit.

Short-Haul Provision (Non-CDL)

Under this provision, you may extend your workday twice in any period of 7 consecutive days and are not required to maintain a record of duty status (logbook) if the following criteria are met:

- You are not required to hold a commercial driver's license (CDL) to operate your vehicle; and

- You remain within a 150 air-mile radius of your normal work reporting location and return to and are released from your normal work reporting location at the end of each day.

Under this provision, you must:

- Comply with the 11-hour driving rule;

- Have at least 10 consecutive hours off duty separating each on-duty period; and

- Comply with the 60-hour/7-day limit or 70-hour/8-day limit (you may use the 34-hour restart provision if applicable).

Under this provision, you must not drive:

- After 14 consecutive hours of duty time during 5 days of any period of 7 consecutive days; and

- After 16 consecutive hours of duty time during 2 days of any period of 7 consecutive days.

You are not required to keep a record of duty status (driver's log), but your motor carrier is required to keep a time record showing the time you report for and are released from duty each day, the total number of hours you are on duty each day, and the total time you are on duty for the past 7 days if you are used for the first time or intermittently.

If you use this exemption you are not eligible to use the 100 air-mile radius exception, the sleeper-berth exception, or the short-haul (16-hour) exemption.

These are the current regulations as of the writing of this manual. The hours-of-service regulations have been in flux since 2003 and to date, still have not been solidified. Your instructor will bring you up to date as to what the latest rulings are pertaining to driving hours, reset hours, etc.

Summary

The purpose of the hours-of-service regulations is to keep tired drivers off the road. The FMCSA and law enforcement in general take these regulations seriously. Drivers and motor carriers are fined hundreds of thousands of dollars each year for violating these requirements.

Operating within legal limits and maintaining a neat and accurate log book will help you operate legally, reducing the chance of a fatigue-related accident and keep you from receiving citations and fines.

Hours of Service Quiz

Directions: Read each statement carefully and mark the response that best answers the question.

1. **You must have 10 consecutive hours off duty after_____ hours of driving, before you are allowed to drive again.**

    A. 8

    B. 9

    C. 10

    D. 11

2. **If you encounter adverse driving conditions, you may ignore the driving time requirements and continue driving until you have reached your destination.**

    A. True

    B. False

3. **After 14 consecutive hours of duty time, you may not drive again until you have 10 consecutive hours off duty.**

    A. True

    B. False

4. **You may use lunch breaks and/or other off-duty time to extend your 14 consecutive hours of duty time.**

    A. True

    B. False

5. **By using the sleeper-berth option, you can accumulate the equivalent of at least 10 consecutive hours off duty in two sleeper-berth periods, provided:**

    A. At least 8 consecutive hours (but less than 10 consecutive hours) are spent in the sleeper berth

    B. A separate period of at least 2 consecutive hours (but less than 10 consecutive hours) is spent either in the sleeper berth, off duty, or any combination of the two

    C. A separate period of 1 hour is spent taking a break to eat a meal

    D. A. and B.

6. You may "restart" your 60-hour/7 day or 70-hour/8 day clock by having at least _____ consecutive hours off duty.

   A. 14

   B. 24

   C. 34

   D. 48

7. The regulations require you to record your duty status (in duplicate) for each 24-hour period.

   A. True

   B. False

8. There are three categories that must be recorded on your record of duty status: behind the wheel, sleeping, and working.

   A. True

   B. False

9. _____ must be recorded at each change of duty status.

   A. Weather conditions

   B. Vehicle weight

   C. City and state

   D. All of the above

10. You must have in your possession a copy of each record of duty status for the last 7 consecutive days as well as the original record for the current day.

    A. True

    B. False

CDL Air Brake Pre-Test

Read each statement carefully and select the most correct answer.

1. **Air brake equipped vehicles must have:**

    A. At least three air tanks

    B. A hydraulic braking system, in case the air system fails

    C. An air pressure gauge, to show the pressure available for braking

    D. An air application gauge, to show air used by the brake chambers for braking

2. **How do you check the free play in manual slack adjusters?**

    A. Stop on level ground and apply the emergency brakes

    B. Park on level ground, chock wheels, release the parking brakes and pull slack adjusters

    C. Park on level ground and drain off air pressure before making adjustments

    D. Apply the service brakes by hand at the brake chambers and watch the slack adjusters move

3. **The most common type of foundation brake found on heavy commercial vehicles is:**

    A. Disc

    B. Wedge and drum

    C. S-cam drum

    D. None of the above

4. **The air compressor governor controls:**

    A. The rpms of the air compressor

    B. Whether the compressor is in good condition

    C. Air pressure applied to the brakes

    D. When the compressor will pump air into the storage tanks

5. **The brake pedal:**

    A. Is the main control in the system

    B. Can be a foot rest during normal driving

    C. Controls the air pressure applied to operate the brakes

    D. Exerts force on the slack adjusters by rods and connectors

Chapter 25
Hours of Service

Chapter 26

International driving

OBJECTIVES

Upon completion of this chapter, you should have a basic understanding of what to expect when crossing international borders and operating in foreign countries, including:

❏ What to expect if operating in Mexico

❏ What to expect if operating in Canada

❏ Types of customs paperwork needed for cargo transported in Canada

❏ General differences in motor carrier safety requirements and vehicle sizes and weights between U.S. and Canada

Introduction

Every day, many professional drivers cross the U.S. borders without incident. For the new professional driver however, the thought of delivering goods into another country might seem like a daunting task. Being aware of and knowledgeable about some of the processes and procedures can help make your border crossing experience smooth and relatively easy. As long as you know your responsibilities, remain patient and professional, and listen to directions, you should not have a problem.

Some advance planning is necessary when transporting goods to another country, such as Canada and Mexico. It may take time to learn the procedures on border crossings and gather information before you leave; this will be time well spent. The more time you spend learning about and preparing the necessary documentation, the less time you will spend delayed at the border.

As a professional driver who may operate in Mexico or Canada, you need to remember that you are driving in a foreign country. This country may have different laws, customs, poverty levels, and education levels. You may find different languages, units of measurement, road signs, and safety standards. It is your responsibility as a professional to make sure you are familiar with these differences before you enter Mexico, Canada, or any other foreign country.

Operating in Mexico

Prior to 2007, U.S. drivers were not allowed to operate freely in Mexico. Instead, U.S. drivers usually dropped their trailer or load at a U.S. warehouse on the U.S.–Mexico border. A Mexican–based carrier would then pick up the load and transport it to its Mexican destination.

Through the actions of the North American Free Trade Agreement (NAFTA), this is slowly changing and a few U.S. trucking companies are now allowed to operate in Mexico. As this may increase, you may find yourself presented with a load bound for Mexico sometime in the future.

You also need to realize that laws and customs in Mexico are changing due to security concerns and NAFTA rules. Because of this, a Mexican customs broker, which will be hired for your shipment, will be the best source for current information about routing, fuel stops, sleeping facilities, restaurants, traveling concerns, etc.

Mexico's telephone system — Domestic telephone service offers 12 main lines per 100 people. Because of this, your phone access may be limited although, service is typically adequate for business and government. The use of cellular phones is common for much of the domestic service. You should check with your service provider ahead of time to determine availability while in Mexico.

Hey driver. Here's the most important thing you can remember when driving in Mexico or Canada. This is not your country! You are a visitor so don't act like this is your country, you have rights, and you can do what you want. If you do, you just might find yourself in jail...or worse

Maybe there is no rule in Mexico, but you plan on coming back to the U.S. sometime, don't you? You would be much better off continuing your log book as if your were driving in the U.S. That way, when you return, everything is still legal.

Reporting an emergency in Mexico — If you have an emergency in Mexico while driving, the equivalent of 911 in Mexico is 060, but this number is not always answered. If you are driving on a toll highway, or *cuota,* or any other major highway, you may contact the Green Angels. This is a fleet of repair trucks with bilingual crews that operate daily. Their number is (01) 55-5250-8221. If you are unable to contact them by phone, pull off the road and open the hood of your truck. They are trained to spot disabled trucks and assist them.

Holidays in Mexico — There are many holidays in Mexico that are different from those in the United States. Independence Day falls on September 16th. Another holiday, the Day of the Dead, is celebrated on November 1st. It is important that you know Mexico's national holidays while traveling in Mexico since in many cases, a holiday means businesses will be closed and delivery may be difficult.

Hours of Service in Mexico — To date, there is no established governmental limit to the number of hours you may drive per shift while in Mexico. However, remember that you will need to abide by all U.S. regulations as you re–enter the United States which includes recording the previous seven days activities.

Basic personal identification needed — The government of Mexico requires all U.S. citizens present proof of citizenship and photo identification for entry into Mexico. A U.S. passport and your valid commercial driver's license should be carried at all times.

Penalties for drug offenses in Mexico — Penalties for drug offenses are strict, and convicted offenders can expect large fines and jail sentences up to 25 years. As in the United States, the purchase of controlled medication requires a doctor's prescription. The Mexican list of controlled substances differs from that of the United States, and Mexican public health laws concerning controlled medication are unclear and often enforced selectively.

The U.S. Embassy cautions that possession of any amount of prescription medicine brought from the United States could result in arrest if Mexican authorities suspect abuse or if the quantity of the medication exceeds the amount required for several days' use.

Penalties for firearms violations — Do not take any type of firearm or ammunition into Mexico without prior written authorization from the Mexican authorities. Entering Mexico with a firearm, some kinds of knives, or even a single round of ammunition is illegal, even if done unintentionally. Firearms and ammunition of a caliber higher than .22 are considered the exclusive use of the military, and their importation carries penalties of up to 30 years in prison. The Mexican government strictly enforces its laws pertaining to firearms and ammunition along all borders and at air and sea ports.

If legal problems occur in Mexico — In Mexico, U.S. citizens are subject to Mexico's laws and regulations, which sometimes differ significantly from those in the United States. The protection available to citizens under U.S. law are not available in Mexico, and Americans who commit illegal acts have no special privileges, as they are subject to full prosecution under the Mexican judicial system. Penalties for breaking the law can be more severe than in the United States for similar offenses. Persons violating Mexico's laws, even unknowingly, may be expelled, arrested, or imprisoned.

Prison conditions in Mexico can be extremely poor. In many facilities, food is insufficient in both quantity and quality, and prisoners must pay for adequate nutrition from their own funds.

Operating in Canada

Canadian border crossing.

Travel into Canada is relatively common for the professional driver. Because U.S. drivers are allowed to operate into Canada without restriction, entry into and operation throughout Canada requires adequate preparation and paperwork. Unlike Mexico, travel by U.S. commercial motor vehicle operators has been allowed in Canada for many years. Border crossing practices have been well established and streamlined in many ways.

Personal credentials/identification — To enter the country, Canada requires proof of identification and citizenship. Similar to entrance into Mexico, your best identification method is a current passport and your commercial operator's license. Passports are expected to become mandatory some time in 2008, so check with the U.S. Department of State periodically. In lieu of a passport, Canada currently accepts a birth certificate.

If you are a permanent resident of the U.S. but not a citizen, then you will be required to present proof of your immigration status and show your visa.

Entering Canada with children — Officials at the Canadian border place an emphasis on ensuring child safety. Because of this, minors are required to possess proof of citizenship; a passport, citizenship card, or a legal resident card, in order to enter Canada, just like all other visitors.

If you are a parent, you must show written proof that you have legal authority to have this child with you, and that the other parent is aware that you are taking them out of the country. This must be in letter form, signed by the other parent.

If you are a parent who is divorced or separated and you want to take a minor to Canada with you, you will need to carry any applicable court documents showing legal custody rights and/or letters from the other parent stating that he/she authorizes the child to leave the country. Also, if you are entering Canada with a minor and you are not the minor's parent or legal guardian, you must have a letter from the minor's parent(s) or guardian(s) giving permission for you to take the minor to Canada.

In all instances, this letter must include the address and phone number of the other parent, legal parent(s), or legal guardian(s). It must also include the name, address, and phone number of any other person who can verify the minor is not being taken against his/her will.

Prior convictions — Certain types of convictions that are considered misdemeanors in the United States may be considered serious criminal (felony) offenses in Canada. If a professional driver has a felony conviction in the U.S., the driver may not be admitted into Canada. Through Canada's rehabilitation program, this "banning from Canada" may not be permanent. If you have been convicted of a crime that is considered to be a felony in Canada, you may be eligible for entry into Canada after five years from the end of your sentence.

Hey, now is not the time to terrorize your children! Plan ahead, make sure you have the proper documentation, and avoid the hassles. Your kid will thank you for it!

Rehabilitation requests can range from $200 up to $1000 based on the level of felony. If you are unsure about whether a crime would make you criminally inadmissable into Canada, you can fill out a rehabilitation request "for information only." By doing this, you would not be required to pay the associated fees until you want to proceed with the official rehabilitation request.

If you have a felony conviction and need to enter Canada for a short time on a very limited basis, a special permit may be issued by the Citizenship and Immigration Canada consulate offices in the United States, but this is not guaranteed.

Declaring personal items — Certain personal items carried over the border into Canada must be "declared" to the Canadian Border Services Agency (CBSA). Personal items that you must declare include:

- Alcohol

- Tobacco

- All animals, plants, and their products

- Explosives, fireworks, ammunition

- Firearms and weapons (certain weapons are prohibited and may be confiscated at the border)

- Prescription drugs with a clearly identifying label (if possible, you should also carry a letter from your doctor indicating your prescription)

Prohibited items — In Canada, professional drivers are prohibited from having alcohol in the cab of their vehicle under any circumstances. Other generally prohibited items include weapons, such as mace and handguns, as well as illegal drugs.

Vehicle credentials/safety compliance — Before leaving for Canada, you need to ensure that your vehicle registration, applicable safety certificates, fuel tax registration, permits, and operating authority are all in order. Carriers will usually provide the necessary credentials to their drivers, but it is the driver's responsibility to make sure that he/she has everything they need and that it is current.

You will also want to make sure that your vehicle and load meet the vehicle size and weight limits for where you will be traveling in Canada. More information on sizes and weights will be discussed a little later in this chapter.

Border station hours — While many border crossing locations are in operation 24 hours a day, 7 days a week, some border crossings in rural areas may have limited operating hours. Be sure to check with your intended border crossing office to ensure the office will be open when you arrive.

Crossing the Canadian Border

Crossing the border into Canada requires patience and a general understanding of the paperwork and procedures required by the CBSA. If you have done your homework in these areas, your border crossing should be relatively painless.

Border station entry — When you approach most border stations, you will find that there are certain lanes specified for the various vehicles entering the station. Use the designated commercial lanes, regardless of how long they are, at the border crossing station. Watch for signs that will direct you to the proper areas. It is important to remember crossing into Canada is a well-established systematic process. If you follow the signs and the directions of the officials at the border, your problems should be minimal.

Questioning — Upon arrival at the border, be prepared to answer a series of questions pertaining to your truck, your freight, your purpose for entering Canada, and your background or citizenship.

Officers will ask you questions to make sure you are not involved in any illegal activity and that

Container port.

you have met all documentation requirements for you, your vehicle, and your load. Some possible questions you may be asked include:

- How long will you be visiting Canada?
- Where will you be staying while in Canada?
- What will you be doing in Canada during your stay?
- What is your date of intended return to the United States?
- Do you have items to declare?
- Do you have any weapons in your possession?
- What are you hauling?
- Are you traveling alone?

Answer all questions directly and honestly. Be sure to listen closely and follow all further instructions from the CBSA officers.

Customs inspections — CBSA may inspect your cargo for illegal drugs/ weapons and plants/animals that are not permitted into Canada. They may also search the cab of your truck for these items and may also search for illegal aliens or undeclared passengers. Last, they may inspect your cargo to insure that what you are carrying matches the paperwork you have provided.

Paperwork — The type of cargo you are hauling can determine what types of paperwork you will be required to submit at the border. Some shipments that are going to Canada are released or cleared by the CBSA at the border, and some shipments are released or cleared at warehouses or other inland locations. The manner in which cargo is released can also change the type of paperwork needed to transport a shipment into and out of Canada.

Some common forms/paperwork required to be submitted or shown at the Canadian border may include the following:

- *Form 7525–V, Shipper's Export Declaration.* Form 7525–V is actually a form required by U.S. Customs Border Patrol (CBP). This form notifies the CBP that you are exporting goods into Canada.

- *Form A8A, United States–Canada Transit Manifest.* This form is used to report shipments traveling through, but not delivering within, the United States and Canada.

- *B232, North American Free Trade Agreement (NAFTA)–Certificate of Origin.* Form B232 is used by importers to report goods qualifying under the NAFTA.

- *Bill of Lading.* The bill of lading describes the property you are carrying, as well as its origin and destination.

Border crossing programs — There are several different types of border crossing programs in which you or your carrier may be involved in. These border crossing programs were created to expedite shipments and drivers across the Canadian border while ensuring the shipments are legal and secure. Some of these programs are:

- *PARS* — The pre-arrival review system (PARS) is an optional program that allows shipments to be released directly into Canada without additional inspection at the border. The exporter/shipper will provide advance cargo documentation to CBSA, who will then look over the cargo documentation for accuracy and validity. When the driver arrives at the border, the driver's paperwork is matched to the information previously sent by the exporter or shipper. If everything matches, CBSA will then usually release the cargo without further inspection.

- *CSA* — Customs Self Assessment (CSA) is a program under which carriers and drivers can take advantage of streamlined clearance options for eligible goods. Carriers must apply for the CSA program and meet certain conditions before becoming a CSA participant.

- *FAST* — U.S. CBP and Canadian CBSA have aligned to create the Free and Secure Trade Program (FAST). This program establishes a harmonized clearance process for low-risk shipments and helps expedite shipments across the border. Dedicated FAST lanes at border crossings allow drivers and carriers with FAST clearance to cross the border much more quickly. Carriers and/or drivers must pre-apply for FAST through the U.S. CBP or the Canadian CBSA.

Hey driver. "I don't know" or "I don't care" are not acceptable answers when it comes to your paperwork and your freight if you are crossing into Canada. It's your job to know what you have and that your paperwork is correct and complete. The border officials do not smile on ignorance!

- *FIRST* — Frequent Importer Release System (FIRST) is an option that allows approved importers with low-risk, low-revenue goods to expedite the movement of their goods across the border. This program must also be applied for by the carrier, and they must meet certain pre-established guidelines.

All of these programs were designed to expedite the movement of freight between the U.S. and Canada and to keep the driver's delay time at the border down to a minimum.

Returning to the United States From Canada

Upon returning to the United States after your trip to Canada, you will be required to show identification, such as your CDL, and proof of citizenship. You should already have these items available, as you needed them to enter Canada.

If you are returning with freight, you will also be required to show proper credentials and paperwork for the freight, similar to what you needed when you entered Canada with a load.

Motor Carrier Safety and Licensing

As referenced earlier, while operating in Canada you need to be aware of some differences in the safety regulations as they apply to the professional driver. As in the United States, you need to be in compliance when operating in Canada.

Canadian hours of service — The Canadian hours-of-service requirements are different from those in the United States. Canadian regulations compared to U.S. regulations can be summarized as follows:

Time, Cycle, Etc	Canadian HOS regulations	U.S. HOS regulations
Daily Driving Time	13 hours	11 hours after 10 hours off duty
Daily on-duty time	14 hours	may not drive after the 14th hour after coming on-duty
Daily off-duty time	10 hours	10 consecutive hours off duty before driving
Length of workday	no driving after 16 hours	no driving after 14 hours after coming on duty
Duty Cycle	70 hours/7 days, 120 hours/14 days	60 hours/7 days, 70 hours/8 days

Split Sleeper (non-team)	10 hours can be split into two periods of no less than 2 hours each	10 hours can be split into two periods with one period in the sleeper berth of at least 8 hours and the other off duty and/or sleeper berth of at least 2 hours
Split Sleeper (team)	8 hours can be split into two periods of no less than 4 hours each	same as split sleeper (non-team)
Cycle Reset	36 hours for 70-hour/7 day, 72 hours for 120-hour/14 day	34-hour restart

Canada also requires additional items to be recorded in the daily log, such as:

- Starting/ending odometer reading and total distance traveled (minus any personal use)

- Drivers cycle identified

- Starting/ending odometer reading for any personal use (up to 75 kilometers, approximately 47 miles travel per day)

- Home terminal and address

Vehicle trip inspections — Canada requires a documented pre-trip inspection of vehicles while the U.S. requires a documented post-trip inspection. The U.S. and Canada have a reciprocal agreement in place for trip inspection reporting. Be sure you have proof of a post-trip inspection before entering Canada.

Operating authority/Canadian safety credentials — Operating authority in the United States is granted by the Federal Motor Carrier Safety Administration (FMCSA). In Canada however, a federal operating authority does not exist. Instead, Canadian carriers must obtain a safety operating authority called a safety fitness certificate. In most Canadian jurisdictions, the requirements for a carrier to obtain a safety fitness certificate only applies to Canadian-based carriers. However, two provinces, Ontario and Quebec, both require U.S.-based carriers to obtain registration within the provinces.

In Ontario, it is called the Commercial Vehicle Operator Registration and in Quebec it is called the Registration Identification Number. Both registrations allow Ontario and Quebec to track the safety performance of U.S. carriers operating in the provinces. While operating in these provinces, you may have to produce credentials showing that your carrier is registered under these programs.

IFTA/IRP credentials — Because the International Fuel Tax Agreement (IFTA) and the International Registration Plan (IRP) apply to the lower 48 states and 10 Canadian provinces, you must have proper IFTA and IRP credentials when operating in Canada. For IFTA, you will have a copy of the IFTA license in your cab and IFTA decals on both sides of your cab.

For IRP, you will have a "cab card" listing at what weights and in what states and provinces your vehicle can travel. If a state or province is not listed on your cab card, you will need to purchase a trip permit to enter that state or province, or the carrier may have the state or province added to the card. The carrier will likely provide you with all necessary documentation and permits.

Canadian enforcement officers are authorized to ask to see your IFTA and IRP credentials at any time.

Vehicle Sizes and Weights

The vehicle size and weight requirements in Canada are different, but similar to, the requirements in the United States.

In Canada, the vehicle size and weight requirements are established by each jurisdiction. For example, the size and weight requirements in British Columbia may not be the same as the requirements in Ontario. In order to create uniformity among the Canadian jurisdictions, all jurisdictions agreed to a "Memorandum of Understanding" (MOU) on vehicle size and weights.

The MOU establishes the following size and weight limitations:

- Height 4.15 m (13 ft. 6 in.)
- Width 2.60 m (8 ft. 6 in.)
- Length -
    1. Straight truck 12.5 m (41 ft.)
    2. Semitrailer 16.2 m (53 ft.)
    3. Truck-trailer 23.0 m (75 ft. 6 in.)
- Weight -
    1. Straight truck 25,250 kg (55,667 lb.)
    2. Tractor-semitrailer 46,500 kg (102,515 lb.)
    3. Truck-full trailer 53,500 kg (117,947 lb.)

Even though the MOU is in place, a Canadian jurisdiction may adopt less restrictive size and weight limits for roads within their jurisdiction. Refer to the individual jurisdictions' size and weight regulations for more information.

Don't get scared when you see that bridge height in meters. Just figure it out and continue on your trip. If you are on a major highway, you are probably OK. If you are on a city street and you are not sure...better pull over and do a little math!

Metric Measurements and Conversions

Canada uses the metric system which is unlike the United States, where the English system is used. Common conversions of the English and Metric systems include the following:

- 1 meter = 3.28 feet

- 1 kilometer = 0.621 miles

- 1 kilogram = 2.2046 pounds

- 1 foot = 0.3048 meters

- 1 mile = 1.6093 kilometers

- 1 pound = 0.454 kilograms

To convert a metric measurement to an English measurement, simply multiply by the English conversion equivalent. For example:

- To convert 80 kilometers to miles: 80 x 0.621 = 49.7 miles

- To convert 20 meters to feet: 20 x 3.28 = 65.6 feet

Canada uses degrees Celsius to represent temperature. To convert Celsius temperatures to Fahrenheit, multiply the degrees Celsius by 1.8 and add 32. For example, to determine the Fahrenheit temperature equivalent to 25° C, multiply (25°C x 1.8) + 32 = 77°F

Common Traffic Signs and Rules

The rules of the road in Canada are similar to that in the United States. In Canada, vehicles operate on the right side of the road and traffic signs and lights look relatively the same as they do in the United States.

Many of the signs on Canadian roads are generally self-explanatory. "STOP," "YIELD," "DO NOT ENTER," and "U-TURN PROHIBITED" signs are similar in design and color. Speed limit signs look the same except they are posted in metric units, such as 80 kilometers/hour.

Because there are many French-speaking regions in Canada, stop signs may be posted using the French word "ARRET" in place of "STOP," or both words may be posted on one sign. While operating in Canada, you may see signs for cities, buildings, parks, etc., posted in both English and French.

One more thing driver...If you ask for "wheat toast" in Canada, you may get a funny look from the server. The correct terminology is "Brown toast." Canadians keep it simple...brown toast or white toast, your choice!

Summary

This chapter has covered many of the differences, similarities, and challenges you will experience while driving in Canada and Mexico. It is most important to remember that planning ahead and remaining professional are two of the most important things you can do to make your cross-border trip a successful and positive experience.

To best summarize what we have covered, here is a list of ten tips for border crossings:

1. Be patient.

2. Listen to directions given by border personnel.

3. Do not argue with border personnel. Be cooperative.

4. Be polite and answer questions honestly.

5. Have your paperwork and documentation completed and in order before arriving at the border.

6. Be familiar with your cargo.

7. Declare your personal items truthfully.

8. Check border crossing hours to make sure the location you will be using is open at the time you plan to arrive.

9. Do not leave your vehicle unlocked or unattended.

10. Report any suspicious or criminal activity at the border crossing.

International Driving Quiz

1. **Regarding suggestions for safe trips in any country, which of the following is not a correct statement?**

    A. Never leave you vehicle unlocked, even when your engine is idling

    B. Do not leave valuables unattended. Lock them in the truck, motel, or truck stop safe

    C. It is safe to walk or go anywhere you like because local police always look out for foreigners

    D. Keep all valuables in your vehicle out of sight

2. **When NAFTA was passed, it _____.**

    A. Provided a continuity in the efforts by the United States and Canada to improve the movement of freight and people over the border

    B. Focused on restricting trade in Europe

    C. Focused on improving trade in South America

    D. Focused on improving world trade

3. **Canadians use the _____ system to measure everything including speed and fuel.**

    A. Imperial (metric)

    B. U.S.

    C. Modified imperial

    D. World trade

4. **The rules and guidelines of the Commercial Vehicle Safety Alliance are used on all roads across Canada just like they are across _____.**

    A. All of South America

    B. All of Central America

    C. All of Europe

    D. The United States

5. **The Free and Secure Trade (FAST) supports moving _____ across the border quickly and verifying trade compliance away from the border.**

    A. Race cars only

    B. Pre-approved eligible goods

    C. All items manufactured in Europe

    D. Any items from South America

6. **Which of the following is not a good practice regarding getting through Canadian customs?**

   A. Have your trailer loaded so it can be inspected easily

   B. Be cordial and helpful with inspectors

   C. You do not have to declare personal goods such as prescription drugs, firearms, pets, etc.

   D. Know what your cargo contains so you can answer any questions the authorities may have

*7. **Regarding commercial drivers in Canada, which of the following is a correct statement?**

   A. Maximum time on duty is 15 hours including driving time

   B. You are allowed to drive 10 hours in a 24-hour period

   C. 8 hours off duty is required before a driver can drive again

   D. In any seven day period, drivers may be on duty for only 60 hours

8. **Because of changes in Mexico brought about by such things as changing political climates, security concerns, and changing NAFTA rules, _____ is the best source of information concerning routing, fuel stops, safe stopping areas, etc.**

   A. The Mexican customs broker hired for your shipment

   B. Other drivers

   C. Newspapers, magazines, etc

   D. Television news

9. **Since fuel in Mexico is sold in liter measures, to convert liters to gallons divide the number of liters purchased by _____ to get an approximate amount.**

   A. 6

   B. 10

   C. 4

   D. 2

10. **Regarding hours of service in Mexico, which of the following is correct?**

    A. Mexican law is the same as U.S. law

    B. Drivers may drive 15 hours with 9 hours off duty

    C. Drivers may be on duty 15 hours with 13 hours of driving and 9 hours off duty

    D. There is no governmental limit to the number of hours driven per shift

CDL Air Brake Pre-Test

Read each statement carefully and select the most correct answer.

1. **What will determine how effectively the spring emergency brakes or the parking brakes work?**

    A. The condition of the service brakes

    B. This can only be tested by highly trained brake service people

    C. The adjustment of the service brakes

    D. Braking power will increase when the service brakes are hot

2. **When a failure occurs in the service brake system, the system you need to stop the vehicle is the:**

    A. Parking brake system

    B. Emergency brake system

    C. Drum brake system

    D. Hand brake system

3. **If your vehicle is equipped with an alcohol evaporator, every day during the winter weather you should:**

    A. Check and fill the alcohol level

    B. Change the alcohol with a new bottle

    C. Oil the system with 5 wt. oil

    D. Drain out the alcohol which has accumulated

4. **What turns on the electrical stop light switch in an air brake system?**

    A. Spring pressure

    B. Hydraulic pressure

    C. Air pressure

    D. The driver, by hand

5. **Which of the following is O.K. to find in the air brake system?**

    A. Oil

    B. Air

    C. Water

    D. All of the above

Chapter **27**

Trip planning

OBJECTIVES

Upon completion of this chapter, you should have a general understanding of the five basic steps involved when planning a trip:

❏   Having up to date paperwork

❏   Selecting a route

❏   Estimating time

❏   Estimating fuel use and fuel stops

❏   Estimating trip expenses

Introduction

The idea behind trip planning is to design the most effective, efficient, safe, and legal route between two points.

A well thought out trip plan can mean a savings of time and money for you and your company. A good plan can also mean a safe trip for you and the load you are hauling. If you have a solid plan before hitting the road, you are better able to relax and devote all of your time to paying attention to the road. If you don't have a plan, you have more than just driving on your mind. You are concerned about when and how you will arrive at your destination.

The Five Basic Steps of Trip Planning

The following are the five basic steps of trip planning.

1. Make sure paperwork is up to date. Have proper freight documentation, current hours-of-service records, and proper permits and licenses.

2. Select the route. Remember, many variables are involved including cargo restrictions, traffic conditions, and weather.

3. Estimate time and plan for stops. Plan to meet the scheduled deadline, but consider driver and vehicle factors as well as weather and road conditions.

4. Estimate fuel use and fuel stops.

5. Estimate trip expenses. Understand the length and nature of the trip, what conditions to expect on the road, and plan for the unexpected.

Paperwork

After driving, paperwork is probably the largest task a driver deals with on a daily basis. Making sure you have all necessary paperwork and that the paperwork is accurate before your trip is essential to planning an efficient and profitable trip.

Generally, the paperwork you should carry with you falls under three categories:

- Driver;
- Cargo; and
- Vehicle.

Driver — As the driver of a commercial motor vehicle, the Federal Motor Carrier Safety Regulations (FMCSRs) require you to carry certain documents to verify that you are a qualified driver.

Operator's license — You are required to have a valid operator's (driver's) license when operating any type of motor vehicle. You must carry this license when operating a motor vehicle.

The class of license you must hold is based on the type of vehicle you are operating.

The commercial driver's license (CDL) classes are federally mandated. (See Sec. 383.91 of the FMCSRs for details.) The CDL classes are as follows:

1. **Class A** — Any combination of vehicles with a gross combination weight rating (GCWR) of 26,001 pounds (11,794 kilograms) or more provided the gross vehicle weight rating (GVWR) of the vehicle(s) being towed is in excess of 10,000 pounds (4,536 kilograms).

2. **Class B** — Any single vehicle with a GVWR of 26,001 pounds (11,794 kilograms) or more, or any such vehicle towing a vehicle not in excess of 10,000 pounds (4,536 kilograms) GVWR.

3. **Class C** — Any single vehicle, or combination of vehicles that meets neither the definition of Class A nor that of Class B, but is designed to transport 16 or more passengers (including the driver) or is used in the transportation of a placardable amount of hazardous materials.

Non-CDL classes of license vary from state to state. Consult state requirements for details.

Hey driver. This stuff should ALWAYS be up to date and it's your responsibility to make sure it is. You should know when your license needs to be renewed, when your medical card expires, and that you have the proper endorsements for what you are hauling. Don't wait for someone else to tell you that your license is expired. It's your license, and it's your fine if you don't get it right!

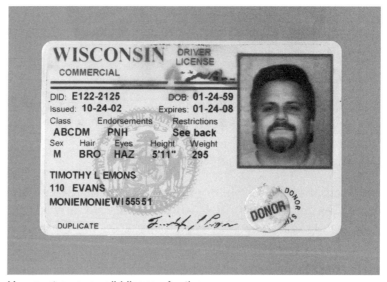

You must carry a valid license for the vehicle you are operating.

Medical exam certificate — The driver qualification regulations place a great deal of emphasis on physical qualifications. This includes a requirement that you possess the original or copy of a medical examiner's certificate stating you are physically qualified to drive.

The medical examiner's certificate is the only certificate that is required by the regulations to be carried by you at all times while operating a commercial motor vehicle.

MEDICAL EXAMINER'S CERTIFICATE

I certify that I have examined _____ in accordance with the Federal Motor Carrier Safety Regulations (49 CFR 391.41-391.49) and with knowledge of the driving duties, I find this person is qualified; and, if applicable, only when:

☐ wearing corrective lenses   ☐ driving within an exempt intracity zone (49 CFR 391.62)

☐ wearing hearing aid   ☐ accompanied by a Skill Performance Evaluation Certificate (SPE)

☐ accompanied by a _____ waiver/exemption   ☐ qualified by operation of 49 CFR 391.64

The information I have provided regarding this physical examination is true and complete. A complete examination form with any attachment embodies my findings completely and correctly, and is on file in my office.

SIGNATURE OF MEDICAL EXAMINER	TELEPHONE	DATE
MEDICAL EXAMINER'S NAME (PRINT)	☐ MD ☐ DO ☐ Chiropractor ☐ Physician Assistant ☐ Advanced Practice Nurse	
MEDICAL EXAMINER'S LICENSE OR CERTIFICATE NO. ISSUING STATE		
SIGNATURE OF DRIVER	DRIVER'S LICENSE NO.	STATE
ADDRESS OF DRIVER		
MEDICAL CERTIFICATE EXPIRATION DATE		

DISTRIBUTION: 1 COPY TO THE DRIVER, 1 COPY TO THE MOTOR CARRIER

Published by J. J. KELLER & ASSOCIATES, INC., Neenah, WI • USA
(800) 327-6868 • www.jjkeller.com • Printed in the United States
650-FS-L2 6046 (3/01)

The medical exam certificate.

Record of duty status (driver's log) — Each motor carrier must require every driver to record his/her duty status for each 24-hour period.

You must complete the record of duty status in your own handwriting (in duplicate) or by using an automatic on-board recording device. The record must be legible and kept current to the time shown for the last change of duty status.

You must submit the original record of duty status to your motor carrier within 13 days of completion.

You must have in your possession a copy of each record for the last 7 consecutive days as well as the original record for the current day. They must be available for inspection while you are on duty.

Note: In-depth information on the record of duty status and hours-of-service requirements is covered in Chapter 25.

Cargo — Paperwork regarding the freight you are hauling should be in proper order *before* you begin your trip. This ensures the safe and accurate delivery of goods to the appropriate party.

Bill of lading — The bill of lading is the document used in transactions between a shipper and carrier. There are three distinct and important functions served by the bill of lading:

1. It is a receipt issued by the carrier to a shipper for goods received for transportation.

2. It is a contract naming the parties involved, the rate/charge for transportation, and the agreement regarding the carrier's liability in the event of damage or loss of goods.

3. It serves as documentary evidence of title to the goods.

Remember, we talked about this before. Drive it legal and record what you drive. Don't play games with your log book and make sure you keep the required copies on-hand. Gettin' "creative" with your log book will eventually get you in big trouble, so just don't do it.

Unless specifically instructed otherwise, the carrier's duty is to deliver the shipment to the consignee named on the bill of lading. Possession of an original "order" bill of lading, properly endorsed, indicates title to the goods.

Bills of lading must be legibly written.

The following information must be included on the bill of lading:

- Names of consignor and consignee;

- Origin and destination points;

- Number of packages;

- Description of freight; and

- Weight, volume, or measure of freight (if applicable to the rating of the freight).

Note: In-depth information on the bill of lading requirements are covered in Chapter 23.

This is an important document so make sure it's right from the beginning. If something looks incorrect, or incomplete, question it. If you are not getting answers, stop what you are doing and call your dispatcher. When you get to the receiver is no time to be trying to explain why the freight on your trailer is not what you are supposed to have!

A straight bill of lading.

Vehicle — Paperwork regarding vehicle operations is completed throughout a trip. Accuracy is important, as the paperwork listed below is required by regulation and/or law.

Driver vehicle inspection report (DVIR) — Though the regulations do not require you to carry this document on your vehicle, you are required to complete a DVIR at the end of each day's work on each vehicle operated and the DVIR must be reviewed as part of your pre-trip inspection process.

Section 396.11 of the FMCSRs requires you to complete a written report covering eleven different parts and accessories.

On the report, you must identify the vehicle and list any defect or deficiency which could affect its safe operation or cause a mechanical breakdown. If you do not find any defects or deficiencies, you need to report that as well. In all cases, after completing the inspection, you must sign the report.

DRIVER'S VEHICLE INSPECTION REPORT
AS REQUIRED BY THE D.O.T. FEDERAL MOTOR CARRIER SAFETY REGULATIONS

CARRIER: _____

ADDRESS: _____

DATE: _____ TIME: _____ A.M. _____ P.M.
CHECK ANY DEFECTIVE ITEM AND GIVE DETAILS UNDER "REMARKS"

**TRACTOR/
TRUCK NO.** _____ ODOMETER READING _____

☐ Air Compressor
☐ Air Lines
☐ Battery
☐ Belts and Hoses
☐ Body
☐ Brake Accessories
☐ Brakes, Parking
☐ Brakes, Service
☐ Clutch
☐ Coupling Devices
☐ Defroster/Heater
☐ Drive Line
☐ Engine
☐ Exhaust
☐ Fifth Wheel
☐ Fluid Levels
☐ Frame and Assembly

☐ Front Axle
☐ Fuel Tanks
☐ Horn
☐ Lights
　　Head - Stop
　　Tail - Dash
　　Turn Indicators
☐ Mirrors
☐ Muffler
☐ Oil Pressure
☐ Radiator
☐ Rear End
☐ Reflectors

☐ Safety Equipment
　　Fire Extinguisher
　　Flags - Flares - Fusees
　　Reflective Triangles
　　Spare Bulbs and Fuses
　　Spare Seal Beam
☐ Starter
☐ Steering
☐ Suspension System
☐ Tire Chains
☐ Tires
☐ Transmission
☐ Trip Recorder
☐ Wheels and Rims
☐ Windows
☐ Windshield Wipers
☐ Other

TRAILER(S) NO.(S) _____

☐ Brake Connections
☐ Brakes
☐ Coupling Devices
☐ Coupling (King) Pin
☐ Doors

☐ Hitch
☐ Landing Gear
☐ Lights - All
☐ Reflectors/Reflective Tape
☐ Roof

☐ Suspension System
☐ Tarpaulin
☐ Tires
☐ Wheels and Rims
☐ Other

Remarks: _____
_____
_____
_____
_____
_____
_____
_____

☐ CONDITION OF THE ABOVE VEHICLE IS SATISFACTORY

DRIVER'S SIGNATURE: _____

☐ ABOVE DEFECTS CORRECTED

☐ ABOVE DEFECTS NEED NOT BE CORRECTED FOR SAFE OPERATION OF VEHICLE

MECHANIC'S SIGNATURE: _____ DATE: _____

DRIVER'S SIGNATURE: _____ DATE: _____

ORIGINAL
© Copyright 2007 J. J. KELLER & ASSOCIATES, INC., Neenah, WI
USA • (800) 327-6868 • Printed in the United States

A driver vehicle inspection report (DVIR).

Before the vehicle can be operated again, any items listed as being defective or deficient that may affect the safety of the vehicle must be repaired.

The motor carrier must certify (on the DVIR) that the defect or deficiency has been corrected or that correction is not necessary to safely operate the vehicle.

Your signature, acknowledging the corrective action, must be on the DVIR before you may operate the vehicle.

Trip report — A trip report or individual vehicle mileage report (IVMR) is used to record trip information including:

- Date of trip (starting and ending);

- Trip origin and destination;

- Route of travel and/or beginning and ending odometer reading of the trip;

- Total trip miles;

- Unit number or vehicle identification number.

The trip report must be accurate as this information is used by International Fuel Tax Agreement (IFTA) and International Registration Plan (IRP) auditors to verify payment of taxes.

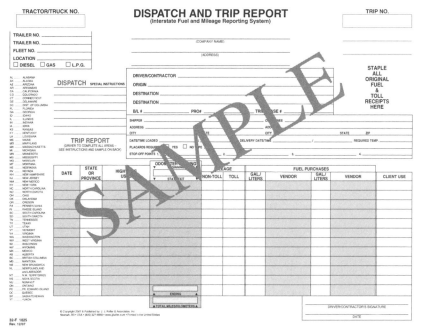

A dispatch and trip report.

You should also complete a trip cost report. It tracks expenses incurred during the course of a trip. A trip cost report includes detailed information on:

- Fuel purchases;

- Brokerage fees;

- Permit fees;

- Tolls; and

- Scale fees.

Route Selection

Many factors go into the selection of an appropriate route. Though, when reading a map, the shortest route (mileage-wise) may appear to be the best, this isn't always the case. Terrain, weather, traffic, road construction, and vehicle and cargo restrictions all play a part in selecting an appropriate route.

Reading maps — Being able to read and understand a road map is the first step in selecting an efficient route.

The road map is a necessary tool for the professional driver.

The road map is a necessary tool, helping you determine routes and locate specific destinations. Essential map reading skills you need to be proficient in include:

- Locating the starting point, intermediate stops, and the destination;
- Laying the route out on a map;
- Estimating point-to-point mileage using the map scale; and
- Reading map symbols.

Maps have many characteristics you need to understand in order to successfully plan a trip.

The majority of maps are set on a box or grid pattern with letters along the top and bottom and numbers along the sides of the map. A box or key within the map lists destinations (cities, towns, streets) and where to find them within the grid system.

All maps include a scale. The scale lists how many inches represent a given number of miles. Map scales are good for figuring a rough mileage estimate. Mileage charts give a better idea of true distance.

O.K. driver...only you really know where you are going. Don't count on your dispatcher, the guy in the booth next to you at the truck stop or the CB to help you get to where you need to be. You need to plan your trip BEFORE you hit the road, and stick to your plan! Know your highways; know your fuel and rest stops; know your customer location. If you don't, you could have a miserable trip. That's not being a professional! Don't just get in your truck and start driving. Plan ahead!

Symbols are also included on all maps. Symbols represent everything from the size of a community to where to find a rest area. Symbols vary from map to map and all maps include a legend explaining the symbols used.

There are two types of maps most drivers rely on, highway maps and city maps.

1. **Highway maps** show an entire state or region. They sometimes include major cities in some detail. Features vary depending on the map, but all include major routes, road types, toll roads and freeways, population centers, and railroad crossings. Highway maps are best used to locate major highways and routes for long distance travel.

2. **City maps** provide the greatest detail. Major street names are readable and secondary streets can often be located on these types of maps.

Maps are also available online via several search engines and other providers.

Keep in mind that maps do not include information on delays caused by road construction or poor weather conditions. This information is available via the Internet from several sources including the Federal Highway Administration (FHWA): http://www.fhwa.dot.gov/trafficinfo/.

Vehicle and cargo restrictions — Even the best planned trip can run into some unplanned delays and/or problems. Issues such as restricted routes and weight limits on roads and/or bridges must be dealt with while on the road.

Legal weight limits — Your vehicle must stay within legal limits. Federal requirements outlined in 49 CFR 658.17 are as follows:

The maximum gross vehicle weight (GVW) is 80,000 pounds except where a lower GVW is dictated by the bridge formula.

The maximum gross weight on any one axle, including any one axle of a group of axles, or a vehicle, is 20,000 pounds.

The maximum gross weight on tandem axles is 34,000 pounds.

Vehicles are not allowed on interstate highways if the gross weight on two or more consecutive axles exceeds the limitations prescribed in the Bridge Gross Weight Formula, described below.

$$W = 500\left[\frac{LN}{N-1} + 12N + 36\right]$$

W = the maximum weight in pounds that can be carried on a group of two or more axles to the nearest 500 pounds.

L = the distance in feet between the outer axles of any two or more consecutive axles.

N = the number of axles being considered.

Hey driver. Do you know the difference between an even numbered road and an odd numbered road? How about the difference between Interstate 94, 494, 694, and 394? Can you name the major interstates from South to North and West to East? A professional driver knows what all this means. If you don't know, ask your instructor!!

This formula limits the weight on groups of axles in order to reduce the risk of damage to highway bridges. Allowable weight depends on the number of axles a vehicle has and the distance between those axles. However, the single- or tandem-axle weight limits supersede the Bridge Formula limits for all axles not more than 96 inches apart.

Know the weight limitations for the roads you travel on.

Note: Each state has its own weight limitations. Be aware of the regulations for the states you travel through. Also keep in mind that weight limits may be posted on individual roads or bridges. Vehicles exceeding the posted weights are prohibited.

Truck routes — Communities often designate certain roads as truck routes, in many cases, prohibiting trucks from operating outside of these routes

Estimating Time

Estimating the time a trip will take is necessary for planning stops, complying with hours-of-service regulations, estimating arrival time, and of course meeting schedules.

Allow two hours for every 100 miles traveled. This amount of time is a reasonable amount to cover driving time, meals, fuel stops, and rest stops.

Distance x 2/100 miles = Hours

If you drive mainly in the western states, you may be able to average better than this figure; however, it's important to understand that this is an average. If you drive 75 mph sometimes and 55 mph other times you may be averaging only 60 mph, so don't plan your entire trip at 75 mph just because that's what the posted speed limit is in the state you are running.

This holds true conversely if you are running mainly in the northeast. Even though most posted speeds in that area are 55 mph, you may only average 45 or 50 due to increased traffic and congestion.

Estimating time is crucial to your success as a professional driver. Most deliveries and pickups have scheduled times. If you miss those times you may have to wait hours or even days to get loaded or unloaded. So when you pick up a load in Boston and you have to deliver it in Los Angeles, how do you know when you will get there? By planning your route and estimating your time!

Keep in mind weather, traffic and other conditions which could affect trip time. Remember, no driver is able to drive the maximum speed limit at all times.

Also take into consideration the hours-of-service regulations. Under these regulations, located in Part 395 of the FMCSRs, the driver of a property-carrying commercial motor vehicle may not drive:

- More than 11 hours following 10 consecutive hours off duty; or

- Beyond the 14th consecutive hour after coming on duty, following 10 consecutive hours off duty; or

- After being on duty more than 60 or 70 hours in any 7 or 8 consecutive days.

Note: See Chapter 25 for complete details.

Estimating Fuel Usage

Fuel usage estimates are needed to plan fuel stops.

The first step in estimating fuel usage is to determine the range of the vehicle. To find the range of a vehicle, multiply the tank capacity (in gallons) by the miles per gallon the vehicle delivers.

Tank capacity (gallons) x Miles per gallon (mpg) = Range

Average fuel usage is based on several factors including:

- Highway driving;

- City (town) driving;

- Slowdowns; and

- Idling time.

There are also factors/conditions that may not occur on a daily basis that you should keep in mind when estimating fuel use including:

- Idling for an extended period of time;

- Driving at higher speeds;

- Driving in the mountains; and

- Headwinds.

There's a sign in Utah on a certain highway that says, "This is the last town for over 100 miles...how's your fuel?" There's another one in Nevada that says, "Nation's loneliest road...how's your vehicle running?" You need to know how much fuel you have at all times and where your next fuel stop is. If not...it could be a very long walk to get help.

Estimating Trip Expenses

Estimating the amount of money a trip will take means planning for food, fuel, tolls, and overnight stops. When estimating expenses, consider the:

- Distance to be traveled;
- Time the trip will take; and
- Possibility that emergency funds may be needed.

Items topping the expense list include meals, layovers, tolls, rest stops, and fuel stops. In an emergency, you may need funds for towing, a service call, or an unexpected layover.

Summary

A well thought out trip plan can save your company time and money. Proper planning can save you from having to worry about certain details while on the road, allowing you to concentrate on driving safely.

Trip Planning Quiz

Directions: Read each statement carefully and mark the response that best answers the question.

1. **When on the road, you do not need to carry the original or a copy of the medical examiner's certificate.**

    A. True

    B. False

2. **Paperwork regarding the freight you are hauling should be in proper order before you begin your trip.**

    A. True

    B. False

3. **The information you record on a trip report must be accurate as it is used by auditors to verify payment of taxes.**

    A. True

    B. False

4. **What do you need to consider when selecting a route?**

    A. Vehicle and cargo restrictions

    B. Local traffic conditions

    C. Weather conditions

    D. All of the above

5. **Maps include information on delays caused by road construction or poor weather conditions.**

    A. True

    B. False

6. **What is best to use when figuring the distance of a trip?**

    A. A map scale

    B. Symbols

    C. Mileage charts

    D. A map key

7. **How many hours should you allow for each 100 miles traveled when estimating trip time?**

    A.   1 hour

    B.   2.5 hours

    C.   2 hours

    D.   3 hours

8. **When estimating a vehicle's fuel usage you need to determine the range of the vehicle.**

    A.   True

    B.   False

9. **When estimating trip expenses, you should consider:**

    A.   Distance traveled

    B.   Time the trip will take

    C.   Emergency funds

    D.   All of the above

10. **A well thought out trip plan can mean a savings of time and money for your company.**

    A.   True

    B.   False

CDL Air Brake Pre-Test

Read each question carefully and select the most correct answer

1. **If the air system should develop a leak, what will keep the air in the air tanks?**

    A. The governor

    B. The tractor protection valve

    C. The emergency relay valve

    D. The one-way check valve

2. **If your truck or bus has dual parking control valves, you can use pressure from a separate tank to:**

    A. Release the emergency brakes to move a short distance

    B. Apply more brake pressure for stopping if the main tank is getting low

    C. Stay parked without using up service air pressure

    D. Balance the service brake system while you drive

3. **In air–brake equipped vehicles, you use the parking brakes when?**

    A. When slowing down

    B. As little as possible

    C. Whenever you park the vehicle

    D. Only during pre-trip and post-trip inspections

4. **During normal operations, the parking and emergency brakes are usually held back by:**

    A. Air pressure

    B. Spring pressure

    C. Centrifugal force

    D. Bolts or clamps

5. **A combination vehicle air brake system cannot leak more than _____ psi per minute with the engine off and the brakes released.**

    A. 1

    B. 2

    C. 3

    D. 4

Chapter **28**

Accident procedures

OBJECTIVES

Upon completion of this chapter, you should have a basic understanding of:

- ❏ Accident procedures

- ❏ Accident preventability guidelines

- ❏ Vehicle fire procedures

Introduction

No matter how safely you operate your commercial motor vehicle, there will always be a chance for an accident as long as there are variables that you have no control over (weather, wildlife, other drivers, etc.)

As a professional driver, it is important that you have a clear understanding of your responsibilities at the scene in the event of an accident, as well as your role afterward.

Defining the Situation

What is an accident? — A DOT reportable accident is defined in Sec. 390.5 of the Federal Motor Carrier Safety Regulations (FMCSRs) as an occurrence involving a commercial motor vehicle (CMV) operating on a highway in interstate or intrastate commerce which results in:

1. A fatality;

2. Injury to a person who, as a result of the injury, immediately receives medical treatment away from the scene of the accident; or

3. Disabling damage to one or more of the vehicles, requiring the vehicle(s) to be towed from the scene.

A fatality means any injury which results in the death of a person at the time of the accident or within 30 days of the accident.

Disabling damage includes vehicles that could have been driven, but would have been further damaged if driven. Excluded from the definition of disabling damage is:

- Damage which can be temporarily fixed at the scene without special tools or parts;

- Tire disablement without other damage (even if no spare is available);

- Headlamp or taillight damage; and

- Damage to turn signals, horn, or windshield wipers which makes them inoperative.

The term "accident" does not include incidents involving getting in or out of a parked vehicle, or which involves only the loading or unloading of a vehicle's cargo.

Accident register — A motor carrier must retain a record of each accident in an accident register for review by the Federal Motor Carrier Safety Administration (FMCSA).

According to Sec. 390.15(b) of the FMCSRs, a motor carrier must retain an accident register for three years after an accident occurs. The accident register must contain the following information for each accident:

1. Date of accident;

You really need to pay attention to this chapter, driver. Why? Because you have been working long and hard to learn how to become a professional truck driver. One accident could cause you to lose your license or even worse your life or the lives of others. Don't let all this go to waste. This truck driving is serious stuff, and if by chance you do have an accident, you need to know what to do to minimize the risk to yourself, your company, and those around you.

2. City/town and state in which the accident occurred;

3. Driver name;

4. Number of injuries;

5. Number of fatalities;

6. Whether hazardous materials, other than fuel spilled from the fuel tanks of the motor vehicles involved in the accident, were released; and

7. Copies of all accident reports required by state or other governmental entities or insurers.

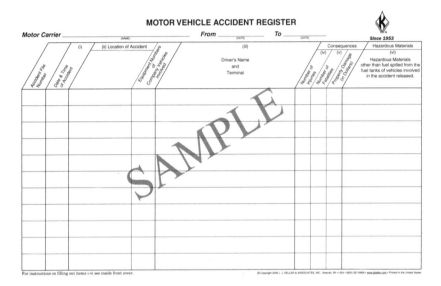

An accident register.

Calculating the Cost

The cost of an accident is more than just repairing and replacing physical damage to equipment and property. There are several other costs, some of which can be hard to measure. When analyzing the cost of an accident, a carrier tracks both direct and indirect expenses.

Direct costs — Direct costs of an accident are those that you can easily put a dollar amount on. They may include:

- **Physical damage** — This area includes all costs associated with repairing and replacing the actual physical damage to vehicle(s) and property.

- **Medical expenses** — These include the total medical costs incurred for all injuries from the time of the accident, until the accident file is officially closed.

- **Cargo damage** — The total expense of replacing lost and damaged cargo associated with an accident

- **Towing** — Depending on the condition of the vehicle(s), towing expenses can run from several hundred to a few thousand dollars.

- **Storage** — Post-accident storage fees for damaged vehicle(s) at a repair facility or impoundment yard must also be figured into the direct cost.

- **Police report** — Generally, there is a fee associated with obtaining an official police report for an accident.

- **Lost capacity** — If the driver involved in the accident is injured or otherwise cannot resume his/her duties, dispatch capacity will decrease.

- **Lost utilization** — If the vehicle is so damaged that it cannot be operated until repairs have been made, the motor carrier will lose the opportunity for that unit to put on revenue-generating miles.

Indirect costs — Indirect costs of an accident are those items that you may not be able to put a dollar amount on, but cost your motor carrier money nevertheless. They may include:

- **Administrative costs** — These include phone calls and personnel hours needed to deal with the accident that would normally be spent on other daily activities.

- **Workers' compensation** — Rates for workers' compensation premiums might be impacted if personal injuries are involved in the accident.

- **Insurance premiums** — A high accident rate, or even one high-profile accident, could mean an increase in insurance premiums, a higher deductible rate, or both. It is also possible that the company could lose its insurance.

- **Customer relations** — Customers' perception of an organization and its drivers may be negatively impacted by a high accident rate. If the customer feels its cargo is not safe with you, other carriers may be considered.

- **Public relations** — The general public's perception of your company, its drivers, and in some cases its product could be negatively impacted. A well-publicized accident may cause the general public to question your company's dedication to safety and/or a quality product.

Securing the Scene

No matter how safely you drive your vehicle, there's always a chance of being involved in an accident. When the unexpected happens, it is important that you know what to do and what to expect.

When an accident occurs, you must deal with immediate problems and gather and report accident information in a timely manner. The following steps can help you accomplish these tasks.

1. **Stop immediately.** Failure to stop is against the law and can result in fines and/or jail time.

Leaving the scene of an accident can also disqualify you as the holder of a commercial driver's license (CDL) from driving a CMV for one year. (See Sec. 383.51 of the FMCSRs for details.)

When involved in an accident, remain calm and pull your vehicle as far off the road as possible.

If the accident involves an unoccupied vehicle, try to find the owner. If the owner can't be found, leave your name, the company's name, address, and phone number in a visible location, such as under a windshield wiper blade, and contact law enforcement. Also write down the make, model, year, license number, and description of the unoccupied vehicle to supply to your company.

Set out emergency warning devices within ten minutes.

No matter what you think, or how you feel, DO NOT say, "I'm sorry" or, "It was my fault." Your feelings are not important at this point, the facts are. Don't argue about who's to blame; let the authorities do their job and cooperate with them, but DON'T point fingers and don't admit guilt. It may not have happened like you thought, and admission of guilt when you may not be guilty can ruin your career in a matter of minutes!

2. **Prevent additional accidents.** Turn on your vehicle's four-way flashers as the first warning signal and then set out emergency warning devices. The devices must be set out within 10 minutes of stopping.

Emergency warning device placement is spelled out in Part 392 of the FMCSRs and is described below:

Warning devices must be placed in the following order:

1. **Two-lane road** — The devices should be placed as follows:

   • The first device should be placed on the traffic side of the vehicle four paces (about 10 feet) from the front or rear, depending on traffic direction.

   • The second device should be placed 40 paces (about 100 feet) behind the vehicle.

   • A third device should be placed 40 paces (about 100 feet) ahead of the vehicle on the shoulder or in the lane the vehicle is in.

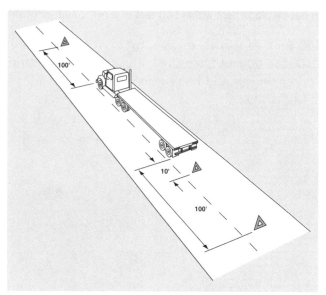

Warning device placement on a two-lane road.

2. **One-way or divided highway** — The devices should be placed 10, 100, and 200 feet from the rear of the vehicle, toward approaching traffic.

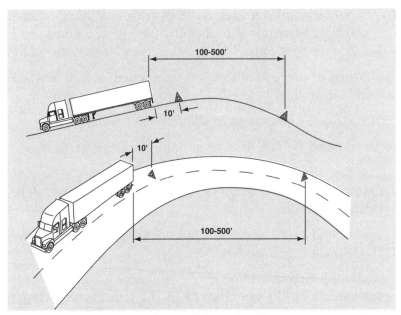

Warning device placement within 500 feet of a hill, curve, or obstruction.

3. **Within 500 feet of a hill, curve, or obstruction** — A device should be placed 100 to 500 feet from the vehicle in the direction of the obstruction. The other two should be placed according to the rules for two-lane or divided highways.

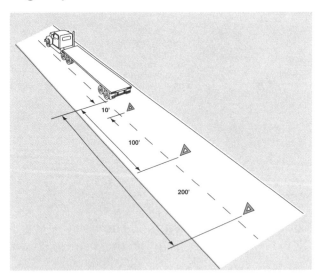

Warning device placement on a one-way or divided highway.

Three bidirectional emergency reflective triangles, six fusees, or three liquid burning flares are acceptable warning devices with which a vehicle must be equipped. The triangles must meet the specifications of 49 CFR 571.125. Fuses and liquid-burning flares must meet Underwriters Laboratories standards. Flame-producing devices are prohibited on vehicles carrying explosives, a flammable gas, a flammable liquid, or a motor vehicle using compressed gas as a motor fuel.

Use caution when setting out warning devices.

3. **Notify law enforcement.** Call law enforcement officials. Provide as many details as possible, including the location of the accident, the number of vehicles involved, and the number of people involved.

Never leave the scene of an accident to notify law enforcement unless there is no means of communicating at the accident site.

4. **Check for injuries.** If anyone is hurt, you should call for medical assistance. Do not move an injured person unless there's a risk of fire or additional injury. Depending on company policy, if trained in first aid procedures you may provide assistance.

hey...STOP! Don't you dare drive away from an accident. That's about the worst thing you can do for your future as a driver and for the reputation of your company.

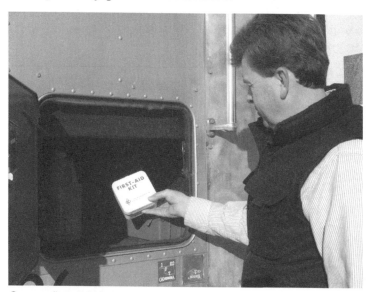

Carry a first aid kit on your vehicle at all times.

At a minimum, you should call for help, ask if the other party wants someone contacted, and keep them warm. Doing too much can be just as dangerous as doing nothing at all. Never attempt to do something you are not trained in.

5.   **Contact the carrier.** Notify your company of the accident as soon as possible. Know whom to call in the event of an accident. These names and phone numbers should always be available, possibly posted in a single place in each cab. Follow all company rules, be cooperative, and answer all questions posed by the company representative (safety director, dispatcher, etc.).

Post-accident testing — If certain conditions are met, your carrier will instruct you to go for a DOT-post-accident drug and alcohol test. The following table notes when a test is required under Sec. 382.303 of the FMCSRs.

Type of accident involved	Citation issued to the CMV driver	Test must be performed by the employer
1. Human fatality	YES	YES
	NO	YES
2. Bodily injury with immediate medical treatment away from the scene	YES	YES
	NO	NO
3. Disabling damage to any motor vehicle requiring tow away	YES	YES
	NO	NO

You are prohibited from consuming alcohol for eight hours after an accident, or until you submit to a post-accident alcohol test, whichever occurs first.

Damaged vehicle — The company representative will also direct you on how to handle a disabled or damaged commercial motor vehicle (towing, repairs, etc.). If the vehicle is not disabled, the carrier may grant permission to drive the vehicle from the scene (providing it is given a thorough pre-trip inspection to ensure safety) to a garage.

Commenting on the situation — Think before you speak. Anything said can and may be used against you. Many carriers have specific policies on what can be said after an accident. But they must be careful not to be too tightlipped as law enforcement could see this as a failure to cooperate. Maintaining a low profile doesn't mean you can't be polite to the parties involved. Be professional at all times. You represent your company, no matter the circumstances.

Hey driver...take A LOT of pictures. Even if the officer is taking his/her own, you need to document the scene as well. Disposable cameras take pretty good pictures and are relatively inexpensive. If your company doesn't give you one to carry in your truck, buy one on your own. It's a minor investment with a major payoff if you need to use it.

6. **Document the accident.** The more detail you can provide can assist with potential future insurance and legal issues. Write down all information regarding the accident and those involved including:

- Time and location of accident;

- Description of damage to vehicles and property;

- Name and address of all individuals involved;

- Name and address of insurance companies of all individuals involved;

- Type, make, model, and license numbers of all vehicles involved; and

- Names and departments of any investigating officers.

An accident reporting kit can help you gather all of the important information you and/or your company may need.

Many motor carriers have accident reporting kits in their trucks. These kits can be used to answer questions in a time when you may not be thinking straight. Also, a disposable camera may be a great resource to record how the event happened. Drawing a simple diagram of the situation is also a good idea.

Photographs — A disposable camera may be the most useful item you can have at the scene. Taking pictures will help determine how an accident occurred and how much damage was involved. But you need to know what to photograph, and what not to:

- Take wide shots from the fog stripe at the edge of the road toward the point of impact, showing the final location of the vehicles.

- Take wide shots from the centerline and all sides of the vehicles, including the damage.

- Take close-up shots of damage and any skid marks or road debris.

- Never take pictures of individuals who have been injured or killed.

Hazardous Materials

When an accident or incident involves a hazardous material, there may be additional risks to safety, health, and the environment. Because of this, there are additional regulatory requirements that must be followed.

If you haul hazardous materials, your employer must provide training to you on proper procedures for responding to leaks, spills, and other emergencies.

If you are involved in an incident or accident, you must immediately report this to your company. Regulatory requirements and company policy will dictate how you handle the situation. At the very least, keep bystanders away from the area.

If a hazardous material response team is called to the scene, follow their instructions.

Also, certain reports must be made by your company (See Sec. 171.15 and Sec. 171.16 of the Hazardous Materials Regulations for details.)

Vehicle Fires

A vehicle fire can be a dangerous and frightening experience. Common sense, good driving habits, and good housekeeping can prevent many vehicle fires but, unfortunately, not all fires can be prevented. You need to be prepared to face this potentially dangerous situation.

Prevention — All fires need fuel, air, and heat to ignite and spread. Fire prevention revolves around keeping those elements from coming together. Most vehicle fires occur in one of the following three areas:

- Cab/engine;

- Tires/brakes; and

- Cargo.

Cab/Engine — Good housekeeping is important. The cab should be clean and free of debris at all times.

The engine compartment should be checked regularly. The engine should always be clean. If oils or fluids are spilled on the engine they should be wiped up immediately. After work is finished on the engine all rags should be removed from the area and all fluid caps should be put back where they belong.

Regular checks should be made of the following items:

- Wiring and electrical system;

- Fuses;

- Battery; and

- Exhaust system.

When refueling, the engine should be turned off and all smoking materials should be extinguished. Turn off your cell phone. The fuel tank should be checked for signs of leakage. Also, make sure you have metal to metal contact while fueling.

Tires/Brakes — Overheated tires are another way vehicle fires ignite. An underinflated tire can overheat, increasing the risk of a tire fire. A soft or flat tire should be changed as soon as possible.

If a hot tire is changed, it shouldn't be placed in the spare tire rack until it cools.

Brakes should also be checked regularly, as worn brakes can overheat, causing a fire.

All brakes (including the parking brake) should be fully released before a vehicle is moved.

Also, never ride the brakes. Riding the brakes can cause a fire in the brake linings that could spread to the tires.

Cargo — Periodically check your mirrors, looking for smoke. Smoking materials should never be used around a vehicle hauling hazardous materials or in the cargo area as freight is being loaded or unloaded.

Know what commodities you are hauling. This information is important so you and/or emergency crews can respond properly.

Putting out fires — The first consideration when a fire occurs is the safety of the driver and others. If possible, move the vehicle to a location away from other people, vehicles, and buildings. Getting the fire under control is the next step, but don't take unnecessary risks. If a fire is too large or dangerous to handle, leave it to the professionals.

Cab/engine fires — The following are basic steps to follow when dealing with a cab/engine fire.

- Turn off the vehicle's engine. If you can do it safely, also look for fuel leaks.

- Disconnect the battery cables from the terminals (if it can be safely done) if the fire is electrical.

- Don't open the hood more than necessary when fighting an engine fire. Remember, air is one of the ingredients that will help fuel a fire.

- Never use water on a petroleum–based fire. The use of water will cause a petroleum–based fire to spread.

- Follow the directions on the fire extinguisher. To avoid smoke and fumes, the extinguisher should be used with the wind behind the extinguisher.

- Never assume a fire is completely out. Fires often smolder, spark, and can reignite.

Tire fires — Tire fires are hard to extinguish, and are dangerous. This is due to the fact that tires are made of highly flammable material. A tire fire can generate an intense amount of heat. There are several things that should be kept in mind when fighting a tire fire.

- Remove the hot tire (if it can be done safely) from the vehicle.

- Use water to fight a tire fire. Water helps cool a tire as well as extinguish flames. Fire extinguishers are good at suppressing flames, but will not be able to put out a tire fire.

Cargo Fires — In many cases cargo fires are discovered by the sight or smell of smoke around cargo doors. There are several things to keep in mind when fighting a cargo fire.

- Do not open the doors if smoke is detected until the vehicle is in a safe place and help has arrived.

- Disconnect the tractor from the trailer (if possible) and move the tractor to a safe place away from the fire.

- Always know what type of cargo is in the trailer. This will help firefighters determine the safest way to extinguish the flames.

General classes of fires — The National Fire Protection Association (NFPA) has classified four general types of fires, based on the combustible materials involved and the kind of extinguisher needed to put them out. The four fire classifications are A, B, C, and D. Each classification has a special symbol and color identification.

1. **Class A.** This type of fire is the most common. The combustible materials are wood, cloth, paper, rubber, and plastics. The common extinguisher agent is water, but dry chemicals are also effective. Carbon dioxide extinguishers and those using sodium or potassium bicarbonate chemicals are not to be used on this type of fire.

2. **Class B.** Flammable liquids, gases, and greases create Class B fires. The extinguishers to use are foam, carbon dioxide, and dry chemical.

3. **Class C.** Class C fires are electrical fires and a nonconducting agent must be used. Carbon dioxide and dry chemical extinguishers are to be used. Never use foam or water-type extinguishers on these fires.

4. **Class D.** Combustible metals, such as magnesium, titanium, zirconium, and sodium fires are Class D. These fires require specialized techniques to extinguish them. None of the common extinguishers should be used since they can increase the intensity of the fire by adding an additional chemical reaction.

There are only two dry chemical extinguishers that can be used on Class A, B, and C fires, and those are multi-purpose ABC extinguishers, either stored pressure or cartridge operated. Multi-purpose extinguishers (ABC) will handle all A, B, and C fires. All fire extinguishers are labeled with either ABC, or A, or B, or C. It is important to know what type of fire is in progress. If you use a fire extinguisher, be sure to use one only on fires for which that fire extinguisher is designed. Using the wrong agent on a fire may increase the intensity of the fire. Check the label on the fire extinguisher. It should list the fire class(es) it is meant to put out.

Fire extinguishers — Section 393.95 of the FMCSRs requires one or two (depending on the rating) properly filled and readily accessible fire extinguishers on all commercial motor vehicles. The extinguisher(s) must be securely mounted on the vehicle and must be designed and maintained to visually show whether the extinguisher is fully charged. If a vehicle is hauling hazardous materials, it must be equipped with one fire extinguisher having an Underwriters' Laboratories rating of 10 B:C or more. If a vehicle is not hauling hazardous materials, it must be equipped with either one fire extinguisher having an Underwriters' Laboratories rating of 5 B:C or more or two fire extinguishers, each with an Underwriters' Laboratories rating of 4 B:C or more.

The FMCSRs require that you carry properly filled and readily accessible fire extinguishers.

Evaluating the Accident

Preventable accident — By reviewing the following industry standard definitions for preventable accident, you will gain a better understanding on how a carrier would evaluate an accident.

> **Federal Motor Carrier Safety Administration (FMCSA):** A preventable accident is "one which occurs because the driver fails to act in a reasonably expected manner to prevent it. In judging whether the driver's actions were reasonable, one seeks to determine whether the driver drove defensively and demonstrated an acceptable level of skill and knowledge. The judgment of what is reasonable can be based on a company-adopted definition, thus establishing a goal for its safety management programs."

> **National Safety Council (NSC):** A preventable accident is "any accident involving a company controlled vehicle which results in property damage and/or personal injury, regardless of who was injured, and what property was damaged, to what extent, or where it occurred, in which the driver in question failed to exercise reasonable precaution to prevent the accident."

Because there are a number of different areas to consider, preventability cannot be defined in a single sentence. First, everyone at a motor carrier must understand that preventable does not necessarily imply blame or fault. Preventable means accountable.

Proper assessment of preventability relies on the active, personal involvement, and sound judgment of supervisors and managers. Preventability usually can only be correctly determined after an appropriate, and in some cases, extensive investigation is conducted. While there may be a difference of opinion in determining preventability, the process should result in sound decision-making.

Most important is that everyone involved understands and accepts the premise that a determination of preventability does not mean simply assessing blame or fault, but is rather a process of determining what actually happened and why, with the primary purpose of trying to prevent it from happening again.

Preventability guidelines — The heart of accident analysis is the determination of preventability. Information must be evaluated in light of all available facts that are pertinent to the cause of the accident. Valuable information can be obtained in many instances by a detailed analysis and reconstruction of the accident sequence. Each accident must be judged individually. However, certain types will generally fall in the non-preventable category, and certain others, in the absence of extenuating circumstances and conditions, fall in the preventable category.

Accident review committee — Generally, for clear-cut preventability decisions, your supervisor will probably make the call without the need to consult with or involve others. However, in a few borderline cases, he/she may need help. For many motor carriers, this help comes in the form of an accident review committee.

An accident review committee is a tool used by some companies to help determine accident preventability in difficult situations, or cases involving many variables or unusual circumstances. Generally, it is made up of representatives from several departments as well as select drivers.

Summary

Even the best driver may be involved in an accident at some point in his/her career. When the unexpected happens, you need to safely and legally deal with the situation in a short period of time. In this chapter, you learned about accidents; the definition of an accident, regulatory requirements, the procedures you should follow when an accident occurs, including documentation and reporting responsibilities and preventing and fighting vehicle fires.

Accident Procedures Quiz

Directions: Read each statement carefully and mark the response that best answers the question.

1. **You should document an accident by getting names, license numbers, and insurance company information from all drivers involved.**

    A. True

    B. False

2. **When taking photos of the accident scene, take shots of:**

    A. The injured or killed

    B. Skid marks and vehicle final positions

    C. The centerline and all sides of the vehicles, including the damage

    D. Both B and C

3. **Disabling damage includes damage to the vehicle's turn signals or horn.**

    A. True

    B. False

4. **At a minimum, when someone is injured in an accident, a driver should call for help, ask if the other party wants someone contacted, and keep them warm.**

    A. True

    B. False

5. **Which is *not* true of Class A fires:**

    A. They are the most common

    B. The combustible materials are wood, cloth, paper, rubber and plastics

    C. Carbon dioxide extinguishers and those using sodium or potassium bicarbonate chemicals should be used on this type of fire

    D. The common extinguisher agent is water, but dry chemicals are also effective

6. **After an accident, make sure that you either apologize or defend yourself, depending on the circumstances.**

    A. True

    B. False

7. **If you are involved in an accident, your company must record this in an accident register.**

   A. True

   B. False

8. **Required warning devices for two-lane roads include:**

   A. One device on the traffic side of the vehicle 4 paces (approximately 10 feet or 3 meters) from the front or rear, depending on traffic direction

   B. One device 40 paces (approximately 100 feet or 30 meters) behind

   C. One device 40 paces (approximately 100 feet or 30 meters) ahead of the vehicle on the shoulder or in the lane the vehicle is in

   D. All of the above

CDL Air Brake Pre-Test

Read each question carefully and select the most correct answer

1. **A straight truck or bus air brake system cannot leak more than ____ psi per minute with the engine off and the brakes released.**

   A. 1

   B. 2

   C. 3

   D. 4

2. **You must make a quick emergency stop. You should brake so you:**

   A. Can steer hard while braking hard

   B. Use the full power of the brakes and lock them

   C. Can stay in a straight line and maintain steering control

   D. Burn up the hand brake first

3. **Why should you not fan the brakes on and off during long downgrades?**

   A. Air usage is less when fanning

   B. Brake linings do not get hot when fanning

   C. The short time off the brakes does not allow for brake cooling

   D. None of the above

4. **Which of the following answers is most correct about using brakes on a long and/or steep downgrade?**

   A. Use the braking effects of the engine and when the vehicle speed reaches the "safe" speed, apply brakes firmly until vehicle speed is reduced to approximately 5 mph below "safe" speed

   B. Use stab braking

   C. Use only the trailer brakes to maintain "safe" speed

   D. Apply brakes when the vehicle speed reaches 5 mph over "safe" speed and then release when speed of vehicle is back at the "safe" speed

5. **To use the stab braking technique during emergency braking, you:**

   A. Pump the brake pedal rapidly and lightly

   B. Brake hard with the pedal until the wheels lock, then get off the brakes until the wheels begin to roll again

   C. Brake hard with the pedal until the wheels lock, then get off the brakes for as long as the wheels were locked

   D. Brake hard with the pedal and hand valve until you stop

Chapter 29

Security of cargo, truck, and driver

OBJECTIVES

Upon completion of this chapter, you should have a basic understanding of:

❏ Current terrorism threats

❏ Cargo security and theft issues

❏ Personal security do's and dont's

❏ Identifying suspicious activity and your responsibilities for notification

❏ In–transit security issues and recommendations

Introduction

Today's trucking environment requires vigilance. The average driver needs to be alert to a variety of security concerns including terrorist threats, cargo theft, and personal security. More and more, vehicles are being considered potential weapons if they are in the wrong hands. A commercial motor vehicle, based on it's size and what it hauls, could be used as a weapon of mass destruction.

Prior to September 11, 2001, and the associated loss of lives and property on U.S. soil, most Americans and most of the world thought that terrorist activities were something that happened in some other country, certainly not in their own back yards. The very real use of a large vehicle, such as a truck or plane, to cause death and destruction within our borders has changed the way we all look at security today. This escalation of terrorism makes all drivers potential targets for terrorists and hijackers.

In this chapter you will learn about security issues and safeguarding practices in the areas of:

- Terrorist threats;
- Cargo and vehicle theft; and
- Personal security.

The intention of this section is to give a realistic picture of the threats that loom on the open highways, at the shipper and receiver, at truck stops, and all points in between.

Terrorism Threats

Because terrorism became so real in this country in 2001, the Department of Homeland Security was established as a branch of the Federal Government, with a mission to prevent terrorist attacks within the United States, reduce the vulnerability of the U.S. to terrorism, and to minimize the damage and assist in the recovery from terrorist attacks that do occur.

This department now heavily regulates and controls the movement of many types of freight, vehicles, and equipment throughout our country. It is a very real assumption that a commercial motor vehicle may be used some time in the future to create mass destruction and lose of life, somewhere within our borders.

O.K. driver. You are not Superman (or Super-woman). Pride and ignorance are two very different things. It's time for you to put the pride of being the "big tough truck driver" in your pocket for a minute and learn how to be an educated security conscious professional. This is not the time to wave your flag and think that you can "take on the world."

Ocean Port Facility

Hey driver, do you think every terrorist activity is driven by some radical group overseas? Think again. Home grown terrorism could be more of a threat to you as a truck driver than what you see every day on the news. As a security conscious truck driver you need to open your eyes, and stop making assumptions!

As a truck driver, you need to fully understand what your responsibilities are pertaining to the nation's security, and must become a trained professional in how to avoid and/or respond to threats and concerns involving your freight and equipment.

The freight you are hauling or the vehicle you are operating could feasibly be used to carry out a terrorist plot. Consider the following:

1. If you are transporting food commodities, product-tampering (bioterrorism) could be a motive to gain entry into your shipment. A terrorist could attempt to taint the agricultural or food product with chemicals, bio-agents, metal, etc. Even if you are transporting animal feed you are a potential target. A terrorist could taint the food supply for animals, providing for a possible chemical or toxic agent to be passed on to humans by way of consumption.

2. If you are transporting chemicals, radioactive materials, or explosives, the motive for terrorism is much greater as your vehicle and/or its cargo could be used as a mobile bomb — targeting national icons, schools, hospitals, and other highly populated areas. Bulk chemicals could be used to contaminate water or food supplies, destroy natural resources, or render vast areas of the country uninhabitable.

3. If you are hauling general commodities that are neither chemical nor agricultural in nature, just the size of your truck, fully loaded with fuel, could still be a force to be reckoned with if hijacked. Regardless of what you haul, you as a professional driver, should always be aware of the happenings around you and your vehicle.

Keep in mind that terrorism is not always international in origin. Many home-grown extremist groups have an axe to grind against certain companies, industries, or the U.S. government. Remember, terrorism, regardless of its motive or origin, is always in someone's backyard. It has become painfully clear that terrorism happens in the United States, not always directed from somewhere else.

Cargo Theft

Cargo theft has been a lucrative business for theft rings for decades. The level of sophistication of these criminals can be startling. It only takes a matter of minutes to:

Cargo Security Threats Are Everywhere

- Take a load to a warehouse and dismantle it for distribution, sometimes to unsuspecting legitimate businesses;

- Repaint a tractor and/or trailer, covering up any identifying markings and reidentifying it for future use; or

- Transfer the load to another truck or trucks for further movement and distribution.

Theft of a trailer or just its contents could occur while;

- The vehicle is unattended during a driver's break or home time;

- The driver is in the sleeper berth; or

- the trailer is staged at a drop-yard or terminal.

Some thefts, including highjackings, are based on someone's inside information or knowledge of what's on your trailer — the commodity being shipped, location, and time. These criminals know the specific target they want, and wait outside the shipper to follow the vehicle, taking advantage of the first fuel or meal stop to act. In some instances, they know the commodity based on a specific distribution center and can identify a trailer hauling the desired cargo based on the trailer's "billboard." No inside information is even necessary if it's common knowledge. It is just a waiting game for the first truck that provides an opportunity.

Hey driver, put that CB down! There is nothing wrong with being proud of what you haul and how you operate your vehicle, but it might not be a good idea to tell the whole world about it! I can't tell you how many times I've heard some diesel dummy (that's slang for a truck driver that has no common sense...that's not you) going down the road bragging about what he's got on his trailer, how much it's worth, where he's going, and when he plans on being there. What a golden opportunity for a highjacker to be listening to that conversation! Remember what I said before about the CB? Use it to "cut up" with a fellow driver or solve all the problems of the world at 2 A.M. DON'T brag about your load. It could get you killed!

Even though much attention is given to million dollar cargo thefts, petty theft robs the economy of immeasurable dollars each year. This type of theft may include local criminals who just want a few of the items and are hoping you won't notice the discrepancy until you reach your final destination. It could also be an unscrupulous warehouse or dockworker at the shipper or receiver, who will take a few items, leaving your carrier (or you) to foot the bill for the shortage. It is always important to verify the load's count against the shipping papers at the point of origin — with someone at the shipper witnessing the quantity — and doing the same at the receiver.

Personal Security

Safeguarding the cargo being transported is important, but it is equally important that drivers protect themselves from physical attacks and the loss of personal items. Consider the following best practices:

Always be Alert

- **Personal possessions** — Drivers obviously want to feel like they are at home while out on the road. This may involve bringing personal electric items, such as PDA's, laptop computers, MP3 players, and televisions. If you bring any creature comforts from home, make sure that anything of value is not left out in the open for a passerby to see. Discreetly put these items in the sleeper berth, if you have one, or under the seat or other less conspicuous location. In the same respect, be careful what you leave in a motel room while you grab a bite to eat or run some errands. Last but not least, you are proud of the things you own, but a truck stop is no place to brag about what latest and greatest gadgets you may have in your truck. This type of talk "motivates" would-be thieves to pay attention to what you are saying and where you parked your truck.

- **Money** — Drivers should never flash large amounts of cash when paying for meals, fuel, or any other purchases. Safeguard your wallets and keep all receipts with account numbers. Local criminals are waiting for the unsuspecting traveler. You do not want to be the victim of a pick-pocket or someone rummaging through an unlocked truck. It is advisable to travel with the least amount of credit cards as possible, leaving the rest at home under lock and key. Leave the check book at home as well. Out-of-state checks are rarely accepted at most places anyway. A debit card would be the better choice if you wanted to use funds directly from your checking account.

- **ATM visits** — When drivers are out on the road longer than expected, they sometimes need large sums of money from an ATM. This seemingly simple task should not be taken lightly. It has its own list of dangers associated with it. Take the following precautions:

  1. Be alert at all times when using an ATM.

  2. Avoid using an ATM in an isolated or poorly lighted area.

  3. Refrain from displaying your cash. Place it in your pocket as soon as the transaction is completed.

  4. Do not make a transaction if you notice someone suspicious. Find another machine or come back later.

  5. Protect your ATM or debit card as you would cash or a credit card. Never let anyone else use it.

  6. Memorize your Personal Identification Number (PIN). Do not write it down on your card or leave it in your wallet.

Identifying Suspicious Activities

Most employees develop a sense of the ordinary within a work environment in a relatively short time. This "normalcy" will help gauge what is not normal or unusual. Anything that appears out of the ordinary or unusual should be a red flag to possible suspicious activity. It is important for employees to question an activity, even if it is just a hunch or suspicion, rather than let it go and later have it become an incident. Remember, if it doesn't look quite right, it probably should be checked out.

The following list may be used to aid and identify suspicious activities while at a terminal, dock, or any location:

- Unidentified person(s) attempting to gain access to equipment.

- Unidentified person(s) seen in a normally restricted or secured area.

I know, I know...you don't work in the building, so why should you care, right? Wrong! Anything that happens inside could affect you and your truck outside. Use common sense, be a professional, and just let someone else know if you see something that doesn't look right. Trust me, it doesn't take a lot of effort, and you'll feel better that you did something rather than just ignored it and hoped that it went away.

- An employee, vendor, or supplier in a part of the office for no known reason.

- An unescorted or unaccompanied visitor anywhere in the building, or wandering around the external facility.

- Any person (employee, visitor, vendor, stranger) who appears to be hiding something or is acting nervous, anxious, or secretive.

- Any employee, visitor, or vendor making unusual or repeated requests for sensitive or important company-related information.

- Any person or group loitering outside the facility.

- Any person claiming to be a utility worker but unable to produce proper identification.

- Anyone not possessing proper identification.

- Anyone claiming to have an appointment that is not listed.

- Any person (employee, visitor, vendor, or stranger) carrying a weapon.

- Any vehicle parked outside the building or near the grounds for a long period or after normal work hours.

- An unfamiliar vehicle appearing to have been abandoned near the building or grounds.

- A disgruntled employee wanting to take revenge on the organization, supervisor, or co-worker.

Motor carrier employees need to use common sense and good judgement when assessing a potential threat. Depending upon the situation, employees will be expected to report suspicious activity to an immediate supervisor, next level manager, corporate safety/security officer, or the police and/or fire department.

While on the road, drivers need to be:

- Cautious when leaving the shipper. The vast majority of highjackings occur within a few miles of the load's origin;

- Conscious of other vehicles that may be following for long distances;

- Suspicious of other motorists that are signaling you to stop; and

- Alert to details in the event you need to file a police report. Be a good witness.

In-Transit Security Tips

The security protocols that most employers have set up were probably created for a reason. They cannot be ignored or viewed as an inconvenience. To do so will put you, your vehicle, your load, and potentially the nation at risk.

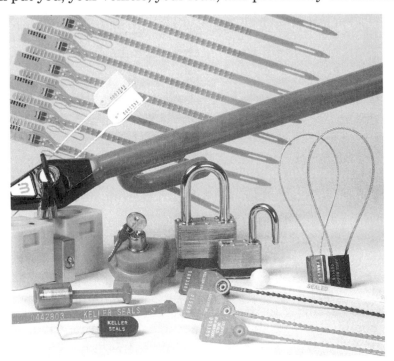

Various Security Devices

The following are just a few security best practices that you as a driver may be called upon to abide by:

- **Communications** — Many carriers require drivers to maintain regular communication either through a phone or some sort of satellite communication system. While checking in, you should make sure the phone conversation is as private as possible and is not for everyone to hear. This includes the use of a cell phone, office phone, or pay phone. You just never know who is listening when you are checking in with the office, family, or friends.

- **Tight lips** — Drivers should never discuss load-related information. Information such as load content, pick-up and delivery schedules, and routing, should never be offered to anyone while on the road. This includes even the friendliest of faces at the counter of the truck stop or a "fellow trucker" on the CB. Criminals can and do listen in on CB conversations between drivers or even pose as a driver to draw information out of you.

Hey driver...so you're a little tired, there's no truck stop at the next exit, but you can just pull off on the shoulder of the on-ramp right? Wrong! That is a highly unsecure and dangerous place to stop. You should never consider stopping there. If you planned your trip (including your stops) you shouldn't have to be thinking about stopping there anyway. Oh yeah, and that person in the car next to you that's waving at you to stop...DON'T DO IT! If you think he or she is being friendly, just smile, wave, and continue on down the road. You probably can't see the person hiding in the back seat waiting for you to stop your truck. It's not worth the loss of your life, your truck, or your cargo, just because you thought you were going to be the "nice guy."

Night Time is Extremely Dangerous

- **Resting and parking** — Drivers should stop at only reputable truck stops or high-traffic rest areas. They should park in well-lit areas where other trucks are present. When possible, the trailer should be backed against a wall, fence, or other closed trailer, for added security to the load. When at truck stops, restaurants, or motels, the load should be parked so that the driver has a clear view of the vehicle and trailer seals, pin locks, and other vehicle security devices should be used. Drivers should avoid stopping on dark freeways or deserted areas while waiting to make deliveries. As simple as it may seem, drivers should always remember to lock their vehicle and keep the keys with them at all times.

- **Strangers asking the driver to stop** — Anyone asking you to stop should be viewed as suspicious. A frequent ploy used by hijackers is to create a scenario that forces or compels a driver to stop. If someone tries to hijack or break into your truck, always assume the criminal is armed and dangerous. Do not try to be a hero. Call the police immediately for help.

- **Inspection of the vehicle** — Your equipment and load should be inspected after each stop or rest period not only for safety-related defects, but also for signs of tampering or intrusion. The padlock or cargo seal should be examined for anything unusual, and the driver should look over the vehicle itself for anything suspicious.

- **Routes** — A well-thought-out trip plan can be a security tool of its own. The best trip plan will involve driving directly to the destination without stopping, if possible, or with the least amount of stops or breaks needed. Drivers should never take a load to or through home or to any unsecured or unauthorized parking area. Also, you should never ask for directions on the CB. You just don't know who you are talking to and they may be directing you right into trouble.

Summary

Security, in general, is common sense. You need to watch what you say and look for anything that looks out of the ordinary or suspicious. You should always keep a look out for anyone watching or listening to you or who is overly eager to learn more about your load or route.

It is also vital that you know who to call in response to a specific threat. Every day, million-dollar warehouses on wheels are making their way down the highway, hidden from authorities. A potentially volatile chemical that could be used as a WMD may fall into the hands of terrorists at any time. Every moment counts, and each detail you can provide will aid in an investigation and in the security of yourself, your equipment, your company, and your country.

Transportation Security Quiz

Read each statement carefully and select the response that best answers the statement.

1. **All terrorist activity has ties to international causes.**

   A. True

   B. False

2. **Cargo theft is:**

   A. A lucrative business

   B. Sometimes very sophisticated in its techniques

   C. Not a problem

   D. Both A & B

3. **It is okay to talk about your load if:**

   A. The person is another driver

   B. The person at the counter of the truck stop is friendly

   C. The person seems interested

   D. It is never appropriate to discuss load-related information while on the road

4. **A truck and trailer cannot be used by a terrorist group if it only contains DVD players.**

   A. True

   B. False

5. **It is a security threat to:**

   A. Pick up hitchhikers

   B. Stop for a stranded motorist

   C. Pull over when another motorist signals for you to do so

   D. All of the above

6. **If you are a victim of a crime while on the road:**

   A. Try to be a hero and fight your way out

   B. Be a good witness

   C. Notify authorities as soon as possible

   D. Both B & C

7. **Most highjackings occur within a few miles of the point of origin (the shipper).**

    A. True

    B. False

8. **Anyone who has been following you for a long distance:**

    A. Just happens to be going the same direction

    B. Should be viewed as suspicious

    C. Should be ignored

    D. All of the above

9. **Drivers do not have to worry about terminal security, just en-route security.**

    A. True

    B. False

10. **A single terrorist event could feasibly:**

    A. Disrupt the American economy

    B. Hurt consumer confidence

    C. Affect your motor carrier's reputation

    D. All of the above

CDL General Knowledge Pre-Test

Read each statement carefully and select the most correct response.

1. **When you are driving through construction zones, you should:**

   A. Speed up and hurry through them so you aren't in them any longer than necessary

   B. Stop before entering them, get in low gear and proceed through

   C. Watch for sharp pavement drop-offs

   D. Reduce your speed only if construction workers are near the roadway

2. **If you break down on a level, straight, four-lane, divided highway, where should you place the reflective warning triangles?**

   A. One 10 feet from the rear of the vehicle, one approximately 100 feet from the rear of the vehicle and another one about 100 feet to the front of the vehicle

   B. One 10 feet from the rear of the vehicle, one approximately 100 feet from the rear of the vehicle, and one about 200 feet from the rear of the vehicle

   C. One 100 feet from the rear of the vehicle, one approximately 200 feet from the rear of the vehicle, and one about 300 feet from the rear of the vehicle

   D. One 50 feet from the rear of the vehicle, one about 100 feet from the rear of the vehicle, and one about 200 feet from the front of the vehicle

3. **According to the Commercial Driver's manual, why should you limit the use of your vehicle's horn?**

   A. If your vehicle has air brakes, the air horn may not work while you are applying your brakes

   B. It may startle other drivers

   C. You should keep both hands on the steering wheel at all times

   D. The Driver's Manual does not say that a driver should limit the use of the horn

4. **Which of the following should you NOT do?**

   A. Turn your headlights on during the day if visibility is reduced due to bad weather

   B. Flash you brake lights to warn vehicles behind you that you are slowing down

   C. Flash your brake lights when entering a construction zone if vehicles are close behind you

   D. Flash your brake lights if someone is following too closely

5. **The proper way to load a vehicle is:**

   A. Keep the load balanced in the cargo area

   B. Place the load at the front of the trailer to give your drive wheels better traction

   C. Place the load at the rear of the trailer so your rear tires have better traction

   D. It makes no difference where the cargo is placed as long as you are not over the allowable gross weight

Chapter 29
Security of
Cargo, Truck,
and Driver

Chapter 30

Personal health and safety

OBJECTIVES

Upon completion of this chapter, you should have a basic understanding of:

- ❏ Healthy lifestyles

- ❏ Driver fatigue

- ❏ Effects of drugs and alcohol

- ❏ Safety and security

Introduction

This chapter will give you an overview of three very important aspects of commercial driving. In order to succeed in this profession, you will need to take care of your health, be conscious of safety practices, and understand the many facets that make up your day-to-day work environment

Personal Health and Driving

A healthy driver is an alert, safe driver.

Life on the road can lead to a lot of bad habits including:

- Minimal exercise;
- Unhealthy eating habits;
- Stress;
- Over consumption of caffeine; and
- Smoking.

It is important to incorporate good habits including eating well, getting plenty of rest, and an exercise routine into your day. Remember, a healthy driver is an alert, safe driver.

Physical qualification requirements — The Federal Motor Carrier Safety Administration (FMCSA) has set physical qualification requirements for a driver in order to operate a commercial motor vehicle. One must keep in mind that these requirements, listed in Part 391 of the Federal Motor Carrier Safety Regulations (FMCSRs), are the minimum standards. Any efforts to improve upon your physical condition will aid in your work performance, stamina, mental health, and long-term success in this industry.

Hey driver, it's time to think about yourself for a little bit. You've been learning everything it takes to become a professional driver, but none of that matters if you don't take care of yourself. Eatin' right, exercising, reducing stress...these are all pretty tough subjects to deal with when you're on the road all the time. Do the best you can. It's not just for you, it's for your family too!

When I was driving, I would only keep water in my truck. Do you want to know why? Because we need to drink A LOT of water every day! If it's there, and you're thirsty, you'll drink it! It's just that simple.

Physical condition — Although the correlation is indirect, general overall health, fitness, and a good attitude can contribute to reduced workplace injury and illness. A healthy and fit person with a good attitude is less likely to get injured or ill, on or off the job. A healthy person who is feeling well is a safer employee, because he/she can focus better on the job, the surroundings, and what he/she is doing. In addition, when you're healthy, you just feel better.

Diet — The first place you can start to work on feeling better and improving your health is with the diet you choose. You should try to eat a "balanced diet" - one characterized by a combination of the right foods that allows you to get all the vitamins, minerals, and protein your body needs to be healthy. The U.S. Food and Drug Administration (FDA) recommends a variety of foods to get necessary nutrients and the right amount of calories to maintain a healthy weight.

To practice healthful eating habits at work, avoid these common nutrition pitfalls while on the road:

- The morning doughnut and coffee;
- Lunch at a fast food restaurant; and
- The afternoon snack break of a candy bar.

Replace these bad eating habits with good ones, like keeping fruits and vegetables handy for munching in the morning or afternoon, and eating a healthy lunch.

Vitamins — Even if you eat properly, you still may need to take dietary supplements in the form of vitamins or minerals. Especially if you are watching your weight, or not eating the number of fruits and vegetables recommended by the FDA, you may need such supplements. Check with your doctor if you think you may need vitamin and mineral supplements.

Water — Water is a key ingredient to health and wellness. You need water to process the nutrients you eat, cleanse your body of toxins and impurities, and replenish you after exercise or physical exertion, especially in extreme heat.

Normally, you should drink at least eight-8-oz. glasses of water every day (you can get some of this water through milk and other drinks and through fruits and vegetables). Instead of going to get a cup of coffee or a soda, grab a tall glass of refreshing cold water. A little bit of water all day long will add up to what you need.

For working in extreme heat, you will need to drink at least 8 ounces of cool water every 15 to 20 minutes.

Exercise — A driver has little opportunity to move around in any given day. With irregular hours, most drivers find it difficult to join a fitness center or have consistent exercise routines. The following exercises can be done right in the comfort of the tractor seat or sleeper. Repeat them three or four times per day or as often as you feel comfortable. They are quick and easy and excellent for exercise beginners:

1. **Crunches** — These require little space and can be done in the sleeper. Lying on your back, cross your arms across your chest so that your right hand is touching your left shoulder and your left hand is touching your right. Now, keeping your head straight, lift your shoulders 6-8 inches off the mattress. Return slowly and repeat. Do as many as you feel comfortable with. Crunches are great for strengthening your lower back and abdominal muscles.

2. **Knees to chest** — Again, lying on your back, bring your left knee up to your chest and hold it with your hands for 5-10 seconds. Repeat with your right knee. This is good for stretching and strengthening back and buttocks muscles.

3. **Shoulder rolls** — This and the following exercises are designed to strengthen your neck, shoulders and upper back muscles and can be done while sitting behind the wheel. Roll your shoulders up, backwards and down as far as you can comfortably move them. Repeat 10-12 times, then reverse your direction.

4. **Shoulder extension** — Bring your shoulders up and backwards to their fullest extent. Hold this position for 5-10 seconds while tightening your upper back and neck muscles. Repeat 3-5 times.

5. **Neck rotations** — Turn your neck one direction to its maximum extension and hold this position for 5 seconds. Do the same in the opposite direction, then repeat 3-5 times.

6. **Neck side bends** — Keeping your head forward, bend your neck to one side and then the other, trying to touch your ear to your shoulder each time. Repeat 3-5 times.

7. **Whole body** — Walking just one mile a day (about 15-18 minutes), along with a moderately low fat diet, can help you lose weight. But there's more. Walking can also help lower your heart rate, cholesterol and blood pressure. It is an effective low impact exercise that is easy on the ankles, knees, and hips.

To increase your daily walking distance, try these suggestions:

*   When at your terminal waiting for dispatch, ask another driver if he/she has time for a quick walk around the yard. Having someone to talk to while you walk will make the experience more enjoyable.

You know, there's nothing worse than seeing some lazy "someone" circling the truck stop parking lot, waiting for that spot right by the front door to open. I've seen some people drive around for what seems like hours, just because they don't want to walk a little ways. When they finally get that front parking spot and get out of their truck...it's pretty obvious that they don't walk much, if you know what I mean. Here's an idea...park in the back and walk! It's good for you. If you happen to get that front spot sometime, get out and walk all the way around the parking lot before you go in. Even a little exercise is better than nothing!

- When parking at a truck-stop or rest area, park as far away from the facility as possible (during the daylight hours only). This will not only force you to do a little extra walking, but it also decreases the chance of fender-bender accidents since parking away from the facility will tend to be less congested.

- When walking, maintain a pace that isn't too strenuous but that will increase your heart rate. Also, try to walk with small weights or dumbbells - a great idea for upper body muscle conditioning

Mental health — In addition to the struggles with keeping your body fit and healthy, you should also consider your mental health and state of mind. Poor mental health can make it difficult to function in your day-to-day work, as well as affecting your physical health and well-being.

Stress — Stress is a physical or mental response to the pressures of an event or factors of living in general. Though we tend to speak of it in a negative context, stress can be positive or negative.

Biologically, when stress occurs, your body releases hormones which accelerate your breathing and heart rate, increase your blood sugar levels and blood pressure, and improve blood clotting. Your body gets into a survival mode, readying itself for a physical emergency. This can be a good thing. You have energy and mental agility to get the job done. You are alert and perform well.

As stress continues, your body temporarily adjusts to the stress. If stress is removed during this adjustment period, your body returns to normal. However, if stress goes on for prolonged periods of time, your body fails to adjust and wears out. This can weaken your defenses and lead to disease. A body cannot run on high speed forever. This can lead to "burnout." Some stress adds challenge, opportunity, and variety to your life. Too much stress can work against you.

Medically, stress can cause you to suffer high blood pressure, pain, breathing trouble, cancer, digestive disorders, insomnia, and fatigue. Psychologically, you may suffer frustration, irritability, anger, impatience, worry, a lack of self confidence, poor listening, and violence, alcohol, or drug abuse.

To compound matters, your job can be affected too. Stress can lead to accidents, a loss of priorities, rushing, and anger or inappropriate behavior.

You can deal with stress by watching for the warning signs. Become aware of when you are under stress. Look for signs of being in survival mode. Once you are aware of what stresses you, you can manage your stress by using one or more of the following stress-reduction techniques:

- Take breaks and learn to relax fully.

- Release stress with exercise.

- Maintain proper rest and diet so that you can deal with stressful situations.

- Practice deep breathing or yoga to relax body and mind.

- Manage your time. Set priorities and do the most important things first.

- Build your self confidence.

- Have fun.

- Laugh and cry to release tension.

- Avoid taking medication or drinking alcohol to eliminate stress temporarily. Your problem will not really be solved.

- Share your stress with others. Talk to a friend. "Cry on someone's shoulder."

Fatigue and Driving

Demanding work schedules are a fact of life in a modern, 24-hour society. Goods are produced and services are provided at all hours of the day and night. Because of this, approximately 15.5 million people in the U.S. work unconventional hours, including permanent nights or rotating shifts.

These schedules help keep businesses running, but for the people who have to function within them, they can have a negative impact if not managed correctly.

A good night's sleep has been characterized as fuel for the brain, and sleep is as important as proper nutrition and regular exercise. Those who have trouble getting enough sleep report a greater difficulty concentrating, accomplishing required tasks, and handling minor irritations.

Hey driver, this is no time for magic pills or potions, whether they're legal or not. If you are tired, GET SOME SLEEP! Don't let anyone push you to the point that you find yourself on your top in the ditch. It's just not worth it. Plan you route, drive your plan, and if you need sleep, then sleep!

Fatigue can be a serious issue for the professional driver.

Every choice that you make in regards to rest will have either a negative or positive impact. Consider the following scientific investigations which have documented negative consequences of both short sleep duration and insomnia:

- Insomnia can lead to increased risk of depression; problems with memory, family/social relationships, and mood; poorer quality of life; increased health care costs; increased absenteeism; and increased risk for coronary disease.

- Insufficient sleep can lead to excessive sleepiness, negative mood changes, reduced performance on standardized tasks, increased accident risk, and acute negative effects on glucose metabolism and immune function.

Causes of fatigue include:

Sleep apnea — A breathing disorder characterized by brief pauses of breathing during sleep. Snoring may be a sign of sleep apnea. The condition causes daytime sleepiness and poor concentration. Early detection and treatment for sleep apnea is important because it may be linked with irregular heartbeat, high blood pressure, heart attack, and stroke. Sleep apnea is more common in men, but it occurs in both sexes and all age groups.

Stress — Fatigue is commonly considered a strictly physical problem, but stress, which can be much more subtle than lack of sleep, is another factor. It can cause fatigue without necessarily making you feel physically tired. It can tire you out mentally and emotionally, eventually wearing you down and making you feel drained.

Highway hypnosis — This happens to everyone at one point or another. You're driving down a dull stretch of highway with very little traffic. Nothing to look at, nothing to get your attention. The lines and the mile markers just keep passing by. Then you suddenly realize you don't remember the last ten miles. You've just been driving on automatic pilot, while your mind has been a million miles away. Experts call this dangerous phenomenon "Driving Without Awareness" or DWA Syndrome. It can happen even when you're well rested, but more often it comes about when you're vulnerable to fatigue. The problem is that you may not come out of the trance until your mind finally registers a hazard ahead of you. And then it may be too late.

Your body clock — As you sleep, your body goes through different stages of sleep from light to deep sleep. When you sleep uninterrupted, your body has a chance to go through several cycles of light and deep sleep, giving you maximum effectiveness. However, if you break up the pattern, you lose some of the recuperative effects of going through the cycles.

Your "body clock" goes through different stages of sleep.

Circadian rhythm — Biologically, humans are day-oriented. We function better during the day and sleep better at night. Our circadian rhythms have regular ups and downs in a 24-hour day and they try to synchronize body functions with behavior. Typically, body functions are high during the day and low at night. Trying to reverse this is difficult. Night shift workers are at work when their circadian rhythms are low and asleep when they are high. These rhythms affect safety because they control how alert we feel. We are more alert when our internal body activity is high, therefore perform best during those times. However, night shift workers are at work when they are low, when their level of alertness is diminished. Add to this a lack of good sleep, and it becomes easy to see how judgment can be affected, increasing the difficulty of making good, effective, and timely safety decisions.

Sleep debt — If you go too long without enough sleep, you begin to build up what is known as a sleep debt. The longer you go without enough sleep, the more sleep you will need to catch up. The only way to pay off this debt is to sleep. Unfortunately, the reverse is not true. You can't build up a bank of sleep time, and then expect to go without. In fact, sleeping too much can leave you as tired as if you hadn't slept enough.

Rotating shifts — Working at night often leads to poor sleep. Workers on rotating shifts are among those who sleep the least of all. Switching from a day schedule to a night schedule is more demanding for these workers, because they are trying to reverse their body's internal clock within a short time frame. Not only does working at night make it difficult to get enough sleep, the sleep gotten is often less refreshing or satisfying than sleep during the normal nighttime hours. This impact on sleep can have immediate, short-term effects such as difficulty in concentrating.

The following practical tips may help reduce the detrimental effects of shiftwork:

Get enough sleep — Everyone needs at least six hours of sleep, but most people need more than that. For night workers, the best time to get enough sleep varies. Try different times to see what works best. It may help to keep a record to identify which time works best.

Added to regular sleep, a short afternoon or evening nap can help fight sleepiness during the night. Naps less than 15 minutes long, however, may actually make a person sleepier. Try to make them 20-30 minutes long.

If a shiftworker switches from nights to days, it is best for them to get most of their sleep the following night. They should sleep just a couple of hours shortly after the night shift to shake off sleepiness. Then stay awake all day long and go to sleep at their regular bedtime that night.

Protect your sleep — A few tricks to protecting sleep during the day include:

- Sleep in the sleeper, not sitting at the wheel.

- If you have to sleep during the day, make sure your sleep area is as dark and quiet as possible.

- Follow your regular bedtime routine every time you go to sleep.

- If you're going to eat before you go to sleep, eat a light meal.

- Try to reduce your stress before you go to sleep by taking a short walk.

- Use a fan or music to act as a sound barrier.

- Keep the temperature in your room between 65-68° F.

Exercise — Keeping physically fit helps resist stress and illness. It also keeps you from becoming tired too quickly. Always consult a doctor before starting an exercise program. It's also a good idea to get an annual checkup with an emphasis on sleeping, eating, and exercise habits. The best exercise schedule is a 20 minute aerobic workout soon after waking, but before work. This is enough to help you wake up and get going, and also keep your heart in shape. Don't forget to warm up before exercising. Your muscles will need time to wake up, too.

This pre-shift exercise raises your body temperature and can help activate your body to produce energy and adjust your internal rhythms to the new work schedule.

Relax — When not at work, take time to relax and get rid of work-time stresses. This could include simply sitting down and closing your eyes for a while. It could also be meditating, reading, taking a bath, or watching TV. If none of these methods work, you might:

- Lie down on a comfortable surface, or sit in an easy chair.

- One by one, slowly tense each muscle group in your body, then slowly let them relax.

- Breathe deeply and go slowly.

- Try to feel all the muscle tension draining away.

Watch what you eat — This means avoiding fatty and sugary foods. Heavy, greasy foods act against sleep because they are difficult to digest and can lead to possible stomach upset.

Caffeine is a mild stimulant that helps you feel more alert. It is the most widely used drug in the world. It is a fairly safe drug if used in small doses. A small dose is one to three cups of coffee, tea, or caffeinated soft drink. However, caffeine can make relaxation difficult.

Another substance to use with caution is alcohol. Although it may make you feel sleepy, it will also wake you up too quickly after falling asleep.

If you have been on the road a while, and begin to feel fatigued, you need to remember this: No matter how many years truck driving experience you have, or how many miles have been logged, you are not a machine. It's an undeniable fact that humans need sleep. It takes a sharp mind and a steady hand to control a commercial motor vehicle.

Alcohol and Driving

Alcohol is a socially accepted drug that has been consumed throughout the world for centuries. It is considered a recreational beverage when consumed in moderation for enjoyment and relaxation during social gatherings. However, when consumed primarily for its physical and mood-altering effects, it is a substance of abuse. As a depressant, it slows down physical responses and progressively impairs mental functions.

Alcohol slows down physical responses and impairs mental functions.

How alcohol affects driving — Alcohol consumption is associated with a wide range of accidents and injuries resulting from the impaired performance of complex mental and motor functions. The skills required to operate motor vehicles make them susceptible to impairment by even low doses of alcohol.

The brain's control of eye movements is highly vulnerable to alcohol. In driving, the eyes must focus briefly on important objects in the visual field and track them as they (and the vehicle) move. Low to moderate blood alcohol concentrations (BAC) (0.03 to 0.05 percent) interfere with voluntary eye movements, impairing the eye's ability to rapidly track a moving target.

Alcohol impairs nearly every aspect of information processing by the brain. Alcohol-impaired drivers require more time to read a street sign or to respond to a traffic signal than unimpaired drivers. Consequently, they tend to look at fewer sources of information. Research on the effects of alcohol on driver performance shows a narrowing of the attention field beginning at about 0.04 percent BAC.

The most sensitive aspect of driving performance is the division of attention among component skills. Drivers must maintain their vehicles in the proper lane and direction while monitoring the environment for vital safety information, such as other vehicles, traffic signals, and pedestrians. Alcohol-impaired subjects who are required to divide their attention between two tasks tend to favor one of them. Therefore, alcohol-impaired drivers tend to concentrate on steering, becoming less vigilant with respect to safety information. Results of numerous studies indicate that divided attention deficits occur as low as 0.02 percent BAC.

Regulations — The FMCSRs address the use of alcohol by commercial drivers. Prohibited behaviors, as listed in Sec. 392.5 of the FMCSRs include:

- Alcohol consumption four hours prior to coming on duty, or while having physical control of, or operating a commercial motor vehicle.

- Alcohol use, being under the influence of alcohol, or having any measurable amount of alcohol concentration or detected presence of alcohol, while on duty, operating, or in physical control of a commercial motor vehicle.

- Being on duty or operating a commercial motor vehicle with alcohol in possession, with the exception of transporting a manifest shipment of alcoholic beverages.

Alcohol testing — Under Part 382 of the FMCSRs, a driver who has a breath alcohol concentration of 0.02 but less than 0.04 may not perform any safety-sensitive functions, including driving a commercial motor vehicle for 24 hours from the time of the reading. If a driver has a reading of 0.04 or greater, he/he must be immediately removed from all safety-sensitive functions and cannot resume until he/she takes the necessary steps in the return-to-duty process found in Part 40 Subpart O of the FMCSRs.

Hey! Listen up...remember what we said about alcohol in an earlier chapter? Not in the truck, not in the sleeper, not in your hand! And if you go out to have a drink, you better not get back behind the wheel until it's out of your system. I know it may sound corny, but big trucks and alcohol just don't mix. When you are in a truck, you are "at work." Would you normally drink at work? I hope not.

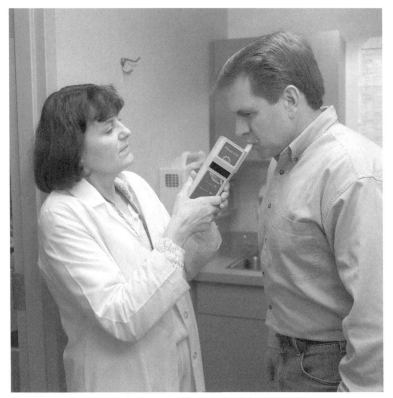

Alcohol testing is required under Part 382 of the FMCSRs.

Disqualification — Offenses occurring in *any* kind of vehicle will be held against a CDL driver. This means that any CDL driver who is convicted of being under the influence of alcohol (in any kind of vehicle) as prescribed by state law will be disqualified from operating a vehicle requiring a CDL for a period of one year for a first offense. If the offense occurred in a vehicle hauling hazardous materials, the penalty is stiffer with a 3-year disqualification. Any subsequent offenses in any kind of vehicle will lead to a lifetime disqualification.

Drugs and Driving

The FMCSA, in its attempt to safeguard the nation's highways, has mandated the monitoring of commercial drivers who operate commercial motor vehicles requiring a CDL by means of random drug testing.

No driver shall report for duty or remain on duty requiring the performance of safety-sensitive functions when the driver uses any controlled substance, except when the use is pursuant to the instructions of a licensed medical practitioner who has advised the driver that the substance will not adversely affect the driver's ability to safely operate a commercial motor vehicle.

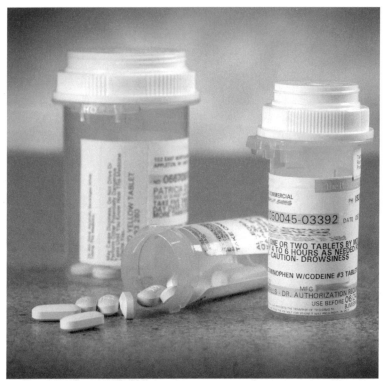

The FMCSA requires certified labs to test for five major categories of drugs, along with any signs of substitution or adulteration. The drugs are:

- Marijuana metabolites;

- Cocaine metabolites;

- Amphetamines;

- Opiate metabolites; and

- Phencyclidine (PCP).

Marijuana — People use marijuana for the mildly tranquilizing and mood and perception altering effects it produces. Marijuana does not depress central nervous system reactions. Its action is almost exclusively on the brain, altering the proper interpretation of incoming messages.

Cocaine — Cocaine is used medically as a local anesthetic. It is abused as a powerful physical and mental stimulant. The entire central nervous system is energized. Muscles are more tense, the heart beats faster and stronger, and the body burns more energy. The brain experiences an exhilaration caused by a large release of neurohormones associated with mood elevation.

Opiates — Opiates are narcotic drugs that alleviate pain, depress body functions and reactions and, when taken in large doses, cause a strong euphoric feeling. They include:

- Natural and natural derivatives - opium, morphine, codeine, and heroin; and

- Synthetics - meperidine (Demerol®), oxymorphone (Numorphan®), and oxycodone (Percodan®)

Same speech, different subject driver. Drugs are no better than alcohol when it comes to driving trucks. Like I've said over and over...just don't do it!

Amphetamines — Amphetamines are central nervous system stimulants that speed up the mind and body. The physical sense of energy at lower doses and the mental exhilaration of higher doses are the reasons for their abuse. Although widely prescribed at one time for weight reduction and mood elevation, the legal use of amphetamines is now limited to a very narrow range of medical conditions. Most amphetamines that are abused are illegally manufactured in foreign countries and smuggled into the U.S. or clandestinely manufactured in crude laboratories.

Phencyclidine (PCP) — Phencyclidine (PCP) was originally developed as an anesthetic, but the adverse side effects prevented its use except as a large animal tranquilizer. Phencyclidine acts as both a depressant and a hallucinogen, and sometimes as a stimulant. It is abused primarily for its variety of mood altering effects. A low dose produces sedation and euphoric mood changes. The mood can change rapidly from sedation to excitation and agitation. Larger doses may produce a coma-like condition with muscle rigidity and a blank stare, with the eyelids half closed. Sudden noises or physical shocks may cause a "freak out" in which the person has abnormal strength, extremely violent behavior, and an inability to speak or comprehend communication.

Refusal to test — If a driver refuses to go in for a test, or shows up to a test site beyond the expected arrival time, he/she falls under the consequences of a refusal to be tested. If a driver is unable to produce an acceptable quantity of urine and cannot present a medical explanation from a licensed medical practitioner, this test is also deemed a "refusal." The consequences of a "refusal" are the same as a positive test.

CDL disqualification — As stated in Sec.383.51 of the FMCSRs, a first-time conviction for being under the influence of a controlled substance in a vehicle will disqualify a CDL-holder for one year, and for three years for operating a vehicle transporting hazardous materials. A second offense in any kind of vehicle will disqualify a driver for life.

A CDL-holder who uses any kind of vehicle in the commission of a felony involving manufacturing, distributing, or dispensing a controlled substance will be disqualified for life after one conviction.

Safety Equipment and Practices

Safety on the job includes more than a general knowledge of the FMCSRs and OSHA regs. It includes common sense and following company safety and security policies and procedures. Because carelessness and inattentiveness on the job can lead to disaster, do all you can to think things over before acting. What are you about to do, and what are the consequences? Review the steps for doing your job safely, and use the right tools for the job.

Accidents often occur when you face a new job or a change at work. When something in your workplace changes, think about your safety. If you are not sure about how to proceed, ask questions. Also, if you discover a hazard, report it.

Vehicle entry and exit — Believe it or not, there are proper ways of climbing up, getting into and out of cabs and seats, and getting down from motor vehicles:

- Always use handrails, face the ladder or steps, and maintain three points of contact (two feet and one hand, or one foot and two hands) at all times;

- Always use anti-slip surfaces for climbing or stepping; and

- Never jump from or to ladders, steps, or walkways.

Maintain three points of contact.

Equipment — Wear the right equipment and appropriate equipment to prevent a disabling injury. Consider the use of:

- Eye protection such as safety glasses and goggles;

- Safety toe shoes;

- Personal protective equipment for hands, including gloves;

- Protective hard hat; and

- Hearing protection.

Also, be conscious of loose clothes which could catch on a vehicle or load.

Using the right equipment prevents injury.

Proper lifting — Injury to the back must be taken seriously, as it can cause a lifetime of pain and discomfort. There are five steps to a proper lifting technique:

Step 1: Size up the load before trying to lift it. If it's too heavy get some help.

- Stretch before you lift, and stretch out frequently during sessions of repeated lifting;

- Test the weight by lifting one of the corners;

- Anything over 50 pounds is considered a heavy lift;

- Request help if you need it; and

- Use mechanical aids - hoists, carts, or dollies - as load warrants;

Step 2: Bend your knees. Let your legs do the work.

Proper lifting technique can prevent back injury.

- Place your feet apart and close to the object;

- Center yourself over the load, bend your knees, and get a good handhold;

- Lift straight up, smoothly; and

- Never bend at the waist, or lift with a rounded back.

Step 3: Never twist or turn your body once you have made the lift.

- Keep the load steady and close to your body; and

- Never carry a load above your head or at your side.

Step 4: Make sure you can carry the load to its destination before attempting the lift.

- Make sure your path is clear of all obstacles; and

- Break up a long carry by stopping halfway to reposition your grasp.

Step 5: Set the load down properly.

- Bend your knees;

- Keep your back upright;

- Let your legs do the work;

- Take your time;

- Keep your head up;

- Tighten the abdominal muscles; and

- Pivot your feet before you move another direction - do not twist.

Always push, don't pull an object.

- Pushing puts less strain on the back.

Cargo security/theft — Whether it's 5,000 pounds of fish, a load of personal computers, or a full truckload of pharmaceuticals, loaded trailers containing virtually any type of cargo are potential targets for theft. Some estimates place annual U.S. cargo losses at $10 billion. Costs from cargo theft include not only the actual value of the cargo itself, but also increased insurance premiums, loss of profit, loss of customers and business opportunity, interruption of freight distribution, and increased overall supply-chain costs.

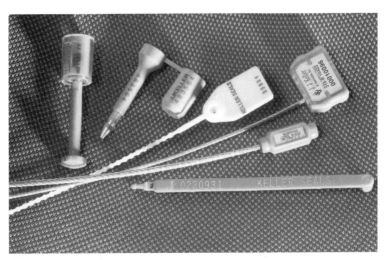

Various cargo seals.

For motor carriers to develop and implement effective cargo security and anti-theft measures, they must first understand the specific techniques and methods used by cargo thieves. These include:

Armed robberies — Armed theft from warehouses, truck terminals, and professional truck drivers are the most common form of cargo theft and fall into three basic categories:

- Theft of loaded vehicles from a trucking facility;

- Theft of a vehicle after thieves compel a driver to make an unplanned stop; and

- Theft of a vehicle when a truck driver stops (at a signal light, truck stop, rest area, etc.).

Burglaries and break-ins — Burglaries and break-ins most often occur at transportation facilities, commercial industrial parks, and intermodal railroad yards.

Counterfeit paperwork and fraud — Generally, this method is used by independent contractors who transport chassis/containers to and from container terminals and intermodal rail-yards. The driver presents counterfeit paperwork to the security personnel and ultimately makes off with an entire container of valuable product.

Grab and runs — Often used by thieves who have inside information about a load of expensive, high-tech merchandise. Involves criminals breaking into a stopped truck and off-loading as much property as possible before the truck driver returns. The Department of Justice estimates that 80 percent of cargo thefts occur while the freight is in transit.

The following tips are provided to help give drivers a better understanding of what to look for when supervising any loading activity:

Pre-trip — Conduct a thorough pre-trip inspection of your equipment prior to entering the shipper's facility, to inspect for safety as well as foreign material and debris.

Unauthorized cargo — You should be prohibited from accepting or allowing any unauthorized or unscheduled box, carton, package, or other cargo (regardless of size) to be loaded on or in your trailer. View all requests to load unauthorized or unscheduled packages as highly suspicious. If this should happen, notify your carrier, responsible shipping personnel, and/or the appropriate authorities immediately.

Cargo inspection — Be sure to get exactly what you sign for. Inspect all cargo before it is loaded. The cargo should be free of any visual damage. Once loaded, the cargo should be properly secured from shifting and falling.

Loading — When possible, load the most valuable cargo into the nose of the trailer and as far away from the doors as possible, as a means of better protecting it from thieves.

Documentation — All load-related documentation should be thoroughly reviewed and verified.

Suspicious activity — Be especially alert when leaving a shipper because the vast majority of cargo thefts and highjackings occur within a few miles of the load's point of origin. Before leaving any shipper:

- Secure the trailer doors with a heavy-duty padlock and/or trailer door seal;

- Keep tractor doors locked and windows rolled up until out on a major road or highway;

- Keep a watchful eye out - if you suspect you are being followed, contact your carrier or the authorities immediately; and

- Be especially alert near signal-regulated highway on- and off-ramps.

Communication — Check in at regular intervals throughout the day (including when loaded and ready to leave a shipper). Report all load-related information, as well as any other company-required information such as trailer seal numbers, hours-of-service data, estimated time(s) of arrival, etc.

Hey driver, did you see that guy standing by your trailer? You need to pay attention when walking through truck stop parking lots, especially at night. Don't walk straight to your truck, never looking around at anyone. Keep your head up, take a "different" route back to your truck than you took when you went inside, and watch out for anyone watching you. Sometimes if you just make eye contact or say "Hi" it's enough to let them know that you're watching them and they'll go bother someone else.

Identification — Before leaving the shipper, have available a list of information on you such as the vehicle identification numbers (VIN) of the tractor and trailer, vehicle license numbers, and insurance information. This list will help law enforcement in the event of a vehicle theft.

Securing the trailer — In general, commercial motor carriers secure loads to provide a measure of theft deterrence and to maintain or ensure the integrity of the cargo. The degree to which a trailer is secured generally depends on the value and type of cargo being transported, from plastic or metal strip seals for a low-value load to steel cable seals and heavy-duty padlocks for a high-value load. Even if shippers supply trailer seals, motor carriers should provide a supply of trailer seals to their drivers. You and a responsible shipping employee should, together, seal the trailer and record the seal number(s) on the bill of lading or other designated shipping document.

Responding to danger en route — What if, even after being careful, alert, and aware, you find yourself in a dangerous situation? What should you do?

For a cargo theft in progress:

- Always assume a criminal is armed and dangerous. Don't be a hero.

- If you encounter a cargo theft in progress or someone trying to break into the truck or trailer, call the police or other authority for help immediately.

For a vehicle hijacking:

- Be very cautious when leaving the shipper. The vast majority of highjackings occur within a few miles of the load's origin.

- Be conscious of other vehicles that may be following the truck over long distances.

- Be very suspicious of motorists that are signaling you to stop or pull over.

- If a hijacking cannot be avoided, always do as instructed. Try to be a good witness by paying attention and listening carefully. After the crime, you may be able to provide law enforcement with vital information with regard to the thieves' methods and where they may have taken the vehicle and cargo.

Driver, pay attention. If you have a "high-value" load, such as electronics, you need to be prepared to drive at least four hours when you leave the shipper. Thieves watch drivers as they leave these kinds of places, loaded for wherever they are going. If you pull out of the shipper and stop at the closest truck stop...it's a good possibility that car that followed you into the parking lot knows exactly what you have on. Don't give them the opportunity to ruin your day!

Re-checking trailer and cargo integrity — Load security ends with you and the responsible receiving personnel working together to unload the trailer. You and receiver should:

- Match the bill of lading and/or other load-related numbers and paperwork;

- Inspect the seal(s), and match seal number(s) with corresponding documentation;

- Break the seal(s);

- Begin and complete unloading; and

- Sign the bill of lading or other load-related paperwork.

Driver supervision of the unloading process is recommended mainly for cargo claims protection for the carrier. During the unloading process, you should be trained to report any discrepancies or damage to the motor carrier as soon as possible.

Summary

A successful, professional driver needs to take health and safety seriously, whether on the road or at the terminal. Health and safety must be a way of life for the commercial driver in order to succeed. It is all a matter of choices, from healthy lifestyles to the conscious effort to follow safety policies and procedures.

Personal Health and Safety Quiz

Directions: Read each statement carefully and mark the response that best answers the question.

1. **A healthy driver is an alert, safe driver.**

   A. True

   B. False

2. **The morning doughnut and coffee and lunch at a fast food restaurant are considered good eating habits.**

   A. True

   B. False

3. **Ways to deal with stress include:**

   A. Taking breaks and relaxing

   B. Maintaining proper rest and diet

   C. Managing your time, setting priorities

   D. All of the above

4. **Alcohol impairs nearly every aspect of information processing by the brain.**

   A. True

   B. False

5. **The regulations allow you to transport a small amount of alcohol on your vehicle for use when off duty.**

   A. True

   B. False

6. **A driver must be removed from all safety-sensitive functions if he/she tests positive for drugs.**

   A. True

   B. False

7. **When entering or exiting a vehicle, you should:**

   A. Jump

   B. Wear a hardhat

   C. Maintain three points of contact at all times

   D. All of the above

8. **Proper lifting technique includes:**

    A. Sizing up the load

    B. Bending your knees, letting your legs do the work

    C. Lifting straight and smoothly

    D. All of the above

9. **As a security precaution, you should load the most valuable cargo into the nose of your vehicle's trailer, as far from the doors as possible.**

    A. True

    B. False

10. **If you suspect you are being followed by a cargo thief you should:**

    A. Confront the individual

    B. Weave in and out of traffic to avoid the thief

    C. Call the authorities immediately

    D. All of the above

CDL Pre-Test

Read each question carefully and select the most correct answer.

1. **When you are driving through construction zones, you should:**

   A. Speed up and hurry through them so you aren't in them any longer than necessary

   B. Stop before entering them, get in low gear and proceed through

   C. Watch for sharp pavement drop-offs

   D. Reduce your speed only if construction workers are near the road-way

2. **If you break down on a level, straight, four-lane, divided high-way, where should you place the reflective warning triangles?**

   A. One 10 feet from the rear of the vehicle, one approximately 100 feet from the rear of the vehicle and another one about 100 feet to the front of the vehicle

   B. One 10 feet from the rear of the vehicle, one approximately 100 feet from the rear of the vehicle, and one about 200 feet from the rear of the vehicle

   C. One 100 feet from the rear of the vehicle, one approximately 200 feet from the rear of the vehicle, and one about 300 feet from the rear of the vehicle

   D. One 50 feet from the rear of the vehicle, one about 100 feet from the rear of the vehicle, and one about 200 feet from the front of the vehicle

3. **According to the Commercial Driver's manual, why should you limit the use of your vehicle's horn?**

   A. If your vehicle has air brakes, the air horn may not work while you are applying your brakes

   B. Blowing your vehicle's horn may startle other drivers

   C. You should keep both hands on the steering wheel at all times

   D. The driver's manual does not say that a driver should limit the use of the horn

4. **Which of the following should you NOT do?**

    A. Turn your headlights on during the day if visibility is reduced due to bad weather

    B. Flash your brake lights to warn vehicles behind you that you are slowing down

    C. Flash your brake lights when entering a construction zone if vehicles are close behind you

    D. Flash your brake lights if someone is following too closely

5. **The proper way to load a vehicle is:**

    A. Keep the load balanced in the cargo area

    B. Place the load at the front of the trailer to give your drive wheels better traction

    C. Place the load at the rear of the trailer so your rear tires have better traction

    D. It makes no difference where the cargo is placed as long as you are not over the allowable gross weight

Chapter 30
Personal Health
and Safety

Chapter **31**

Public and employer relations

OBJECTIVES

Upon completion of this chapter, you should have a basic understanding of:

❏   The image of the trucking industry

❏   Appropriate contact with the public

❏   Good customer relations

❏   Job requirements

❏   How to apply for a job

Introduction

A professional is defined in the Merriam Webster's Collegiate Dictionary as a person "exhibiting a courteous, conscientious, and generally businesslike manner in the workplace." As a professional driver, your workplace is the nation's highways and the facilities you travel to when making deliveries. A successful driver maintains his/her professionalism at all times. This chapter will address the skills, techniques, and regulatory requirements you need to master in order to be a true professional and land a job within the trucking industry.

Trucking Industry Image

As with any group or industry, it only takes the actions of a few individuals to give the whole group a poor public image. This is especially true for the trucking industry. Drivers who are rude and aggressive, including those who speed, tailgate, and hog the road are responsible for leaving fellow motorists with a bad impression of the professional driver and the trucking industry.

There are many consequences for an industry that has a poor public image. Public and media outcry can have a strong effect, in some cases spurring new or changed laws and regulations that can be costly to the trucking industry. How does this effect you? Legislation that is unfavorable to the industry (increased use taxes, road restrictions, etc.) can lead to less profit, which can mean fewer jobs.

Remember, it is often said that when something bad happens to someone, that individual tells ten others of his/her experience.

Contact With the Public

Obey the law — Laws and regulations are intended to protect everyone. Follow all laws and regulations as this helps project that professional image.

Law enforcement.

Truck drivers used to be called, "Knights of the Highway." Now we are referred to as "Road Hogs, Killer Truck Drivers, and Billy Big-Riggers." This is because a few bad apples lost site of what it used to mean to be a truck driver...a guardian of the road. You can help change the public's opinion of truck drivers, but only by being a professional in everything that you say and do. Don't be a "Billy Big-Rigger." We just don't need them any more.

Your vehicle should be clean and well maintained.

Make a good appearance — Often, the first impression is a lasting one. Vehicle and personal appearance are important factors when it comes to first impressions.

Your vehicle should be clean and well maintained. A dirty vehicle, loose tarp, or dragging chains all send the message that you don't care about your job. Use your pre-trip inspections and other inspections throughout the day to ensure that your vehicle is in good shape.

Look at your vehicle as a rolling advertisement for both the trucking industry and your employer. Anyone who comes in contact with your vehicle will come away with an impression of the industry and your company.

When it comes to your personal appearance, neatness counts. You are a representative of your company. Your clothes should be neat, clean, and appropriate for the workplace. Your hair should be neat and if you have a beard or moustache, keep it trimmed.

Share the road — Good driving habits are top priority. This includes:

- Following posted speed limits;
- Maintaining a safe distance between vehicles;
- Making sure there is a clear path when changing lanes;
- Making sure there is adequate space to safely pass;
- Giving early warning when planning to turn;
- Not using the vehicle's size to intimidate other drivers;
- Being courteous when using high-beam headlights — don't blind other drivers; and
- Being aware of other drivers, vehicles, and the flow of traffic when stopping your vehicle.

Hey driver. Wash your truck, wash your clothes, take a shower! There's absolutely no reason to look like a slob going down the road. And when you see a customer, you are representing your company. Take pride in your ride and you'll feel better all day!

Remember, operate safely, legally, and courteously. Stay calm and act professional. Help others when needed and as company policy allows. Treat other motorists the way you would like to be treated. Negative reactions can make a situation unsafe.

Customer Relations

The majority of contact between a business and a customer is made via phone, fax, or computer. Often, you, the professional driver, are the only representative of a company the customer deals with face-to-face.

Be on time. The customer is probably setting his/her work schedule around when you will arrive. If you are going to be late, you or your dispatcher should make a short phone call to the customer letting him/her know you will be late. This can save a lot of time and problems for both you and your customer.

Be polite and friendly when dealing with customer personnel. Never take out your frustrations on, or argue with the customer.

Be honest with the customer. If you can't answer his/her question, assure the customer that you will check with your company and report back with the answer. Once you have the answer to the customer's question, promptly share the answer with him/her.

A customer's impression of you can lose or gain business for your company. Make every effort to be courteous at all times.

Follow company rules in handling cargo and documentation. Also, know your company's procedure for dealing with freight problems. A prompt solution is good customer service.

Be aware of what types of services your company offers. Customers may ask if your company can handle a certain type of shipment, deliver to a specific area, or carry a specific product.

You, the professional driver, represent your company.

Always respect your customer's property. Put yourself in your customer's shoes. Think about how you would feel if a driver making a delivery to your home tracked dirt on your carpeting or broke a window. Make all deliveries as you would like deliveries made to your home. Handle all cargo carefully. No one wants to see their order mishandled.

Respect the requests of your customer. Make every effort to follow the rules of the company where you are making the delivery. Be aware of special delivery or pick-up instructions.

Use extra caution when driving on your customer's property. Watch for low telephone and power lines as well as porches, overhangs, steps and loading docks that stick out from buildings. Use the same care when driving on a

The guy on the dock is not the person you should be arguing with if the load is not right. Call your dispatcher and find out what you need to do to take care of the customer in the right way. If it wasn't for him, you wouldn't have a job; you'd be surprised how far a little professional courtesy goes when you need to get something done. Try it, you'll like the results!

customer's property as you would on other roads. Follow posted directions. Don't speed and watch for pedestrians.

When a customer is angry, how you handle the situation can make or break your company's relationship with the customer. Do not take a customer's anger personally. Focus your energy on fixing the problem that caused the customer's anger. Be courteous and remain calm. This will help you think clearly.

Apologize for the situation, even if it isn't your fault. You don't have to take blame for the situation, but do apologize for the situation. Express your concern that things didn't go as planned, but never be patronizing. An angry customer wants to know that you care.

Even if you or your company aren't at fault, accept responsibility and assure the customer that you will do your best to make things right.

Determine what steps your company can take to make things right. You may need to contact your supervisor for advice and/or directions as to what can or can not be done.

Try to come to some sort of solution with your customer before leaving. If you need to return to your company to work with your supervisor or others at the company to correct the problem, assure the customer that you will contact him/her as soon as possible and make sure you follow up on that promise.

If you are able to offer solutions to the problem before leaving, let the customer choose the course of action that is most convenient for his/her company.

Follow up with the customer to make sure the course of action agreed to worked out as planned. Following up shows that your company cares about the customer and wants to continue a positive business relationship.

Employer Relations/What Do Employers Look For?

As mentioned earlier in this chapter, you, the professional driver, are a representative of your company. You are the individual the general public associates with your company. Because of this, employers are looking for just the right professional to fit their company's image when hiring. They are looking for someone who is qualified based on federal regulations and company policy.

The FMCSRs — The Federal Motor Carrier Safety Regulations (FMCSRs) mandate that a driver of a commercial motor vehicle meet certain qualification standards. Section 391.11 states that you are qualified if you:

- Are at least 21 years old;

- Can read, write, and speak English well enough to do your job;

- Can drive your truck safely;

- Can pass a DOT physical exam;

- Have only one current commercial driver's license (CDL);

- Have given your company a list of any violations you have been convicted of in the last 12 months;

- Are not disqualified to drive a commercial motor vehicle; and

- Passed a road test.

The FMCSRs require a driver to meet certain qualification standards.

An employer may not permit you to drive a commercial motor vehicle (CMV) unless you can determine whether the cargo you transport is properly loaded, distributed, and secured. You must also be familiar with methods and procedures for securing cargo in or on the CMV you drive.

Driver Qualification File — Section 391.51 of the FMCSRs states that an employer is required to maintain a driver qualification file (DQ) for each driver it employs. The following documents must be included in your DQ file:

- Application for employment;

- Motor vehicle record from state(s);

- Road test form and certificate, or a copy of the license or certificate accepted in lieu of a road test;

- Medical exam certificate (original or copy);

- Skill Performance Evaluation (SPE) certificate or medical exemption document;

- Response of each state agency to the annual review of driving record inquiry;

- A note relating to the annual review of your driving record; and

- List of violations.

Your DQ file must be kept by your employer for the whole time you are employed by your employer plus three years.

Your employer is required to maintain a driver qualification file.

Section 383.51 of the FMCSRs states that you are disqualified from driving if you are convicted (including forfeiture of bond or collateral) of any of the following **major offenses** while operating any type of vehicle (commercial or non-commercial):

- Being under the influence of alcohol, as prescribed by state law;

- Being under the influence of a controlled substance;

- Refusing to take an alcohol test, as requested by a state or jurisdiction under its implied consent laws or regulations;

- Leaving the scene of an accident;

- Using a vehicle to commit a felony; or

- Using a vehicle in the commission of a felony involving the manufacturing, distributing, or dispensing of a controlled substance.

You are disqualified from driving if you are convicted (including forfeiture of bond or collateral) of any of the following **major offenses** while operating a CMV:

- Having an alcohol concentration of 0.04 or greater;

- Driving a CMV when, as a result of prior violations committed operating a CMV, your CDL is revoked, suspended, or cancelled, or you are disqualified from driving a CMV; or

- Causing a fatality through negligent operation of a CMV.

The disqualification period ranges from one year to life depending on the severity of the offense and your previous disqualification record.

*You are disqualified from driving if you are convicted of any combination of two or more of the following **serious traffic violations** while operating any vehicle (CMV or non-CMV):

- Excessive speeding (15 mph or more over posted limit);

- Reckless driving;

- Improper/erratic lane changes;

- Following the vehicle ahead too closely; or

- Violating state or local law relating to motor vehicle traffic control (other than a parking violation) arising in connection with a fatal accident.

You are disqualified from driving if you are convicted of any combination of two or more of the following **serious traffic violations** while operating a CMV:

- Driving a CMV without obtaining a CDL;

- Driving without a CDL in your possession;

- Driving a CMV without the proper class of CDL and/or endorsements;

- Violating a state or local law or ordinance on motor vehicle traffic control prohibiting texting while driving a CMV; or

- Violating a state or local law or ordinance on motor vehicle traffic control restricting or prohibiting the use of a hand-held mobile telephone while driving a CMV.

The disqualification period can range from 60 to 120 days.

*__Note:__ A driver convicted of two or more serious traffic violations while operating a non-CMV is disqualified only if the convictions result in the revocation, cancellation, or suspension of the driver's license or driving privileges.

During a trip, you may be placed out of service by an enforcement officer for a certain period of time or until a given problem has been corrected. Conviction for __violating such an out-of-service order__ subjects you to a fine and disqualification period.

The disqualification period ranges from 180 days to 5 years with penalties for drivers of vehicles carrying hazardous materials being more severe. Fines for violating an out-of-service order range from $2,500 to $5,000.

You are disqualified from driving if you are convicted of operating a vehicle requiring a CDL in violation of a federal, state, or local law or regulation pertaining to certain offenses at a railroad-highway grade crossing.

If you are convicted of a __railroad-highway grade crossing violation__, you are subject to a disqualification period of between 60 days and 1 year. See Chapter 17 for details.

__General job qualifications__ — The following are some of the things a prospective employer is looking for when hiring a driver:

- A general knowledge of the various types of vehicles used by the trucking industry as well as vehicle systems and components;

- An understanding of the language of the industry;

- General knowledge about required paperwork (record of duty status, inspection reports, etc.);

- The ability to safely drive assigned vehicles;

- A basic understanding of cargo handling techniques and procedures; and

- A prospective employer is also looking for an individual who has a good, positive attitude. This means being interested in the job, mature, responsible, enthusiastic, and safe.

__Company policy__ — Each company that hires drivers has its own policies and procedures. Know your company's policies and follow them. Some of the policies may vary from what you have learned in this driver training program, but do keep in mind that you should always operate safely and legally.

It is illegal for an employer to require you to violate federal, state, or local laws/regulations.

A typical company policy covers:

- Hours of work;
- Compensation (pay and benefits);
- Safety rules;
- Vehicle inspection and maintenance requirements;
- Rules for trips; and
- Public/customer relations.

Whistleblower protection — If employees have knowledge of wrongdoing on the part of their employer, the employees may take steps to point out the activities and be free from fear of retaliation. This is the basis of whistleblower protection laws. A "whistleblower" is someone who reports a company or someone in the company or otherwise seeks to stop actions by the company, which he or she believes to be illegal or improper. "Whistleblowing" activities may include such things as making a report to management or the board of directors, or reporting the activity to a government agency.

There are many statutes that protect employees who engage in whistle-blowing activities. A recent example is the Sarbanes-Oxley Act, which mandates a number of reforms in the field of corporate governance and which include broad whistle-blower protection to those who report violations. Other examples include various federal discrimination statutes, which prohibit retaliation against individuals who file a claim or who oppose discrimination by other means.

Department of Labor regulations (29 CFR 1978) prohibit an employer from discharging, disciplining, or discriminating against an employee (you) regarding pay, terms, or privileges of employment because you did one of the following actions:

1. You filed a complaint related to a violation of a commercial motor vehicle safety regulation.

2. You have testified in or will testify in a proceeding related to a violation of a commercial motor vehicle safety regulation.

3. You refused to operate a commercial motor vehicle, because of one of the following two items:

    - You would have violated a federal safety or health regulation.

    - You had a reasonable apprehension you, or someone else, would have been seriously injured or impaired had you operated the unsafe vehicle.

4. You accurately report your hours on duty.

5. You cooperate with a safety or security investigation by a federal agency.

6. You furnish factual information to a regulatory or law enforcement agency related to an accident or incident resulting in injury or death to an individual or damage to property occurring in connection with commercial motor vehicle transportation.

Retaliation — "Retaliation" refers to claims on lawsuits which assert that an employer took action such as discipline or harassment against an employee because that employee made a claim against the employer or supported a claim. Although the most common claims are under the federal and state discrimination laws, such claims may be brought under many other statutes which protect "whistleblowers." The laws and regulations regarding discrimination and harassment prohibit employers from retaliating against individuals who oppose unlawful employment discrimination, participate in employment discrimination proceedings, or otherwise assert their rights under the laws enforced by the Equal Employment Opportunity Commission (EEOC).

Most state anti-discrimination laws include similar protections. Retaliation complaints have become a large problem for employers. After a charge has been alleged, employers or supervisors sometimes take actions against the charging employee, and the employee may bring a retaliation claim. At this point, the employer or supervisor may bear responsibility for proving that the action was based on legitimate employment concerns, and was not founded in retaliation.

A charge of retaliation can be established even if the alleged discrimination was not founded. It is not uncommon for an employer to win the underlying discrimination case, but still be found guilty of retaliation. Title VII of the Civil Rights Act of 1964, the Age Discrimination in Employment Act (ADEA), the Americans with Disabilities Act (ADA), and the Equal Pay Act prohibit retaliation because an individual has engaged in protected activity.

An individual who alleges retaliation need not claim that he or she was treated differently because of race, religion, sex, national origin, age, or disability. An individual who alleges retaliation for protesting discrimination against persons in the protected group need not be in the protected group themselves. Employees can charge retaliation even if it occurred after their employment relationship ended. A charging party can bring an ADA retaliation claim against an individual supervisor, as well as an employer.

This is because Section 503(a) of the ADA makes it unlawful for a "person" to retaliate against an individual for engaging in protected activity. Elements of a retaliation claim

There are three essential elements of an employee retaliation claim:

- The charging party opposed discrimination or participated in covered proceedings;

- The employer or supervisor took adverse action; and

- There is a causal connection between the protected activity and the adverse action.

Examples of employee opposition to discrimination include:

- Threatening to file a charge or other formal complaint alleging discrimination;

- Complaining to anyone about alleged discrimination against one-self or others;

- Refusing to obey an order because of a reasonable belief that it is discriminatory; and

- Requesting reasonable accommodation or religious accommodation.

The manner of opposition must be reasonable for the anti-retaliation provisions to apply. For example, opposing an employment practice through unlawful activities such as acts or threats of violence to life or property would not be protected. In applying a "reasonableness" standard, courts and the EEOC balance the right of individuals to oppose employment discrimination and the public's interest in enforcement of the EEO laws against an employer's need for a stable and productive work environment.

Courts have found that the following activities were not reasonable and thus not protected:

Searching and photocopying confidential documents relating to alleged ADEA discrimination and showing them to co-workers

Making an overwhelming number of complaints based on unsupported allegations and bypassing the chain of command in bringing complaints

Badgering a subordinate employee to give a witness statement in support of an EEOC charge and attempting to coerce her to change her statement.

If an employee's protests interfere with job performance to the extent that they render him or her ineffective in the job, the retaliation provisions do not immunize the worker from appropriate discipline or discharge. Opposition to perceived discrimination does not serve as license for the employee to neglect job duties. A person is protected against retaliation for opposing perceived discrimination if the person had a reasonable and good faith belief that the opposed practices were unlawful. Thus, a violation of the retaliation provision can be found even if the challenged practice is not found to be unlawful.

There must be proof that the respondent took an adverse action because the charging party engaged in protected activity. Proof can be through direct or circumstantial evidence. Direct evidence of a retaliatory motive is any written or verbal statement by a respondent (such as a supervisor against whom a charge was made) that he or she undertook the challenged action because the charging party engaged in protected activity. Such evidence also includes a written or oral statement by a respondent that on its face demonstrates a bias toward the charging party based on his or her protected activity, along with evidence linking that bias to the adverse action.

Such a link could be shown if the statement was made by the decision–maker at the time of the adverse action. Direct evidence of retaliation is rare. The most common method of proving that retaliation was the reason for an adverse action is through circumstantial evidence. If circumstantial evidence indicates retaliation, and the respondent can not produce evidence of a legitimate, non–retaliatory reason for the action, then a violation is established.

Many times, the timing of the action is important. If the discipline occurs soon after the protected activity, it may be difficult to convince the agency or court that one deed did not cause the other. On the other hand, charging parties have great difficulty convincing the court or agency that actions which occurred years after the protected activity were caused by it.

Employers must recognize that supervisors and fellow employees who are charged with improper actions, whether fairly or unfairly, have a tendency to want to fight back and may retaliate out of emotion or anger. To avoid such claims, the employer should meet with those involved, talk about retaliation claims, and ensure a "business as usual" approach. It may also be useful to meet with the complaining employee to confirm that no inappropriate actions have occurred, to resolve any misunderstandings, and to establish a line of communication in the event an issue arises.

Opportunities for advancement — Experience plays a part in the hiring process. As with any type of job, the higher paying, more lucrative jobs go to drivers with a certain level of experience and skill as well as a safe driving record.

Know that completing your driving education is a solid first step in achieving whatever driving goal you may have. Many experienced drivers will tell you that their first job was hauling local freight or working in a motor carrier's yard jockeying trailers, spotting trailers, and/or loading and unloading freight.

When working in this type of situation, put your best foot forward, show enthusiasm, and above all do a good job. This will help you in advancing your career.

Applying for a job — The application process for a tractor-trailer driver involves a certain amount of paperwork, tests, and an interview process.

Much of the paperwork you will be required to fill out is mandated by the FMCSRs.

1. **Application for employment** — Section 391.21 of the FMCSRs requires a motor carrier to obtain certain, specific information from you including (but not limited to):

   - Your name, address, date of birth, and Social Security number;

   - The issuing state, number, and expiration date of your CDL;

   - Information on your experience operating motor vehicles;

   - A list of all motor vehicle accidents in the past 3 years;

   - A list of all violations of motor vehicle laws in the past 3 years; and

   - A list of all employers in the past 10 years.

2. **Investigations and inquiries** — Section 391.23 of the FMCSRs requires a motor carrier to obtain information about your work and driving history. You will be required to fill out paperwork giving your permission to the motor carrier to conduct these investigations.

The motor carrier is also required to check your drug and alcohol testing history for the past 3 years. You will be required to fill out paperwork giving your permission for the motor carrier to obtain this information from your past employers (driving jobs only).

You will also be required to complete a certain battery of tests before you can operate a commercial motor vehicle for a prospective employer.

1. **Road test** — Section 391.31 of the FMCSRs requires that you complete a specific road test before operating a commercial motor vehicle for an employer.

   Exceptions: An employer may accept another employers road test if it was conducted in the last 3 years. Also, your valid CDL may be accepted if you do not have a double/triple or tanker endorsement. Keep in mind that an employer may still require a road test even though you could meet the exception.

2. **Written exam** — Though a written exam hasn't been required for several years, some carriers still require this test as a way of evaluating a driver's understanding of the FMCSRs.

3. **Physical exam** — Section 391.41 of the FMCSRs requires you to pass a physical exam before you can operate a commercial motor vehicle. You must carry a certificate signed by a medical examiner that states you are physically qualified. The motor carrier must also keep a copy of this certificate in its files.

4. **Pre-employment drug test** — Section 382.301 of the FMCSRs requires you to pass a pre-employment drug test before driving a commercial motor vehicle. Though a pre-employment alcohol test isn't required by the FMCSRs, some companies do require this as company policy.

The job interview is an important part of the application process. Be prepared for the interview:

- Learn all you can about the company. Ask current and past employees and/or visit the company's website.

- Be prepared to ask intelligent questions.

- Make sure you have the necessary paperwork and information with you, including information to fill out the paperwork mentioned earlier in this chapter.

- Dress neatly.

- Be well rested.

- Get to the interview site a little early.

- When asked, present your qualifications honestly.

- Be positive and responsive to questions asked.

- Keep the conversation focused on the job and why you are the best candidate.

The interviewer should volunteer information about the company, work conditions, and company policies. If they don't, you should ask. Don't wait until you are on the job to find this out.

Keep in mind that most people are nervous in job interviews. Be yourself. Try to relax and enjoy the experience. Make sure you end the interview on a positive note. Thank the interviewer(s) for their time and interest and make sure you express your interest in the job and company. Before leaving, ask what will happen next, including what procedure the company will follow in making a decision.

Summary

In this chapter, you have learned what it takes to become a trucking professional. This includes professional image, good customer service, and the skills required to land a job within the trucking industry.

Public and Employer Relations Quiz

Directions: Read each statement carefully and mark the response that best answers the question.

1. **A successful driver maintains his/her professionalism at all times.**

   A. True

   B. False

2. **Good driving habits include:**

   A. Giving little or no warning when planning to turn

   B. Using the vehicle's size to intimidate other drivers

   C. Following posted speed limits and maintaining a safe distance between vehicles

   D. All of the above

3. **You should look at your vehicle as a rolling advertisement for both the trucking industry and your employer.**

   A. True

   B. False

4. **Good customer relations includes being:**

   A. On time

   B. Polite, friendly, and honest with the customer

   C. Knowledgeable of your company's services

   D. All of the above

5. **When searching for a new employee, a motor carrier is looking for someone who is qualified based on federal regulations and company policies.**

   A. True

   B. False

6. **According to the FMCSRs _____ must be included on a driver application.**

   A. Your mother's maiden name

   B. A summary of your high school achievements

   C. A list of all motor vehicle violations in the past three years

   D. All of the above

7.   **The FMCSRs require a motor carrier to obtain information about your work and driving history.**

   A.   True

   B.   False

8.   **The FMCSRs do not require a physical exam prior to operating a commercial motor vehicle.**

   A.   True

   B.   False

9.   **In preparing for a job interview you should:**

   A.   Learn all you can about the company

   B.   Dress neatly

   C.   Make sure you have necessary paperwork with you

   D.   All of the above

10.   **Always try to end a job interview on a positive note.**

   A.   True

   B.   False

CDL Pre-Test

Read each question carefully and select the most correct answer.

1. **When driving a vehicle with a height over 13 feet, you should:**

   A. Assume all clearances are of sufficient height

   B. Height clearance is not a concern as long as you stay on state or federal roadways

   C. If you are unsure of the clearance, stop and check before proceeding

   D. All of the above

2. **Controlled braking is:**

   A. Applying brakes hard enough for the wheels to lock up

   B. Pressing the brakes hard enough to lock-up the wheels, then releasing and then reapplying again

   C. Applying firm brake pressure but not to the point of lock-up

   D. Only used if the vehicle does not have anti-lock brakes

3. **You are driving on a straight and level roadway at 60 mph and suddenly a tire blows out on your vehicle. What should you do first?**

   A. Immediately begin light, controlled braking

   B. Immediately begin stab braking

   C. Grip steering wheel firmly with both hands and stay off the brakes until the vehicle has slowed down

   D. Immediately begin emergency braking

4. **Which of the following is true?**

   A. It is permissible to use radial and bias-ply tires together on the same axle

   B. Tires which are mismatched sizes should not be used on the same vehicle

   C. $4/32$ inch tread depth is the maximum allowed on drive tires

   D. $2/32$ inch tread depth is permissible for steering tires

5. **Why do hazardous materials regulations exist?**

   A. To provide for safe drivers and equipment

   B. To communicate a risk

   C. To contain the product

   D. All of the above

Chapter **32**

Basic business practices for truck drivers

OBJECTIVES

Upon completion of this chapter, you should have a basic understanding of:

- ❏ Cost determination and control

- ❏ Fuel management

- ❏ Growing revenue

Introduction

In a world that measures your success in terms of capacities, mileages, utilization percentages, rates, revenue realizations and losses, costs per mile, profits and losses, and return on investments, it is difficult to be aware of everything involved in the business of trucking. This is the world you have been studying so hard to be a part of. Your goal in this world is to try and bring order out of chaos and operate a safe and profitable operation. And you thought you were just going to go drive a truck!

Paperwork can be time consuming.

In this final chapter we will touch on just a few of the many business concepts and ideas that you should be aware of in operating a profitable trucking business, whether you are a company driver, a one-truck owner/operator or an entrepreneur that wants to grow a trucking business.

Cost Determination and Control

Cost is the greatest single issue that you will deal with as a trucking professional. Excessive costs, or lack of an effective cost control program, can cause any truck driver to become unprofitable.

One of the first things to understand as a business person, is that not all costs are bad. Some costs are actually an investment, reducing costs in other areas. Many time new drivers (and old) are so caught up in trying to save pennies that they end up losing dollars. Remember you're in this business to make money, but it doesn't matter how much you make if it all gets spent before you get home.

An example of this is equipment purchases. Newer equipment can create a significant cost, both figured monthly and per mile. However, newer equipment requires less maintenance, operates more efficiently (fuel mileage, oil consumption, etc), operates with less down time, and has a positive effect on driver retention.

Looked at independently, new vehicle purchases may appear to be an unnecessary expense, but when other factors are taken under consideration the cost situation changes.

There are two main categories of Costs that you should be familiar with as a business person; Rolling (or variable) costs, and Fixed costs.

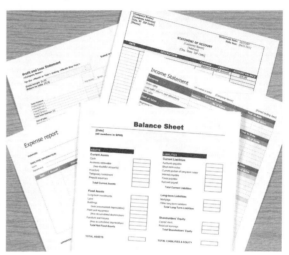

Various forms.

Rolling costs — also referred to as variable costs, are difficult to predict because they are always changing. These types of costs typically get budgeted as an "estimate" or assumption of what they will be. When you look at what type of freight you want to haul, and where you want to run, rolling costs can become a substantial factor in your decision.

Rolling costs included such things as:

- Your pay
- Fuel
- Tires
- Road tax
- Tolls & Scale fees
- Vehicle depreciation
- Loading and Unloading fees
- Fines
- Accidents and claims

O.K. driver. You really need to stop and think here. Do you drive Uncle Fred's 1976 Mack because he said you could have it..."just needs a little oil", or do you get into one of those "lease-to-own" programs with your favorite trucking company, or do you buy that shiny new Pete that you've been looking at since you started this course. If you're going to be an owner/operator, the vehicle you own could make the difference between success and failure. Do your homework, make cost comparisons, and make an educated business decision.

As you can see from this list, there are many rolling costs that can use up a substantial portion of your revenue. How you control these costs will have a direct impact on how successful you are as a truck driver and professional business person.

Fixed costs — are those costs that can be placed into a budget and don't change over time. They are known costs that do not change based on how many miles you drive, or how long you sit at home. This is important to remember as these costs will continue, even if you decide to take a vacation, or just don't feel like driving for a month.

Fixed costs include:

- Vehicle payments
- Finance charges
- Liability insurance
- Health insurance
- Vehicle insurance
- Cargo insurance
- Facility rent or mortgage (if you have one)
- Property taxes
- Professional services (legal, accounting, etc)
- Professional dues and subscriptions

Fixed costs are the easiest to "see" because they are always there and don't change. This can be good and bad. If you are motivated to succeed, and realize the commitment necessary to become a successful trucking professional, your fixed costs will just become a base for what you need to create in revenue each month to succeed. If you are more of a "hobby trucker" and are doing this just for the glamour, then your fixed costs will eat you alive.

So which is it? Are you going to be a professional trucker or a "want-a-be" I think you decided that before you started this course, but only you know for sure.

Fuel Management

Fuel costs will be one of the highest costs you will deal with as a truck driver. Even if you don't own your own truck, it's important to understand how fuel and fuel mileage strategies can affect your bottom line.

Driver habits and performance — can be one of the largest factors in fuel mileage. The driver's driving techniques can influence fuel mileage as much as a mile per gallon.

Hey, just because you may not own this truck doesn't mean you shouldn't care about how much it costs to operate it! Do you want a raise? Do you like bonuses? If so, then get involved in the operating costs of your truck. Drive it like you own it, and the rewards can be substantial.

Here is a list of driving techniques that can improve fuel mileage:

- Progressive shifting
- Low RPM driving
- Operating at a slower speed
- Idle reduction

Many companies currently have fuel bonus programs in place for their company drivers. This incentive could create thousands of dollars in extra revenue for you, as a company driver, just by doing some of the things that you have been taught in this course about proper driving techniques. As an owner/operator, your "fuel bonus program" is the realization that you have saved thousands of dollars in fuel costs every month just by exercising good driving practices. Whether a company driver or owner/operator, spending less money on fuel means more money in your pocket. We're not talking a few dollars a week, fuel savings over the course of a year can be thousands of dollars!

Growing Revenue

Whether you get paid by the mile, the trip, or the hour, revenue is controlled by you, the driver. How much you make is directly determined by how much you want to do and what you want to pay others to do for you.

You may think that as a company driver or even as an owner/operator you have little control over what you get paid. That is incorrect. While you may not be able to adjust your rate per mile when ever you want to, you can control how many miles you run, how you run those miles, what "extra" things you will do to create additional revenue, and how you schedule your time off.

As we talked about earlier, your creation of revenue should initially be driven by your costs; how much do you need to make to break even. In addition to that, you should have an amount in mind as to what you want and/or need to realize an acceptable standard of living for yourself and your family. Keeping this in mind, you can now determine how much revenue is necessary to accomplish these benchmarks, and operate accordingly.

There's lots of ways to make additional income as a driver, driver. I used to run out west a lot. Often I would see drivers who were trying to adjust their brakes to go down a mountain, but obviously didn't know how. You can make a fast $20 by offering to show some poor lost soul how to keep their brakes adjusted and may just save their life in the process. Be creative! You'd be surprised what other people will pay you to do. You're the professional. Use that knowledge and make some money!

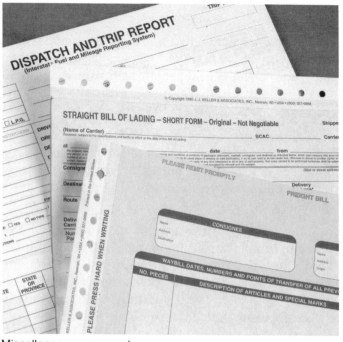

Miscellaneous paperwork.

As an owner/operator, how you run your truck affects your bottom line. Remember those fixed costs? Well, they don't change as you drive more or less each month. If you want to realize a larger net revenue (what's in your pocket at the end of the month) this month, then try running more miles than you did the previous month. The fixed costs won't increase but your gross revenue will. This in turn, creates more money to you.

How do you do this? Run smart, not hard. Decide ahead of time where it makes the most sense to run, based on freight availability, and schedule accordingly. You may like to run to Southern California every trip but if that means you are going to sit there for three days until you find a reload, that's not good business sense. Look at where the freight runs, plan your trips accordingly, and spend your three days at home. The end result could be a greater realization of income without sacrificing home time.

As a company driver, you may not be able to control where you run, but you can control other areas of revenue. When you have a "driver unload" do you do it yourself, or do you pay a lumper to do it? Depending on what type of freight you haul, and your company's policies, this could be a way to create hundreds of extra dollars monthly in your pocket. And besides, it's good exercise! Also, remember that you came into this business to make money to provide for yourself and your family. You should realize that the longer you stay out on the road, the more income you will bring home.

Don't get me wrong, I feel that home time is extremely important. However, try and be practical about your schedule. If you insist on being home every weekend, your paycheck will reflect a limited commitment to the driving profession. You may be better off staying out two or three weeks and enjoying that home time when it comes because you won't be spending all your time arguing about expenses! I've been there...I know.

Don't believe everything you hear, particularly when it comes to how "terrible" the driving profession is and how little money there is to be made out there. The funny thing about those guys that are complaining all the time...They're the same guys that are braggin' about how great it is the next time they pick up the CB mic or talk to a friend in a restaurant. They're just talkin'...let them talk! You'll be out of range soon, thinkin' about how great it is to be doing what you're doing!

Summary

In this chapter, you have learned just a few of the business concepts involved with being a company driver and/or owner/operator. Although there are many other business concepts and practices, far too many to mention in this manual, the ideas of costs and revenue are the most important for you to know.

Everything you do in the future as a professional in the transportation industry will be associated to either a cost or revenue. If you look at your truck driving career not as a job, but as a business, you can be extremely successful and can realize a level of income that may not have been available to you elsewhere.

You will hear many truck driver stories of failure; of financial loss and misery. Yes that can happen in trucking, just like it can happen in any other profession. That's not you. You are a professional and you entered this program to learn how to be a successful truck driver. That success is not just realized in knowing how to physically handle a big rig going down the road, but also in the realization that you are doing something that you love and making good money at it too!

Learn how to be a professional truck driver, but learn how to be a professional business person as well. It will make all this learning seem worthwhile and you will realize a life that many others only dream of.

Business Quiz

Read each statement carefully and select the most correct answer.

1. **There are many types of costs associated with trucking but you only need to worry about variable costs.**

   A.   True

   B.   False

2. **Fuel cost is considered to be a fixed cost.**

   A.   True

   B.   False

3. **Which of the following is not a rolling cost?**

   A.   Tires

   B.   Road Tax

   C.   Vehicle payment

   D.   Scale fees

4. **Fuel is one of the highest costs that a owner/operator has to deal with every day.**

   A.   True

   B.   False

5. **Methods of improving your fuel mileage include _____.**

   A.   Driving fast

   B.   Revving the engine to get the oil to flow better

   C.   Coasting

   D.   Progressive shifting

6. **Both company drivers and owner/operator can affect their revenue in positive ways.**

   A.   True

   B.   False

7. **One suggested way for a company driver to increase his/her revenue is to _____.**

   A.   Sell parts off the truck

   B.   Work a part time job

   C.   Unload his/her own trailer rather than paying someone else to do it

   D.   Spend all day unloading other drivers' trailers because it's fun

8. **Owner/operators should increase their revenue by selling extra fuel to other drivers.**

   A.   True

   B.   False

9. **Home time is very important. A driver who schedules his/her time correctly can make money and enjoy quality home time.**

   A.   True

   B.   False

10. **When buying a truck, you should always buy the biggest one with the most chrome. Chrome makes trucks go faster and you'll make more money.**

   A.   True

   B.   False

CDL Pre-Test

Read each question carefully and select the most correct answer. This is your last chance!

1. **Which of the following statements about backing a commercial vehicle to a dock is NOT true?**

    A. Since you can't see behind you, you should back slowly until you bump the dock

    B. Use a helper and communicate with hand signals

    C. You should always back toward the driver's side when possible

    D. Both A and C

2. **As alcohol begins to build up in the body, which of the following is affected first?**

    A. Muscle control

    B. Coordination

    C. Kidney control

    D. Judgment and self-control

3. **Which of the following is true concerning cold weather driving?**

    A. Exhaust system leaks are not of concern during cold weather

    B. If the temperature is below 32 degrees Fahrenheit, the engine cannot overheat

    C. Using bleach on tires will provide increased traction

    D. You should use windshield washer fluid which contains an anti-freeze

4. **Placarding, the use of hazardous material placards and labels, is an example of:**

    A. Containment

    B. Controlling the hazardous materials risk

    C. Communication

    D. All of the above

5. **Controlled braking is used when:**

    A. The goal is to keep the vehicle in a straight line while braking

    B. You must stop as quickly as possible

    C. Is only used with hydraulic brakes

    D. Is only used when the vehicle is equipped with anti-lock brakes

6. **What is hydroplaning?**

   A.   An emergency situation created when an aircraft must make an emergency landing on a highway

   B.   Excessive heat built up in the radiator

   C.   Something that only occurs at high vehicle speeds

   D.   When your vehicle wheels lift off the roadway on a thin film of water

7. **It you are being tailgated you should:**

   A.   Motion for the tailgater to pass you when it is safe

   B.   Increase your following distance

   C.   Turn your 4-way flashers on

   D.   Slam on the brakes

8. **Which of the following conditions may produce a skid?**

   A.   Driving too fast for conditions

   B.   Over braking

   C.   Over steering

   D.   All of the above

9. **When fighting a fire, which is most correct?**

   A.   Get downwind of the fire before using the fire extinguisher

   B.   Get as close to the fire as possible

   C.   Aim the fire extinguisher at the base of the fire

   D.   Aim the fire extinguisher at the top of the fire

10. **When starting a commercial vehicle on level, dry pavement, it is not usually necessary to:**

   A.   Apply the parking brake

   B.   Use a slower acceleration

   C.   Press on the accelerator while popping out the clutch

   D.   Both A and C

Chapter **33**

CSA

OBJECTIVES

Upon completion of this chapter, you should have a basic understanding of:

- ❏ What CSA is and how it affects your professional driving career

- ❏ The four major components of the CSA system

- ❏ CSA-related data

Introduction

When it comes to topics of importance in the motor carrier industry, Compliance, Safety, Accountability (CSA) is at the top of the list. So what is CSA and how does it affect you and your future as a professional driver? This chapter will help you answer this and many more questions about this issue.

What Is CSA?

CSA is a compliance and enforcement program implemented by the Federal Motor Carrier Safety Administration (FMCSA) that focuses on both motor carriers and drivers. CSA applies to:

- Any interstate motor carrier that operates commercial motor vehicles and has a US DOT number;

- Any interstate or intrastate motor carrier that operates vehicles transporting hazardous materials; and

- All drivers who drive commercial motor vehicles in interstate commerce.

A commercial motor vehicle is defined in Section 390.5 of the Federal Motor Carrier Safety Regulations (FMCSRs) as:

- Having a gross vehicle weight rating or gross combination weight rating, or gross vehicle weight or gross combination weight of 10,001 pounds or more, whichever is greater; or

- Designed or used to transport more than 8 passengers (including the driver) for compensation; or

- Designed or used to transport more than 15 passengers (including the driver), and is not used to transport passengers for compensation; or

- Transporting hazardous materials in a type or quantity requiring placarding.

The goal of CSA is to improve large truck and bus safety by reducing crashes, injuries, and fatalities on the nation's highways. It addresses enforcement in a way that allows for contact with a larger number of motor carriers and drivers earlier in the safety evaluation process. This allows FMCSA to address problems before they become serious.

In the past, FMCSA's enforcement system focused on motor carriers and didn't include drivers. Under CSA, FMCSA's focus includes both motor carriers and drivers. FMCSA believes that by tracking both motor carriers and drivers the agency has a more complete picture of compliance.

The CSA system consists of four major components:

- Data collection;

- Safety measurement;

- Safety evaluation; and

- Interventions.

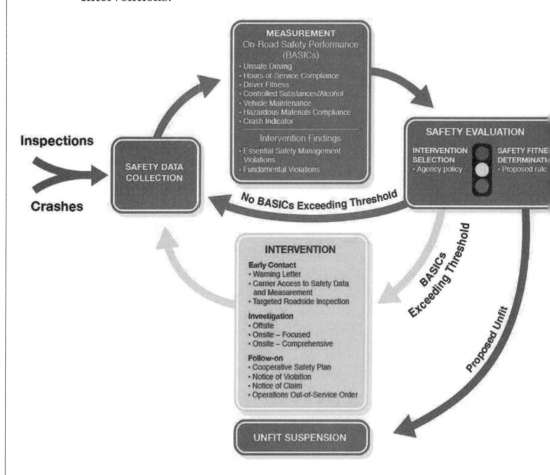

CSA Operational Model

Data Collection

The first component in the CSA system is data collection. FMCSA uses three data sources to gather information about motor carrier and driver compliance:

- Roadside inspections;

- Crash reports; and

- Investigations.

The roadside inspection is where the majority of data about motor carriers and drivers is gathered. The roadside inspection is an examination of both the driver and his/her commercial motor vehicle by law enforcement. This examination determines if the driver and his/her vehicle are in compliance with the FMCSRs and Hazardous Materials Regulations.

The roadside inspection.

Data collection takes place during all roadside inspections. Violations found during the roadside inspection are entered into the system. When no violations are found, that is also entered into the system.

Safety Measurement System (SMS)

The second component of the CSA system is the Safety Measurement System (SMS). The SMS quantifies the on-road safety performance and compliance history of motor carriers and drivers to:

- Identify candidates for interventions;

- Determine the specific safety problems exhibited by a driver or motor carrier; and

- Monitor whether safety problems are getting worse.

Every month, the SMS measures roadside violation and crash data performance and calculates a score in the seven Behavior Analysis and Safety Improvement Categories (BASICs).

Motor carriers are measured on the previous 24 months and drivers are measured on the previous 36 months.

Behavior Analysis and Safety Improvement Categories (BASICs)

The Behavior Analysis and Safety Improvement Categories (BASICs) are seven categories of safety behaviors measured in the SMS. The BASICs are behaviors that can lead to crashes. The seven BASICs are:

- Unsafe driving;

- Hours-of-service compliance;

- Driver fitness;

- Controlled substances and alcohol;

- Vehicle maintenance;

- Hazardous materials (HM) compliance; and

- Crash indicator.

Unsafe driving addresses the operation of commercial motor vehicles by drivers in a dangerous or careless manner. Examples of violations that fall under this BASIC include:

- Speeding;

- Reckless driving; and

- Improper lane change.

Hours-of-service compliance covers the operation of commercial motor vehicles by drivers who are ill, fatigued, or in non-compliance with the hours-of-service regulations. Examples of violations that fall under this BASIC include:

- Operating a commercial motor vehicle while ill or fatigued;

- Hours-of-service violations; and

- Logbook violations.

Driver fitness addresses operation of commercial motor vehicles by drivers who are unfit due to a lack of training, experience, or medical qualifications. Examples of violations that fall under this BASIC include:

- Failure to have a valid and/or appropriate license;

- Failure to have proper endorsements;

- Failure to have a valid medical certificate/card; and

- Failure to train hazmat employees.

Speed and space management, visual search, and communication are just some of the topics related to safe driving. See Chapters 9 through 15 of this Manual for information on these and other safe driving issues.

The most cited offense during a roadside inspection is the log book violation. It is important that you understand and follow the hours-of-service regulations. See Chapter 25 of your Manual to learn more about the hours-of-service regulations.

Your overall health and how it relates to a successful driving career is discussed in Chapter 30 of this Manual.

Controlled substances and alcohol covers operation of commercial motor vehicles by drivers who are impaired due to alcohol, illegal drugs, and misuse of prescription or over-the-counter medications. Examples of violations that fall under this BASIC include:

- Use or possession of drugs; and

- Possession, use, or under the influence of alcohol within four hours prior to duty.

Vehicle maintenance addresses failure to properly maintain a commercial motor vehicle and prevent shifting loads. Examples of violations that fall under this BASIC include:

- Defective brakes, lights, and other mechanical components;

- Failure to make required repairs;

- Failure to inspect the vehicle or prepare inspection reports; and

- Improper load securement.

The condition of your vehicle is an extremely important issue, as the roadside inspection is where most data will be gathered. See Chapter 4 of your Manual for detailed information on vehicle inspections and Chapters 20 and 21 for information on preventive maintenance and diagnosing and reporting vehicle malfunctions.

Make sure your cargo is properly secured.

Hazardous materials (HM) compliance addresses the unsafe handling of hazardous materials on a commercial motor vehicle. Examples of violations include:

- Leaking containers;

- Improper placarding;

- Failure to have proper hazmat documentation; and

- Hazmat routing violations.

As well as preventing accidents and incidents, proper cargo securement allows you to deliver your loads on time and damage-free to your customer. See Chapter 22 of your Manual to learn more about handling cargo.

Crash indicator covers histories or patterns of high crash involvement, including frequency and severity. It is based on law enforcement crash reports.

Each safety-related event is assigned to one of the seven BASICs. It then receives a number value between one and ten. This number value is based on the violation's relation to causing a crash. Violations not often related to causing crashes receive a low value and violations that have a high relation to causing crashes receive higher values.

Examples of low value violations include:

- A general form and manner violation on your record of duty status;
- A defective/inoperative windshield wiper on your vehicle; and
- Not carrying spare fuses on your vehicle (when required).

Examples of high value violations include:

- A false record of duty status;
- No or improper load securement; and
- Violating an out-of-service order.

As well as receiving a number value between one and ten, safety-related events are also time weighted. This means that recent events count more than events that occurred a year earlier.

Safety Evaluation

The safety evaluation is the third component in the CSA system. This is where FMCSA determines what, if any actions will be taken against the motor carrier or driver.

After a score is determined, the carrier and driver are then placed in a peer group of carriers and drivers. Percentiles of 0 to 100 are then determined by comparing the BASIC scores to the scores of others in the peer group. A score of 100 indicates the worst performance. In other words, the lower the score the better.

If one or more of the BASIC percentiles exceed a threshold, the carrier or driver becomes a candidate for an intervention.

Interventions

Interventions are the fourth component in the CSA system. Interventions are actions FMCSA can take against a motor carrier and driver based on safety measurement scores and enforcement history.

Motor carrier interventions can be triggered by one or more deficient BASICs, a high crash rate, a complaint, or a fatal crash.

Intervention selection is influenced by safety performance, hazardous material or passenger carrier status, and intervention history.

Remember, under this system, both the driver and motor carrier are scored. Data stays with the motor carrier for 24 months and with the driver for 36 months.

Interventions range from mild to severe. Interventions include:

- Warning letter;
- Targeted roadside inspection;
- Off-site investigation;
- Focused on-site investigation;
- Comprehensive on-site investigation;
- Cooperative safety plan;
- Notice of violation;
- Notice of claim/settlement agreement; and
- Operations out-of-service order (unfit suspension).

Generally, **driver** interventions are triggered by an on-site investigation of the motor carrier for whom the driver is working. During an on-site investigation, the investigating officer reviews the safety performance of the drivers who work for the company. This review determines whether any drivers will be subject to intervention.

Your Role in CSA

As you can see, your actions (or inactions) can play a huge part in the scoring of both you and your motor carrier under CSA. So, how do you ensure positive scores?

Since the majority of data will be gathered during roadside inspections, it is important to have roadside inspections with no violations. How do you do this?

Take care of your vehicle:

- Conduct thorough pre-trip and post-trip vehicle inspections;
- Get problems with your vehicle repaired as soon as possible; and
- Make sure your vehicle is on a regular maintenance schedule.

Also, make sure all of your paperwork is current and up to date including your:

- Records of duty status (drivers logs);
- Commercial driver's license; and
- Medical certificate/card.

Remember, positive scores will reflect well on you as a professional driver.

CSA-Related Data

As part of the CSA initiative, FMCSA has been working to make accurate and timely information about motor carriers and drivers available to the industry.

As a new driver who will be applying for work with motor carriers in the near future, it is important that you are aware of and understand one of these initiatives, FMCSA's Pre-Employment Screening Program (PSP).

PSP allows motor carriers to electronically access driver inspection and crash records as part of the hiring process.

Drivers must give their written consent before records may be released to a motor carrier and records will be protected in accordance with federal privacy laws.

Drivers may also access this data to verify its accuracy and correct any discrepancies. The information provided includes the most recent five years of crash data and three years of roadside inspection data from FMCSA's Motor Carrier Management Information System (MCMIS).

MCMIS is comprised of driver data including:

- Inspection and compliance review results;
- Enforcement data;
- State-reported crashes; and
- Motor carrier census data.

FMCSA states that by accessing this data, motor carriers will be able to better assess the potential safety risks of prospective driver-employees.

Summary

Safe driving practices, maintaining a safe vehicle, and accurate paperwork all have a role in your success as a professional driver. Maintaining positive scores in the CSA Safety Measurement System and making sure prospective employers are able to receive and review positive records under the PSP will go a long way in forwarding your career as a professional driver.

CSA Quiz

Read each statement carefully and select the most correct answer.

1. **Compliance, Safety, Accountability (CSA) is a program designed to improve truck and bus safety.**

    A.   True

    B.   False

2. **CSA applies to:**

    A.   Any interstate motor carrier that operates commercial motor vehicles and has a US DOT number

    B.   Any interstate or intrastate motor carrier that operates vehicles transporting hazardous materials

    C.   Drivers who drive commercial motor vehicles in interstate commerce

    D.   All of the above

3. **The majority of CSA data is collected during:**

    A.   Interviews at truck stops

    B.   Inspections at motor carrier terminals

    C.   Roadside inspections

    D.   All of the above

4. **In the CSA Safety Measurement System (SMS), motor carriers are measured on the previous _____ months of roadside violation and crash data.**

    A.   12

    B.   24

    C.   36

    D.   48

5. **The Behavior Analysis and Safety Improvement Categories (BASICs) are seven categories of safety behaviors measured in the SMS.**

    A.   True

    B.   False

6. **The unsafe driving BASIC addresses commercial motor vehicle incidents resulting from the unsafe handling of hazardous materials.**

   A. True

   B. False

7. **_____ is an example of a violation that falls under the driver fitness BASIC.**

   A. Speeding

   B. Defective brakes

   C. Failure to have a valid and/or appropriate license

   D. All of the above

8. **A false record of duty status (log book) is an example of a low value violation in the SMS.**

   A. True

   B. False

9. **Interventions are actions that can be taken against a motor carrier and driver based on safety measurement scores and enforcement history.**

   A. True

   B. False

10. **To ensure a positive score under CSA you should:**

    A. Take care of your vehicle

    B. Make sure your records of duty status are up to date

    C. Always carry a current and valid license and medical certificate

    D. All of the above

WHAT'S THE SYMPTOM	WHERE'S THE PROBLEM	WHAT COULD BE WRONG	WHAT SHOULD YOU DO
Ammeter shows continuous maximum charge	Electrical	Short circuit in wiring. Regulator malfunction.	Disconnect battery, check regulator, find short
Ammeter shows discharge while motor is running	Electrical	Loose wiring connection. Alternator malfunction. Bad battery.	Tighten connections, check battery, check alternator, check belts
High engine temperature	Cooling	Low water level. Broken fan belt. Defective fan clutch. Defective thermostat.	Add water, replace fan belt, check fan clutch, check/replace thermostat
Coolant, oil, or fuel dripping	Cooling, Lubricating, or Fuel system	Bad connections and/or hoses. Loose filters. Bad fuel pump or water pump.	Identify source of leak and repair
Excessive exhaust smoke	Exhaust or turbo system	Air filter dirty. Poor grade fuel. Fuel pump malfunction. Return fuel line blocked.	Change filter, check fuel pump, treat fuel, check return line
Excessive black smoke	Engine, fuel system	Restricted air supply. Malfunctioning injector(s). Overloading engine.	Change fuel filters, check/replace injectors, use better shifting technique
White exhaust smoke	Engine, fuel system	Engine is cold. Worn injector. Water in fuel. Fuel is beginning to gel.	Treat fuel, warm up engine, check/replace injectors
Blue exhaust smoke	Engine, fuel system	Worn valves. Malfunctioning turbo. Excessive oil overfill.	Check oil level, have turbo checked, have valves and rings (compression) checked
Low oil pressure <20 psi	Lubricating system	Cracked engine seals or rings. Oil temperature very high. Worn oil pump. Dirty filters. Worn bearings. Oil leak.	Change oil and filters, have engine components checked, check oil pump
Mettalic click in time with wheels revolving	Suspension, wheels, tires	Loose wheel. Loose lug nuts. Object in tire.	Check and tighten lug nuts, tighten axle nut, check wheel bearings, check tire for object/damage
Dull thud in time with wheel rotation	Wheels or tires	Flat tire. Loose lugs or wheel. Rock between duels.	Change tire, tighten lugs, remove rock

WHAT'S THE SYMPTOM	WHERE'S THE PROBLEM	WHAT COULD BE WRONG	WHAT SHOULD YOU DO
Dull thud or loud rap in time with engine	Engine	Burned out connecting rods or main bearing. Piston slap.	Shut off motor immediately. Contact mechanic for instructions.
Air escaping or hissing noise	Tires, air system, braking system	Damaged tire. Open air petcock. Air lines or fittings leaking. Brake application valve sticking. Ice in brake valves or lines. Air bag going bad.	Change/check tires, check all air lines and connections, apply brakes several times to dislodge ice, apply heat to brake canisters and/or lines carefully, check and/or replace air bag
Snap or click when starting from dead stop	Drive train, fifth wheel	Loose u-joints. Excessive wear in differential. Worn or broken fifth wheel lock. Loose or broken mounting bolts.	Tighten bolts, adjust fifth wheel, check differential and u-joints
Clunking or grinding noise under floor	Drive train	Clutch going bad or out of adjustment. Bad throw-out bearing. Bent or damaged drive shaft. Broken teeth in transmission.	Have all listed parts checked by mechanic
Whine - harsh high pitch	Drive train at engine	Worn accessory drive. Loose belts	Check drive gears, tighten belts
Whine - short high pitch	Engine	Ball bearing in housing. Generator or Alternator malfunction. Water pump malfunction.	Shut off engine. Check listed parts
Clicking sound in engine with loss of power, sluggishness, or overheating	Engine	Broken valve spring. Worn timing gear.	Shut off engine. Contact mechanic
Sudden loss of power	Brake, drive train, engine, or fuel system	Brakes dragging. Clutch slipping. Engine severely overheated. Blocked fuel filter. Fuel pedal linkage failure.	Adjust brakes, adjust clutch, determine cause of overheating and fix, change fuel filters, check fuel linkage
Engine surges	Fuel or engine system	Air or water in fuel system. Throttle linkage loose. Fuel level low.	Check fuel for air and/or water, check throttle linkage, refill fuel
Brakes grab	Braking system	Grease on brake lining. Brakes adjusted improperly. Ice in brakes.	Cleans brake drums of grease, check and readjust brakes, thaw (warm) brake system

WHAT'S THE SYMPTOM	WHERE'S THE PROBLEM	WHAT COULD BE WRONG	WHAT SHOULD YOU DO
Brakes don't hold	Braking system	Brakes out of adjust-ment. Grease on lin-ings. Water or ice on linings. Air tanks full of oil or water. Broken air line or fitting.	Readjust brakes, check linings for grease, warm brake system to remove ice, drain air tanks, repair and/or replace air lines and/or fittings
Constant pull to right or left on steering	Tires, suspen-sion, braking, or steering system	Soft tire. Broken spring. Front brake dragging or our of adjustment. Axles out of alignment.	Check tires, check springs, readjust brakes, align all axles
Tractor does not want to come back straight after lane change or turn	Steering or fifth wheel	Dry fifth wheel.	Grease fifth wheel
Excessive vibration in engine	Engine system	Broken valve. Blown cylinder head gasket. Unbalanced or dam-aged fan. Engine mount loose. Clutch out of bal-ance. Bad injectors. Air in fuel.	Check all listed parts and sys-tems for damage or wear.
Gradual loss of power	Fuel or engine system	Fuel filter dirty or clogged. Air filter dirty or clogged. Faulty valve. Jelling fuel. Freezing fuel filter. Injectors going bad.	Check fuel system, replace bad or blocked fuel and/or air filters, treat fuel for jelling, check and replace injectors

**Trouble
shooting
guide**

A

A Train — Combination of vehicles composed of a tractor and a semi-trailer towing a full trailer: 1) connected with an A dolly; or 2) without a convertor dolly.

Accelerator pedal — Located on the floor under the steering wheel. Operated by driver's right foot. Driver depresses accelerator pedal to increase engine speed.

Agent — A person authorized to transact business for and in the name of another. A driver becomes an agent of the trucking company when signing for freight.

Aggregated shipments — Several shipments from different shippers to one consignee that are consolidated and treated as a single consignment.

Agitator body — Truck body designed and equipped to mix concrete in transit.

Agreed valuation — Freight value mutually agreed upon by shipper and carrier as a basis for transportation charges. It also may represent an agreed maximum amount that can be recovered in case of loss or damage.

Air application pressure gauge — Indicates how much air pressure is being applied by the brakes during brake operation.

Air brakes — Brakes that utilize compressed air to activate brakes.

Air cleaner — Air or filter device for cleaning air entering engine. There may be two, one on each side of the tractor.

Air compressor — Device to build up and maintain required air pressure in the brake system reservoir.

Air dryer — A device for cleaning and removing moisture from air systems.

Air filter restriction gauge — Provides indication of filter's obstruction by dirt and other contaminants which would restrict the flow of air to the engine.

Air intake manifold — Distributes air to the various cylinders of the engine. It attaches to the cylinder heads at the intake ports.

Air lines — Used to carry compressed air from one part of the air brake system to another and from tractor to the trailer. One line is called the emergency or supply line and is always charged with compressed air. The other line is called the service or control line. When the air brake treadle valve is depressed, air flows from the supply reservoir through the service line and causes the brakes to apply.

Air operated (fifth wheel) release — Located under the fifth wheel plate, but operated by a release lever in the cab, this device locks and unlocks the sliding fifth wheel's locking mechanism.

Air pressure gauge — Indicates the amount of air pressure in the air tanks.

Air reservoirs — Storage tanks for compressed air, used in tractor and trailer air systems.

Air slider — A cab-controlled sliding fifth wheel that can be unlocked by air to be moved backward or forward. See sliding fifth wheel.

Air suspension — Located between the axle and the frame of a truck, the suspension system uses air bags to cushion vibration and road shocks and dampen the ride. See air tag.

Air tag — A tag axle that has two bellows-like air bags that, when filled, force the tractor's rear axle harder against the ground for a smoother ride and for weight distribution between the two axles of the tractor.

Ammeter — An instrument that measures the amount of battery being charged or discharged.

Anti-lock brake system (ABS) — While the driver holds the brake pedal firmly down during a hard stop, the computer operated system senses wheel speeds and rapidly applies and releases the brakes to each wheel, thus avoiding wheel lock-up, providing steering control during the stop.

Articulated — Having parts connected by joints. A tractor-trailer is an articulated vehicle.

Authority — Operating rights granted to for-hire, common, and contract carriers by the FMCSA.

Authorized carrier — Person/company granted common or contract carrier operating rights by the FMCSA.

Automobile transporter — Company authorized to transport motor vehicles on special vehicles or by driving them.

Automobile transporter body — Truck or trailer body with ramps for loading and low-road clearance, designed for the transportation of vehicles, also known as a car carrier.

Auxiliary transmission — Second transmission connected with the main transmission to provide a wider range of speeds and gear ratios.

Average speed calculation — Average speed (miles per hour) may be calculated by dividing the distance driven (in miles) by time (the number of hours it took to drive that distance).

Axle — The housing or beam that connects opposite wheels. There are two types of axles: 1) live axles, which transmit power from the drive shaft to the wheels; and 2) dead axles, which do not transmit power and are used only to help carry the load or to steer.

Axle group — Any number of consecutive axles on a vehicle through which weight is: 1) intended to be equally distributed for transmission to a public highway; and 2) transmitted to a public highway.

Axle load — Weight existing on a motor vehicle's axle; an axle weight limit on a highway refers to the maximum weight allowed on the truck's heaviest axle.

Axle ratings — Rear axles on a truck generally carry three ratings: 1) carrying capacity rated at the ground; 2) total weight the axle is capable of carrying/pulling in service, gross combined weight; 3) the maximum horsepower limit the axle is capable of carrying in normal service.

Axle ratio — Ratio of axle to drive line; the number of turns of the drive line in relation to one full turn of the drive wheels. The higher the numerical ratio, the slower the road speed. See gear ratio.

Axle spread — The distance between the extreme axle centers of an axle group.

Axle temperature gauges — Indicate temperature of lubricant in drive axles.

Axle weight — The gross weight of a rig that rests on any truck axle; axle weights are used as part of the bridge formula when setting bridge weight limits.

B

B Train — A combination of vehicles composed of a tractor and a semi-trailer towing another semi-trailer attached to a fifth wheel mounted on the rear of the first semi-trailer.

Backhaul — 1) Return transportation movement, usually at less revenue than the original move (headhaul); 2) movement in the direction of lighter traffic flow when traffic is generally heavier in the opposite direction; or 3) to move a shipment back over part of a route already traveled.

Baffle — A perforated divider or wall inside the tank of a liquid cargo tanker truck that moderates the movement or surging of liquids carried in a less-than-full tank.

BASIC(s) — See Behavior Analysis and Safety Improvement Categories.

Battery — An electrochemical device for storing and supplying electrical energy.

Bead — The inner edge of the outer wall of a rubber tire, fitting on the rim. The "foundation" of a tire. It is made of high tensile steel wires and wrapped and reinforced by the plies.

Behavior Analysis and Safety Improvement Categories (BASICs) — Seven categories of safety behaviors measured in the Compliance, Safety, Accountability (CSA) Safety Measurement System (SMS). The BASICs represent behaviors that can lead to crashes: unsafe driving, fatigued driving, driver fitness, controlled substances/alcohol, vehicle maintenance, cargo-related, and crash indicator.

Belly dump — Trailer that unloads by opening an air-operated gate in its bed; bulk materials like sand, grain, coal or other dry products are usually belly-dumped.

Berm — The shoulder of the road.

Bill of lading (B/L) — The written transportation contract between shipper and carrier. It identifies the freight, who it is consigned to, the place of delivery, and gives the terms of the agreement. The straight bill of lading provides that goods be delivered to the consignee indicated. The consignee does not have to surrender his copy to receive the goods.

Bill of sale — Formal document issued by a seller to a buyer as evidence of transfer of title to an item of personal property.

Binders — 1) Load stabilizing equipment such as chain, wire/manila/synthetic fiber rope, steel strapping or nylon webbing used to secure a load; or 2) slang term for brakes.

Bingo card — Slang term for authority cab card; designed with open squares on the back where driver places vehicle's authority identification stamps (or PSC#) as received from various states. Card is to be carried in the cab of the power unit to which it has been assigned. See cab card.

Black ice — A very dangerous, nearly invisible patch of ice on a clear road formed when temperatures drop very rapidly when the road surface is wet.

Blanket permit — A master type permit issued to a carrier by a state or province and which does not have any particular vehicle identification indicated. The permit may be photocopied, with a copy placed in the carrier's vehicles as the required permit for those vehicles in that state.

Blanket waybill — A waybill covering two or more consignments of freight.

Bleed the air tanks — To drain the accumulated water out of the air tanks of a tractor to prevent the condensed water from reducing air tank capacity and thus cutting braking efficiency.

Bleed the fuel lines — To remove trapped air from the fuel lines.

Blocking or bracing — Pieces of wood or other material used to prevent movement of goods in rail, vessel, or truck shipments in order to prevent breakage.

Blood Alcohol Content (BAC) — A measurement or calculation of the amount of alcohol in the bloodstream. The blood alcohol content is considered an indirect indicator of the level of someone's intoxication.

Blower — A device that forces additional air into the engine to increase its efficiency and horsepower.

Bobtail — Slang term for a tractor driven without its trailer, can also refer to a straight truck or a truck with a short rear overhang.

Bogie — 1) An assembly of two or more axles; or 2) removable set of rear axles and wheels used to support a van container.

Bogie truck — Low skeleton platform mounted on two centrally located load-carrying wheels and fitted with two or four smaller diameter stabilizing wheels; also known as a restless dolly.

Boomers — Slang term for the binder devices used to tighten chains around cargo on flatbed trailers.

Booster axles — An axle generally having an air or hydraulic cylinder suspension system that can be actuated independently to assume a portion of the load that would otherwise be carried by adjacent axles.

Bottom dump — Trailer that unloads through bottom gates; same as belly dump.

Brake chamber — Air chamber mounted near each wheel and connected to the brake itself by a push rod and slack adjuster (cam brake) or a push rod (wedge brake).

Brake drum — Metal, drum-shaped compartment that revolves with the wheel and provides a friction surface for the brake lining.

Brake horsepower — The actual horsepower of an engine, measured by a brake attached to the drive shaft and recorded on a dynamometer.

Brake lining — Material designed to create friction when pressed against the brake drum. It is fastened to the brake shoe and contacts the drum during the braking process.

Brake shoe — The nonrotating unit of the brake (to which the brake shoe is attached) that contacts the rotating unit to supply braking force.

Break down the unit — Slang term for the process of uncoupling a tractor from a trailer.

Breakaway protection — Process which applies brakes on the trailer(s) in case of a broken air hose or some other emergency.

Breakaway valve — Valve positioned between the tractor and trailer; automatically cuts off air going to trailers if pressure drops below 60 pounds, causing trailer brakes to activate.

Bridge — The distance between one axle and another, or between two sets of axles. Used in some states to ascertain the permissible gross weight for the vehicle. Also called spread. See spread tandem.

Bridge formula — Formula used to determine maximum gross weight that can be carried on any given arrangement of consecutive axles.

Broker — A broker arranges, for compensation, the truck transportation of cargo belonging to others, utilizing authorized for-hire carriers to provide the actual truck transportation. A broker does not assume responsibility for the cargo and usually does not take possession of the cargo.

Brokerage license — Granted by the Federal Motor Carrier Safety Administration to allow licensee to arrange for transportation in interstate commerce.

Bulkhead — Found on each end of a tanker, it is used to seal the tank. Also a wall or metal divider used inside a tanker to divide it into smaller compartments.

Bulk cargo container — Shipping container employed in handling/hauling dry fluid materials.

Bulk freight — Dry or liquid freight not in packages/containers and transported in bulk, e.g., potatoes, grain, citrus, ore, etc.

Buttonhook turn — A right turn procedure for tractor-trailers that lets the trailer's rear wheels clear the inside corner of the turn. The rig proceeds through the intersection until the rear tires will clear the corner and then the driver sharply turns right and holds the turn (creating the "hook" of the turn) until the tractor can be turned left to straighten itself in the turn lane.

C

C Train — A combination of vehicles composed of a tractor and a semi-trailer towing a full trailer connected with a C dolly.

C Dolly — A converter dolly with two parallel arms which connect to two hitches located on a towing unit so as to prevent any rotation in a horizontal plane through the hitch points.

Cab — Driver compartment of a truck or tractor-trailer.

Cab card — Registration document issued by base jurisdiction for a vehicle in an apportioned/prorated fleet which identifies vehicle, base plate, registered weight by jurisdiction (if IRP); also shows jurisdictions where vehicle is registered.

Cab-over-engine (COE) — Truck tractor unit with engine located under the cab; face of the vehicle is flat.

Camber — Inward or outward tilt of wheels on vertical axis of truck or other motor vehicle; proper camber affects tire wear.

Camshaft — Long, straight shaft covered with elliptical knobs called cams; as the camshaft turns, cams push the push rods and open the cylinder valves.

Carbon monoxide (CO) — A colorless, odorless, highly poisonous gas, produced by the incomplete combustion of fuel. It is usually expelled by the exhaust system.

Carburetor — Device in an engine to mix air with gasoline spray; mixture is then distributed to cylinders by intake manifold so it can be ignited by a spark.

Cargo — Freight transported in a vehicle.

Cargo manifest — Document listing all consignments on a truck, vessel or aircraft and giving quantity, identifying marks, consignor/consignee of each item.

Cargo-related BASIC — One of seven categories of safety behaviors measured in the CSA Safety Measurement System. Commercial motor vehicle incident resulting from shifting loads, spilled or dropped cargo, and unsafe handling of hazardous materials are included in this BASIC. Violations include improper load securement and hazardous material handling.

Carrier — Individual, partnership or corporation engaged in the business of transporting goods or passengers.

Casing — The tire structure, excepting tread and sidewall rubber.

Caster — Forward (or rearward) inclination of kingpin or support arm of wheel; amount of tilt in axle beam.

Center of gravity — The point within the length and width of a vehicle around which its weight is evenly distributed or balanced.

Cetane number — Rating applied to ignition properties of diesel fuel; the higher the number, the better the ignition quality. See octane number.

Chain binders — A device used to remove slack from chains used to tie down loads. See boomers.

Check valve — Device to automatically isolate one part of the air brake system from another. A one-way check valve provides free air flow in one direction only. A two-way check valve permits actuation of the brake system by either of two brake application valves.

Chocks — Block or stop barriers placed behind/in front of wheels to keep vehicle from rolling.

Circuit breaker — A device that automatically interrupts the flow of an electric current when the current becomes excessive.

Clutch — The part of the drive train that allows the driver to disconnect or connect the engine to the transmission.

C.O.D. — Collect on delivery. The payment for goods is made at the delivery point. The driver must collect payment before the cargo is unloaded.

Code of Federal Regulations (CFR) — U.S. Government Printing Office publications containing regulations various federal agencies have created/promulgated. Combination ramp and arrester bed — An emergency escape ramp built off of steep road grades to slow and stop a rig in emergency situations. The ramp uses loose surface materials and/or an upward grade and ramp length to safely slow and stop the rig.

Combination vehicle — Truck/truck tractor coupled to one or more trailers, including semi-trailers. Also referred to as a "rig". See rig.

Combined gross vehicle weight — The total unladen weight of a combination of vehicles plus the weight of the load carried on that combination of vehicles.

Commercial carrier — Any motor carrier transporting persons or property for-hire on the public highways.

Commingling — Mixing types of goods from separate shipments and sending them as a combined shipment.

Commodities — 1) Articles, goods, or merchandise; or 2) goods shipped.

Common carrier — A for-hire carrier that holds itself out to serve the general public at reasonable rates and without discrimination. To operate, the carrier must secure a Certificate of Public Convenience and Necessity from the FMCSA.

Compliance, Safety, Accountability (CSA) — A Federal Motor Carrier Safety Administration initiative to improve large truck and bus safety and reduce commercial vehicle-related crashes, injuries, and fatalities.

Compression pin — Hardware used to join two 20-foot containers into a single 40-foot unit.

Compression ratio — Volume of air above the piston at bottom dead center compared with volume of air at top dead center.

Compression stroke — A phase of the four-stroke cycle when the air-fuel mix is compressed.

Compressor — See air compressor.

Compressor belt — Belt running between engine pulley and air compressor that uses power of engine to operate air compressor.

Connecting carrier — Carrier that interchanges trailers/freight with another carrier to complete shipments.

Connecting rod — Rod that connects the piston to the crankshaft.

Consign — To send goods to purchaser or agent to sell.

Consignee — Person who receives goods shipped from the owner.

Consignment — Goods shipped when an actual purchase has not been made, but when the consignee agrees to sell the goods

Consignor — The person or company (usually the owner) that ships goods to customers.

Consolidation — Practice of combining less-than-carload (LCL) or less-than-truckload (LTL) shipments to make carload/truckload movements.

Container (van body type) — A truck or trailer body provided with means for ready removal from and attachment to a vehicle.

Containerization — 1) Practice/technique of using box-like device to store, protect, and handle a number of packages as a unit in transit; or 2) shipping system based on large cargo-carrying containers (usually 20 or 40 feet in length) that can be interchanged between trucks, trains, and ships without rehandling contents.

Continuous seal — A term denoting that the seals on a truck remained intact during the movement of the truck from origin to destinations or, if broken in transit, that it was done by proper authority and without opportunity for loss to occur before new seals were applied.

Contraband — Illegal or prohibited traffic or freight.

Contract carrier — A for-hire carrier that does not serve the general public but serves shippers with whom the carrier has a continuing contract. A Permit from the FMCSA is required.

Controlled substances/alcohol BASIC — One of seven categories of safety behaviors measured in the CSA Safety Measurement System. The operation of commercial motor vehicles by drivers who are impaired due to alcohol, illegal drugs, and misuse of prescription or over-the-counter medications are included in this BASIC. A violation under this category could be issued for use or possession of controlled substances or alcohol.

Conventional tractor — Power unit with engine under the hood of the tractor, in front of driver compartment.

Converter gear or dolly — The coupling device composed of one or two axles and a fifth wheel by which a semi-trailer can be coupled to the rear of a tractor-trainer combination, forming a double-bottom rig, i.e. it converts a semi-trailer into a full trailer.

Convex mirror — A type of mirror having a convex shape in order to show a larger field of view than can be obtained from a flat mirror of the same size.

Coolant — The fluid that circulates around an engine to help it maintain a safe working temperature, usually it is a combination of antifreeze and water.

Coolant alarm — A warning light that indicates if the level of coolant in the engine's system is too low.

Coolant temperature gauge — Indicates the current temperature of the coolant in the engine.

Coolant temperature warning — A warning light that indicates if the coolant is overheating causing severe internal engine damage.

Coupling — Act of connecting truck (or tractor) and trailer.

Coupling device — Any mechanical means for connecting trailer or semi-trailer to truck or truck-tractor, e.g., fifth wheel.

Crash indicator BASIC — One of seven categories of safety behaviors measured in the CSA Safety Measurement System. Histories or patterns of high crash involvement, including frequency and severity are included in this BASIC. It is based on information from state-reported crash reports.

Creeper gear — Lowest gear/combination of gears on a tractor used when extra power is needed.

CSA — See Compliance, Safety, Accountability.

Cubic capacity — The carrying capacity of a truck measured in cubic feet.

Cubic foot — A common measure of the capacity of a truck, 1,728 cubic inches.

Curb weight — The weight of an empty tractor-trailer minus driver and cargo but including fuel, oil, and all standard equipment.

D

DOT — See Department of Transportation.

Dead axle — An axle that does not transmit power. Used to steer and support the load.

Deadheading — Returning to home base without a load after delivery has been made.

Declared combined gross vehicle weight — The total unladen weight of any combination of vehicles plus the maximum load to be carried on that combination of vehicles for which registration fees have been paid.

Delivery — The act of transferring possession of a shipment. This could be from consignor to carrier, one carrier to another, or carrier to consignee.

Demountable body — Box of motor freight vehicle (chassis or trailer) constructed so it can be used interchangeably on railroad flatcars for piggyback hauling or on trucks for highway loads.

Department of Transportation (DOT) — A cabinet-level executive department of the United States government. The DOT consists of the Office of the Secretary and eleven individual Operating Administrations, including the Federal Motor Carrier Safety Administration (FMCSA).

Depth perception — The ability to judge distances.

Detention — Delay of a driver and freight vehicle or container beyond a stipulated time.

Diesel engine — An internal combustion engine that uses compression to raise air temperature to the igniting point, whereas fuel is ignited by a spark in a gasoline engine.

Differential — The part of the power train that permits one wheel to turn at a different rate of speed from the other, as occurs when going around a turn.

Differential lock, interaxle type — Used on twin-screw tractors, this valve can be set to lock both rear axles together so that they pull as one for off-the-road operation. Never used for over-the-road operation.

Direct current (D.C.) — Electrical current that always flows in one direction only and is the type used in automotive equipment.

Direct drive — Refers to a condition in which the transmission is in a gear having a 1:1 ratio, that is, when the engine crankshaft is turning at the same rate as the vehicle drive shaft. See overdrive and underdrive.

Disc brakes — Brakes that function by causing friction pads to press on either side of a disc rotating along with the wheel.

Dispatcher — Person in charge of dispatching trucks and drivers to and from destinations.

Dispatching — The scheduling and control of freight distribution.

Distance calculation — Distance traveled can be determined by multiplying driving speed (miles per hour) by time (the number of hours driven).

Diversion — A change made in the route of a shipment in transit. See reconsigment.

Divisible load — Any load consisting of a product, material or equipment which can be reduced to meet the specified regulatory limits for size and/or weight.

Dock — A platform where trucks load and unload.

Dock plate — Removable ramp used between dock and trailer/railcar so forklift can drive into unit, used for ease/safety in loading/unloading.

Dock receipt — A receipt given for a shipment received or delivered at a pier or dock.

Documentation — 1) The supplying of anything printed, written, etc., relied upon to record or prove something (documents); or 2) the documents that are supplied.

Dolly — 1) Auxiliary axle assembly equipped with fifth wheel used to convert semitrailer to full trailer; 2) small square or rectangular platform on rollers/wheels used to handle freight in warehouse; or 3) landing gear on a trailer (dolly wheels).

Double-axle — See tandem axle.

Double bottom — Combination of tractor, semi-trailer and full trailer, also called twin trailers or doubles.

Double-clutching — Shifting the gears of a nonsynchronized truck transmission without clashing them, by depressing and releasing the clutch pedal twice.

Double drop frame — A drop frame trailer with one drop behind the kingpin and one in front of the rear axles. See drop frame.

Driveaway operation — Transportation of new/used motor vehicles where units being transported are loaded with the front axles resting on the back of the power unit being driven and the wheels of the rear axles on roadway, one or more units can be transported in tandem; or power units can be driven on their own.

Drive axle — An axle that transmits power to the wheels. A drive axle is a powered axle that actively pulls the load.

Drive shaft — A heavy-duty tube that connects the transmission to the rear-end assembly of the tractor.

Drive train — A series of connected mechanical parts for transmitting motion.

Driver fitness BASIC — One of seven categories of safety behaviors measured in the CSA Safety Measurement System. The operation of commercial motor vehicles by drivers who are unfit to operate a commercial motor vehicle due to lack of training, experience, or medical qualifications are included in this BASIC. Violations include failure to have a valid and appropriate commercial driver's license and being medically unqualified to operate a commercial motor vehicle.

Driver's daily log — Daily record required to be kept by driver which shows driving, on-duty/not driving, sleeper berth, and off-duty time. See record of duty status.

Drop frame trailer — Open flatbed trailer sometimes equipped with van body (household goods movers) designed with minimum floor-to-highway distance except for raised section for rear wheel housings and raised forward section. This increases cargo capability without increasing the vertical clearance of the vehicle.

Dry tank — Part of brake system. Air passes from wet tank to dry tank. Dry tank is the air reservoir from which the air is drawn for operating the brake system.

Dual wheels — Wheel assembly with two wheels on each side of axle, generally found only on rear.

Dummy coupler — A fitting used to seal the opening in an air brake hose connection (glad hands) when the connection is not in use. Sometimes called a dust cap.

Dump body — Truck body which can be tilted to discharge load.

Dunnage — The material used to protect or support freight in trucks. The weight of dunnage is shown separately on the bill of lading since it is material used around cargo to prevent damage. Often, it is transported without charge.

Duty — A tax levied by a government on imports and exports.

DVIR — Driver vehicle inspection report.

Dynamometer — A device for measuring the work output of an engine. See brake horsepower.

E

Embargo — To resist or prohibit the acceptance and handling of freight. A formal notice that certain freight will not be accepted.

Emergency (air line) — See air lines.

Emergency brake release — Will override the spring brake control in the event air pressure is lost. You must hold it while pulling out on the spring brake control. For emergency use only.

Emergency engine stop — See Stop (Engine) and emergency stop.

Emergency movement — Movement by motor carrier in an instance which is not covered by ordinary circumstances, law, regulation or permit, which usually requires the acquisition of authority from a regulatory body.

Emission — Refers to gases and other materials vented to the atmosphere by the exhaust system.

Encroachment — The act of intruding or going beyond the proper limits, such as encroachment on another lane of traffic or off-tracking.

Engine brake — Sometimes called a Jake Brake or compression brake. Part of the truck's retarder system, activated by a switch on the dash or by taking your foot off of the accelerator pedal. The engine brake changes valve timing so instead of providing engine power, it acts as an air compressor, powered by the wheels, which slows the truck vs. total reliance on wheel brakes. See exhaust brake, hydraulic retarder and retarder systems.

Engine oil temperature gauge — Indicates the temperature of the engine oil.

Engine water jackets — Hollow chambers that surround the cylinder liners and other parts exposed to high temperatures in the engine. The coolant circulates within these chambers to cool the engine.

En-route inspection — See inspection.

Escape ramp — A ramp on a steep downgrade that can be used by a truck driver to stop a runaway truck when brakes have failed. The ramp often has a soft gravel surface and forms a steep upgrade to stop the truck. Sometimes called a runaway truck ramp.

Excess freight — Freight in excess of the quantity shown on the freight bill.

Exempt carrier — Motor carrier engaged in for-hire transportation of commodities exempt from federal economic regulation under 49 USC 13506 and 49 CFR 372.115.

Exhaust brake — Part of a truck retarder system. It closes a valve in the exhaust system which restricts the flow of exhaust gases, creating back pressure and slowing the engine. See engine brake, hydraulic retarder and retarder systems.

Exhaust manifold — That part of the exhaust system that carries the exhaust gases from the cylinders to the turbocharger.

Exhaust ports — Connecting passages from the inside to the outside of the cylinder heads.

Exhaust stack — Pipe connected to the muffler through which exhaust gases are released.

Exhaust stroke — The last phase of the four-stroke cycle when waste gases are pushed out of the exhaust valve.

Exhaust valves — Open to discharge the burned gases from the combustion chambers.

Export — To send goods to a foreign country.

Eye lead time — Term used to describe the distance that a driver is looking ahead on the road. A 12-second eye lead time means that the driver is looking ahead the distance he/she will travel in 12 seconds time.

F

Fatigued driving BASIC — One of seven categories of safety behaviors measured in the CSA Safety Measurement System. The operation of commercial motor vehicles by drivers who are ill, fatigued, or in non-compliance with the hours-of-service regulations are included in this BASIC. Violations include hours of service, logbook, and operating a commercial motor vehicle while ill or fatigued.

Federal Motor Carrier Safety Administration (FMCSA) — An administration within the U.S. Department of Transportation. FMCSA's primary mission is to reduce crashes, injuries, and fatalities involving large trucks and buses. FMCSA develops and enforces the Federal Motor Carrier Safety Regulations (FMCSRs).

Federal Motor Carrier Safety Regulations (FMCSRs) — Federal regulations that establish safe operating requirements for commercial vehicle drivers, carriers, vehicles, and vehicle equipment.

Federal Register — Government publication that prints rules/regulations of federal agencies on a daily basis.

Fifth wheel — The coupling device located on the tractor's rear frame that is used to join the front end of the trailer to the tractor. It is a flat, rounded plate with a V-shaped notch in the rear.

First aid — The immediate and temporary care given to the victim of an accident or sudden illness until the services of medical personnel can be obtained.

Flatbed — Trailer with level bed and no sides or top.

Flexi-van — Trailers with detachable container bodies that are loaded on specially constructed flat cars equipped with two turntables.

FMCSA — See Federal Motor Carrier Safety Administration.

FMCSRs — See Federal Motor Carrier Safety Regulations.

Fog lamps — Amber colored auxiliary lights for use during foggy and misty conditions.

Foot brake valve — Valve which the driver depresses with his foot, which controls the amount of air pressure delivered to or released from the brake chambers. Also called a treadle valve.

Forklift — A self-propelled vehicle for lifting, stacking, etc., heavy objects that may be loaded on pallets or skids; it consists typically of projecting prongs that are slid under the load then raised or lowered.

For-hire carriage — Motor carrier services in which charge is made to cover cost of transportation, generally provided by common or contract carrier.

For-hire carrier — A company that can be engaged to haul cargo by truck.

Foundation brake — A type of brake designed with the brake shoes on the inside of the braking drum to expand against the inner surface of the drum. A common braking mechanism for trucks.

Frame or chassis — A metal support for the body, power unit, and running gear; the backbone structure around which the vehicle is assembled. Contains the engine mounts, fuel tank supports, etc.

F.O.B. (Free on board) — Contractual terms between a buyer and a seller which define where title transfer takes place and the exchange point where responsibility for risk/expense transitions from seller to buyer.

Freight — Goods being transported from one place to another.

Freight bill — The carrier's invoice for payment of transport services rendered.

Freight charge — The rate established for transporting freight.

Freight claim — A charge made against a carrier for loss, damage, delay, or overcharge.

Freight forwarder — 1) Individual/company that accepts less than truckload (LTL) shipments and consolidates them into truckload lots on a for-hire basis; or 2) agent who helps expedite shipments by preparing necessary documents/making other arrangements for moving freight. Forwarders must obtain operating authority from the FMCSA.

Front haul — 1) The front portion of a trip, from start to destination; or 2) freight carried on the front portion of the trip. See back haul.

Fuel filter — Device for cleaning engine fuel.

Fuel gauge — Registers amount of fuel in fuel tank. One for each tank.

Fuel pump — Pump that moves a fuel from the fuel tank to the engine.

Fuel taxes — Excise taxes on gasoline and other fuels.

Full trailer — A trailer with both front and rear axles; used as the second trailer in a double-bottom rig or hooked behind a straight truck to form a truck-trailer combination. A semi-trailer can be converted into a full trailer by the use of converter dollies. See semi-trailer.

Furniture van body — Truck body designed for the transportation of household goods; usually a van of drop-frame construction.

Fuse — A wire or strip of easily melted metal, usually set in a plug, placed in a circuit as a safeguard; if the current becomes too strong, the metal melts, thus breaking the circuit.

Fusee — A colored burning flare used as a signal to warn other road users.

G

Gear box temperature gauge — Indicates temperature of lubricant in transmission.

Gear pump — Located at the rear of the fuel pump. Driven by the fuel pump main shaft. Consists of a single set of gears to pick up and deliver fuel throughout the fuel system. From gear pump, fuel flows through the filter screen and to the pressure regulator.

Glad hands — Connectors mounted on the front of a trailer for connecting air lines from the tractor.

Gooseneck — Part of a lowbed trailer that reaches up from the deck to attach to the fifth wheel.

Governor (air) — Device to automatically control the air pressure being maintained in the air reservoirs. Keeps air pressure between 90 and 120 psi. Prevents excessive air pressure from building up.

Governor (fuel) — Maintains sufficient fuel for idling with the throttle control in "Idle" position, and cuts off fuel above maximum rated rpm.

Grain body — Low side, open-top truck body designed to transport dry flowable commodities.

Gross combination weight (GCW) — The weight of the tractor, trailer, and cargo.

Gross combination weight rating (GCWR) — The value specified by the manufacturer as the loaded weight of a combination motor vehicle.

Gross ton — 2,240 pounds. More commonly called a long ton.

Gross vehicle weight (GVW) — The weight of an empty tractor or trailer.

Gross vehicle weight rating (GVWR) — The value specified by the manufacturer as the loaded weight of a single motor vehicle.

Gross weight — 1) The weight of an article together with the weight of its container and the material used in packing; 2) as applied to a truck, the weight of a truck together with weight of its entire contents. See gross vehicle weight and gross combination weight.

H

Half-cab — A tractor having only a half of a cab along the left side of the engine.

Hand valve — The valve that controls only the trailer brakes. See trailer brake.

Hazardous materials — Substance/material determined and designated by Secretary of Transportation to be capable of posing unreasonable risk to health, safety and property when transported in commerce.

Hazmat — Slang for hazardous materials.

Headache rack — Slang for a heavy bulkhead mounted behind the tractor cab to protect the driver from a shifting load.

Header bar — A hinged, rear cross piece on open-top trailer, that can be swung out of the way to load high objects.

Heavy hauler — A trucking company authorized to transport articles which require special equipment for loading/unloading/transporting because of size/shape/weight/other inherent characteristics.

Hopper body — Truck or trailer body capable of discharging its load through a bottom opening without tilting.

Hose tenders — Devices that keep air and electrical lines between the tractor and trailer suspended and out of the way. Also known as "pogo sticks."

Hours of service — The number of hours tractor-trailer drivers may drive and be on duty after meeting off-duty requirements, according to Part 395 of the Federal Motor Carrier Safety Regulations.

Household goods carrier — Motor carrier authorized to transport furniture, household goods and other properties involved in change of residence. Includes moving offices, stores, etc.

Hydraulic brakes — Brakes that depend on the transmission of hydraulic pressure from a master cylinder to the wheel cylinders.

Hydraulic retarder — A driveline retarder consisting of a spinning rotor enclosed in a stationary housing with vanes. Oil (transmission fluid or engine oil) is pumped into the retarder and movement of the oil by the rotor, and against the fixed vanes, uses up energy and creates a slowing action. Part of a truck's retarder system. See engine brake, exhaust brake, and retarder systems.

Hydrometer — An instrument used to determine the state of charge of a battery.

Hydroplaning — Action produced by water on the roadway, in which tires lose traction (contact with the road) and skim along the water's surface, thus causing dangerous loss of directional control.

I

In bond — Storage of goods in custody of government/bonded warehouse or carrier from whom goods can be taken only upon payment of taxes/duties to an appropriate government agency.

Independent trailer brake (trolley valve) — Located on the dash or steering column, this hand operated brake applies brakes only to the trailer.

Indivisible load — Any vehicle or load which cannot be dismantled, disassembled, or loaded to meet specific regulatory limits for size and/or weight.

Initial carrier — The transportation line that picks up a shipment from the shipper; in other words, the "first" carrier.

Initial point — The point at which a shipment originates.

Injector — A device found in a diesel engine that changes liquid fuel oil into a mist or spray and meters it to each cylinder.

Injector pump — A pump used to deliver fuel to the injectors under very high pressure.

Inner bridge — The distance between the extreme of any group of two or more consecutive axles, e.g., between the front and rear axles of a tractor, or between axles 2 and 5 of a tandem tractor and tandem trailer. The measurement, taken at the center of the wheel hubs, is used to determine the gross weight that can be carried on any consecutive set of axles.

Inspection (vehicle) — Checking over the vehicle parts and systems for problems and malfunctions and to see that everything is in order and in place. Pre-trip inspection is a thorough inspection done before the trip. En-route inspections are made periodically during the trip. Post-trip inspections are done after the trip, so that problems and malfunctions can be reported to maintenance personnel.

Intake manifold — That part of the fuel system that carries the air or air/fuel mixture to the cylinders.

Intake ports — Provide the connecting passages from the outside of the cylinder heads to the inside head openings (the valves).

Intake stroke — Phase of the four-stroke cycle when fuel and air enter the cylinder.

Intake valves — Valves used in an engine to admit air into the combustion chambers of the cylinders.

Interaxle differential lock — See differential lock.

Interaxle differential lock control — Used for slippery conditions, it is activated by the driver from the cab by a switch which locks or unlocks two differentials. When the differential lock is engaged, it maximizes the traction output of both axles. Do not engage if wheels are spinning.

Interchange point — A station at which freight in the course of transportation is delivered by one transportation line to another.

Interline — Transferring loaded trailer from one carrier to another to avoid loading/unloading. Daily rental/lease agreement usually used in this circumstance.

Internal combustion engine — Any engine that burns fuel within itself, as a source of power.

Intermodal transportation — Using more than one mode to deliver a shipment.

Interstate commerce —- Trade, traffic, or transportation in the United States — 1) Between a place in a state and a place outside of such state (including a place outside of the United States); 2) Between two places in a state through another state or a place outside of the United States; or 3) Between two places in a state as part of trade, traffic, or transportation originating or terminating outside the state or the United States.

Interstate operating authority — The right to transport regulated goods across state lines issued by the FMCSA and required by all for-hire interstate carriers of regulated commodities.

Interventions — Action FMCSA would take under Compliance, Safety, Accountability (CSA) to correct unsafe behavior and achieve safety compliance. An intervention is triggered by: (1) one or more BASICs above a predetermined FMCSA threshold/score, (2) a high crash indicator, (3) a complaint, or (4) fatal crash.

Intrastate commerce — The transportation of persons or property between points within a state having origin, destination, and all travel within the same state. A shipment between two points within a state may be interstate if the shipment had a prior or subsequent move outside of the state and the shipper intended an interstate shipment at origin.

Intrastate operating authority — Permission granted by an individual state to conduct intrastate transportation within that state. Some states require authority registration for for-hire, private, and exempt carriers.

Invoice — An itemized list of goods shipped to a buyer stating quantities, prices, fees, shipping charges, etc., often with a request for payment.

J

Jackknife — 1) To place the trailer at a sharp angle to the tractor; or 2) a type of skid in which either the tractor or the trailer loses traction and slides sideways.

Jake Brake — Slang for the Jacobs engine brake. Used as an auxiliary braking device on a tractor. See engine brake.

K

Kingpin — The "peg" or "pin" permanently attached to a trailer which is inserted and locked into the pulling frame of a fifth wheel or the power unit, and serving as the attachment by which the trailer is pulled.

Kingpin weight — Weight of the trailer at the kingpin or the trailer weight applied to the fifth wheel.

L

Laden weight — Weight of vehicle and its load.

Lading — That which constitutes a load. The freight in a vehicle.

Landing gear — The support legs that hold up the front end of a semi-trailer when it is disconnected from a tractor. See dolly.

Layover time — The non-working time that a road driver spends away from his home terminal before being dispatched to some other destination.

Lift axle — Normally kept in the raised position unless heavier loads require it to be used. The axle can be raised or lowered, to meet the requirements for the load.

Line haul — The movement of freight between major cities or terminals. Line haul operations do not include pick-ups or deliveries. Line haul service is also commonly referred to as over-the-road (OTR) operations.

Live axle — Same as drive axle or powered axle.

Livestock body — Truck or trailer designed for the transportation of farm animals.

Lock ring — In two-piece wheel rims, the lock ring holds the side ring firmly on the rim base.

Log book — See record of duty status.

Log body — Truck or trailer body designed for the transportation of long items. See pole trailer.

Long ton — 2,240 pounds. Also called a gross ton.

Low bed — An open trailer with drop frame construction used primarily to haul heavy equipment. Also known as flat bed or low boy.

Low boy — See low bed.

Low-air warning device — Any mechanical means of warning a truck driver that his/her vehicle is not maintaining the proper amount of air pressure needed to operate the brakes, etc. Can be a buzzer, a flashing red light on the instrument panel, or a small red metal flag that drops into the driver's line of vision.

Lumber body — Platform truck or trailer body with rollers designed for the transportation of lumber.

M

Manifest — See bill of lading.

Mixed truckload — A truckload of different freight articles combined into a single shipment.

Mode — Frequently used to refer to the basic divisions of the transportation industry. The principal modes of transportation are truck, rail, air and water.

Motor carrier — A for-hire motor carrier or a private motor carrier. The term includes a motor carrier's agents, officers, and representatives as well as employees responsible for hiring, supervising, training, assigning, or dispatching of drivers and employees concerned with the installation, inspection, and maintenance of motor vehicle equipment and/or accessories.

Motor vehicle — Any vehicle, machine, tractor, trailer, or semi-trailer propelled or drawn by mechanical power and used upon the highways in the transportation of passengers or property, or any combination thereof determined by the Federal Motor Carrier Safety Administration, but does not include any vehicle, locomotive, or car operated exclusively on a rail or rails, or a trolley bus operated by electric power derived from a fixed overhead wire, furnishing local passenger transportation similar to street-railway service.

Muffler — Noise-absorbing chamber used to quiet the engine's noise.

N

Net ton — 2,000 pounds. Also called a short ton.

Net weight — 1) The weight of an article clear of packing and container; 2) as applied to a truckload, the weight of the entire contents of the truck; or 3) as applied to a rig, the weight of a tractor-trailer when empty or curbweight.

Non-divisible load — A unit load which cannot be broken down into smaller, more convenient units for transportation.

Nozzle — See injector.

O

Occupational Safety And Health Administration (OSHA) — The regulatory and enforcement agency within the Department of Labor (DOL) responsible for ensuring safe and healthy workplaces in the U.S.

Odometer — An instrument attached to a power vehicle to measure the distance traveled.

Off-road recovery — The use of the road shoulder as an escape way by a truck that is then able to safely return to the highway.

Off-tracking — A term used to refer to the path taken by the rear end of a vehicle when turning. The path of the rear wheels is shorter than the path of the front. The off-track is much shorter on a tractor-trailer. Drivers must compensate for off-tracking in turns and on curves.

Oil filter — Device for cleaning and purifying the engine lubricating oil.

Oil pressure gauge — Measures pressure of engine lubricating oil. Pressure varies with engine speed and oil viscosity. Sudden drop of pressure indicates a problem.

Oil seal — A device used to retain lubricant in the bearing area of the wheel. The sealing part of the seal is usually made of a resilient material such as synthetic rubber or leather, which is assembled into a wheel or the hub bore.

Open top (trailer) — A truck or trailer body with sides but without any permanent top, often used for heavy equipment that must be lowered into place by crane.

Out-of-service order — A declaration by an authorized enforcement officer of a Federal, State, Canadian, Mexican, or local jurisdiction that a driver, a commercial motor vehicle, or a motor carrier operation, is out of service pursuant to Sections 386.72, 392.5, 395.13, 396.9 or compatible laws, or the North American Uniform Out-of-Service Criteria.

Outer bridge — The distance from the center of the wheel hub of the steering axle to the center of the wheel hub of the last axle of the rig. The measurement is used to determine gross weight limits and meet the requirements of bridge law.

Outriggers — Devices used for increasing width of low boy trailer.

Overage — Freight in excess of the quantity or amount shown on the bill of lading or other shipping document.

Overdimensional (OD) — Term which denotes a vehicle that exceeds a state's maximum, allowable length, width, height, and/or weight.

Overdrive — Refers to a condition in which the vehicle's transmission is in a gear having a ratio greater than 1:1, that is, the engine crank shaft turns at a slower rate than the vehicle drive shaft.

Overdriving the headlights — Driving at a speed that will not permit you to stop your vehicle within the distance you can see ahead.

Overriding the governor (overspeeding) — When the weight of the vehicle drives the engine beyond governed speed. Happens on hills when vehicle is not in a low enough gear and is not supplemented as necessary by light, steady brake application. The governor does not control the engine speed when the vehicle is driving the engine.

Oversized vehicle — Any vehicle whose weight and/or dimensions exceeds state regulations.

Owner-operator — Driver who owns and operates his own truck; he may be a common carrier, contract carrier or exempt carrier; such contractor may lease vehicle and driver to another carrier.

P

Packing list — A detailed specification of packed goods.

Pallet — A portable platform for holding material for storage or transportation.

Pallet jacks — Powered or manual mechanical lifts for loading or unloading cargo shipped on pallets.

Palletized — Stacked on pallets.

Parking brake control valve — Controlled from the dashboard by either a switch or a push-pull control, this valve engages the springbrakes.Use theparking brake anytime the rig is parked and engage only after it is completely stopped.

Payload — The cargo or freight that a vehicle hauls.

Peddle run — Truck route with frequent delivery stops.

Piggyback — Transportation of a highway trailer on a railway flat car.

Pigtail — Slang for the electrical cable used to transmit power from the tractor to the trailer.

Pintle hook — Coupling device at rear of truck or trailer for the purpose of towing trailers.

Piston — A device that moves up and down in the engine cylinder and provides power to the crankshaft.

Placards — Diamond-shaped signs required by regulation to be displayed on all four sides of a motor vehicle when it is hauling hazardous materials.

Plane or west coast mirror — Flat-surfaced side mirrors positioned on both sides of a truck tractor so the driver can see both sides of the rig and its immediate environment from the cab.

Platform body — Truck or trailer body with a floor, but no sides or roof. Also called a stake truck.

Point of origin — The terminal at which a shipment is received by a transportation line from the shipper.

Pole trailer — Trailer composed of a single telescopic pole, a tandem rear-wheel unit, and a coupling device used to join the trailer to a tractor. Pole trailers are used to transport logs or similar items. When chained together it becomes a rigid unit and thereby serves as its own trailer body. Pole trailers are adjustable in length.

Post-trip inspection — See inspection (vehicle).

Power-lift tail gate — A power-operated tailgate capable of lifting load from street level to the level of the truck or trailer floor.

Power stroke — Phase of the four-stroke cycle when fuel is ignited and combustion take place.

Power train — The series of parts that transfer the power of the engine to the wheels. Same as drive train.

Powered axle — Commonly called a live axle. See drive axle.

Prepaid — A term denoting that transportation charges have been or are to be paid at shipping point.

Pre-trip inspection — See inspection (vehicle).

Preventive maintenance — A systematic checking and care of equipment to keep repairs to a minimum.

Private carrier — A company that carries/hauls its own property in its own vehicles.

Progressive shifting — A process of shifting high torque rise engines that involves shifting at lower rpms at slower speeds, and at progressively higher rpms as the speed of the vehicle increases.

Pro number — The abbreviation of the word progressive and is usually prefixed to an agent's record numbers on freight bills, which are used to identify the freight bill.

Proof of delivery — A motor carrier establishes proof of delivery from delivery receipt copy of freight bill signed by consignee at time of delivery. This is legal proof of delivery.

Property broker — A company that arranges for the truck transportation of cargo belonging to others utilizing for-hire carriers to provide the actual truck transportation. The broker does not assume responsibility for the cargo and usually does not take possession of the cargo. Brokers must obtain operating authority from the FMCSA.

PSI — Pounds per square inch. A measurement of pressure, for example, the amount of air pressure in a tire.

Pup — Slang term for short semi-trailer used in combination with dolly and another semi-trailer to create twin trailers.

Pusher axle — Dead axle (non-powered) mounted in front of powered axle, single or tandem, increases weight-carrying capacity of vehicle.

Pyrometer — An instrument that registers the temperature of the exhaust gases.

R

Radiator — A device of tubes and fins through which circulating water from the engine water jackets passes to give off excess heat and thus cool the engine.

Ragtop — Slang term for open-top trailer using a tarpaulin cover.

Rain cap — Protection device used on exhaust stacks to prevent rain entry when the engine is stopped.

Reaction time — The time that elapses between the point that a driver recognizes the need for action and the time that he takes the action.

Recap (tires) — 1) To recap a tire by bonding new tread rubber to the used tire; or 2) a tire that has been recapped.

Reciprocity — 1) An exchange of rights, in motor transportation may involve granting equal rights to vehicles of several states in which reciprocity agreements are in effect; or 2) to give preference in buying to vendors who are customers of a buying company.

Reconsigment — A change (made in transit) in the route, destination, or consignee as indicated in the original bill of lading.

Record of duty status (Driver's log) — Daily record required to be completed by driver which shows driving, on-duty/not driving, sleeper-berth, and off-duty time. See driver's daily log.

Reefer — Slang for refrigerated trailer.

Refrigerated trailer — An insulated van-type truck or trailer body equipped with a refrigeration unit. Used for carrying perishable goods. Also called a reefer.

Regular route common carrier — Motor carrier operating over definite routes between specified points with fixed termini on regular schedule.

Relay emergency valve — A combination valve in an air brake system, which controls brake application and which also provides for automatic trailer brake application should the trailer become disconnected from the towing vehicle.

Relay valve — Valve used to speed up the application and release of the rear wheel brakes.

Repower — When dispatch sends a replacement tractor and driver to recover a load in transit.

Reshipment — Goods sent to another destination under conditions which do not make the act subject to reconsignment rules and charges of the carrier. See reconsignment.

Restricted articles — Types of freight that cannot be handled at all or may only be handled under certain specific conditions.

Retarder systems — Retarders supplement diesel truck service brakes and assist in reducing brake shoe overheating and resulting brake fade on long, steep downgrades. See engine brake, exhaust brake and hydraulic retarder.

Revolutions per minute (RPM) — The number of turns or rotations the engine makes in a minute. Engine RPM is expressed in hundreds on the tachometer.

Rig — Slang for truck, tractor-semi-trailer, truck and full trailer, or other combination vehicle.

Rocky mountain double — A tractor pulling a 40 to 53 foot semi-trailer and a 26 to 29 foot full trailer. Overall lengths range from 80 to 100 feet.

Route — 1) The course or direction that a shipment moves; 2) to designate the course or direction a shipment shall move; or 3) the carrier or carriers over which a shipment moves.

Runaway truck ramp — See escape ramp.

S

Saddle tanks — Barrel type fuel tanks that hang from the sides of the tractor's frame.

Saddlemount combination — Is a combination of vehicles in which a truck or tractor tows one or more trucks or truck tractors, each connected by a saddle to the frame or fifth wheel of the vehicle in front of it. The saddle is a mechanism that connects the front axle of the towed vehicle to the frame or fifth wheel of the vehicle in front and functions like a fifth wheel kingpin connection.

Safety evaluation — FMCSA's process of determining how to address motor carriers with poor safety performance.

Safety measurement system (SMS) — Quantifies the safety performance of motor carriers and drivers under Compliance, Safety, Accountability (CSA) to identify candidates for interventions, to determine the specific safety problems exhibited by a motor carrier or driver, and to monitor whether safety problems are improving or worsening.

Security seals — Seals used by shippers to ensure a cargo container, and/or the truck's rear doors haven't been opened while in transit

Semi — Slang for either a tractor-trailer combination, or for a semi-trailer.

Semi-trailer — A trailer that has only rear axles. The front of a semi-trailer either rests on the tractor or is supported by its landing gear when coupled. See full trailer.

Service brake system — Under normal braking conditions the braking system uses air pressure controlled by the brake pedal on the floor to move the brake shoes against the brake drum to slow a vehicle or bring it to a stop.

Severity weighting — Places a value on each safety-related violation in Compliance, Safety, Accountability (CSA) that is determined by its association with crash causation.

Shipper — A person or agent that ships freight.

Shipper's load and count — Indicates that the contents of a truck were loaded and counted by the shipper and not checked or verified by the carrier.

Shipping papers — Papers used in connection with movement of freight.

Shock absorber — A device added to an axle that dampens axle momentum and tire bounce caused by rough road surface.

Short ton — 2,000 pounds. Also called a net ton.

Shortage — When quantity of freight received is actually less than that shown on the documents.

Sight side — The side of the tractor visible by driver, i.e., driver's side. Opposite of blind side.

Single axle — Term commonly used to refer to a power unit (tractor) having only one rear axle, thus, actually a two axle unit (one axle steering at the front and one at the rear), or a semi-trailer having one axle only.

Single drop frame — A drop frame trailer with one drop, immediately behind kingpin. See drop frame.

Skid — 1) A wooden platform or pallet on which heavy articles or packaged goods are placed to permit handling; or 2) failure of tires to grip the roadway because of loss of traction.

Slack adjuster — An adjustable device located on the brake chamber pushrod that is used to compensate for brake shoe wear.

Sleeper berth — Area in a tractor where a driver can sleep. Sleeper berths must meet standards set by the Federal Motor Carrier Safety Regulations.

Sleeper — Tractor cab equipped with bunk facilities so a driver may rest.

Sliding fifth wheel — Fifth wheel assembly capable of being moved forward/backward on tractor to give desired load distribution between tractor and trailer axles.

Sliding tandem —An adjusted bogie beneath the trailer that can be moved forward or backward to distribute the weight between tractor and trailer axles.

Space management — Maintaining a safe distance between your vehicle and other vehicles, people or objects above, below ,and around your truck.

Speedometer — An instrument that indicates the speed of a vehicle.

Splitter — Mechanism that divides a gear into two or more ratios such as direct, overdrive, or underdrive. Controlled by a switch on the gearshift.

Spotter — 1) Someone who assists another driver in a backing maneuver; 2) a worker in terminal yard who parks vehicles brought in by regular drivers; or 3) a supervisor who checks the activities of drivers on the road.

Spread tandem —A two-axle assembly in which the axles are separated by distances substantially greater than that in conventional assemblies.

Stabilizer — Device used to stabilize vehicle during turns. Also called a sway bar.

Stake body — Truck or trailer platform body with readily removable stakes which may be joined by chains, slats, or panels.

Starter motor — An electric or air powered motor used to set the crankshaft in motion in order to start the engine.

Steering axle —Axle through which directional control of vehicle is applied. It may be powered or non-powered and there may be more than one steering axle on the unit.

Stop (engine) and emergency stop — Some tractors are equipped with a starter button and an "engine stop" switch. The engine stop is used to shut off the engine. Some tractors are equipped with an "emergency engine stop" switch to be used only when the engine starts to "run away" (exceeding the safe upper RPM limits). Once the emergency stop has been used, the engine will not start again until a mechanic has made repairs.

Straight bill of lading — See bill of lading.

Straight truck — Power unit/cargo body mounted on the same chassis.

Supercharger —A type of blower, connected to the engine crankshaft, that forces air into the intake manifold at higher than atmospheric pressure to increase engine power and performance. See blower.

Supply lines (fuel) — The lines that carry a supply of fuel to each injector. Fuel enters the inlet connection and then the injectors.

Suspension — The system of springs, etc., supporting a vehicle upon its undercarriage or axles.

Sway bar — See stabilizer.

Synchronized transmission —A transmission in which the gears are so constructed as to allow smooth shifting without the need to double-clutch.

T

Tachograph — A recording device in a tractor that automatically records the number of miles driven, the speed, the number of stops, and other pertinent statistics.

Tachometer — A device in the tractor, located on the instrument panel, that indicates the revolutions per minute of the engine's crankshaft.

Tag axle — The rearmost axle of a tandem-axle tractor if that axle serves only to support additional gross weight. A tag axle does not transmit power.

Tailgating — Following the vehicle ahead of you at an unsafe distance i.e., less than your total stopping distance.

Tandem axle — An assembly of two axles, either, none or both of which may be powered.

Tank trailer — Any trailer on which tanks are mounted to contain fluid commodities in bulk, tanks may contain baffles to stop liquid from surging while in motion, pumps for loading/unloading may be self-contained.

Temperature gauge — A device that indicates the temperature of such things as coolant, lubricating oil, and gear lube.

Terminal — A building for the handling and temporary storage of freight as it is transferred between trucks, i-e., from a city pickup to a line haul truck.

Terminal carrier — The line haul motor carrier making delivery of a shipment at its destination. Terminal carrier means the last or final carrier.

Throttle — Controls the engine speed.

Through bill of lading — See bill of lading.

Tie rod — Part of the tractor's steering system, it is the connecting rod between the steering arms.

Time weighted — Assigning a value to a violation based on when it occurred under Compliance, Safety, Accountability (CSA). The time weight of an event decreases with time, resulting in more recent events having a greater impact on an entity's BASIC than events from the more distant past.

Toll — A charge made for the use of a facility such as a bridge or turnpike.

Ton-mile — A unit of measure. The movement of a ton of freight one mile.

Tonnage — Number of tons.

Total stopping distance — The distance the vehicle travels between the time the driver recognizes the need to stop and the time the vehicle comes to a complete stop. Total stopping distance includes perception distance, reaction distance, brake lag distance, and braking distance.

Traction — Adhesive friction, as of tires on pavements.

Tractor — Power unit designed primarily for pulling other vehicles and not constructed to carry load other than part of weight of vehicle and load being drawn.

Tractor protection valve — Controls flow of compressed air from tractor to trailer; when closed, stops flow of air to trailer. When this happens, the trailer brakes will apply. Used to make sure that air is always available for tractor brakes.

Trailer — See full trailer; semi-trailer.

Trailer brake — A hand-operated remote control that applies trailer brakes only. Located on the steering column or dash. Must never be used for parking. Also called hand valve, trolley brake, trolley valve handle, trailer hand brake, and independent trailer brake.

Trailer-on-flatcar — Popular piggyback arrangement which features conventional highway trailers placed on rail flatcars.

Transfer pump — A pump used to move fuel from fuel tank to injectors.

Transmission — Selective gear box providing various combinations of gear ratios.

Treadle valve — See foot brake valve.

Tri-axle — An assembly of three rear axles, any or all of which may be powered.

Triple-bottom — Double-bottom unit, plus an additional trailer.

Triples — A combination consisting of a tractor, a semi-trailer and two full trailers, coupled together.

Truck — 1) Vehicle for hauling; or 2) weight-bearing, wheeled device used to move goods from place-to-place.

Truck tractor — Motor vehicle used for drawing other vehicles (trailers and semi-trailers), built so that the only load it carries is part of the weight of vehicle it draws.

Truckload — 1) Quantity of freight that will fill a truck; 2) quantity of freight weighing the maximum legal amount for a particular type of truck; or 3) when used in connection with freight rates, the quantity of freight necessary to qualify a shipment for a truckload rate, which is cheaper than a less-than-truckload rate..

Turbocharger — A type of blower, powered by engine exhaust gases, that forces air into the intake manifold at higher than atmospheric pressure to increase engine power and performance. See blower.

Turn around — A type of trip or "run" in which the driver returns to the origin point immediately after his vehicle is unloaded and reloaded.

Turnpike double — A tractor pulling two trailers between 35 and 48 feet in length. Total length is about 100 feet or more.

Twin screw — A truck or tractor with two rear axles, both driven by the engine. Same as tandem drive axles.

Two-speed axle — A drive axle capable of being shifted through two gear ranges in order to double the number of gears available from the transmission

U

Unclaimed freight — Freight which has not been called for by the consignee or owner, or freight that cannot be delivered.

Underdrive — Refers to a condition in which the vehicle's transmission is in a gear having a ratio less than 1:1, that is, the engine crankshaft turns at a faster rate than the vehicle's drive shaft. Opposite of overdrive. See direct drive.

Underpass and bridge clearance — The minimum vertical clearance from the surface of the roadway to an overhead structure.

Unladen vehicle weight — See curb weight.

Universal joint — A joint or coupling that permits a swing of limited angle in any direction; used to transmit rotary motion from one shaft to another not in line with it.

Unsafe driving BASIC — One of seven categories of safety behaviors measured in the CSA Safety Measurement System. The operation of a commercial motor vehicle in a dangerous or careless manner is included in this BASIC. Violations can include speeding, reckless driving, improper lane change, and inattention.

V

Valve — A device that opens and closes openings in a pipe, tube, or cylinder,.

Vehicle identification number (VIN) — The numbers and letters assigned to a vehicle for the purpose of titling and registration.

Vehicle maintenance BASIC — One of seven categories of safety behaviors measured in the CSA Safety Measurement System. Commercial motor vehicle failure due to improper or inadequate maintenance is included in this BASIC. A roadside inspection report might show violations associated with brakes, lights, and other mechanical defects, and failure to make required repairs.

Vehicle scale — Scale designed to determine weight of motor truck or other vehicle, loaded or unloaded.

Voltage regulator — A device that controls the voltage output of a generator.

Voltmeter — indicates output of alternator in volts.

W

Warehouse receipt — A receipt for goods placed in a warehouse (may be issued as a negotiable or non-negotiable document).

Water level warning light — Lights up when coolant level in radiator drops below required level. Similar lights will indicate low oil pressure or high coolant temperature, depending on the type of engine.

Water pump — Pump that circulates the coolant through the engine cooling system.

Water temperature gauge — Indicates temperature of engine coolant.

Waybill — A document prepared by a transportation line at the point of origin of a shipment, showing the point of origin, destination, route, consignor, consignee, description of shipment and amount charged for the transportation service. Forwarded with the shipment, or sometimes direct by mail, to the agent at the transfer point or waybill destination. The waybill is basically a description of goods and shipping instructions.

Weigh station — Permanent station equipped with scales at which motor vehicles transporting property on public highways are required to stop for checking of gross vehicle and/or axle weights. Many states also use portable scales to check compliance with the state's weight limits. Also often combined with port of entry facilities.

Western double — Standard A-train with two equal-length trailers, typically 24-31 feet long, and an overall length of 60-75 feet.

Wet tank — Part of the air brake system. Compressed air produced by the compressor goes to the wet tank, which collects any water and engine oil that the air has in it.

Wheelbase — Distance in inches from center of hub of front wheel of a vehicle to center of hub of back wheels or the center of the space between the tandems.

Wrecker — Truck designed for hoisting and towing disabled vehicles.

Y

Yard jockey — Slang for person who operates a yard tractor or yard mule, a special tractor used to move semi-trailer around the terminal yard.

Yard mule — Slang for tractor used to move semi-trailers around the terminal yard.

Numerics

A

C

E

S

U

Index

Notes

Notes

Notes

Notes

Notes